ADA TERRITORY, 1861

ioneer Drug Store and Langton's Express; the residences of L. Hermann and G. Maldonada; Black
Howell's provisions, hardware, groceries and liquors; Fleishhacker's store; Paul and Bateman's In-
ernational Hotel; Piper's Old Corner Saloon; Mining Agency of Atwill and Company; Grosetta and
company's Virginia Saloon; Edwards, Hughes and Company's hardware, stoves and tin-ware; Collins
nd Darling's blacksmith shop; Gaylord's Building; Billet and Ferris, mining claims agents; Kelly &
Aott, hardware, stoves and tin-ware; and Horche's Fulton Market.

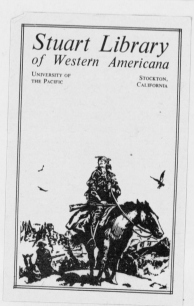

THE SAGA OF THE COMSTOCK LODE
BOOM DAYS IN VIRGINIA CITY

"Levabo oculos meos in montes undi veniet auxilium mihi."
—*Psalmus CXXI.*

"I always hear Abraham Lincoln saying, 'It is easier to admit [Washoe] than to raise another million of soldiers.'"
—*Charles A. Dana's "Recollections of the Civil War," p. 175.*

"Even such is time, that takes in trust
Our youth, our joys, our all we have,
And pays us but with age and dust; . . ."
—*Sir Walter Raleigh.*

Courtesy Wells Fargo Bank and Union Trust Company, San Francisco.

"LINCOLN'S ELECTED."

From the painting by Maynard Dixon, in possession of Wells Fargo Bank, San Francisco.

THE SAGA
OF THE
COMSTOCK LODE

BOOM DAYS IN
VIRGINIA CITY

BY
GEORGE D. LYMAN
Author of "John Marsh, Pioneer"

ILLUSTRATED

CHARLES SCRIBNER'S SONS
NEW YORK · LONDON
1934

TO

DOROTHY QUINCY VAN SICKLEN

MY WIFE

CONTENTS

Book I: "Blue-Stuff"

Book II: Bonanza

CONTENTS

ILLUSTRATIONS

xi

BOOK ONE

"BLUE-STUFF"

CHAPTER I

AT DEVIL'S GATE

1849-1850

Clouds of dust rolled in from the east. Out of them stepped youth such as the world has rarely seen. Youth that had been tried in the furnace and freed of coward and weakling; youth with down just appearing on lips—youth with splendor and sheen—whole-souled— great-hearted—rollicking youth. They came in twos and fours— they came muleback—horseback—high in prairie-schooners. With them they bore an image—an image bequeathed them by their mothers—by their fathers—by their mothers' mothers—by their fathers' fathers. An image that was old that historic December day on the shingle of Plymouth. They were seeking El Dorado.

With every step they kicked up such clouds of white choking alkali dust as all but stifled them. Thick—constant—penetrating dust. Beyond experience. Beyond comparison. It filled the air—it *was* the air—it covered their bodies—it penetrated them. It soared to almighty altitudes. It became omnipresent. In spite of everything the boys could do to the contrary it seeped through canvas curtains and begrimed—every one—everything. It seeped under lids of half-closed eyes; crept up nostrils; gritted between teeth. It filled mouths with its salty taste. It was a cruel country—this utmost rim of western Utah. It choked. Stifled. Smelt acrid. Tasted bitter.

Along with these boys, one bright May morning in the spring of 1850, crept John Orr's train of white-covered wagons. Slowly it filed over the alkali of Twelve Mile toward Spafford Hall's Station on the Carson River. The panting oxen, with tongues lolling and eyes rolling in blood-shot sockets, pulled one weary hoof after another out of the heavy sand, with every step all but obliterated by dust.

In spite of it, the orderly file of white-topped wagons crawled forward as steadily as a centipede intent on its prey—in and out of mounds of sand—round and about clumps of sage.

Behind John Orr lay the worst part of his journey, the Humboldt, that River of Death,[1] and the Forty-Mile Desert—that graveyard of hope and desire. Forty God-forsaken miles—haunted by hunger and thirst, pestilence and Piutes, death and dust.

3

Ahead, in all its grim grandeur, loomed Sun Mountain—the loftiest point of Washoe Range—the sun-dial of the desert—arising with one majestic sweep from desert sands to terminate in a rocky finger—a gray, arresting finger that pointed straight into hot blue sky. For countless days, through dust of endless deserts, each more horrible than the last, John Orr had been directing his prairie-schooners toward that mountain. For days he had seen it streaked with dawn at sunup, splotched with crimson at sundown and had gazed enraptured at eve when its shadow stalked across the desert to tryst with those of night. All nature pointed toward that mountain with prophetic gesture. Not only was it the beacon of the waste, but like the Olympus of the Greeks, it was the dwelling-place of gods—such gods as the desert demands—the green-eyed Goddess of Chance—the grim-visaged Genii of Solitude.

Orr might well keep his eyes fixed on Sun Mountain, towering as it did 8000 feet above the rim of the sea, 5000 above the floor of the desert. At its foot, as Orr knew, flowed the Carson River and along-side ran the immigrant road that was leading him to El Dorado.

By noon, John Orr's wagons were moving up that road in the very shadow of the mountain. Finally they came abreast a cañon, a cañon down which a creek tumbled—a deep cañon that twisted upon itself as sinuously as a serpent from the summit down to a great yawning mouth that spewed its watery contents into the Carson River. When John Orr saw that cool-walled cañon and the water pouring out of it he halted his caravan and shouted through his cracked lips. His women laughed and cried. His oxen lowed with passionate thirst. Before they could be unyoked they broke all re-straints and bolted for the bunch-grass in the creek-bottom.

While John Orr went to Spafford Hall's Station, which stood nearby, and the women prepared the noonday meal of bacon and potatoes, William Prouse, one of the young Mormons in the party, took a tin milkpan and going down the gulch picked up a handful of dry creeksand, placed it in the pan, faced the wind and whirled it rapidly. The wind blew off the superincumbent dust and left in the bottom of the pan a few flecks of yellow. Prouse saw that they were gold—bright—yellow—glittering gold.[2] Gold in the soil that burned and smarted—gold in the soil that tasted bitter! It was unbelievable! Gold at the foot of Sun Mountain and El Dorado 150 miles away!

Prouse was thrilled at his find. He ran with his pan back to the covered wagons and displayed its contents to his companions. But it started no fever in the blood of the Saints. To them it had little significance. Besides they saw nothing attractive in those burnt hills clothed in ragged sage, nor in the piles of tawny rock that jutted, bonelike, through its rags.[3] A bird in the hand meant nothing to these prophets of Brigham—they wanted only one bird—the fabulous phœnix in the legend land of El Dorado.

Had they been told that day that they stood at the gates of one of nature's greatest treasure-houses, that already they held a key to those gates, but that every revolution of their creaking caravan-wheels would take them farther from it, they would not have lent ear nor halted. They had one-way minds with only one goal—El Dorado. Even though the track thither lay over the "Mountains of the Moon," over that track they would go as swiftly, as directly as possible. With its potentialities of delay the show of color in Prouse's pan irritated them. "Throw it away," the more impatient called out in disgust. "Throw it away, Prouse, and come on."

Although Prouse had labored in California placers, his chispa of gold bore no message to him. It was not evidence to be traced to a source. What did he know of outcroppings? Of their disintegration? Of fissure veins? Or of overflows?

Had an experienced, red-blooded, quartz-miner on that May noontide of 1850 found that show of color in his pan, he would have been out in the middle of the cañon and with hand-shaded eyes gazed up its course to the peak of Sun Mountain. He would have seen the Goddess of Chance smile alluringly, beckoning him to come on. "So! Ho! Up there. Eh?" he would have said to himself, and up there he would have gone, El Dorado or no El Dorado. Nothing would have restrained him.

But Prouse lacked imagination. He had no eye for chance. No blood for adventure. Worst of all he knew none of the secrets of geology save those that were divulged by pan or rocker. If he looked up that cañon at all, he saw only grim-visaged solitude enthroned in the midst of wild and desolate hills. That was sufficient. He wished to be gone as speedily as possible. So he threw away his specks of Gold—spurned Midas—mounted his wagon, cracked his blacksnake over the backs of his oxen and lumbered on up the valley towards California's last barrier—the high Sierra.

But the Goddess of Chance seemed loath to part with one to whom she had proffered a key to her secret. Before John Orr's train had scaled the Sierra Summit his outriders dashed up. The passes were blocked with snow! They could not break through the drifts, or locate the divide to El Dorado! They must go back!

Forthwith John Orr gave orders to turn about. Down he reled his caravan into the Valley of the Carson. Brought it again to a halt near Spafford Hall's Station. At the very mouth of the cañon where Prouse had discovered his gold. That night when Orr was mapping out his chart of the day's progress he set down that spot as "Gold Cañon" and Gold Cañon it has remained.[4]

The next day, having nothing better to do, Orr went prospecting in the gulch where Prouse had discovered his gold.[5] Rapidly up the cañon, he worked. Until, on the first day of June, he reached a point where the opposing banks of a ravine approached so near to one another that only a narrow defile was left between—a gate, as it were, leading to a wild, virgin region, above and beyond. At a long-previous period that passage had been barred by a wall of stone; but some subsequent cataclysm of nature had rent it suddenly apart, leaving cliffs on either side so glowering and precipitous that the sun rarely penetrated their deeper recesses and giving it an aspect of such dreary desolation that, had Pluto himself appeared in the opening and barred the way, Orr could not have been surprised. Through the cut tumbled a creek of clear, foam-sprayed water so broad that it left no room for a path and Orr was forced to scramble as best he could over gray rocks.

Probably the stones upon which Orr trod had never felt before the foot of a white man. Orr reached the gate and stood leaning against one of its rocky pilasters. He gazed idly down at the water cascading at his feet. At the edge of a diminutive cascade he noted a slab of slate with a diagonal crack across its face. What prompted him to action he never knew. He had a feeling that he wanted to sink his knife into that crack and split the slate wide open.

He dropped to one knee. He pulled out his bowie-knife, flexed his arm and plunged the blade through the crevice and deep into the earth beyond. There was a splintering sound. The slate cracked. Opened. A corner of it fell away.[6] The water, running over the place where the slate had been, washed away the underlying dirt and disclosed beneath, a nugget! *A nugget of gold!* Orr thrust in his hand and drew it forth before the swirling waters could steal it away. He held it up in the fading light. A big, round nugget of gold! A nugget the size of a gold-eagle coin! The first one he had ever seen! He would cherish it to his dying day—a symbol of his one great chance—the chance that comes but once in a lifetime. But Orr was deaf to the voice of Opportunity that day. He argued that if there were nuggets of gold the size of a hazelnut in this forbidding cañon what must there be in El Dorado? He looked through Devil's Gate to the virgin land beyond—scoria—slag—cinders—ash! Pluto's realm! No place for one of Brigham's Angels!

Orr shivered and retraced his steps down the cañon and showed his find to all the emigrants congregated about the station. They were dumfounded at his luck. But a few days later when the Sierra passes opened, Orr clucked to his oxen, turned his back on Gold Cañon and led his wagons down into the land of promise.[7] How the Goddess of Chance must have chortled as she saw him depart, choosing a mess of pottage in lieu of her pot of gold!

Again Solitude held sway over the virgin territory above Devil's Gate. Again winds moaned through the opening. Coyotes cried. And the Piutes gave praise to Pah-Ah that the paleface had passed on.

By July, a steady stream of California-bound emigrants flowed past the mouth of Gold Cañon—flowed past as a mountain stream flows to the sea. Now and again the flow eddied about Spafford Hall's Station. A prairie-schooner slowed up and stopped. Those within heard the miraculous story of John Orr's nugget and having heard passed on. Umph! Many more in California! Hall would have liked to divert even a little trickle from the steady stream that glided by his station, would have liked to direct it up Gold Cañon.

Once in a while he succeeded. One lucky wayfarer, that summer, took $30,000 out of a pocket at the very spot where John Orr thrust in his bowie-knife. Another adventurer, working near Devil's Gate, washed out 600 ounces of gold-dust in a single day, sold it for $8000 and then passed on over the ridge![8] "The gold was too flakey," he complained. "Too ragged," said others. "It's alloyed with some fake 'blue-stuff' that chokes our rockers and carries away our quicksilver."

When they learned that "blue-stuff" was unknown in golden California, over the Sierra they went. As yet no one had dared to explore the forbidding territory above the gate.[9]

By August 60,000 emigrants, foot-sore and weary, had swept by the mouth of Gold Cañon. Sixty thousand emigrants watched the sun rise and set on Sun Mountain. Sixty thousand looked up Gold Cañon and shivered. They were glad they did not have to live in the shadow of that appalling mountain. It seemed as though the procession would never stop—all summer, ceaselessly, it flowed westward with its droves of cattle, its flocks of sheep, its horses, mules, oxen, men, women and children carried along on its outgoing current. An Empire on the move!

Among those 60,000 was Horace Greeley, one-time editor of *The New York Tribune*. The country was so "defiant" that he couldn't take himself out of it fast enough. "Faster!—Faster!" he urged his stage-driver. "This desert," complained he, "ought to be good for precious metal. It's not good for anything else." On to El Dorado! "Faster!—Faster!"

Unheralded, came a rollicking, hard-eyed, swarthy-skinned young Irishman, a lad of eighteen—Jimmy Fair—a giant in stature—with curly head uplifted on a pair of broad shoulders. He rushed by the cañon afoot, the leader of his band, his eyes fixed on El Dorado, with never a glance for Sun Mountain.[10]

Along came William Sharon, college-fostered, astride a fine sleek steed. A pack animal trailing behind. What a strange accretion to El Dorado! Nothing of man's size about *him!* Short in stature, with features as finely chiselled as the features on a cameo—feet too small for stirrups—hands too soft for bridle rein! What use could hardrock make of such a puny man?

At the mouth of Gold Cañon, Sharon dismounted. For days he camped within the shadow of Sun Mountain before he dared attempt the last labor with which California confronted the contenders for her fleece.[11] Any number of times he looked up Gold Cañon to where the mountain towered above him—a pigmy loking at Olympus! Then he, too, speeded on toward El Dorado. Who, ever, would have dreamed that in him the mountain was to find a master, a master who would conquer her with reins of steel?

Through broiling midsummer heat, tall, spare, wide-eyed, George Hearst staggered toward Gold Cañon, exhausted. His tongue so swollen, he could hardly speak. Pestilence and death had stalked his caravan across the cruel desert. Many an erstwhile pal had he left, in whited sepulchre along the great salt way. Hearst's last dollar had gone for flour at Ragtown. His last shred of hope had withered under the brazen August sun. His brain was fired—his imagination ran wild. Billowing sand became waves of water. Ghostly caravans swept by. Once his own image tottered toward him. Suddenly his own voice jeered at him: "Gee!—Whoa!—Haw!" Only stamina was left. He mumbled into his beard. Speed! Speed! The only escape from this desert hell-hole lay in speed. No matter how he hungered or thirsted he must make speed to El Dorado.[12]

Past Gold Cañon he crawled. Sun Peak shimmered in waves of

metallic heat. Who could tell that mountain would change the trend of United States history? Who knew that cañon would fill Hearst's empty pockets to bursting? Who could foresee that Washoe would make the name of Hearst one with which gods might conjure? To which Fortune would bend the knee? Certainly not George Hearst. The tenor of his prayer as he staggered by was for speed toward El Dorado.

Along with empire-makers and -breakers passed Bill Thorrington! Broad shouldered—powerful—with glossy black hair—mirthful gray eyes—a man cast in a man's mould. He went by like a prancing colt—all youth—vitality—stamina—the zest of the party with which he was travelling. Because of the felicitous result that followed his every action, his fellow argonauts hailed him as "Lucky Bill." For a night he pitched his camp under Gold Cañon's starry sky. "We'll stay here and help our comrades over," suggested Bill. "Naw," said his fellows. "On to El Dorado!"[13]

Setting steadily westward, the tide let no one drop anchor on the "Eastern Slope." Ultimately the current caught them all. The good. The bad. The indifferent. Thorrington, Hearst, Sharon, Fair. And a host of others. Whisked them over the Sierra and set them down in California.

In its passage by Gold Cañon this human tide swept up every green thing in its way—stripped Gold Cañon cleaner than a cloud of locusts could have stripped it. By September there was not a blade of grass that the eye could discern. The water in the Carson was foul and stagnant. Men grew weak, faint, fell sick, ignominiously died and were carelessly buried in numberless graves. Oxen fell in their traces, their lifeless eyes fixed on the Sierra. Before the great yawning maw of the cañon lay a shambles. It was almost as though the cañon had seen more, heard more, smelt more than even a cañon could endure, and that, sickened from sight, sound and odor, it had spewed forth a jumble of human wreckage: abandoned wagons, broken wheels, discarded yokes and rotting carcasses—of cattle and horses. The terrible effluvium from decaying bodies tainted the air for miles around.[14] Summoned by this carnival of putrid flesh, buzzards blackened the sky, circled and wheeled over their prey; perched, gorged and surfeited, on bovine horns; pecked out the sightless eyes and leered at the lowering Sierra.

Still this human tide flowed toward its destination, discarding the weak and useless—sustaining the stout and strong.

By late September no water trickled down Gold Cañon to wash

gold-dust free of "blue-stuff." The miners threw aside their rockers. Prices for foodstuffs became prohibitive.[15] Relief parties were rushed over from California. Privations increased—no water—no gold-dust—no bacon—no flour, only buzzards and the accursed "blue-stuff" that stuck tighter than glue to their rockers. . . . Snow began to fall. . . . They must hurry. . . . Sierra passes would be blocked.

Blaspheming and reviling the "blue-stuff" the miners trekked over the ridge into California, leaving Gold Cañon in the merciless grip of winter, wolves, and solitude.

CHAPTER II

"BLUE-STUFF" IN GOLD CAÑON

Winter passed. Spring tripped down Gold Cañon. Spring, with neither leaf nor blossom for raiment. Yet, in all her nakedness, Spring, with the beauty of blue sky—shadow-enshrouded mountains and the pungent odor of sage.

With the spring came the Saints again. Colonel John Reese and a well-equipped party of Mormon agriculturists to hold the rich valley of the Carson against the host of gathering Gentiles. Among the teamsters, who bowled them across the alkali, were Sandy Bowers, a good-natured, illiterate Irishman, and James Fennimore, a young Virginian, equally illiterate, equally feather-brained, but more bibulous.

Fennimore had killed his man over in California. To escape the brand of Cain, he had fled to Utah and changed his name to Finney. When the sheriff had failed to overtake him he allowed Finney to be corrupted into "Virginny." "Old" was added by his intimates by way of recognizing a vast capacity for "tarantula juice." Although still in his youth he was hailed up and down the cañon as "Old Virginny!" [1] Fennimore was an inveterate miner. Along with his gun he always balanced a shovel on his shoulder, provided a bottle for his pocket, and "aimed," he said, "to keep in advance of civilization." But alas! his hankering for liquor kept Fennimore chained to the oasis at Spafford Hall's bar. [2]

The Mormons settled at the most fertile spot in the valley, Mormon Station, and devoted themselves to farming. But there was no water. Drought was the curse of Washoe—the name the region received from the Indian tribe that roamed it. So the Mormons imported a hundred Celestials, with pigtails down their backs, to dig an irrigating ditch from the Carson to their farms. But when the placers in Gold Cañon grew richer and richer, Celestial and Saint deserted their irrigating ditches to lave the auriferous gravels that lay fallow in its gulches. Here, when one of the Celestials infringed on the prior rights of his white companions, he was unceremoniously strung up by his pig-tail to the nearest cottonwood, there to pendulate as a warning to others to be wary. To protect themselves, the

Orientals built their cabins about the mouth of the creek. Thus Spafford Hall's Station became Chinatown.

The apostates in the cañon were soon joined by a motley throng—the flotsam and jetsam of California's placers—criminals and outlaws driven from El Dorado, and by winter-bound immigrants who had left all observance of law east of the Rockies. Here came Pete O'Riley, Pat McLaughlin, Manny Penrod, Jack Bishop and Joe Winters.[3] Mostly a worthless lot of louts.

Back into the springtime valley from a profitable winter in California came Bill Thorrington. "Lucky Bill," whose every action fortune smiled upon. Bill "made good" in the cañon placers and was soon in control of the Carson Cañon Toll Road. Here, beside the way to California, he built a station, collected toll and dispensed an even-handed charity to those less fortunate than himself. Always in favor of "the underdog in a fight," regardless of the cause, Bill had his hands busy. But, as long as a man was in trouble—log cabin, pocketbook, and belongings were at his disposal. In addition to his toll road pursuits Bill ran a faro table, the winnings of which went to any adventurer who had lost his "roll" on the way. Whatever his faults—Bill Thorrington aimed to be a friend to man.[4]

Into these surroundings from over the desert straggled a herder and his flock of sheep, a Canadian—loud-mouthed—haggard—slothful—braggart. By name he was Henry Thomas Paige Comstock, "son of Old Noah Comstock" of Cleveland, Ohio. "H. T. P." grew up, he said, "a regular born mountaineer." He was a singular genius, unburdened with virtues, a spontaneous being with little conception of right or wrong as abstract principles regulating life. Good-natured, liberal in prosperity, but as one of his acquaintances said: "A hell of a liar."

From the direction of Salt Lake came a woman—one of the first women—to the Gold Cañon placers, Eilley Orrum, a visionary Highland lassie, who in her stride westward had loved—and surrendered to a pioneer divorce-mill—two husbands, both Mormons, both polygamists—and one a bishop! But when both, after a reasonable period, had failed to gratify Eilley's ambitions for motherhood she discarded them to become a mother to the miners in Gold Cañon. Possessed by a mother-complex, the girl would not be frustrated in every woman's urge. To satisfy it she nested at a place called Johntown, a camp that had sprung into being four miles up the cañon from Spafford Hall's Station.

Here she built a log cabin and let it be known that she would take boarders, but not "sleep" them. In the course of a few weeks her pork, beans, and batter biscuits became so famous that she numbered among her boarders such Johntowners as, "Sandy" Bowers, "Old Pancake" Comstock, "Old Virginny," Pat McLaughlin, Pete O'Riley, Joe Plato and many others. All spring and summer she cooked for them; but as soon as the water ran low in the gulches she collected the yearly laundry of her boarders, packed it in the panniers on her donkey and betook herself to the hot-water springs in Washoe Valley where she had pre-empted a location and erected a log cabin wash-house. Here Eilley Orrum gave up the winter to scrubbing, mending, and pressing for her boys.[5]

In summer, from sunrise to dusk, the hairy, brawny Johntowners, in red shirts, blue jeans, and heavy boots, splashed, knee-deep in cold mountain water, rocking their cradles back and forth, damning the while the "blue-stuff" that clogged their riffles. Picking up the cobalt mass by the handful they hurled it as far down the gulch as they could throw. "That damned 'blue-stuff,'" they cursed, "is spoiling these diggings."

They noted with alarm that the higher they worked up the cañon the bluer and heavier became the "stuff" while the paler and lighter grew the gold. Had they been good quartz-miners, that fact would have excited their suspicions. At once they would have searched for outcropping. Instead, the pale yellow gold mixed with heavy "blue-stuff" angered them. In the beginning, Gold Cañon dust had brought $14 to $15 an ounce at Hangtown. Now, on account of this blue alloy, it brought only $11 an ounce. The Johntowners were disgusted. A few gave up the struggle and drifted across the desert to more profitable "pickings." But the majority worked on up the cañon, breaking their backs over their rockers and filling the air with azure maledictions. But they earned enough to keep body and soul well pickled in "tarantula juice."

One day a Mexican miner came to work in their placers. He could speak no English, but was a master of Latin gesture. Even the Johntowners understood what he meant when he examined a handful of "blue-stuff" with popping eyes and loudly exclaimed, "Bueno!" Then waving his arm dramatically toward Sun Mountain, he cried out, "Mucha plata! Mucha buena plata!"[6]

Although the Johntowner knew no Spanish, the Mexican's pantomime proclaimed plainer than words that high up on Sun Mountain was plenty of gold. Taking him on their interpretation, they worked doggedly toward that mystical region that would flood their industry with plenty of "tarantula juice." Afterward, when it was too late, they recalled that the Mexican had not said, "Mucho oro," but had distinctly reiterated, "Mucha plata! Mucha buena plata!"

Even after a peon, who had worked in the mines of Sonora, came upon them throwing away buckets of "blue-stuff" and remonstrated, "You keep one dollar but throw away two!"—even those significant words failed to register on Johntown minds.

The prodigal Johntowners had no ambition for wealth, so long as they could wash out an ounce or two of gold-dust during a day. That was enough. Why worry about what they threw away? A yellow ounce would insure a wild time behind the red-lights of Spafford Hall's bar.

Spafford Hall's was the centre of Gold Cañon gaiety, the mecca of Johntowners.[7] Every night just as soon as Eilley Orrum's pork and beans were dispatched they mounted their jennies and raced for Chinatown.[8] Here, over green baize tables, they "bucked the tiger and wrastled with the beasts of the jungle," squandering the gold-dust they had broken their backs to obtain during the day.

Although the Johntowners ate with Eilley Orrum, drank at Spafford Hall's, they slept in the purple sage. The danger lurking about their sleep-quarters was the reason they gave for drinking so much "tarantula juice." If they drank enough before retiring, no coyote, scorpion, tarantula or other beast that lived in the sage would tackle them, but—if they lay themselves down insufficiently fortified, they were in mortal peril.

It was not always gambling at Hall's Station. Every Saturday night the miners forsook Monté for the ballroom on the second floor. Promptly at eight o'clock a "yaller-backed fiddle" struck up, Spafford Hall mounted the platform and called out in stentorian phrases: "Take your partners for the French-four." Then there was a scramble for Eilley Orrum, Laura Ellis, and the other queens of the greasewood. Women were scarce. When the pale supply was exhausted the enthusiastic Johntown "hoss" balanced with equal fervor in front of "Princess Sarah,"[9] the daughter of "Old One"—moccasined Winnemucca, chief of all the Piutes. Just because she was red was no reason for economizing in shoe leather.[10] Underneath she was woman, wasn't she?

Sometimes these Saturday nights ended with fireworks and the spilling of blood. Once, while they danced, the Piutes stampeded their mustangs. When two of the Johntowners became obstreperous,

Courtesy John A. Fulton.

A COMPLETE PLACER MINING PLANT, INCLUDING POWER PLANT, TYPICALLY GOOD-HUMORED.

From the author's collection.

OLD WINNEMUCCA: CHIEF OF THE PIUTE INDIANS.

DISCOVERING COMSTOCK LODE—JUNE 12, 1859.   THE MAN SEATED AT THE LEFT IS COMSTOCK.

the redskins transfixed them with arrows.[11] Sometimes the miners struck back and killed a brave or two. "Bad medicine," growled the Piutes. "Bad medicine."

The Johntowners were not averse to murder; if the murder was well executed and the corpse was not "mussed up." But heaven help the killer who mangled his victims! Even if it did "serve him right," as Washoe juries were wont to pronounce over their corpses, Johntowners demanded perfect finesse from their "gun-toters."

Manslaughter was as nothing in comparison to thieving. "Claim jumping" and "cattle rustling" were the most heinous crimes on the Johntown calendar. You could steal a man's wife. If he couldn't hold her—that served him right; but you couldn't steal his ox nor his ass, nor anything else that was his without getting into trouble. The Johntowners would not abide a thief. Several times they sliced the ears off refractory horse-thieves and sometimes it was a nose. Once they even hanged an innocent man named Snow for a thieving crime one Edwards had committed.[12] Before they could rectify their mistake Edwards had fled to Bill Thorrington and Bill had given him sanctuary. Thus "Lucky Bill" fell afoul their suspicions. They accused him of shielding a horse-thief. So far as they were concerned that finished Thorrington. Bill was tried before a people's court and found guilty. "Accessory after the fact," the court said. Forthwith he was sentenced to be hanged.[13] Bill didn't argue or cringe or whimper. What was the use? The cards were stacked against him. That was all. He must play out the hand dealt him. When one morning his erstwhile friends came for him in a wagon he climbed cheerfully aboard. When they drove under the limb of a cottonwood tree, Bill adjusted the hemp noose about his own neck. When the wagon drove off from under him Bill stepped into Eternity singing blithely at the top of his lungs: "The Last Rose of Summer."

Such was the sanctity of life and the majesty of law in the sage.

CHAPTER III

THE SECRET OF THE GROSCHES

1851–1857

Into these unhallowed surroundings in the spring of 1851 came the Grosch brothers—Allen and Hosea, sons of A. B. Grosch, a Universalist clergyman of considerable note, and editor of a Universalist paper at Utica, New York.[1]

They were a fine pair of youths, chaste and honest, worthy of the Grail, worthy of the best Washoe had to offer. Still in the prime of early manhood—slim, blond-headed, ruddy-cheeked, blue-eyed, eager—they represented the finest type that America was producing. They were there to make their "pile" and then go back home and ease up the pressure on their old father. They knew considerable about metallurgy and assaying and in the saddle-bags of their "pack" were several technical books on mining and on chemistry. They didn't loiter long at Chinatown, nor at Johntown. Spafford Hall's gaming-tables held no attractions. Up through Devil's Gate, further up the cañon than any one had heretofore ventured they went, and set to work with a rocker. Before long they, too, found their riffles clogged with the "blue-stuff" which the Johntowners anathematized so roundly. Instead of throwing it away, they picked it out carefully. They wanted to know what it was. They took it home, put it in a mortar, wet it and ground it to fine powder. Then they baked it in an improvised oven. When they found a small dark colored button in the bottom of their crucible they could hardly trust their eyes. "It's unbelievable," said Hosea, "we must test it further."[2]

Thrilled, they filled a beaker with nitric acid and dropped the button into the liquid. Everything depended on that last final test. If it disappeared. . . . Their faces were flushed from the glare of the cupel furnace as they held the beaker toward the light the better to see what went on inside the glass. Hosea's hand trembled a little. They scarcely breathed. It could hardly be . . .

Slowly but surely the button disappeared in the acid-solution. They were overjoyed. Hosea's hand was steady now! What a mo-

16

ment it was! On the result of that assay hung the fortunes of thousands, national welfare, the future of a race, the outcome of a great war! Out of that assay sprang dozens of millionaires! Blocks of San Francisco's marble buildings! A telegraph cable to girdle the earth! A State—legislation—a great mining school—a mining code! Engineering enterprises that were to make the mountain famous! Out of that assay sprang the pomp of kings, the power of principalities, the glitter of coronets!

Out of that little beaker came a giant of the earth more powerful and relentless than the awful spectre that sprang from the pan in the Arabian tale; and that giant still lives, still makes, still breaks the destinies of countless thousands.

Long after the button had dissolved in the nitric acid the Grosch boys held their glass to the glare of the cupel furnace. They couldn't believe their button had disappeared in its contents.

The next day they wrote their father a jubilant letter—about their discovery—about the great vein they had found in Gold Cañon. "A perfect monster," they wrote. "It resembles thin sheet lead—broken very fine, and lead the miners suppose it to be, tarnished from sulphuric acid in the water."[3]

Then Hosea and Allen held a conference. Should they tell the Johntowners the real nature of the "blue-stuff" that they were cursing and throwing away?

They decided they would keep their secret. What was the use of telling men a secret they could not possibly understand? What did they know about assays? They detested every "color" but gold.

Thus the two lads kept the secret of the "blue-stuff" to themselves. Summers they prospected in the cañon. Winters they spent in Mud Springs, El Dorado County, California, trying to earn money enough to develop their claims. For they realized that the development of "blue-stuff" meant the earning of gold![4]

By the fall of 1855 they had worked up the cañon to a bold outcropping above a spot they designated as the "Divide." It was virgin ground. No one had prospected there before. They found a spring. They dug a pit. There was the "blue-stuff"—bluer than ever. It sparkled with gold and disappeared in a great vein that dipped into the earth.[5] They realized that they needed machinery—a horse—a whim.

That fall, when the Johntowners went down to Chinatown to "wrastle" with beasts of the winter jungle, the Grosches went over the ridge to Mud Springs. That winter they were determined to organize a stock company in El Dorado County. They must develop the "blue-stuff." There were millions in it.

Down into Washoe in the spring of 1857 came Hosea and Allen Grosch, leading their jenny with all their belongings strapped in the saddle-bags on her faithful little back. They were full of plans.

During the winter at El Dorado, they had organized a company to develop their discoveries. With them on their return came Richard Bucke, a young Canadian, to work for them. But they told him nothing of their monster vein. Only to their partner—George Brown —station-master at Gravelly Ford at the sink of the Humboldt, was imparted that secret. So enthusiastic was he over their prospects that he had promised to join them immediately and devote all his savings, some $600, to developing the monster lode which they had unearthed in the cañon.[6]

On their way up Gold Cañon, Hosea and Allen stopped at Laura Ellis' ranch-house, near Chinatown, for dinner. After a good meal the Grosch boys waxed confidential with the good motherly woman. With Brown's money, they assured her, they could start developments on their monster vein, which ran from cañon mouth to mountain crest. They swore her to secrecy. And because she had been so kind they promised to stake out a claim for her right next to their own—the "Pioneer." Then they hurried up the road toward Chinatown. They must reach camp that night.

Off and on that summer the boys boarded with Eilley Orrum. Sometimes they talked about their claims. When they were gone Eilley's brain fairly buzzed with hornblend, quartzite, crystaline limestone, and propylite. But never once did they mention the "blue-stuff."

Along the wash of American Flat, at the very base of Grizzly Peak, the Grosch boys built themselves a stone house, using the native tawny, yellow rock to construct its walls. It was a comfortable little hut with built-in bunks and a fireplace with a crane where they could cook. Every night they piled the crude andirons high with sage-brush, studied by its flame, made notes, and, in the afterglow, discussed the time when the monster vein would make them all rich. In the same room they installed a crude retort for reducing ores, a cupel muffle-furnace with canvas bellows, a work-bench and over it shelves for chemicals, assaying apparatus, and scientific books.

The boys were so busy gold-washing in the cañons and on the adjacent hillsides that they had little time to devote to the Johntowners. Owing to their aloofness, those diggers regarded them as a mysterious pair.[7] They laughed at them for taking life seriously. Ambitions! Hell! The aim of life was pleasure! As such they suffered the Grosch boys to think their own thoughts and go their own way—unquestioned—unheeded.[8] But not Comstock. He was intrigued by their comings and goings. Something was up. He watched them covertly.[9]

In June, 1857, Allen wrote to his father regarding their progress. "We struck the vein without difficulty," he wrote, "and have followed two shoots down the hill. . . .

"We have pounded up some of each variety of rock and set it to work by the Mexican process. . . . The rock of the vein looks beautiful . . . soft . . . violet-blue . . . indigo-blue . . . blue-black and greenish-black."

Their first assay, they wrote, gave unheard of returns—$3500 per ton! Think of it! It was altogether too much of a good thing. They notified George Brown; but they didn't mention those assays to Bucke. The fewer people who knew your business the better.

Soon their savings were exhausted. They needed more machinery. They needed food. George Brown had not "come in" as he had promised. They got so hungry that they left off prospecting, to work in the placers. It was rough work. Worse still, the surface gold showed signs of exhaustion.

By then it was August. The days grew shorter—colder. Everything worked against them. Not only was free gold "petering out," but the sun sank earlier and earlier and came up later and later. Snow would soon be flying. The cañon would be blotted out. The creek would be frozen. They would be forced to "make tracks" for California. More and more men would drift into the diggings. Some one else would happen upon the secret of the "blue-stuff." Then all their work would go for nothing! The Johntowners would reap the reward. Such a secret could not be kept forever. They grew desperate.

One night Allen sat down and wrote to George Brown. Their resources were gone. They needed his help. "For God's sake, join us," he urged, "as soon as possible."

Brown replied that he would sell out at once. He had more than $600 to devote to their claims.

The Grosch boys waited. Brown did not come. Then it was the middle of August. Still he had not arrived.

On the 19th while Hosea was out prospecting he struck the hollow of his foot a glancing blow with his pick. The injury did not seem to amount to anything. Hosea ignored it. He was strong. The wound would soon heal. He forgot that he was underfed and worried. Erysipelas set in. A red line raced menacingly up his leg. He was wracked with fever. There was no doctor in the cañon. Allen left his gold-washing to poultice his brother's foot with cloths wrung from a kettle of hot water on the crane. He scalded his hands doing it. But he kept at it. Finally one day, Comstock, who was always snooping around their cabin and never seemed to have anything to do, drifted in. He told Allen to go back to his rockers. He would stay with Hosea and continue the compresses.

Under the hot water treatment the inflammation receded. The fever abated. Except for occasional chills and some difficulty in chewing and swallowing his food, Hosea rapidly improved. Sometimes he mentioned a stiff neck. The muscles about his jaws were tight, he complained. But that didn't worry the brothers—there was no connection between swallowing and a sore foot. One day Hosea felt so much better that he got out of his bunk, hobbled to the open door, dragged his chair after him, and sat down with his leg propped up on a candle box.

Along came Laura Ellis. She had news for the boys—bad news. George Brown, station-master at Gravelly Ford, was dead. Thieves had rifled his post, found his $600, and murdered him. That was a terrible blow to Hosea. They loved him like an older brother. How they had counted on his counsel! Hosea never knew how much until then! Allen came back to the cabin. George Brown murdered? What chance had they without him![10]

"Never mind," said Laura Ellis, seeing how crestfallen the boys were. "I've saved up $1500. If you're so sure of your 'blue-stuff' I'll devote every cent of it to the development of your claims." That offer cheered the boys, grieved as they were over the fate of their friend.

Allen went to a box, drew out a piece of blue-quartz and handed it to Laura Ellis. "Keep this," he confided. "It's from the claim you're on. . . . We've put your name down for three hundred feet."[11]

Then taking her by the arm and passing by Hosea he led her through the door and up a piece of rising ground. Pointing up the cañon toward Sun Mountain's crest he indicated one particular spot —a bold outcropping—"Down at the base of that point," he said.[12]

Back in the cabin again, he took down a book—the kind of a book in which miners file locations. He turned over a few leaves, and pointing here and there to notations on the pages, indicated to her where their locations and where hers were entered.

Mrs. Ellis was satisfied. Convinced of the value of their ledges, she agreed to furnish them with her $1500. Picking up her piece of blue-quartz, she put it in her pocket. Bidding the brothers good-by, down the cañon she went and out of sight toward Chinatown.[13]

That night Hosea grew perceptibly worse. His fever mounted. He felt chilly—looked blue. Allen was alarmed over the change in his brother's expression! Hosea's eyebrows were raised in surprise! At the same time the lines about his mouth were drawn out into a grimace—a horrible sardonic grin. He was suffering agonizing pain, yet he grinned as if he were going to burst into laughter. Chills shook him from head to foot. Allen could force neither food nor drink between his teeth. They were locked. His suffering grew intense. Held as in a vise, he was unable to utter a sound. Allen sat courageously by—ministering—encouraging—praying—until September 2. That day Hosea died.

Allen was overwhelmed. Crushed into the dust with sorrow. He had no money, no clothes in which to bury his brother. A red shirt and blue jeans for the tomb! They would never do! He borrowed $60 from sympathetic Johntowners, bought a new suit, made a pine box and laid Hosea out. Two days later, while Allen read the service of the dead, the Johntowners lowered Hosea's coffin. On the coffin-lid Allen piled the heaviest boulders he could find. No coyote should have his brother!

By September 7, all was over. Forlornly, Allen sat down to write to his father.

"In the first burst of my sorrow I complained bitterly," he wrote. "I thought it most hard that he should be called away just as we had fair hopes of realizing what we had labored for so hard for so many years. But when I reflected what a debt of gratitude I owed to God in blessing me for so many years with so dear a companion, I became calm and bowed by head in resignation. 'O Father, Thy will, not mine, be done!'[14]

"Well I know your heart is full of the great hope which caused Paul to shout in triumph, 'O death, where is thy sting! O grave, where is thy victory!'"

On September 11, Allen wrote, "I feel lonely and miss Hosea—so much that at times I am strongly tempted to abandon everything and leave the country forever, cowardly as such a course would be. But I shall go on. It is my duty. And I cannot bear to give anything up until I bring it to a conclusion. By Hosea's death you fall heir to his share in the enterprise. We have, so far, four veins. Three of them promise much."

Every day was now precious. It was dangerous to cross the Sierra after October. Yet he must go over the ridge. He must organize another company, raise more money, buy more machinery and develop the lead that had already cost Hosea's life. Still Allen was loath to leave until he had paid off Hosea's funeral expenses. He didn't like debts hanging over him. Foolishly, back he went to gold-washing in the cañon. Not until the middle of November had he satisfied his debtors.

Then Bucke, who was anxious to return to California, and Allen made ready to depart. Although Allen was anxious to get away from the cabin, its lonely desolation, and all that was associated with so much grief, still he disliked leaving until he had made some plans for its care during his absence. He made two bundles of his papers and paraphernalia. In one he placed specimens from his claims, diagrams of the veins in Gold Cañon, charts, his assay books, and the book in which he had filed notice of his and Laura Ellis' claims to the ledges at the base of Sun Mountain. These he wrapped in water-proof paper and laid aside to take with him over the Sierra.

Into the other he packed his assaying apparatus, more samples, his books, some notes on his assays, and drawings of his claims. These he put in a box, nailed on a cover, and stood the box in a corner of his cabin. Then he called Comstock—the one Johntowner who seemed most available for the purpose—to his cabin. Allen did not tell him the secret of the "blue-stuff" but he told him about his claims and a shaft—not very much, not even exactly where they were, but enough to convince Comstock of their great value. Allen promised him that if he would stay, alone, in his cabin all winter, protect his box of belongings and keep his cabin from being rifled during his absence, he would reward him with a one-fourth interest in his hill claims in the spring.

Then Allen drew up a contract stipulating these things. He even went so far as to make a rough diagram of the ground he claimed —"3750 feet north of a ledge and extending beyond a ravine on the north side of the Sun Peak."[15]

Comstock did not know to what ledge Allen alluded nor where it was located. But he could see the box. He agreed to every provision. And when Allen said—"Sign here!"—Comstock wrote his name.

Finally all was in readiness. The little jenny was loaded down with blankets, provisions, guns, and specimens. Last of all Allen stored away in the saddle-bags the water-proof-covered package containing the secrets of the "blue-stuff," and his claims thereto. That was more precious than life itself.

It was November 20. Midafternoon. A warm, beautiful day. Comstock stood in the cabin door. Allen gave him some last instructions. Ran to Hosea's grave—piled more stones upon it. Then he and Bucke and the little jenny went down the cañon. A long trek over the Sierra to Mud Springs, El Dorado County, California, lay ahead of them.

Comstock watched them until they were out of sight. Then he went into the cabin—closed and locked the door.

CHAPTER IV

THE CLEW LOST

1858

Their first night out, the donkey broke her hobbles and strayed back to the diggings. That delayed them. Four days were lost finding her. Finally Allen and Bucke left Washoe Valley and took the Indian trail which crossed the eastern ridge of the Sierra, an ascent to some nine thousand feet in nine miles. It commenced to snow before they reached the Summit. Thence, in a blinding storm, they descended some three thousand feet to Lake Tahoe.[1] The trail to the Truckee was obliterated. Passes were buried under deep snow-drifts. But finally they stumbled into Squaw Valley and found themselves surrounded by white relentless walls of snow. They kindled a camp fire with great difficulty—strung up a blanket for a tent—and sat by to wait. Snowstorm after snowstorm overwhelmed them.

Provisions were soon exhausted. But to turn back was more hazardous than to push ahead. On all sides, now they were hemmed in by inexorable walls, walls so light and fleecy they seemed to hold their prisoners by weakness rather than by strength. The boys dug through them in search for blazed trees and the outgoing trail, but it was useless. The pass was irretrievably lost. It commenced to rain. Grew colder. Froze. Then snow fell again—soft, light, snow, but the fall was heavier now.

The poor little jenny floundered belly-deep through drifts, in a helpless way. She was hungry but there was nothing to feed her but dried twigs of trees. Allen scraped up all he could find. Even climbed a great piñon and shook down some green cones—roasted them—but she spurned pine-nuts. She grew weak and emaciated. She could never reach California, Allen said. Sorrowfully he unloaded her. Into the drifts he threw the bulkiest part of her pack—specimens—charts—books! Out he drew his precious package of claims and assays, and hid them in the bosom of his shirt.

Then he shouldered his gun. God, how he hated to do it! But it was mercy! With his eyes closed he sped a bullet into the little faithful beast of burden. By the camp fire, they roasted as much of her meat as they could carry; packed it in a canvas-lined knapsack and set out again. This time on rudely whittled-out snowshoes. Crude as they were, they delivered them from those unyielding prison walls. Now for the ranges ahead. There were two of them. So far they had travelled less than half the distance. El Dorado was still miles away!

They climbed from point to point. Often waist-deep in snow. Dragging themselves up by bushes. Letting themselves down by jutting rocks. All the time Allen was conscious of that package that lay heavier than lead against his chest. Sometimes its sheer weight seemed to press the air out of his lungs.

Then it was November 29. Already they had been nine days on the trail. The day was clear—icy clear. The sky was blue—cold —remote. Limbs of great trees boldly etched themselves in black against it. Wind moaned through frozen branches—blew hail into their faces—choked them with sleet. Allen was benumbed. So numb that he could not tell whether his package lay on his chest or not. At times, he would clutch wildly at it with his free hand. He must not lose it now. The key to Gold Cañon lay there. . . . Not one living soul knew its secrets but him, not even Bucke. Nothing must happen to it.

They started down the mountainside—half sliding—half falling. Snow-shoes were useless. They took them off. Threw them away. It had grown bitterly cold—blowing hard from the west. They found the trail. They lost it again. Near sundown Bucke saw fresh tracks in the snow ahead. They were overjoyed. Other people were in the neighborhood. They were near help. A moment afterward the truth dawned upon them. Those were their own tracks. They had gone in a circle. They had feared they were off the trail. Here was the proof. What to do next? Furiously the snow whirled and swirled. They could not see a hundred yards ahead. They sat down in despair. Allen felt weak. His pack was too heavy. He took off his heavy outer-coat. Threw it away. His blankets were wet—useless. He threw them away. With both hands pressed to the package on his chest, he fled down the frost-bitten ridge. With difficulty Bucke kept up.

They reached a stand of trees. Allen gathered a bundle of faggots. He must build a fire and thaw out his fingers. He reached for his matches, found them. They were damp and would not light. He threw them away. After repeated trials Bucke lighted a fire by a flash of powder from his gun. They warmed themselves and fell asleep with their feet towards the flames.

Before morning another storm broke over them, so soft that it melted as it fell. It wet them to the skin. Their powder became damp. They fired off their guns—again—again—just a hollow plop —no flash—no fire. With wet powder, their guns were a useless burden. They threw them away.

Allen worried over his precious papers and charts. The wet would penetrate their coverings, blur the writing, obliterate lines on his maps and charts, blot them out. Nobody would be able to read them. That would be worse than losing them. A mass of damp papers, no word or figure decipherable.

He took them out of his bosom. Wrapped them securely in the canvas of his knapsack and deposited them in the hollow of a great, fallen pine. "A fallen tree is safer," Allen chattered as he covered his package with dry moss and broken twigs. "A standing one might be uprooted in a storm."[2] Then with his knife he cut a great mark on the fallen monarch. "See," called Allen. Bucke looked and saw— the rough sign of a cross. Then Allen rolled a huge stone in front of the hollow.[3] Taking a last survey of the surrounding landmarks they picked up their butcher's knife and a tin cup and ran from the spot at top speed. The next day brought another big snowstorm. The weather grew colder. The wind wailed through the trees. They were nearly demented from cold, hunger, and exposure.[4] Allen was perceptibly weaker. Bucke went ahead to break a track for him.

That night, to keep themselves warmer, they dug a hole in the snow, covered the bottom with evergreen boughs and crawled in. Huddled close to one another to conserve the heat of their bodies, they dropped off to sleep. Suddenly, with a start, they awoke. Wolves were sniffing at the entrance to their dug-out. Thus passed the night of December 2.

On December 3, they made only two miles. All the donkey-meat was gone—but they didn't care. They could hardly swallow the tough, sinewy stuff. It choked them.[5]

That night they were too weak to dig a hole in the snow. Exhausted, they threw themselves down on a bare spot at the foot of a pine-tree. They could not sleep. At daybreak they arose, ate a handful of snow and pushed on. They reached the middle fork of the American River. That landmark gave them hope. For two days, half-dazed, they wandered through its rugged cañons. As closely as possible they followed the course of the stream but could find no muddy water—see no miner's cabin, discern no sign of smoke. Hopelessly on the night of the 4th of December they dug themselves into the snow. For four days they had had no food.

Dawn came on the morning of the fifth. They were no longer hungry. Just a horrible sinking feeling in the region of the stomach. Bucke was in despair. Sinking in the snow, he burst into tears.

"Let us lie down where we are," he sobbed, "and die. We can never make it."

Allen would not hearken to him. He patted him on the shoulder.

"No," he said, "we will keep going as long as we can walk." They could not fail—no one in Utah would look for them—no one in California would make the effort—no one in the East would know what had become of them. They could not—they must not fail Hosea. . . .

After a little Allen persuaded Bucke to get up and make another effort.

That night, the 5th of December, when they reached the spot where they were going to camp, Bucke broke down again. "Make up our bed for the last time," he faltered. "We shall never leave this spot." In wordless silence Allen spread the boughs. Hopelessly Bucke sank upon them.

Almost immediately, Bucke dropped off to sleep—to be tortured by horrible, extravagant dreams. He was feasting—feasting on quail. At his side, Allen lay still but open-eyed. At daybreak he tried to get up. He could not stand. He fell back in the snow. He awakened Bucke. Together they crept out of their hole. On hands and knees they crawled ahead—side by side. Not a word passed between them. Hope was dead. Hunger was gone. All that was left in Allen's mind was a sense of momentum—to keep going—and a dim remembrance of things past—of Hosea—a grave—boulders—claims—a company—California—help.

Bucke was seized with an overmastering faintness.

"Let us rest," he faltered.

"No," whispered Allen defiantly. "We will drag ourselves along, while we can move hand or foot."

They moved on—on all fours—across the snow field, painfully, slowly. Allen was fagged. Bucke watched him anxiously. Finally he got in the lead. He must break a path for Allen. From daybreak until noon they crawled less than a mile. They were exhausted. They fell. They pulled themselves to their knees . . . sank in the

lee of some rocks . . . closed their eyes in overwhelming weakness
. . . slept.[6]

A dog barked . . . they awoke with a start . . . they heard shots.
"There is smoke," Allen whispered—but made no attempt to get
up. Bucke roused himself—arose—and went in the direction of the
shots. He came on a party of miners hunting deer. He could not
speak. He waved his arms. They followed. He led them to where
Allen was lying, only a few hundred yards away. Then he sank
down beside him in the snow.[7]

Placing Allen and Bucke tenderly on sleds, the miners pulled them
over the snow to Last Chance (Placer County)—a near-by camp—
and put them in their bunks. But neither could sleep. The diggers
brought them food. Neither could eat. The smallest quantity made
them sick. The miners questioned them. Neither could speak. They
grew worse and worse. All day—all night—they lay in a semi-con-
scious stupor. Once Allen sat bolt upright in his bunk. "Bucke,"
he mumbled. He had something to tell him—the ledge on Sun
Mountain—"blue-stuff"—two hundred feet north—he fell back
babbling incoherently. Bucke had not caught a word.

Bucke's legs were frozen well above the knees. The miners examined them—gangrene was setting in. There was no doctor within
miles—no anæsthetic. But something must be done quickly.
Crudely, with hunting knife and saw, the miners removed one of
his legs, and part of the other foot.[8] Then they turned to Allen.
Both his legs were badly frozen. Amputation was the only way
to save him. Allen could not speak but he could hear, and struggled. At last he fought them off. His lethargy increased. He
could only be roused when disturbed. In his lucid moments he
babbled of Hosea—"blue-stuff"—"Gold Cañon"—and a "company."
On, he fought tenaciously—without food—without drink—until the
morning of December 19, when he opened his eyes—looked curi-
ously about—closed them again and slept. With him slept the secret
of the "blue-stuff" in Gold Cañon.[9]

As soon as the miners had buried Allen in a roadside grave they
carried Bucke to the home of his friend, Alpheus Bull, at Michigan
Bar. There he had a long-lingering illness.

When he was well enough to travel, the miners took up a collection and returned him to his family in Canada, where he studied
medicine, graduated, and became one of the well-known nerve spe-
cialists of the Dominion. At one time he was in charge of the Insane
Asylum at London, Canada. Although in later years he erected a

monument over the grave of Allen Grosch, never did he return to the Sierra country, nor join in any search for a fallen pine that was marked with a cross.[10]

Thus with Allen's death and Bucke's illness the clew to the "blue-stuff" in Gold Cañon was apparently lost. Singing and carousing, the unsuspecting, heedless Johntowners stumbled on—up toward the Sun Peak—up toward the lap of the gods, cursing with every step the "blue-stuff" that choked their rockers; the "blue-stuff" whose secret had cost the lives of the flower of the Cañon.[11]

CHAPTER V

FOOLS OF FORTUNE

1858-1859

One day in the following spring Comstock learned that Allen Grosch was dead—dead and buried beside the road that led to El Dorado.

All winter, alone in the stone hut, Comstock had contemplated Allen's box. What was in it? Alternately its unknown contents had tempted and maddened him. For days at a time he would meditate on it. It had conjured up visions of riches beyond expectation. At night when winds howled down the cañon and coyotes cried about Hosea's grave and Comstock stretched his long gaunt frame on his bunk, he could think of only one thing. What was in Allen's box?

The news that Allen would never come back gave Comstock the opportunity he wanted. With great strides he paced the cabin—one thought uppermost in mind. Now he was the proprietor. The Johntowners knew nothing about the box. They need never know. He picked up Allen's axe—walked over to the box—dealt it a vicious blow and knocked off the lid—nothing popped out. He tiptoed forward and peered within. Not even hope lay there—nothing but books, rock specimens, assaying apparatus, and a mass of papers. Comstock took out the specimens: red rock, blue rock. Blue rock with white lines darting through it which sparkled in the firelight. "Iron pirates," said Comstock eyeing the pyrites disgustedly. He stuffed the specimens into his pocket. He must find the ledges from which those rocks came.

Then he gave his attention to the papers—diagrams, figures. He couldn't make head or tail out of the maps. They were a mess of zig-zag lines. His disappointment angered him.

Anger flared to fury. He seized the papers, tore them to shreds and threw them in the fireplace. He grabbed up the hatchet and pounded the assaying apparatus and the two furnaces to shards. About the cabin, like a madman, he ran, hacking and destroying everything that recalled the Grosches or that might remind any one else of the brothers. The debris he buried under a mass of mud and sand.[1] Last of all he took out the contract, reread it, and gave it to the flames. Whatever had belonged to the Grosches was his now. He had only to locate their claims. Then he would be a wealthy man—the nabob of Washoe.

The next morning, Comstock set out to locate the lost Grosch ledges—ledges that must contain rock as red or as blue as the specimens in his pocket. Every day he walked for miles. Neither fatigue nor bad weather deterred his search.[2]

On the strength of his stolen knowledge Comstock began to have expansive ideas. He was as rich as Monte Cristo. He boasted of his wealth in ledge and mine. His sanctimonious expression lent credence to his words. As he explained to the Johntowners, he no longer had time to prospect for himself, so he hired two Piute braves to wash gravel for him. He paid out more in wages than they could make in the placers. And the Johntowners began to note his preoccupied air. Sometimes they would find him, mixing pancakes, spoon poised in air, utterly oblivious of his batter, his mind lost in speculation on the flanks of the distant Sun Peak. From then on they dubbed him "Old Pancake" and wondered what change had come over him to make him such a "hell of a liar."

One spring day "Old Virginny," who had knifed his man over in California, decided to investigate the spot which absorbed Comstock's attention. He climbed up the cañon. When a tawny-yellow outcropping captured his eye, he took out a piece of yellow paper, scrawled on it a notice of location, signed it James Fennimore, February 22, 1858, and cached it under a flat piece of quartz. Although he never attempted to develop his claim, ever after the tawny-yellow pile was known as "Old Virginny's" ledge.[3]

Comstock feared that "Old Virginny" had stolen a march on him. So he decided to locate every likely spot on the mountain. A few days later he ascended Gold Cañon to the head of Six Mile. When he came to a natural amphitheatre in the hills he stopped and flung his restless eyes around. There was a spring and, nearby, a prospect hole. He ran to it—made a cairn of stones, drove in a stake, and stuck up a sign of location. "For ranching purposes," read the notice he filed in the claim book one of the Johntowners started to keep in Gold Cañon.[4]

With all his "locations," Comstock was in more of a quandary than ever. What was that red rock? What was the "blue-stuff"? He must send samples to California.[5]

The next time one of the Johntowners was going over to Grass

Valley, he took with him a piece of Comstock's blue rock to Richard Killala, an accomplished metallurgist, to assay. Killala's Irish eyes gave a great start when their gaze fell upon those blue pebbles. "Come back tomorrow," he said to the Johntowner, "and I'll give you a report."

The next day when the miner went for the report he found Killala dead in bed—murdered during his sleep.

Comstock despaired of ever learning the significance of his blue rock.

Once, Snow-Shoe Thompson, the blond Norwegian-Viking, who carried the mail between Washoe points and California settlements, took a piece of blue rock, wrapped in check-sheeting, to Frank Stewart, geologist connected with *The Placerville Observer,* considered a great authority on minerals.

"What's this blue-stuff?" said Thompson. "There's lots of it in Washoe."

Stewart looked at the rock. That blue cast puzzled him. "Looks more like common blue limestone than anything else," he hedged. "Better take it to Sacramento."

Thompson did so. The Sacramento assayer reported it worth $2200 to the ton in gold![6] But he neglected to identify the "blue-stuff."

Comstock was baffled. Even with the knowledge of its astounding richness in gold, he had not the least notion how to proceed. Depressed and exalted by turns he was beset by fear that some one would steal a march on him. Especially was he suspicious of "Old Virginny."

When these fears became unendurable, Comstock would throw his shotgun over his shoulder, station himself at Devil's Gate, walk back and forth like a sentry, and challenge every one passing through.

"Where you going?"

"Why?"

One warm January day Gold Cañon's walls echoed and re-echoed to wild shouts of joy. Instinctively Comstock knew that the long-lost Grosch claim had been rediscovered. He dashed up the cañon. Down in Crown Point Ravine he found "Old Virginny," "Big French John," Aleck Henderson, and Jack Yount with a pan of "blue-stuff" sparkling with gold in their midst, all yelling like a band of Comanches. They had found a pocket of gold in a mound of red sandstone near the Divide.

"Old Virginny" was beside himself with excitement. He had been rambling along a ridge when a red mound, partially covered with snow, caught his eye.

"There's some good diggings over there!" "Old Virginny" had shouted.[7] When he had scurried forward, scraped off the sleet, found a gopher hole, plunged in his fist and had drawn out a handful of loose earth, he was sure of it. The stuff literally sparkled with gold spangles. Unwittingly he had unearthed the Gold Hill outcroppings of the famous Lode, and Gold Hill the red mound became.[8]

Comstock was exasperated over "Old Virginny's" find. The mound was red. By rights it belonged to him. All Washoe was his. He told them so. But the four Johntowners paid him scant attention. They staked out four claims of fifty feet each, the limit allowed by Washoe's mining law. "Old Virginny," as the discoverer, took first choice. And Comstock, to his chagrin, was compelled to take what was left.[9] But Comstock got even. Always afterward in recounting the discovery Comstock insisted it was his hand that had pulled out the golden blue dirt. And the Johntowners themselves alluded to it as Comstock's vein.

Before night the news of the Gold Hill discovery swept Johntown. Nick Ambrose, the barkeeper, pulled down his groggery and made tracks for the red mound.

Eilley Orrum, with the aid of her boarders, Jim Rogers, Joe Plato, and Sandy Bowers, packed her boarding-house on a pack-train, trotted up Gold Cañon, and set it up with its rear walls abutting on "Old Nick's" Bar.

When Jim Rogers, paralyzed with too much "tarantula juice," failed to pay his board bill, Eilley graciously took over his claim. It bordered on that of Sandy Bowers and Eilley had designs on Sandy.[10]

Day after day the contents of Comstock's rockers grew richer. Every few hours he washed out from $300 to $500 in gold. Every minute he cursed the "blue-stuff." With the muscles of his face twitching, his hands trembling, voice shaking, he boasted about his discovery. "Comstock's Diggings," crowed he, "are the biggest thing in Washoe." Every night he stretched his long gaunt frame across the roofs of such future golcondas as the Belcher, Crown Point, Yellow Jacket, Imperial, Empire, and Kentuck.[11] Every morning his delusions increased in grandeur.

One June evening Comstock learned that Pete O'Riley and Pat McLaughlin, two former Johntowners, were mining over in Spanish

Ravine near the spring where he had staked off a ranch for grazing purposes. Full of sound and fury, he decided to take a look at their rockers.

Mounting his half-blind mustang, and with his long legs dangling through the sage, Comstock galloped over the Divide. As he approached he saw O'Riley and McLaughlin cleaning up. Alongside their waterhole lay the result of their day's work—a mound of gold-dust—the first output of the world-famous "Ophir" at the opposite end of the Lode.

Comstock's eyes almost popped out of their sockets when he beheld the mound of gold. Without a word he sprang from his mustang, threw himself into the hole and fell upon his knees. Scooping up the blue earth by the handful he let it trickle slowly between his fingers. It sparkled, like diamonds, in the setting sun.[12]

There was no mistake this time. Here was the lost ledge—the lode Allen and Hosea Grosch had discovered. The ledge that he knew existed but never could find. Tremulous with excitement, he struggled to his feet. "You have struck it, boys!"[13] he managed to say in a choked voice. Then he coolly informed the two astounded Irishmen that they were trespassing on his land.[14]

"Look here," said Comstock, "Manny Penrod and me located this claim last winter and sold a tenth part to 'Old Virginny.' You gotta let Manny and I in on equal shares." But he didn't mention letting "Old Virginny" in.

O'Riley and McLaughlin objected strenuously. But they were terrified of Comstock as he stood before them with lips twitching, hands trembling, and the unequal pupils of his eyes dilating. Besides, fifty feet of a placer claim was more than they could work in a season.

When Comstock saw that they had posted up a notice calling for 300 feet for each and a third claim for the discovery he jumped up and down in his rage and swore he would have none of it. Loud and louder, he fumed. Finally he declared that they could not work there at all unless they would agree to locate him in the claim. Rather than have a row about the matter, the two easy-going Irishmen yielded and Comstock's name appeared on their notice of location.

This being arranged to his satisfaction, Comstock demanded one hundred feet for water rights. Knowing the claim was useless without water the Irishmen were forced to agree. This hundred feet afterwards became the Mexican Mine, a bonanza that yielded millions of dollars.[15]

Having provided for himself, Comstock bethought himself of "Old Virginny." Something must be done, at once, to cancel those twenty feet. Wheeling his mustang about and laying on a heavy lash Comstock bolted for Gold Hill. That night before "Old Virginny" learned of the strike he had exchanged potential millions for Comstock's bobtailed mustang and a bottle of whiskey. When the effects of the drink wore off, and "Old Virginny" could see again, he discovered that the mustang was blind.[16]

A year afterward when Ophir stock went up to $3000 a foot "Old Virginny" used to say that he was the most startling example of magnificence and misery the world had ever seen, because he was able to ride a $60,000 horse and yet had to ride him bareback because he could not scare up cash enough to buy a saddle. "If fortune," he would conclude, "were to give me another $60,000 horse it would ruin me."[17]

Within a week of buying "Old Virginny" out, Comstock formed the firm of Penrod, Comstock & Company. He insisted on calling the property the Comstock but finally compromised on the Ophir— the first claim recorded on the Lode.[18]

Having obtained his gold and silver by sheer brass, Comstock's one worry was how to get rid of it.

In July when a party of Carson ladies came upon the Ophir claim, Comstock presented one who had taken his fancy with a pan of gold-dust worth $300. And he was just as profligate of the property to which he brazenly alluded as "Comstock's Lode." Everything that took his fancy he "staked out" and called his.

One day he "staked out" the Chollar and gave it to Billy Chollar. On another he went down to the Carson and brought back Old Daddy Curry and put him and one Alvah Gould in possession of the fabulous Gould and Curry property. He "staked out" the Savage property and presented it to Old Man Savage. "I also owned the Hale and Norcross," he boasted, "and kept Norcross for a year to work on that ground."[19] Unaware of the significance of these delusions the Johntowners called him a "hell of a liar."

One morning Comstock "staked out" a woman, a wisp of a thing in calico and sunbonnet. That she was the wife of a puny, sore-eyed Mormon who had drifted into the camp in a covered wagon made no difference. Comstock wanted her and decided to appropriate her just as he had the claims. To get rid of her husband during his courting, Comstock gave him an underground job in the Ophir. Then he lay siege to the lady's affections with many a pan of "salted dirt" and poke of gold-dust. The sunbonnet wasn't unresponsive either. Before long she was sitting on the tongue of her husband's wagon combing Comstock's long black hair. Soon thereafter Comstock persuaded her to elope with him to Carson. There Comstock found a minister of the gospel to his liking, one who did not recognize the marital bonds of the Mormon Church. "That's no tie," claimed this accommodating man of creed. "The Mormons are 'sealed' to their women, not lawfully 'spliced.'" Delighted with this interpretation of spiritual values Comstock donned a pair of red carpet slippers and a new linen duster and was joined in lawful wedlock with the accommodating "Mrs. Mormon."

The marriage was hardly consummated before the irate husband came tearing down the mountain. But Comstock, being an experienced horse-trader, had provided a mustang—with the spring-halt—for this very emergency. When the proposition was fairly put to him, the Mormon preferred the horse to his woman. When Comstock threw in sixty dollars, the Mormon gave him a bill of sale and rode back to the Ophir content.

All went merry as the proverbial wedding-bell until along came the next spring. When bunch-grass sprouted and grasshoppers jumped over the sage and jack-rabbits went leaping and bounding in the air, the bride grew restless. She, too, wanted to be on the wing. One day when business called Comstock over the ridge, his little wife went eloping with a hairy Johntowner. Hearing of her flight Comstock went in pursuit of his love-bird. Overtaking her, he brought her back to a Carson City hotel, locked her in a room on the second floor, and repaired to the barroom with his cronies. Sometime later when he returned he found his room stark empty, the window open, and the bird flown—this time, it transpired, with a long-legged passerby.[20]

Women were powerful scarce in the sage! But even if he had suffered a serious loss, "Old Pancake" still insisted on calling the whole region "Comstock's Lode."

But one night "Old Virginny" changed the face on the barroom floor. By one fatal step Comstock's bombastic guns were spiked forever!

CHAPTER VI

THE CHRISTENING

1859

It was a moonlit night in October. "Old Virginny," Comstock, and their gang, all a little "mellow," were making tracks toward their bivouac in the sage. "Old Virginny" was in the lead with a bottle of "tarantula juice" snugly tucked under his arm. Suddenly an unlucky boulder happened to jump in "Old Virginny's" way. Over it he stumbled.[1] Away went the bottle, whiskey, "Old Virginny," and all into the dust. In falling the bottle hit a rock and broke. The parched mountain lapped up the whiskey thirstily leaving only a few spoonfuls in the jagged, cup-shaped bottom of the bottle. Comstock laughed in inebriated glee. But not so "Old Virginny." That laugh settled the question of the name of the diggings. "Old Virginny" pulled himself unsteadily erect. Over he bent, picked up the broken bottle and swung it to and fro. As the remaining drops fell upon the sage, he hiccoughed and solemnly uttered: "I baptize this spot Virginia Town."[2]

The baptism took. A reveller's shout went up. It was decided to repair to Jones' bar and make a night of it. As the hours progressed, many was the cup quaffed to "Virginia Town—Queen of the Placers."

During that summer Virginia Town went ahead, like one of her own jack-rabbits, by leaps and bounds. With their budding love of absurdity the miners spoke of their collection of wretched hovels not as a camp but as a city. And so Virginia Town became Virginia City.[3]

At first the "city" hovered about the Ophir "cut" but finally, like a startled covey of quail, it scattered, hit or miss, into the sage. For all its bravado it seemed to be trying to hide its head, ostrich-like, in the brush. It was mostly constructed of canvas. Although gunnysacks, old shirts, and piñons were not ignored. Gradually the growing camp's needs denuded the flanks of Sun Mountain. Piñon after

37

piñon went the way of firewood until there wasn't a tree within miles fit for shade.

With sorrowing eyes and gaunt cheeks the Piutes saw their piñon orchards destroyed. What would they do that winter for food? "Bad medicine," they muttered, as they sharpened their arrow-heads. "Bad medicine," they reiterated, as they stretched fresh gut on their bows.

The fame of Virginia City spread far and wide. Crowds of people dropped in to see for themselves: the herdsmen came in from the foothills; prospectors from distant ledges; desert rats from hideouts in the waste.

In mid-June a man named Stone, from Stone and Gates' Crossing on the Truckee, rode over to Washoe to make an inspection. Everything was covered with blue dust. The very air he breathed was blue with it. He saw Comstock and his gang throwing away masses of it, cursing it as they threw. He saw it piled sky-high about the Ophir "cut" and on Gould and Curry dumps. Stone was curious about it. Its heft convinced him that "blue-stuff" was valuable. With all they threw away, Stone saw each one of those lotus-eaters take from $500 to $1000 a day in gold out of his rocker and not work hard at that. He went to Comstock.

"How about that 'blue-stuff'?" queried Stone.

"Worse'n useless," replied Comstock. "If it weren't for that damned bogus 'blue-stuff' my diggings might amount to something." Visionary and thriftless, Comstock alternately magnified and belittled everything, all in the same breath.[5] Sometimes Sun Mountain's output was prodigious. Again, it was a "puny little thing."

But at that, Stone was curious about the "blue-stuff." He picked up a few specimens, put them in his pocket, and rode away. A few days later when his friend B. A. Harrison went over the ridge to Grass Valley, Stone gave him the samples of blue rock. "Take them to some good assayer over there and have them tested," he said. "I'm curious."

Harrison arrived in Grass Valley on a Sunday. That night he showed the "blue-stuff" to Judge James Walsh, the best mining expert in those parts. Walsh was nonplussed. Never had he seen anything like that stuff before. Together the next morning they took the specimens to Melville Atwood's assay office. "Make an assay of this 'blue-stuff,'" ordered Walsh.

"By tomorrow night I will be able to give you an exact written report," Atwood returned. "Come back then."

That day Atwood made assay after assay. He was dumfounded. He could scarcely credit his own figures. Again and again he tested. Never before had he had any ore like that "blue-stuff." He could hardly wait for Walsh and Harrison. "That 'blue-stuff'," he said, as soon as they had poked their noses inside the door, "runs $4791 to the ton, $3196 in silver, the rest in gold! It's silver. Almost solid silver!" Judge Walsh and Harrison were stunned at the news! Silver! Almost solid silver!

Thus was the nature of the bogus "blue-stuff," so long despised by Washoe's guileless miners, disclosed. Such was the "blue-stuff," whose secret the Grosches had fathomed. Silver was the explanation of those tarnished buttons in their retorts; the cause of their joy when it dissolved in the beaker of nitric acid. That was the "stuff" over which the Mexican miner had exclaimed, "Buena plata!" The "stuff" Snow-Shoe Thompson carried over the Sierra; that no one in Placerville recognized. That was the "stuff" Dick Killala, the accomplished Irish metallurgist, had identified but had never been able to disclose; the "stuff," a piece of which, Laura Ellis still cherished; the "stuff" Old Comstock had found in the Grosch cabin; the "stuff" that was piled mountain high about the Ophir "cut"; the "stuff" Old Comstock was throwing away even now and cursing with every breath he drew! That "stuff" could make millionaires—billionaires! Judge Walsh was flabbergasted.

If he was going to profit by that assay—the Judge knew what must be done *and done quickly*. And Judge Walsh had presence of mind to insist on one condition—utter—profound—secrecy. Until he and Harrison could get across the Sierra no one must breathe a word of that assay. Comstock, "Old Virginny," and the others must be kept in ignorance of the value of the "stuff" they were throwing away until he and Harrison could secure control of the Ophir, and Gould and Curry. For his secrecy the Judge promised to take up two hundred feet for Atwood. More if Washoe laws would allow. Then he hurried into the darkness.

It was nearly midnight when the Judge hammered on the door of his friend Joe Woodworth, got him out of bed, and hurriedly imparted the story of the "blue-stuff" assay.

"Hurry—put on your boots and come with me to Washoe," he urged. "We have no time to waste. We must reach Gold Cañon, buy up all the Lode before the Johntowners find out what 'blue-stuff' is."

Together they seized a mule, packed him tail to ears with provisions, picks, shovels, and rockers, mounted their own mountain ponies and dashed off for Washoe. Long before daylight streaked the east with crimson they were on their way to the pot of gold at the foot of their rainbow. They could not have travelled faster had the vigilantes been on their trail.[8]

CHAPTER VII

CALL OF WASHOE

1859

Although he had agreed to keep the assay of the "blue-stuff" a profound secret, nevertheless before he turned in that night Atwood sat down, wrote and mailed a letter to Donald Davidson, the Rothschilds' London representative at San Francisco, telling him the news of the great silver discovery in Washoe. "I do hope Walsh will be in time to secure our ground," he concluded. "My assay gave from 15 to 20 per cent silver."[1]

It was too good a story to keep. Anyhow Davidson wouldn't tell. Davidson also had a few bosom friends in whom he had the utmost confidence. These bosom friends had confidants. Thus the news spread. Soon everybody knew that a silver mine of astounding magnitude had been discovered over the ridge in Washoe. With startled ears they learned the very hour that Judge Walsh and Joe Woodworth had departed. They surmised just how far they had progressed in their passage of the Sierra, and what chance there was of overtaking them.

By nine o'clock the morning of the 28th half the towns of Grass Valley and Nevada City were on the qui vive over the secret. Nor did the news of the discovery stop there. It spread like a tidal wave through Nevada, Placer, Sierra, and El Dorado Counties, gathering momentum as it went. It eddied down Sierra passes, swirled through cañons, down the Yuba, Sacramento, and San Joaquin Rivers and broke in pent-up fury among the settlements about San Francisco Bay. Everywhere, in mining camps, agricultural centres, along wharves, in business sections, about gambling-tables, in gilded brothels, it caused unparalleled excitement. Everybody was astounded. Nothing was heard or talked of but silver! Silver! Silver in Washoe!

The boys were jubilant. At last they were released from the spell of gold. Silver in Washoe! They had developed into a great crowd, those boys of '49. For ten years they had been ridden, possessed by one word—gold—until they had grown afraid of the very

41

sound. How many times had they sworn never to be gulled by that sound again? How many times had they broken over? Let any piper, however faintly, pipe of gold and they were off. They could not help themselves. Obsessed by that sound, they would go wherever such a one led, over mountain and dale, through fire or water. They would desert any task, no matter how remunerative; any responsibility—wives—mothers—children—jobs—the instant they heard that word.

It had grown to be a frightful sound in their ears. Try as they would they could not resist its influence. In ten years, it had ridden them to shadows. Like the recurring theme of a melody it had kept running through their heads. In spite of everything they could do they were slaves to it.

Gold was a contagious word with magnetic qualities. Repeat it, no matter how many times, and the result was the same: fever—rush—hallucination—mania. Knowing the result, they had grown to dread it. Napoleon once said there was nothing he feared so much as the repetition of any word. That was the way the boys felt about that word—gold. Iteration and reiteration had made it fearsome.

Look what it had done to San Francisco! After ten years of unprecedented munificence she had been reduced to penury and left in sack-cloth and ashes to cower beside the Golden Gate—bewailing her fate. And all on account of that word gold.

Look what it had done to the boys! In '49 it had set them marching across 3000 miles of mountains, valleys, prairies, waste, and desert. Even after that tremendous trek the word had not expended its force. In June of that very year they had followed that mad-mountaineer, Greenwood, far into the Sierra in search of a gold lake he had glimpsed in some Bacchanalian nightmare. For seven destitute, endless weeks they followed him for naught. But even that bitter experience had failed to rob the word of its power.

Weak from that torture they were at its mercy still—waiting—harking—for the next piper.

One night, fever-stricken, mad, Deloreaux stumbled into Downieville. He had a stirring tale to tell. He was a French-Canadian voyageur. He had lost his way in the wilderness. Smitten with thirst, he had leaned over the brink of a mountain lake to quench its fire. When lo and behold! His eyes were blinded by the sun's reflection upon immense boulders of gold that lay on its bottom.

Open-mouthed the boys received the impact of that story—gold in water—the dream of alchemists—and were lost. By thousands they set off in the piper's wake for Gold Lake. Even before they started they were gambling among themselves as to how they were going to transport such great masses of gold.

"I'll bet my mule," said the owner of a little, short-backed institution, then a quarter of a century old, "that my jenny can pack $150,000 worth."

"Gold Lake is hidden among inaccessible crags and solitudes above the snow-belt," prattled mountain-mad Deloreaux. It's guarded by wild beasts and savage men."

"Lead us on," retorted the boys.

"It can only be reached by the pure in heart and iron-souled," he babbled.

The story smacked of Olympian myths but the boys still believed in fairy stories. The tales of Arabian Nights were to be divested of all their romantic extravagance in the eerie fastnesses of the Sierra. After Coloma all things were possible! With popping eyes and bated breath they besought their leader to get under way. For eight days and nights they followed him over as wild and rugged a country as ever existed. On the ninth day, the mountain-mad man looked at his stalwart followers and announced that they had taken the wrong "divide."

"If you've deceived us," announced one of his followers, "we'll blow the top of your damn'd head off."

That night the wilderness swallowed up Deloreaux, swallowed him as utterly as if he had never existed. Never again was he seen in the Sierra. When they came to their senses the boys were in a pitiful condition—a hundred miles from Downieville.[2]

Back the boys went to their rockers—waited—hearkened. They didn't want to listen, but they couldn't help but hear. Then it came —out of the North—the Call of Trinidad—clear as a bell—gold beyond the Trinity! A sailor aboard a coast-freighter saw him first— Old Neptune—rolling golden bowls along the Humboldt shore. The sailor called the mate. Told him what he had seen. The mate watched. He, too, saw the phenomenon—Neptune bowling down a shore paved with gold. Why shouldn't the Argonauts see the god of waters at his sport? Didn't the Crusaders see St. George on the walls of Jerusalem? It was contagious agoraphobia. All the sailors on that freighter saw gold at Trinidad. When the boat tied up at the wharves in San Francisco all the wharf-rats heard it, then *The San Francisco Alta* and the boys.

Any man could go there with hat, umbrella, or fishing-net and catch more gold than he could carry, announced *The Alta* in an early issue. Millions of dollars could be obtained any day in the year. John A. Collins, secretary of the Pacific Mining Company, measured a patch of golden sand estimated to yield to each member of his company $43,000,000. Affidavits in proof of its riches were offered to the boys. *The Alta* of January 11 announced that a flotilla of eight vessels was sailing the next day for Gold Bluff! Avast! Ye Jasons! Yo! Ho! For Gold Bluff![3]

Gold on the Trinity! It set the boys by the ear! There was nothing to do but go. Trinidad fever seized them. Thousands bought tickets. It was a 300-mile tack—but it made no difference—they had heard the call—they must go. But when the boys reached Gold Bluff and saw peaceful waves lapping sand-strewn shores and heard the sea-winds whipping the pines, the bubble burst with a terrible bang, and the boys regained their senses. Neptune was a humbug.

These continuous remittent fevers were playing havoc with the boys' constitutions. Every attack left them more at the mercy of the next cry of "gold." By the spring of 1855 they were beginning to feel that they were free of the obsession when they caught the sound of siren voices, in the direction of Kern River, singing of gold. Wives and mothers besought their men to stop their ears with wax —so that they might not hear those alluring sounds.

But it was too late, the boys had heard the master call. Five thousand set off for Kern River. Cradles, long-toms, claims, and homesteads were deserted. But by the time the boys reached the river the voices had ceased their calling. Those who had gone in stages walked back. Those who had walked, returned on blistered feet.

With all their suffering, still those boys were not cured of goldfever. Still that word had the power to invoke Aladdin-like dreams. Still in their heart of hearts they knew they had not learned to resist that cry—and all the time they were listening, listening for the faintest of pipings.

In March of 1858 they caught it—a high, shrill sound from the Fraser River. Gold in British Columbia! Hundreds of miles away. Desire banished distance. They heard that call—sure and peremptory—"Gold on the Fraser." Every purser, on every ship from the north, arrived in San Francisco with pockets bulging with nuggets. There was no doubt about it this time, Caledonia was Ophir! The doubters could even see the gold, could bite it if they doubted. The Valley of the Fraser was as rich as the Valley of the

Sacramento in '49! Newsboys ran through San Francisco streets shouting, " 'Ere's the extra *Alta!* Latest news from Fraser River! Gold by the bushel!"

Fraser River fever became epidemic. It raged with unabated fury. All classes were afflicted: miners, farmers, clerks, bankers, teachers, all came down with it. In the course of four months 18,000 people left San Francisco. Everything failed but transportation. Business was paralyzed. Grass grew between cobblestones in the streets. Every other house was "for rent." Confidence was gone. Trade was killed. Mountain communities were deserted. One inland town was in the throes of a religious revival when the "call" was heard. Religion was knocked cold. Forgetful of their professions, revivalists broke into ribald songs of the trail.

"Oh, I'm going to Caledonia, that's the place for me;
I'm going to Fraser River with the washbowl on my knee."

California was depopulated. In vain, ministers exhorted from the pulpit on the ungodliness of gold-fever; to no avail! In vain, doctors delivered tirades against the fever-ridden banks of the Fraser. In the end the physician forgot his agonizing patient, the lawyer laid aside his brief, the minister ignored his God, to answer the call of mammon! Coroners complained that Fraser River had put an end to suicides![4] Undertakers deplored a falling off in funerals! The dying arose from death-beds, wrapped themselves in winding sheets, and sailed. Better the fever, they said, than mould! Better the Fraser, than the Styx!

When they got there the boys found the Fraser in flood—the placers under water!

In the end California had to go after her boys. But only a part came back. Some had been drowned in the flood, some had starved on the plains, many had been stamped into unmarked graves. All were destitute. It cost over $30,000 to get them back. But California was glad to retrieve them at any price.

Afterwards, to ask one of those spirited fellows if he had been to Fraser River was taking a chance of getting a gory nose! The boys were through with gold now, they swore, for ever and ever! They avoided the sound as they did the plague. They never wanted to hear about gold again. Henceforth the word *gold* would fall cold upon their ears! They would expunge it from their vocabularies. Pluck it from their memories. In the whole of California there was not a sheep who could be gulled by that cry![5]

Such were their resolutions, when their ears were smitten with the Washoe call—a new call—a call they could not disregard. A call that made the thrills run up and down their spines! A call the boys had never heard before. Not gold, this time, but silver! Silver! Pure, virgin silver! Silver beyond Sierra passes! Silver beyond belief! Silver in Washoe! Silver in the very cañon they once had spurned!

Oh! You beloved vagabonds! You fever-ridden '49ers! You gold-racked Californians! You have never hearkened to that call! It takes you unawares—sweeps you off your feet. Listen—silver! Beds of it 10,000 feet deep! Mountains of it! Ravines of it! Acres of it! Miles of it! Chimneys of it—straight through into the heart of the earth! Hundreds of millions of dollars ready to be pocketed![6] Ledges! Lodes! Veins! Fissures! Croppings! Bonanza! Bonanza!

Being a new disease, silver-fever took the boys unawares. There was no known immunity against it. Silver! Silver! As contagious as microbes, it spread far and wide. It swept their ranks like fire. All came down with the new disease. It was a blessing in disguise. It cured them of the curse of gold. After ten slavish years they found themselves no longer at the mercy of that word gold. Freed —its shackles fell from them forever.

In October a pack-train of eighty mules loaded down with tons and tons of Washoe ore came scurrying through Sierra passes, through Placerville, through Sacramento and dumped the contents of their sacks into the smelters of the Mosheimer furnaces in San Francisco.[7] It was worth $5000 per ton! It was beyond belief! Silver-fever raged with fury up and down every street.

When the squat bars of bullion, white, smooth, and glistening, were borne through the streets a milling crowd of boys followed. Never had their eyes beheld so much silver. Some had never seen silver before. When the bars were displayed in the windows of the bankers, Alsop & Company, the crowd stood there for hours, gazing, feasting, enraptured.[8]

Visions of Solomon's mines; of the ransom of Montezuma; of Spanish galleons sinking under the weight of solid silver altars and crucifixes; of cities plundered for their vast wealth; of Captain Kidd and Treasure Island; of half-savage miners who boiled their frijoles in kettles of silver[9]—a whole cinema of vaguer memories reeled through their brains.

A new Mexico lay just over the Sierra. Their eyes bulged! Those bars of bullion sent the blood singing through their veins. There was romance! There was adventure! A prize worth the striving! What enterprising, red-blooded, self-respecting '49er could resist them? No humbug this time! No chance of it! They could see it, feel it, touch it, bite it! The sight of those bullion bars was like the smell of brimstone in the nostrils of fire-horses. Gold Lake, Gold Bluff, Fraser River! All forgotten! They were hypnotized! Agoraphobia again gripped them. They were in the grasp of an earth-monster more terrible than the giant octopus! "Washoe! Washoe!" they cried. "Glory, Glory to Washoe!"

All California rang with the call. Merchants closed their stores, clerks left their desks, teachers their schools, sailors slipped overboard and swam ashore, mechanics threw down their tools, lawyers forsook their briefs, doctors deserted their pills, gamblers quit gambling, whoremasters abandoned their brothels, ministers and priests renounced their altars, to join the silver-seekers. It was a universal summons! A call to all creeds, to all manner and condition of men! A call as peremptory as the summons of a bugle! "To Washoe!" it ordered. "To Washoe, charge!"

CHAPTER VIII

BILL STEWART

1859

William M. Stewart, "Bill," the boys on the Yuba called him, hearkened to that cry—"Silver in Washoe!" He recognized it as the cry of destiny.

Bill was a lawyer. In nine years he had developed a tremendous following about the northern mines. He had crossed swords with all the big lawyers in Sacramento and San Francisco and was making plenty of money. But Bill wanted something besides money. He felt Washoe would offer it to him. So he listened carefully to that call. Then he packed his law books in his saddle bags, put on a slouch hat, stuffed his buckskins in his top-boots, opened his red shirt on his muscular chest, and announced to his wife that he must go to Washoe. His future lay over the ridge. Friends and clients were hot on the trail of Judge Walsh and Woodworth. If he wanted to overtake them, he would have to travel fast.

"If there are ledges there of that value," he said to his wife, "there will be litigation a-plenty and I must be in on it."

In ten years the cream had been skimmed from Yuba River bars. At the "Call of Washoe" those who had worked them left as precipitately as rats desert a burning ship. From Bill's standpoint the Yuba was a "played out" camp.

Bill had come to the mines directly from Yale—a magnificent long-limbed specimen of manhood. Broad-shouldered, thin-flanked, sunburnt, ruddy complexioned, quick on his feet, quicker with his fists and, for a collegian, quick with the trigger. That kind of a man. He had a thatch of reddish gold hair, a pair of eyes like an eagle's, and a long beard like Moses'! And like Moses he was a lawgiver. No, he wasn't a giver—if you didn't accept Bill's pronouncements he believed in stuffing them down your throat. If you didn't understand you received a good punch on the nose by way of bringing you to your senses. He was a master of men, was Bill, and a master of circumstance. He believed in taking time and opportunity both by the forelock, at one and the same time.

It was because he was master of men, as well as circumstance, that Bill Stewart had lived down a New Haven heritage and had sprung triumphantly from the Yuba River bottom to the distinction of being District Attorney of Nevada County.

At Yale, Bill had begun the study of law. On the Yuba he had become a miner. But circumstance, as well as acumen, had proved to him that California jurisprudence was missing a good member so long as Bill Stewart worked with pick and pan.

In the spring of 1852 Bill was prospecting at Rough and Ready, a reckless mining camp ten miles from Nevada City. One day he found cause to go into the city. So he mounted his mule and for safety's sake poked a pair of "navies" in his holsters. On the outskirts of Nevada he stopped at a trough to water his mule. As he sat watering his steed Bill observed a mob of excited men, fifty or more, leading a handsome young fellow, over six feet tall, stripped naked except for pantaloons. At the heels of the well-set-up chap came a husky miner swinging a huge horse-whip.

"Hallo!" said Bill. "What's up?"

"They're hanging him," said a bystander.

"What for?"

"Stealing 300 Mexican doubloons from his bunkey."

"When?"

"Last night. Dare you stop them?"

"Yes," retorted Bill without stopping to think. "If I can get a word in . . ."

Dismounting and grabbing up his "navies," Bill plunged into the midst of the mob.

"There's a mistake," he shouted. "You've got the wrong man."

At the instant the mob was passing under a building still under construction. There was no roof, but the sides were up and cross stringers with some boards on them, and a ladder reaching to the platform.

"Take him up that ladder." And the crowd, swayed by the authoritative tone in Bill's voice, obeyed.

"Now choose a committee and try him," directed Stewart.

And the mob named Bill the first of a committee of six.

Bill took the ladder at a leap.

"What's your name?" he asked the naked man.

"Owens," came the reply.

Then word by word Bill drew from the accused the proof of his innocence. Long before he had adduced the last bit of evidence the mob was convinced that the wretch who had accused Owens of stealing did so to get the sack of gold he knew Owens was carrying. At that very moment Bill saw the guilty accuser running down the street, trying to make his escape.

"There's your man," yelled Stewart to the mob. "Go get him."

Away went the mob.[1] And Bill helped Owens down from the ladder and later to invest his money in a profitable lumber mill.

That fall Bill sold his mining outfit, bought a Blackstone, and began reading law in the offices of J. R. McConnell, District Attorney of Nevada County. There were those who, having seen him handle his ore wagon and oxen, drew a gloomy picture of the future of an accomplished "bull-whacker" who tried to be a lawyer.[2]

Never sensitive and always sanguine, Bill worked on the theory that a man who could successfully engineer an ox team could, if he tried, succeed in other fields of effort.

In November Bill passed his bar examinations. McConnell resigned from office. On the same day Stewart was appointed to fill the vacancy.

Never having practised law, Bill found himself unfamiliar with technicalities, although able to cope with general principles. During the trial of his first case the defense attorney cornered Bill and called him a liar. Whereupon, Bill drew back his fist and struck his adversary a terrific blow between the eyes, knocking him to the floor. The attorney was removed, unconscious, from the courtroom. Bill was fined and sent to jail. The court adjourned. That night Bill mastered the technicalities of his case. Next morning he made his apologies to the court and won the decision. From then on no lawyer ever questioned Bill's ability to extricate himself from legal difficulties.

Bill did so well in the law game that he established a chain of offices. Beside the one in Nevada he opened branches in Downieville and San Francisco. In the latter place Bill formed a lawpartnership with Hon. Henry S. Foote, an ardent Southerner, a Democrat, and ex-United States Senator from and ex-Governor of Mississippi.

His partner's attractive daughter, Miss Annie, made San Francisco an alluring place. But when Bill's mountain practice became demanding, Bill abandoned tidewater California without a pang.

Shortly after his return, Bill started the construction of a fine twostorey house with wide balconies, on Nevada City's main street.

"What you want of so pretentious a structure?" asked one of his friends.[3]

"The finest girl in all the Golden West has consented to marry me," retorted Bill without revealing the lady's identity. "And I'm going to San Francisco to get her and bring her up here."

When the prospective bridegroom took the down-stage to the Bay the boys promised a mountain chivaree for the bride's homecoming, with plenty of champagne and oysters.

Arrived in San Francisco, Bill found his intended bride in a dilemma. She had found another man—more to her liking. She was humiliated but there was nothing to do about it. It would be wrong to marry any other man than her new love.

It was a bitter pill to swallow. But Bill made no comment, uttered no reproach, expressed no sorrow, merely asked the name of the favored suitor.

The lady told him. Bill bade her good-bye, went back to his hotel, and threw himself down in a lobby chair to think. The worst of it was those boys in Nevada City. He would be the laughing-stock of the Yuba. He couldn't go back to that pretentious house and tell the boys he had been jilted. Even in San Francisco he could hear them jeering Bill Stewart!

While Bill was sitting there his old partner, ex-Senator Foote of Mississippi, came along and seeing Stewart, asked him to take a drink. Bill acquiesced, then asked Foote to drink with him. And so they made a night of it. At a late hour they threw themselves down in Bill's room and went to sleep.

"Stewart," said the fiery Foote on awakening the next morning, "your political principles are a disgrace to the world, but personally I like you. And it will be a pleasure to me at any and all times to serve you personally."[4]

"You can do me a great favor right now," said Bill. "I want your permission to ask your daughter Annie to be my wife."

"Well," said Foote, "as I told you, your political principles are a disgrace, but I never go back on my word. Go and see if you can fix things up with Annie all right. She might do worse."[5]

That afternoon Bill called on Miss Foote and asked her to be his wife.

"I must have time to consider the matter," said the young lady.

"Every day you are considering," insisted Bill, "will be a day lost for us both."

Bill won the point. Within a week they were married and were off to a triumphant entry into Nevada City.[6] And the chivaree that the boys gave to welcome the bride is still remembered on the Yuba.[7]

Bill's prosperity increased. He and his wife agreed perfectly on every subject except secession. On slavery they were hopelessly divided and agreed to avoid the subject.

Bill's friendships included the most prominent men on the Pacific Coast. Once John Bigler, then Governor of California, came to Nevada City to make a campaign speech. When Bill heard the executive grossly insulted by Whigs in the audience, he jumped upon the stand and censured his friends for their treatment of the governor. During Bill's denunciation a pistol shot rang out in the audience. Unperturbed, Bill continued his scorching invective. Six months later a grateful governor appointed Bill Attorney-General of California.[8]

Then came 1859 and the "Call of Washoe." Bill saw Nevada and Downieville empty themselves of population and potential clients. As a place of opportunity the Yuba was exhausted. Beyond the Sierra Bill visioned fresh possibilities. He must be on his way. Like a lion, stalking up and down his cage, he dreamed of the day when he would be lord of a new jungle. Washoe might be wild—but he sensed opportunities among its granite crags.

Tossing back his tawny hair, Bill bade his bride adieu. "I'll be back before winter sets in," he promised as he joined the rabble that was surging over the Sierra passes.

Six-feet-two-inches in his stockings, and weighing above 200 pounds, Bill towered head and shoulders over the average man on the trail. When those adventurers saw him striding confidently toward them, they recognized him as a superior being and compared him to the colossus of Rhodes.

"Bill's one of the wonders of the West," they declared with grim humor. "He has more brass in his make-up than that statue ever had."[9]

And they made haste to keep abreast with him.

CHAPTER IX

THE BOYS

1859–1862

George Hearst heard Washoe's secret from the agitated lips of Melville Atwood.[1]

"The ore is almost pure silver," Atwood had confided, "with a heavy percentage of gold. It's too incredibly rich to be possible. It's worth $3000 a ton. Washoe miners are throwing it away. Come. We must go."[2]

Hearst consulted his friend, A. E. Head. He was loath to leave Nevada City. He had just acquired the rich Lecompton mine. Fortune was already assured. Why go back to that terrible desert country? The very thought made him recoil.[3]

"You're bound to become rich," Atwood coaxed.

Hearst realized he must go. Washoe was too amazing to be neglected.[4]

He mounted his mule. With Head and Atwood in the lead he started off for Washoe. They must overhaul Judge Walsh and Woodworth. It would take four days.[5]

Somewhere in a Salt Lake gambling hole Langford Peel heard the Washoe call and pricked up his ears. Washoe was the place for him. Some of the boys said he was a Harvard graduate. But it is more likely that his wits had been sharpened by grinding contacts with Mississippi cane-brakes.[6] Nevertheless he was highly respected. His great physical strength, manly proportions, undoubted bravery, overflowing kindness, and repose of manner gave him unbounded influence in his sphere. He was another golden-man, golden beard, golden hair, slender of figure, soft-spoken, with wide blue eyes and a gentle way, a strange blend of recklessness and kindness; but he was gentle only when he was sober—in his cups he was a hellhound. Who would have ever taken him for a frontier "Big Chief," a Czar of the underworld? Yet before he reached Sun Mountain there were six notches on his gun-butt. After that—well for years Sun Mountain had a killing every morning for breakfast and Peel brought in his quota. He knew how to shoot from the hip and his aim was deadly. "The secret of shooting," he once ex-

53

plained, "is to shoot first." And his golden rule was: *"Do unto others as they would do unto you—only do it first."* Of course he was speaking of shooting, not deeds! He took no chances. He picked no quarrels. He brooked no insults. An eye for an eye. And he shot quick. God help the other man who started something he couldn't finish! There would be good pickings over in Washoe—plenty of flotsam and jetsam such as "El Dorado" Johnnie, "Sugarfoot" Jack Davis, "Fighting" Sam Brown, and other alumni of the Mississippi basin.[7]

Sam Brown was a "bad man." The first and worst of his breed. The sire of the Southwest tribe. A great, thick-witted, human Saurian with a booming voice and red side-whiskers which he kept tied under his chin. With long Spanish spurs rattling at his heels and a huge bowie-knife slung to his belt, the boys made way when they heard him coming. Why shouldn't they? Before he ever took the Washoe trail Sam Brown had fifteen notches on his gun-butt. He let it be known he intended to add more when he reached Washoe. For killing to Sam Brown was an art—a profession. He intended to be "Chief" there. Like an ogre, his appetite for blood was insatiable. When he couldn't shake money out of his victims he could at least squeeze a little blood. "Fe, Fo, Fi, Fum!" He was a living counterpart of that bed-time story of the nursery. When he walked into a saloon, sidewise, with his big Spanish spurs clanking along the floor and his six-shooter flapping under his coat-tails, the little "Chiefs" hunted their holes and talked small. He was a "bad man" but he had an Achillean heel! With all his artillery he was an arrant coward, never insolent to those with friends or to those who went armed like himself. He heard that Washoe call with joy.

Adolph Sutro, the cigar dealer, heard the Washoe cry. Should he go over the ridge or should he stay in San Francisco and sell tobacco? Sutro could not decide. Was Washoe an unsurpassed El Dorado or another Gold Bluff? Who knew? But being interested in mining and feeling considerable curiosity to see the spot for himself, Sutro decided to go.[8] Sutro was a Jew—a Jew with the eyes of a dreamer—the vision of a seer—the heart of a Viking—the faith of a child—and of a metal that not even hard-rock could wear down. He had a lion-like face, a brain that never slept. Nothing could dismay him—not even the English language. To the day of his death a "W" was a "V". But he thought along logical lines. When he got an idea it stuck. You couldn't root it out.

Jim Fair heard that call—"Silver in Washoe!" He did not hesitate. It was ten years since he had passed the mouth of Gold Cañon. In that period he had progressed from "mucker" to mining superintendent. On the way up he had learned a thing or two about quartz, veins, croppings—reduction. Those who knew said he had a fine nose for ore. He could "smell it out." Sometimes they called him "Slippery Jim." Especially when he said that he could not "smell" any ore though subsequent facts proved that he had. But those were his enemies. "Slippery Jim" didn't tell everything he knew by a long shot. He had that rare faculty of keeping his eyes and ears open and his mouth shut. Those times when he appeared the most indifferent marked the occasions when he was absorbing the most information. For two years he had been in charge of a mine at Angel's Camp. There he had married Teresa Rooney, the comely daughter of an Irish tavern-keeper. Teresa had blessed him with offspring, a small daughter Tessie and a smaller son, Jim, Jr. When the news of Washoe broke around Angel's, Jim told his wife that he wanted to go over there. He would stake out a good claim for her. And Teresa said go.[9]

John Mackay was at Downieville, mining on a bar, when the news about Washoe swept over the Yuba dam. Mackay had been there eight years, ever since he was sixteen, but had accumulated nothing except experience and hard knocks. He knew all about placers, though little enough about quartz veins. But he made up his mind to master that form too. Throwing his blankets over his shoulder he started up the trail, with the sure, nimble tread of youth.

Whatever he set his mind to Mackay could master. He might work with his muscles but he conquered with his brain. He carried his head high—on a pair of well-knit shoulders. His features were clean cut, tanned with sunshine, ruddy with health. They called him John, but they blended familiarity with respect because Mackay was handy with his fists. You couldn't get smart with John Mackay, not unless you wanted a fight. He wouldn't start one, no, nor look for one, but he knew how to wage one. By his side, when he answered the Washoe call, was Jack O'Brien. They were pals—in everything—thought, purse, ambitions. They even "bunked" together on the Yuba. "All we want out of Washoe's millions is $25,000," said Mackay. "Twenty-five thousand will fix us for life."[10]

"Oh, be rasonable now, John," returned his partner.

When Colonel Daniel Hungerford heard the call, he buckled on his armor and made ready for Washoe. Though far fonder of Mars than of Midas, he liked knight-errantry. He loved the smell of gunpowder, the tumult of battle, and was one of the best tacticians of his time. Already he had distinguished himself at Vera Cruz, Cerro Gordo, Contreras, and Chapultepec. Gallant conduct had placed his name on the roll of honor of more than one government dispatch. At Downieville he had organized the Sierra Guards, one of the first military organizations in the state. When he took the Washoe trail his command presented him with a magnificent gold sword, handsomely inscribed, as a memento.[11] With that sword he would hew a path for Washoe civilization to follow.

Physicians and surgeons hearkened to the Washoe call—Doctor S. A. McMeans, an intrepid Tennesseean and a rabid secessionist, lost no time in reaching Sun Mountain. With Terry, he had designs on Washoe. Edmund Gardner Bryant, M.D., a cousin of the poet William Cullen Bryant and a graduate of one of the best New York medical schools, was one of the first on the Washoe trail.[12] For years his silk-hat, frock coat, and polished boots had made him a distinguished figure in mountain mining camps. Early in the fifties he had drifted into Downieville and had married beautiful Marie Louise Hungerford, the clever daughter of the colonel. But when the Washoe excitement came the doctor felt the call. "That will be a fine place to start practising," said he. "Go with my father," urged Mrs. Bryant, "Eva and I will come in the spring." Off he started.

Charlie Fairfax heard that call and turned his face toward Washoe. The boys called him "Baron." Had he been in England he would have been Lord Fairfax as he was the lineal descendant of the British peer who played some part in our colonial history. Repeatedly he had been urged to return to England, assume the title, and restore the prestige of his family.[13] But he preferred the slouch hat, boots, and excitement of the Washoe trail to the white wig and strawberry leaves of the House of Lords. The gamble of life: more chance and less certainty appealed to Charlie!

There was Bill Stewart's partner, Henry Meredith of Nevada City, late of Richmond, Virginia—a tall, dark, handsome Southerner, a graduate of Columbia, a lawyer, distinguished for his skill in handling mining cases.[14] He was a knightly person—better adapted to a crusade than to the incredible Washoe trail. He kept his honor as unsullied as a knight. Of all those mad adventurers, Meredith was worthy of the best that Washoe had to offer.

There was Almarin B. Paul, a young Hercules who owned a

quartz mill at Grass Valley. He didn't want to listen to that call. But when George Hearst wrote him to sell—"sell at any price"— Paul sold out at a sacrifice to join his friend and build the mill that would bring him fabulous riches.

There was Donald Davidson, the Englishman, the representative of the London Rothschilds. As soon as he received Atwood's letter telling him of the assay he started out to get an option for his clients.

Judge David S. Terry, late of the California Supreme Court, harked to Washoe's call. Never was a clarion call so gratefully heard. *Persona non grata* in California courts, the news of Washoe came at an opportune moment. He was a fire-eating Southerner; a devotee of the chivalry-wing of Democracy and a rabid secessionist. In a way he was like "Fighting" Sam Brown, Langford Peel, and "El Dorado" Johnnie, a killer but a "gentleman" killer—a duelist. He had several notches on the butt of his derringer to point to when he started over the ridge. Hadn't he stuck a bowie into the jugular of police officer Hopkins during the Vigilante riots of 1857? For days after that stabbing, life was a gamble for Terry, only a few pulse-beats between him and the gibbet. Had those beats stopped there would have been another necktie party at Fort Gunnybags. On top of that escapade Terry resigned from the bench to kill United States Senator Broderick who was opposing slavery in California. Some men whispered that it was a political necessity. Others called it downright murder. But how else could slaves come? With a man like Broderick blocking the way! But they whispered it— not loud enough for Terry to hear. They didn't want a bowie in their jugulars nor a bullet in their lungs. Terry had ears more sensitive than his hair-trigger touch, and even as resentful! It was further rumored that in his partition of the West, Jefferson Davis had slated Terry for the governorship of Washoe.[15] Thus Terry had a threefold intention in taking the Washoe call: to get away from California, to set his rebel kingdom on its feet, and to get his share of law cases. With a body-guard of five rabid Southerners, all mounted on fine horses and armed to the teeth with rifles, off he charged to take possession of Washoe and establish slavery.

Then there was the Reverend Patrick Manogue, once a quartz miner at Moore's Flat near Grass Valley,[16] now a Jesuit priest fresh from the Seminary of Saint Sulpice in Paris, France.[17] Stalwart-limbed, courageous as a crusader he was. Back in California just in time to carry the Cross to silver-mad Washoe.[18]

There was Tom Peasley of New York, a member of a crack New York regiment, a member of an outstanding Manhattan fire company. In San Francisco, too, he had been enrolled in one of those pseudo-aristocratic fire companies. He was a finished athlete, could throw the discus further than any Greek, outdistance any runner. He didn't want silver—no, nor gold. He wanted adventure—deeds of daring—romance.

Then there was the frail Reverend Franklin Rising, an Episcopal Missionary-clergyman; Joe Goodman, editor—poet—littérateur! Rollin Daggett, founder of the San Francisco *Golden Era;* Duane Bliss, a Yankee lumberman; Henry Yerington, a Canadian youth with snow-white hair; Marcus Daly; "Lucky" Baldwin; Frank Tritle; Edward Visscher, the artist; J. Ross Browne, the humorist; Sandy Baldwin of "Flush-Times-In-Alabama" fame; all bent on making their "pile" and getting back to "the States."

These were only a few of the men who joined the rush to Washoe —but they give you the flavor of the troupe. Among them were those who were destined to take leading parts in the melodrama that was about to begin in the amphitheatre at the base of Sun Mountain. There were hundreds of others, thousands—ten thousand—twenty thousand—forty thousand, boys from "the States"; hellions from river towns; Yankees; secessionists, clerks, sailors, soldiers, lawyers, doctors, poets, authors, miners, artists, merchants, gamblers, swindlers, good men, bad men, lords, parvenus, women in men's clothing, wolves in the garb of sheep, hetaerae under the protection of the silk-hatted, velvet-cuffed gentry. Yes, and there were painted women with wreaths of roses in the rims of their poke bonnets, wreaths that should have been halos. Winged harbingers of civilization who would preserve more than they would destroy.

One of the noblest of them all was Julia Bulette. Some said she was French, some said she was English. Others, who had known her in New Orleans, claimed she was plain "Gulf." Whoever she was, her identity was never disclosed. But the boys were all devoted to her. "Her skin may be scarlet," one asserted, "but her heart is white." She was bad, but paradoxically good. By worthy deeds Julia seemed anxious to compensate for those by which she earned her bitter bread.[19]

Most of these adventurers left profitable businesses in California to answer the call of Washoe. Many were men of means. Some were "bummers." But as a whole they were the pick of California, the pick of the '49ers, the pick of America! Strange, but the majority were of the Anglo-Saxon race, natives of the Old South or of New England, with plentiful off-scourings from the Mississippi River brakes. They had given California freely of their "image." They had founded schools—churches—government. Now they were ready for Washoe.

CHAPTER X

RUSH TO WASHOE

1859-1863

Thus they started out, that heterogeneous collection of mortals, for the argent kingdom of Washoe, with no other ostensible purpose than the pot of silver at the end of the rainbow. Silver and adventure were the bonds that bound them together.

Every night the Sacramento River boats steamed across San Francisco Bay loaded to the gunwales with pilgrims bound for Washoe. Disembarking at Sacramento the boys picked up their staffs, walked or staged to Placerville, the favorite starting point for the silver mines.[1] From there the Washoe trail followed the old emigrant route over the Sierra to Dayton and Gold Cañon, some hundred and fifty transalpine miles. There were other passes over the mountains: the Downieville route through Beckworth's Pass, the Sonora, Big Tree or San Joaquin passes; but the favorite, most travelled and best maintained route was the Placerville one through Sportsman's Hall, Pete's, Dirty Mike's, Berry's Flat, Johnson's Pass, Lake Valley, and so on down into the Valley of the Carson.[2]

By the fall of 1859 these mountain roads were jammed with silver-mad bound for Sun Mountain. They poured through Sierra passes like pent-up streams that had gotten out of bonds. It was the greatest exodus since the days of '49. It surpassed that migration in one particular. The goal of the Washoe crusaders was one lone spot on the flank of a barren mountain a mile and a half above the sea. All the mules, jackasses, and oxen in California grunted their transport up the Sierra. Gamblers and confidence men travelled on priceless thoroughbreds. Some went in coaches, some in stages, a few in covered wagons, but the vast majority travelled on foot. Captain Richard Watkins, hero of Nicaragua, where he lost a leg, went on crutches. All carried packs, a blanket, frying-pan, and coffee-pot lashed to their backs. Some trundled wheelbarrows before them. There were flocks of sheep and herds of cattle in the rush,[3] driven upward by Mexican vaqueros yelling "Caramba"—"Carajo"—"Sacramento"—"Diablo"—until the air was blue. There were organ-grinders grinding out music; there was Bacchanalian dancing and singing, hallooing and shouting, reviling and cursing. But it was a procession of youth, youth such as the world has rarely seen, youth such as had followed Roland; or sought the Grail; or accompanied the crusader. Youth with heart as stout as oak, youth whose soul sang a saga of the trail, but youth that wanted not the Chalice, the Holy Sepulcher nor Washoe silver nearly so much as it wanted pure and unadulterated adventure.

As the boys left Placerville, a crowd of onlookers lined the highway yelling, "Go it Washoe!" And the pilgrims went—by gradual and continuous ascent—up—up the warm, forest-clad foothills of the Sierra and disappeared into clouds of red dust. The air was balmy, fragrant with flowers. Golden bees winged from bloom to bloom. Golden tanagers sang their merriest roundelays. Yellow butterflies fluttered down bars of sunlight. Quail scurried to cover. Wind whispered with Æolian sweetness. Springs gushed out of rocks, gurgled across the road, and tumbled in silvered spray hundreds of feet below. Sturdy pines shot out of mossy slopes, straight and inflexible as rods of iron, impregnating the air with the pungency of their balsam. Nature was joyous and gay.

Through the forests the cavalcade went, up avenues of resinous pine, in spring through budding corridors fragrant with azalea and lilac, in autumn through desiccated aisles hung with red toyon and ochre madrone, in winter over frozen passes, white and all but impassable with snow. Up—up, they went. Stewart, Terry, Sutro, Mackay, Fair, Manogue, gamblers, miners, doctors, lawyers, murderers, and traders, rich men, poor men, lords and ladies of high and low degree. A motley throng of players, they seemed, but they had hot blood, cold nerve, and high courage. In and out of the trees they wended their way like a procession of old-time mummers about to make their initial bow in some woodland amphitheatre. A Mid-Summer Night's Dream perhaps or some other mad frolic. It is seldom that a whole cast moves en masse through the wings at one and the same time. It is rare that the future population of a State descends on its location, like a falcon on its prey, in one fell swoop.

By the grave of Allen Grosch they passed and read the inscription, "Ethan Allen Grosch, Son of the Reverend A. B. Grosch. Born at Reading, Pennsylvania. Died January 28, 1857."

"And who might he be?" they wondered as they clambered on.

Up, up they climbed. To their right was the south fork of the American River now 500 feet below. Still higher they climbed.

The river was a thousand feet below, plunging through a rocky chasm on its way to the sea.[4] Happy river, fulfilling its destiny, on the way to the sea! So on from dawn to dusk, one joyous climb after another. The first night out from Placerville they reached Pete's, a tavern provided with a broken mirror, a common toothbrush on one string, a common comb on another. The second night out and they threw themselves, wrapped in their blankets, into the chaparral and slept like babes in the wood, or they crawled into compartments, made of dry-goods-boxes piled one above the other, and lay until dawn like the tenants of those rock-hewn catacombs of Taormina—utterly oblivious to all about them.

All day long, sometimes all night long, a counter-current of woebegone, weather-beaten, heart-broken men passed. They had been to Washoe. They had seen the elephant. Footsore, weary, surfeited, they went slowly by on their way to Placerville.

"Don't go on," begged one tattered, bedraggled æsthetician, "turn back before it is too late. Washoe is a terrible country. It has space but no atmosphere, soil but no verdure, mountains but no inspiration, sky but no clouds, no climate save that which blows over the Sierra in fragments, no seasons but winter, no title to property, no property worth having, and no shadows save those cast by mountains. Think of a country without shadows! Take my advice and stay away from Washoe."

But the pilgrims went on; they were determined to see the elephant for themselves.[5]

Often they passed saddle trains without riders; long lines of pack-mules tied one to the other and laden heavy with sacks of "blue-stuff" from the Ophir, Mexican, Gould & Curry, or Central, all bound for San Francisco smelters. Every mule had a string of bells strung from an arch over the collar. The pilgrims could hear those tintinnabulous bells miles away, warning them that a pack-train was coming and to make way. Those trains filled the boys with joy —they scattered pieces of quartz like largesse in their wake. They picked up the vagrant pieces. "Sulphurets of silver!" they mimicked with bated breath.

Once they overhauled a "customer" driving a jenny. He was Washoe all over. A mutual "good day" passed.

"Bound for Sun Mountain?" the "customer" queried.

"You bet," from the boys.

"It's a regular '49er over there."

"What do you think of Washoe?" asked one of the boys.

"HE WAS WASHOE ALL OVER."

From the painting by Nahl, in the author's possession.

TOLL HOUSE, DEVIL'S GATE.

Here Bill Stewart had a set-to with the bad-man Sam Brown.

"Richest country in the world," unhesitatingly.

"How do you hold your leads over there?"

"Oh! Be good on the shoot," returned the "customer." "There's no law there—no title. The best man on the shoot takes the best claims. No disputing over there."

The boys had learned what they wanted to know of Washoe. "The richest country in the world"—that was music to their ears. They could take care of the shooting. They spurred on and left the "customer" far to the rear.

Some of them passed M. Lauer, a French engineer sent out by his government to examine and report upon the mines of Washoe. He had no faith in them. "Sell out," he advised, "just as soon as you realize the smallest profit."[6]

"In the name of common sense," he said, "in the name of your great Continental Congress, if you have a claim in California hold on to it. Don't go pirouetting off to Washoe. Not one man in fifty there has a job."

But no one could give those Washoe-wild boys advice. No! Nor discourage them. They were mad—stark-mad for silver.

George Hearst, Head, and Melville Atwood toiled up the Sierra. Hearst's enthusiasm for Washoe had waned. Even though Gold Cañon would make him incredibly rich, what of it? He could never forget that desert—the white, blinding sand, the blistering heat, the sparse soil, the dusty sage, the sun that had fired his brain. How could he crawl back over that terrible way!

Lost in thought, Hearst fell behind his companions. He got off his mule—sat on a log—picked up a handful of dirt—let it run through his fingers. For a seeming eternity he toyed with the dust. In the Lecompton his future was secure. Up that desolate Gold Cañon what was secure but death and dust? Washoe was a wild goose chase! "Blue-stuff" a hoax!

Suddenly a "lucky" feeling came over Hearst. The "blue-stuff" seemed to summon him. Remounting his mule, he went galloping full-tilt toward Washoe.[7]

Towards evening on his third stage-day out from Placerville, Sutro drew near to Berry's Flat. Through the trees, as the stage galloped forward, he could see the camp-fires of those Washoe pilgrims who were ahead of him. Once in a while he glimpsed a view of lighted windows in Berry's Tavern. It was a welcome sight. The stage drew up before the door. Sutro alighted; *mein herr*, Berry, stood in the open door. Sutro elbowed his way through a mob of milling men and strode into the main room. A tremendous fire was burning in the fireplace. Blazing logs five feet long lay across the andirons, throwing out heat of such intensity that the occupants of the room were ranged against the further wall, screening their faces with bended elbows, squirming like a batch of half-cooked lobsters.

"Why such a tremendous fire?" asked Sutro.

"So's to prevent you from hanging over it," retorted the unsociable Berry.

After dinner, Sutro mounted a mule and pressed on rapidly until caught in a terrible mountain storm. The hail, sharp as a shower of needles, stung his face and nearly blinded him. Trees swayed to and fro. The noise of the wind tearing through the branches was fearful. His mule seemed instinctively to know that he must hurry on. On he went, as if fleeing before an implacable enemy. On the very summit Sutro met a lonely rider dashing along at tremendous speed. He wondered what could possibly induce any man to ride so fast through such a gale. The rider passed him at a mad gallop. He must have some very urgent business. "Who rides tonight through such a storm?" Sutro asked the first man he met.

"The Pony Express," came the reply, "the Pony Express." [8]

Terry and his five "secesh" friends, well mounted and armed to the teeth, clattered into the yard of Berry's Tavern. It was night. Terry was impatient. He wanted to get to Washoe, to take possession of those silver mines for the Confederacy.

"Here," ordered Terry as he alighted and handed over his horses to Berry, "take these horses, and see that you feed them well."

The Tavern was packed to the doors. Terry and his cronies fought their way within; fought their way to the dining-room; fought for food; fought for a place to sleep on the floor of the common bedroom, where they were packed as tightly, side by side, as sardines in a can and just about as oily and oozy. The next morning Terry and the rest, as one man, awakened and arose from their hard couch. Unwashed, unshaven, unkempt, bitten by bugs and vermin, they fought their way into breakfast, fought, like demons, for their beans and coffee and then fought their way into the great outdoors. Terry's horses were waiting, poorly groomed, straw hanging to their tails and manes. Terry was out of sorts. He looked them over with disgust.

"See, here," he said to the landlord, making no effort to disguise his displeasure, "these horses are only half fed. They have had nothing to eat but straw."

"See here, yourself," retorted Berry, "if I hear any more complaints, I'll knock the daylights out of you."

"Do you know who you are talking to?" said one of the Judge's friends, taking Berry aside and whispering in his ear. Before the explanation was finished Berry fled and was never seen again.

Terry was tremendously amused. Connecting the straw, the threat, and the man, he dubbed the place "Strawberry" and, to this day, so the place has remained, Strawberry Valley.[9]

From Strawberry to the summit was a short hike through a granite, boulder-strewn country. When they had climbed that last eminence, the impassioned Washoe pilgrims had a chance to pause, catch their breath, and look backward over a glorious scene of forest, vale and stream. The last look many of them would ever have of California. What a magnificent vista it was! What a heritage to leave! Poetic! Inspiring! What a setting for one of Rubens' Olympian fairy-tales! A judgment of Paris perhaps! California, sprung from the foam of the sea, would have received the apple. How Rubens could have interpreted that scene that the boys looked back upon! How he would have revelled in California! Her charm! Her graciousness! Her changing color! Her texture! Her vitality! Her dimpled mounts—luxurious curves—flowing lines! How generously he would have revealed those lineaments! In all that warm coloring in which he excelled—crimson, olive-brown, cool blue—a California as opulent-breasted as an Ephesian Diana!

How could they desert California for this Washoe siren? Would the high adventure on Sun Mountain—the rainbow and the pot of rainbow gold—compensate them? For none of these Jasons had any idea of staying in Washoe—a month—a year—would suffice to make their "pile"—then they would come back.[10] There was only one California and they left her, like a lover, that they might return, renewed at the fonts of life, more fervent, more ardent—to enjoy the feast spread before them.

Over the rocky summit the boys scrambled—then blithely, gaily down into the emerald-and-sapphire magnificence of Lake Tahoe.[11] Then up another ascent to where they could look over the rim of the Sierra and peer down into the land of Washoe. How forbidding! How disconsolate it looked! How repellent! Gaunt, hostile, gray as a coyote! After California, Washoe took their breath away. They were leaving Eden for this. Giving up Elysian wine for a mess of pottage! An arid, efflorescent waste, stippled with sage, was out-spread before them. For all the world it looked like the realm of Pluto. Broken mountains, cinders and scoria, burnt earth and crater-like hills showed that volcano, earthquake, and other terrific forces of nature had been active there at no remote period of the past. There were no signs of life. Aghast—the Washoe pilgrims stared down at that sterile scene. It was inexorable! An abode of Hades! As desolate as death! Around the head of the valley and running out into it were long barren ridges covered with rock and mountain drift—barren of every scrap of vegetation except artemesia and an occasional spike of bunch grass. A guide pointed over the dreary waste. "There," said he, "there are the great llanos. There is neither water nor grass—every animal that goes out upon them dies." [12]

Among them Almarin Paul gazed down upon that devastated area. "The fag-end of Creation," he mused. "The Almighty had some great idea when He planned Washoe, but half-way through He forgot. It was never finished. His creative power was exhausted. All that He had left was mineral. Regarding it of the least benefit to mankind He held onto it until He reached Washoe, then ·He emptied His lap." [13]

Over there was the Washoe Range, now only a short distance away. The boys looked with fixed eyes. Across the void, they could see the gray isolated magnificence of Sun Mountain rising, from the plain, in one majestic sweep to terminate in a stony finger that pointed into sapphire sky. As a mountain she was awe-inspiring. At her feet ran a wavering blue ribbon of a river. Arising about her were thin spirals of yellow smoke. Ascending in the same manner as incense, smoldering before some placid goddess, curls upward. Half-way up the mountain was their destination. To reach Virginia they must slide down three thousand feet, cross Carson Valley and then scramble two thousand feet up again.

A deep valley separated the Washoe Range from the Sierra. It was connected with the Sierra, only, by a series of low, twisted spurs, the umbilical cord, as it were, connecting it with California. Cut that cord and Washoe would have starved—starved as ignominiously as any unborn child. Perhaps that was what was the matter. Perhaps Mother Earth had bungled. Perhaps Washoe had starved. Perhaps during the final hours of gestation something had gone wrong in her womb. Perhaps Old Earth had been seized with volcanic con-vulsions, and, in the throes of her agony, Washoe had been born—premature, blighted.

It hardly seemed to be the earth at all that those boys gazed down upon. Some shivered. Others laughed. What a picture Washoe presented! Imbued with hues of ruin, she was monstrous—moody. Washoe had beauty and sublimity. But her beauty was of ashes, and her sublimity of desolation. She never was designed to be the abode of man. She was a nether-world. No brush or pigment could depict her. Washoe demanded harsher media, sterner treatment—bronze or porphyry, a chisel or a mallet, and the inspiration of a Saint-Gaudens. He could have interpreted her. A Washoe in sackcloth—crouched by the Carson—holding an urn of ashes—gazing with inexorable eyes into a region of bitter waters—and immemorial silence.

The most pitiless tyrant would have hesitated to exile his worst enemy into such a region. But undaunted, that torrent of silver-mad adventurers, Stewart, Sutro, Mackay, Fair, Terry, Manogue, and thousands of others, gazed over the ridge—then plunged below. Sliding, slipping, rolling over rocks and sage-brush, down they went into the Valley of the Carson. The odor of crushed sage was appalling. Like incense it arose to their nostrils. Forever after, that bitter odor would fill them with a vast nostalgia!

At Carson the jealous residents buttonholed the boys. "Don't go up to Virginia," they pleaded. "There's no food there; the water'll poison you; they shoot each other just out of fun." [14]

The boys laughed, and turned into the old emigrant road that led eastward toward Dayton and Gold Cañon. On their way they passed some springs disgorging hot water that sputtered and gurgled out of the earth with a deep, guttural, subterranean sound. From jagged fissures spurted jets of yellow steam, ejected with a forcible sound, like the hiss of a snake. The ground was red with cinnabar, yellow with sulphur, and black with tar. A stream of pitch-blackened fluid edging off into the desert stank worse than putrid eggs. [15]

Lizards with yellow backs slithered under their feet. Horned toads scuttled into the brush. Jack-rabbits bolted in ridiculous alarm. Wraith-like coyotes slunk through the greasewood. It was a hopeless, deformed country. The heart of more than one of those impassioned pilgrims sank into his boots, to be bruised and lacerated with every step its owner took toward the mouth of Gold Cañon. The more desolate it became, the hotter the sun grew—the more bitter arose the aroma of sage.

As he was passing the springs, Sutro caught the stench of sulphur. He, too, smiled. "A fitting odor for this country," he said. When he came to a wayside saloon with a sign "Nick's Tavern" placarded over the door he burst into laughter. Brimstone and Nick's on the way to Washoe! What next?

The hills began to rise toward Sun Mountain. The brush grew rank and tall. The boys came to the mouth of the Cañon and turned up its rocky defile. "That's the Devil's Gate," some one announced. Sutro read the sign that stretched across the road: "Devil's Gate Toll Road—50c—Pass on and up." There was no doubt in his mind now as to where he was headed.[16] Had a cavalcade of imps armed with pitchforks rushed out to grab him, he would not have resisted. A terrible tumult came down the Cañon to greet them. Shrieks and yells. Men were pummelling one another with clubs and bottles.

"Vas ist it?" asked Sutro.

"A question of title," he was answered.

Sutro was positive now. He was in the realms of Pluto. That was it. And he was headed straight for Hell. That was that incredible Cañon's only excuse for existence. It was the corridor of Purgatory!

Up the boys went. Straight up the mountain. The Cañon became deeper, gloomier, colder, windier, dustier. Its walls rose sheer and steep. Up Gold Cañon the boys clambered. By the unmarked sage-brush-covered grave of Hosea Grosch. By Eilley Orrum's boarding-house on Gold Hill. On up to the Divide. They looked over the top. Virginia burst into view, shaking and fluttering as if undecided whether or not to stay or to run to cover and hide in the earth. Yes, it was '49 over again. Forty-nine without wind in the trees, '49 without the gurgle of water—but all else was there; frame shanties, like a deck of cards, pitched together by accident,[17] tents of canvas, of blankets, of old shirts.

The empty sleeve on one of those hovels flapped back and forth as if in distress. It beckoned the boys to come on. They went. Miners in blue shirts with unkempt beards, Piutes with arrows, saloons with open doors, touts with clubs, gamblers with cards, speculators with "wildcats," confidence men with loaded dice, women with painted cheeks and gold teeth—all—were waiting for them.

Thus Virginia, sired by adventurers, daughter of old Mother Earth, met the startled gaze of those impassionate pilgrims. Virginia lying on the lap of Sun Mountain, noisy and raucous. Virginia without beginning; Virginia without end; Virginia without pattern, without God, without law!

Jack O'Brien looked down at the tumultuous city and turned to his pal John Mackay:

"John, have yez any money?" he queried. "I'm broke."

"Yes," said Mackay, "four-bits."

"Hand it over, thin," and Mackay passed the coin to his pal.

O'Brien took it, curved his right arm and sent the half-dollar skimming over the sage-brush down the Cañon as far as he could throw.

"What you doing?" said Mackay. "That's my last."

O'Brien took his arm. "Let us inter the city loike gintlemen," he replied.[18]

BOOK TWO

BONANZA

CHAPTER XI

ARRIVAL

1859

On the last day of June, Judge Walsh and Joe Woodworth urged their exhausted jenny up Gold Cañon.[1] By superhuman effort they had crossed the Sierra in two days. The jenny was winded. But the twain hastened to Spanish Ravine and went into negotiations with Comstock, O'Riley and McLaughlin for the sale of the Ophir.[2]

Judge Walsh had arrived in the nick of time. Already Comstock had sold a sixth interest in the Ophir to a heavy-lidded Mexican, Gabriel Maldonado, for a couple of jackasses.[3]

That sixth interest became the Mexican bonanza. Millions in dollars flowed from its shaft-head. It is estimated that each of those jackasses had cost Comstock $3,000,000. But Comstock wasn't bothered about such trifles as millions. Alternately exalting and belittling his possessions, he went the way of his delusions. He was a multimillionaire. The richest man in Washoe! The nabob of Washoe! Sometimes his good fortune moved him to laughter; sometimes dissolved him in tears.

While Walsh was carrying on pre-buying investigations, Comstock, one day, deeded over his entire interest in the Ophir to one Herman Camp for a small sum, one dollar of which was paid down.[4] That night, at Jones' Bar, when Comstock boasted of his deal the Johntowners hailed him as a "crazy damn'd fool." The next morning, at the point of their shotguns, they helped Comstock regain his property. When a law suit followed the Johntown jury jeered at Camp's claim. Amidst derisive jests the deed was returned.[5]

On August 10, after the first consignment of Ophir ore, smelted in San Francisco, had yielded $114,000, or $3000 per ton, Judge Walsh went into final negotiations with Comstock.

From where they sat in Spanish Ravine both had a good view of the incredible city as it serpentined crazily toward the peak of Sun Mountain.

"We'll give you $5000 for your share of the Ophir," tempted Walsh.

Although, at the time, Comstock believed that the Ophir was only a rich pocket of ore, he shook his head. And getting to his feet, he pointed with a shaky index finger down at the ragged camp.

73

"The Comstock is worth millions," bragged the old gasconader in a thick voice. "It's bound to become a great city. The Ophir will become one of the greatest producers in the world."[6]

Walsh gazed down at the camp. Perhaps Comstock spoke the truth. "We'll make it $11,000." Trembling all over at the mention of a sum of money that seemed to him a fortune, Comstock accepted their offer.

That night with his drink-sodden cronies in Jones' bar, Comstock bragged of how he had fooled "that California Rock Shark," as he called Walsh.[7] So Comstock, on the strength of stolen knowledge, made his exit with a pittance when he might have had millions.

A few years later, when limelight failed and the ears of erstwhile listeners had grown inattentive to his importance, Comstock looked down the muzzle of his "navy," pulled the trigger, and bespattered the Bozeman trail with his brains.

Three days after Walsh and Woodworth had arrived, George Hearst, Head and Atwood galloped up Gold Cañon and tore down on the Ophir cut. The Johntowners were still incredulous over the "blue-stuff."[8] Doubters claimed that Mexican swindlers had salted the earth with lead. Hearst had worked in lead mines. He knew they were mistaken. His practised eye could discern the difference between lead and silver ore. The "blue-stuff" was incredibly rich. But he had no available money with which to purchase an interest. The temptation being great, he borrowed a thousand dollars from a hotel keeper, sold the rich Lecompton mine, and proffered McLaughlin $2500 for his Ophir interests. Promptly his offer was accepted. During that bitter winter, Hearst, Head, and Atwood took forty-five tons of "blue-stuff," muleback, to a San Francisco smelter; then rushed the resulting precious "black-stuff" to the mint. Days of nervous waiting passed. Were they credulous fools? Or about-to-be millionaires?

Finally, C. H. Hemstead, the mint superintendent, sent them a message: *"Boys, come up tonight and I'll give you some money."*[9] The boys went.

Their Ophir ore had yielded $2200 a ton. Eighty thousand glittering, clinking Sun Peak dollars were waiting for them. The "blue-stuff" was good! The belly of Sun Mountain was bursting with more! Hearst and his friends crammed their pockets full of dollars, and rushed down to the nearest saloon on Montgomery Street in San Francisco to find out whether Washoe dollars would pass for Bourbon whisky. They did.[10]

During the next few years Hearst amassed more than a million dollars[11]—the first of the emigrants to establish the legend of Washoe millionaires.

Once, during those hectic early days, Woodworth declined an offer of a million dollars for his interests.[12] Walsh could have cashed in for more than twice as much. But the goddess was against them. She was reserving her favors for younger, more daring gamblers.[13]

While the prospect-hole of the two Irishmen was yielding $17,-655,000, Pat McLaughlin became cook in a sheep-herding camp at $40 a month; Pete O'Riley, who had realized some $40,000 on his interests and had built a stone hotel on "C" Street and lost it boring a tunnel through a near-by granite mountain under spirit guidance, died in an insane asylum and was buried at public expense;[14] and Alvah Gould, part owner of the enormously rich Gould & Curry, sold his half-interest to a Californian for $450, then went cavorting down Gold Cañon yelling, "I've fooled the Californians!"[15]

The long-suffering goddess was tired of wooing such stumbling loafers. From the emigrant road she had picked them up. Through Dayton, up Gold Hill, over the Divide to the portals of her treasure-house, she had beguiled them. Throwing wide the doors she had permitted them a glimpse of wealth, such as the world had never seen, only to hear Comstock bellow that he had taken in "the California Rock Shark"; and to hear Gould shout, "I've fooled the Californians!" Such ingratitude was too much even for a goddess. In disgust she discarded them. With derisive laughter she saw them go stumbling down Gold Cañon to penury and oblivion. For ten years she had been courting swashbucklers! As she turned away, she paused to powder her nose and straighten her bodice. After all, even a goddess is human. She must look her best. For beyond the forests, where the body of Allen Grosch lay, there ascended the sound of an advancing army. Candidates more worthy of her favors were thundering at her gates. Thither she looked. Such horsemen she had never seen in Washoe! Such knights as now came trooping up Gold Cañon! The audacious Bill Stewart, the jester Rollin Daggett, the knightly Meredith, the peerless John Mackay, the indomitable Adolph Sutro, the courageous Patrick Manogue, the sleek Jim Fair, the bold Dave Terry, the superb Tom Peasley!

The goddess looked them over. On which would she cast her favor?

CHAPTER XII

THE IMAGE

1860

As soon as Sam Brown arrived on the Lode he made a tour of inspection.[1] His spurs could be heard jangling along the floor of every bar on Sun Mountain. He had an ambition to fulfill. He must consecrate the Lode—draw the first blood—be the first "Chief" of the Comstock. He must show the boys what great sport murder was. He was proud of his killings. He intended to "get" the first man of the season. Just as a keen sportsman yearns for the first deer.

One day leaning against a bar he found his quarry—one Bill Bilboa —a misfit—without following. There had been no quarrel between them but Sam saw that his man was friendless. Deliberately he picked a quarrel with him and glutted his thirst for blood by stabbing him again and again. Sam always selected a lone solitary individual from that class for his "man for breakfast." Never did he attack an armed man or one with supporters. They might strike back. Start a Washoe vendetta? That would be taking unnecessary chances. Sam never took any, like braver and more reckless men do. In January of 1860 he stabbed Homer Woodruff—a bit of wanton butchery, but nothing was done about it.[2] Altogether, that winter, Sam carved up some sixteen men and bragged about it. He was maintaining his own private cemetery.[3] With such a record he swaggered from bar to bar, vain of the fact that every one gave him a wide berth.

One day one of the boys dropped into a station that Sam maintained on the Carson. He was hungry and asked for something to eat. Sam pointed to a strip of bacon hanging from a rafter. "Help yourself," he said.

"Where's your knife?" asked the traveller.

With an odd smile Sam pulled his immense bowie out of his bootleg—whetted it. "I've killed five men with that knife," Sam boasted, "and am superstitious about lending it to cut bacon."[4]

When Bill Stewart saw how the Lode was located he laughed and

76

laughed. From crest to base Sun Mountain was so driven with signs of location that it looked like the sole of a pegged boot. More land was taken up than Washoe could provide. Claims overlapped three and four deep. All was confusion both on the mountain and in the recorder's office. Swindlers were happy. They didn't want to develop a claim—only a lawsuit.

With no law but the shotgun, Bill saw that Washoe was in a pretty mess. Before long rival claimants would be at each other's throats. With calumny, crime and subornation, he would have his hands full. But he must hold the reins and whip Washoe into shape. Washoe must serve his purposes.

Soon after his arrival the roughs "jumped" a valuable mine at Devil's Gate. Being against murder, the boys who owned it turned towards some one with authority. They wanted a leader. Instinctively one of them suggested Bill Stewart. Yes—Bill was the man—trained in the intricacies of the law. They would search him out—appeal to him. Bill could always find a way out.

They located him. "Arbitration," advised Bill, "was the thing." He would go down to Devil's Gate with them. Bold—brave—strong, Bill gave the boys confidence. Immediately they had faith in him. He could move mountains. They multiplied his strength tenfold.

Throwing on a thin overcoat, Bill dropped a Texas derringer into each of the long side-pockets. "No use taking chances on a mountain ruled by the shotgun," laughed Bill. "If we come to close-range work, a derringer or a bowie is the only piece of artillery worth having. Pistols carrying a small ball maim but rarely kill. In the meantime your antagonist has a chance to 'get' you with a knife or gun; but if I hit a man with one of these one-ounce balls, I'll knock him 'cold.'" Into another pocket Bill emptied a handful of one-ounce balls. No use taking chances.

Thus fortified, they started down Gold Cañon to Devil's Gate. On arrival Bill went over the ground with the boys. When his inspection was finished, Bill suggested that they go to the Devil's Gate Toll House to talk the matter over. They walked up the Cañon and entered the little stone building used as a tollhouse. It was divided into two rooms. The larger, the one they entered, contained the bar. Adjoining it was a smaller room. Into it Bill walked and sat down with his back against the wall, near the door, which opened into the barroom. "Here," he said, "we'll have a chance to talk the situation over quietly." He picked out three arbitrators, and called in a Utah justice of the peace to swear the witnesses. Proceedings commenced. All of a sudden Stewart heard the clattering of Mexican spurs on the barroom floor. A voice, out there, boomed out:

"How are you?"

Stewart pricked up his ears. Instantly—instinctively he knew that hoarse voice. He knew those spurs—that clanking accompanying sound. They belonged to Sam Brown, the notorious killer whom the Utah authorities dared not arrest. Sam was out there in the barroom. He always had everything his own way. Stewart knew what had happened. Sam had come to be a "witness."

He knew only too well that if Sam Brown came into that small room and anything displeased him, some one would be killed—probably Bill Stewart.

Quietly Bill slipped his hands into his pockets, cocked his two derringers, pointed their muzzles at the door, and waited. Anyhow they gave him a feeling of confidence. If one of those one-ounce balls hit Sam he would quit his nonsense. When Sam came through the door Stewart trained them on his heart.

Without noticing Stewart, Sam swaggered up to the justice of the peace, and raised his hand. "Swear me," he ordered.

"Swear the witness," called out Stewart. The judge timidly complied.

"What have you got to say, Brown?" demanded Stewart. "What do you know about this case?"

"Know about it," said Brown, "I've got an interest in that ground." He gave his testimony and went out.

The referees adjourned to the barroom to consult. Stewart following behind the others, brought up the rear.

As Stewart passed through the door he confronted Brown, who stood facing him with his elbow on the bar. Expecting at every step that Sam would open up, Stewart continued to hold his derringers in front of him.

Brown barred the way, cursing with every breath. "I like your kind, Stewart," he drawled. "Come—take a drink with me."

Stewart stepped up to the bar, one derringer still trained on the "killer's" heart. With the other hand he poured out a drink, touched glasses with Brown, "Here goes!"

"You and I," said Sam, "could get justice in a mining camp."

"You're right," replied Stewart. "We could."[5] Holding Brown with his eyes, he swallowed his liquor straight, and the danger-point was passed.

In a few months, Bill's unflagging energy, unfaltering nerve, hard sense, bold ambition, and colossal self-assertion lifted him above the "muck" and gave him a good grip upon the reins and whip of those lunging forces that he had set himself to control—those forces to which he had hitched his chariot.

The Reverend Franklin S. Rising of New York—"the fragile, gentle, new fledgling"—the minister of Mark Twain's famous Buck Fanshaw episode—was determined to establish an Episcopal church on Sun Mountain. With the help of his brother, Judge Richard Rising, he held forth on Sundays in the improvised court-house. He had scarcely installed himself in his lodgings when there came a hammering on his chamber door. A gambler stood on the threshold. There had been a "shooting" in the saloon below-stairs. The hours of one of the duelists were numbered. The dying man wanted a minister. Would he come at once?

"Do you think that your friend," said the Reverend Rising with some hesitancy, "would like to have the Eucharist administered to him before he passes away?" The pal was more familiar with faro than with theology.

"Well, it seems to me a queer time for that sort of thing," replied the puzzled sport. "Howsoever, you know your business, and it ain't for me to interfere. If you choose to take your deck along, I reckon it will be all right."

As soon as Terry and his henchmen reached Sun Mountain they took up three commanding points along the Lode, had them surrounded with high stone walls and well fortified. Sentries with guns over their shoulders marched day and night, up and down, calling out "All's well," at all hours.

There was not any doubt in the boys' minds. Terry intended to hold Washoe for the Confederacy. Hadn't he killed Broderick to make way for slavery in California? Hadn't he boasted that slaves were coming to Washoe? He wanted slaves on Sun Mountain—not to work the mines for himself but in the cause of the South. The boys spoke of these fortifications as "Terry's Forts."

It so happened that one of the three walled points belonged to George Hearst and was part of his Ophir holdings. When Hearst discovered Terry there, knowing who he was, he employed a man named Tom Andrews, a fighting Kentuckian who practised under the shotgun and revolver code, to run Terry off his property. Andrews was a man of nerve, of cool and desperate courage. He wasn't afraid of that fire-eating Texan. Seeking Terry out he came directly to the point. "The best thing you can do, Terry, is to get away," he said. "If you suppose this is 'jumpable' ground you're mistaken. I'm here to defend Hearst's property, so clear out." Tom looked as if he meant every word he said. Terry knew it. He left, remarking that if the ground was Hearst's property he did not want anything more to do with it.

Shortly thereafter two Irishmen, taking courage from the reports of this encounter, "jumped" another of "Terry's Forts"—the one up on the Divide. When the Fenians proceeded to stake off a portion of it for a notorious woman known as "the Sage Hen," Terry came upon them. There was blood in his eye. "Get out," he ordered, without mincing matters. When they undertook to whip him Terry turned upon them and knocked them both cold.[6] Thus two of "Terry's Forts" remained in the possession of the South.

As soon as he arrived, Donald Davidson, the Rothschilds' representative, secured an option on the Mexican Mine. "Hold it," he said to heavy-lidded Maldonado, "until I can hear from London." Immediately he wrote his employers reporting its vast richness, and waited. In the course of time the Rothschilds sent out to Washoe their best mining experts, graduates of Freiberg, to examine the ledge. When these experts finished their examination they reported the Mexican worthless. "It is a contact vein," they wrote, "and utterly worthless." Whereupon Davidson surrendered the option to the Maldonados. One of whom expressed his gratification at getting it back.

"For," said he, "we can get three times the amount your option calls for."

"I am glad of it, boys," retorted Davidson, "but you know the Rothschilds do not speculate, they invest."

In less than five years from that time the Rothschilds, like all the speculative world, were "investing" in Comstock. For the Mexican made millionaires by the bushel.[7]

On one of his Comstock trips, Davidson accompanied a party of hilarious boys to the summit of Sun Mountain. On their way up they located every outcropping of promising appearance. That evening when champagne corks were popping in old Topliffe's palatial "shebang," it was unanimously agreed to christen their grand old mountain, Mount Davidson, in honor of their generous provider.[8]

But the boys would have none of it. They still continued to call it Sun Mountain.

One evening, during those wild early days, Father Manogue was called to see a woman who was dying and wished to make her peace with God. Having arrived at the woman's home in one of the lower quarters of the city, an infuriated man met him at the door, a revolver in his hand. "No damn'd priest," he yelled, "shall enter here," and he jabbed the muzzle into the Father's ribs.

"I have come," called the Father through the door to the woman he could see lying on the couch within.

"Quick, Father!" sobbed the dying woman. "I have sinned . . ."

Like a flash the Father grappled with the man, grabbed the gun, overpowered him and threw him on the floor. "Now stay there," ordered the prelate, "until I have finished." Having captured the fort and thrust the revolver into his pocket, the Father's manner changed to a gentler one.

Approaching the pallet, where the dying woman, breathing faintly, lay, he handed her the Cross, found two candles, drew up a table to the bedside, spread his clean linen handkerchief over it, placed the candles, lighted them, heard her confession, anointed her, administered the Last Sacrament and knelt in prayer by her side until the tired breathing ceased and her eyelids closed. Then he tiptoed softly out of the room, leaving the man on the floor, the two candles flickering at the head of what was now the woman's bier.

It took a man to carry the Cross on Sun Mountain as well as a gentleman to administer it.[9]

On arrival Henry Meredith set up law offices with his partner Bill Stewart. There was plenty to do—with "jumping" and litigation. One day he learned that a poor woman was lying desperately ill in a near-by camp. Penniless and abandoned by a brute husband, she had given up hope of ever seeing her children again. Meredith heard of her plight, located her cabin, opened the door, put a hundred dollars into the woman's hand and was gone before she could learn his name. Before that hundred was gone he was back again. When she was well enough he returned her to her children.[10] That was Henry Meredith, always doing deeds of kindness—searching out the suffering—helping the needy—encouraging the failures—heartening the misfits.

It was distressing to Sam Brown, Langford Peel, and "El Dorado"

Johnny to see Father Manogue, Bill Stewart, and Henry Meredith making their way on the Comstock. For with them came the Cross —rules and regulations.[11] Church bells! School bells! The tocsin of the Vigilantes! Order out of chaos! Soon the minie-ball would be losing its whine.

Julia Bulette's palace became the only real home the boys had. All social life went on within her well-lighted, well-regulated, fragrant walls. Julia would put up with no nonsense. When the boys entered her parlor, they left their rough manners at the door—they behaved or out they were hustled. She taught them to distinguish between the bouquet of the French wines she served and the odor of "tarantula juice." She created an appetite for French cooking. She showed them what was worn on the Rue de la Paix. She caressed Sun Mountain with a gentle touch of splendor.

Their money gone, John Mackay and Jack O'Brien built themselves a flimsy little cabin over in Spanish Ravine and went to work as day-laborers. Mackay cared nothing for cards, less for liquor, and none for gambling. Every day he saw a game played in the heart of the great lode which dwarfed all other games of chance, seeing that health, fortune, and life itself were staked on the turn of a drill or the strike of a pick. The whirl of the mighty lottery wheel beneath his feet riveted his eyes. He longed to be one of the puissant croupiers who turned the wheel and questioned fate. Not to make money for the pleasure of money-making alone, not to be enabled, like Sandy Bowers, to scatter gold broadcast with prodigal hands, not to be known as a "nabob" or "bonanza king," but to win a name as master and manager of the greatest mines in the world—this was what John Mackay wanted; wealth as a world-moving lever, for with money he could, so he thought, attain any end which seemed to him worth prizing. That was what he must have—power.[12]

While Jack O'Brien was off with the boys having a good time, Mackay's attention was centred on the drifts under his feet. His restless eye surveyed the lode from end to end, and he studied every move of those in charge. For John Mackay intended to come up in the world. And the goddess was with him. Here was a knight after her own heart.

Soon after Sutro's arrival he visited the Ophir cut. The miners were bringing rock to the surface in buckets.[13] A joint shaft had been sunk in connection with the adjoining Central Company. The dividing-line between was marked off with a plumb-line. Quantities of ore lay on the dumps. Selected pieces ran $10,000 to the ton.[14]

Then Sutro visited the Gould & Curry. Hundreds of thousands of dollars lay in sight. The Chollar was paying from sage-brush roots down. He was dumfounded at its richness. Heavy-lidded Gabriel Maldonado was working the Mexican with peon labor. Mexicans, with leather buckets strapped to their foreheads, ran up and down slippery ladders, lithe as monkeys. Gould & Curry had been offered a million dollars for their claim. "The Comstock's barely nicked," claimed experts and the offer was refused.[15]

Sutro had expected to witness an extraordinary deposit, but he was dumfounded at its magnitude. Forty tons of Ophir ore had yielded $200,000! That piece of news took Sutro's breath away! It was colossal!

Sutro turned his attention to the topography of the country. He recognized at a glance that nature had so fashioned the locality that the greatest facilities existed for the construction of a deep tunnel. That was the way Sun Mountain should be mined. From down there on the Carson. From the bottom up. He could engineer it. He had inspected the greatest tunnels in Germany. He knew all about them. As there was no law and no capital in Washoe all the companies had to be organized in San Francisco under California laws and with California money. Sutro determined to take up his plan with the directors.

"The working of the mines," he wrote, "is done without any system as yet. Most of the companies commence without an eye to future success. Instead of running a tunnel from low down on the hill, and then sinking a shaft to meet it, which at once insures drainage, ventilation, and facilitates the work by going upwards, the claims are entered from above and large openings made which require considerable timbering, and expose the mine to all sorts of difficulties."

"That Sutro is a bright man," said the San Franciscan who read that article. "Watch him."

No arrangments had been made for crushing or milling. All the richest ore was sent to San Francisco en route to Wales or Freiburg. With a practical eye, Sutro wrote, "Smelting-furnaces, quartz-crushers, and all the machinery required for the successful reduction of ore, could be erected in the valley, and an inexhaustible supply of wood and timber furnished by floating it down the Carson River from points some distance above, where there is abundance."

Sutro sought out the superintendents of the Ophir and Gould & Curry and told them about the tunnel. But they wouldn't listen!

"Impractical," they said. To every mining operator he could button-hole, Sutro talked "tunnel." But he only met with indifference. "A tunnel to the Carson!" miners said with a sneer.[16] "Why, it's six miles away!"

After that, when they saw him coming, mine operators avoided him. But with prophetic vision Sutro continued looking down Six Mile Cañon to where he could see the river fringed with green alders. "A railroad from the Comstock to the Carson," he said, "could be built at a very small expense, the country sloping as it does so gently toward the river." Nobody would listen. He was too chimerical.

"He's crazy," the boys laughed, "absolutely crazy."

"Cars loaded with ore," Sutro continued, "could be made to pull up a train loaded with provisions. Once at the river, the ore can be easly worked."

"Poor devil," they mocked.

Suiting action to vision, Sutro went down Six Mile and took up an immense tract of desert land along the Carson.

"What're ye going to do with that desert?" a prospector asked.

"Raise vegetables," replied Sutro.

"Where'll ye git the water?"

"Out of that mountain," and Sutro indicated the base of Sun Mountain.

The prospector looked at the sterile slopes of the rising upland, dry as bone and covered with sun-shrivelled sage. He was dum-founded.

"Crazy," he muttered. "Crazy as a loon."[17]

CHAPTER XIII

VIRGINIA
1859–1860

Out of the mines, "wildcat" or sound, emerged a city that had known neither infancy nor adolesence. Like Minerva from the brow of Jupiter, Virginia had sprung, full grown, from the loins of Sun Mountain and sprawled, an ulcerous chaos, across her breasts.

But the boys liked their lofty perch among Washoe's granite peaks. Above them, 2000 feet into bright-blue ether, projected the stony finger. To north and south were more mountains, tier on tier of them, grim, gloomy, gray. Ossa piled on Pelion trying to scale the heavens. To the east, the boys looked down upon the western rim of the Great Basin—looked down, as one in a lofty loge gazes upon a low-flung stage.

Two thousand feet below and six miles away through a purple rent in battlemented hills the boys could glimpse the Carson River, the Twenty-six Mile Desert, the Forty Mile Desert, countless ranges of parallel-running buttes, basins within basins, wastes beyond wastes. A vast panorama 200 miles in extent, hemmed in by huge overwhelming mountains. A region so lone, so tormented, so titanic, that it took their breath away.

It was a region of color, worn velvety gray, with glinting threads of silver running through it, rimmed by purple, blue, ruby, and snow-capped mountains whose crests fell away until merged in the blue haze of a distant horizon. Over this boundless waste was flung a colossal turquoise-tinted sky—flushed with splendor at noon—twinkling with thousands of incandescent lights at night.

It was a heartless region of mirage. It deceived the boys. Great ships under full sail rose and fell on palpitating ether. Seagulls cruised through throbbing light. Gigantic castles, evanescent as bubbles, violet, rose, and purple-tinted, shimmered for an instant on pulsing air then crashed into nothingness. It was a region of frustration; of rivers that never reached the sea; of lakes that had no outlets; of trees forever stunted. It was a region of amazing paradox:

85

aridity and oasis, sulphurous valleys and sun-bathed summits, lonely buttes and rocky chasms, light and shadow, eternal winter and perennial spring, life and death. It was a region of sublimation; of supreme beauty, of grandeur, of awfulness. It was a region of defeat; of death and despair. Day after day, the boys looked down on that scene with inexorable eyes until some part of its implacable relentless qualities entered, like iron, into their souls.[2]

When first Sutro, Mackay, Manogue, and Stewart looked down upon it, it was a region unconquered, savage and hostile. No man had ever subdued it. Many had tried. All had failed. It defied the best that any man had to offer. It called for their resourcefulness and expediency. They felt the challenge and gritted their teeth in response.

Sutro meant to harness the Carson River, to make its water power turn the wheels of lumber, ore, and flour mills. He intended to raise hay and vegetables and water them from the subterranean floods in the Ophir and Mexican.

Beyond the desert's frown Bill Stewart saw a smile. Beyond the waste the makings of a state, ranches in the valleys, cattle on ranges, a domed city down by the water. He would harness that region to his own lofty ambitions. On the buttes of that waste he would mount uncharted pinnacles and plant an American flag on the loftiest point.

In wasted tailings and slimes in yonder sloughs and sinks, Mackay saw his $25,000. How recover them? John spent his days working on the problem, his nights pondering over every mining and milling book in Washoe. He burned his candle, both ends, reading them.

Father Manogue looked down on those Plutonian wastes. Only the mercy of the Cross would avail! He made long horse-back trips out beyond the Carson and Humboldt to plant the symbols of Christ.

Had it not been for the defiance expressed by that vast area stretching north, south, and east of Sun Mountain, these boys would have thrown up the sponge and gone back to California. They had already subdued California. She was easy to live with. She worked like a slave to please. But Washoe defied them. She was hard to subjugate. Why waste their lives on such a savage country? But because of her opposition they stayed. Washoe defied them! Challenged them! They would not be driven out. No! They would stay and fight her, harness her deserts, her brackish lakes, her frustrated rivers, take salt out of her arid wastes, cultivate her soil, rear schools, courts, and churches. Just as they had done in California.

Just as pilgrims had conquered the Plymouth shingle, just as cavaliers had vanquished southern swamps, so would they subdue Washoe. There was joy in conquering the unconquered. They had the stuff of conquering pilgrims and cavaliers with them. But little they gauged their antagonist. Washoe was a wily, subtle enemy. They might subdue her, but could they ever conquer such an alien?

Fall advanced. Sun Mountain became more desolate. A land without women or children—light and warmth became a pitiful thing as winter closed in. The boys felt the loneliness of their lofty perch among Washoe's granite peaks. Not a bird flew over the mountain. Once in a while a coyote slunk by. At night, wolves cried hungrily in the brush. Still the boys kept on laughing—joshing—joking. But their laughter had a false ring, their jesting a hollow sound. When one of them heard the mules, tethered on the hillsides, braying at the tops of their lungs, they christened them "Washoe canaries." After that Comstock mules were known as "Washoe canaries." When you had Washoe zephyrs, Washoe canaries, Washoe water to contend with, there was only one thing for these boys to do—laugh! And they laughed and joked and developed a grim humor of their own! If there was one man they respected above all others, that man was a humorist who looked at all things through laughing eyes.

By November a tortuous street straggled along the supposed line of the Comstock ledge. Running north and south it tottered over the Divide and catapulted down the Cañon. It became the main street of Gold Hill and of Silver City. It threaded Devil's Gate. At Dayton it lost itself in the overland trail. At no time did it run straight. Many a detour it made to avoid the cabins of such miners as refused to make way.[3]

·Along this zigzag course staggered a row of flimsy cabins, canvas houses, and mud-covered huts pierced by bent and rusty stove-pipe. Among them was a lodging house, every inch of whose interior was lined with bunks. From floor to ceiling they ranged, one above the other. Down the centre ran a double tier. Of nights the room was jammed with hairy, grimed, perspiring miners, reeking of stale tobacco and "tarantula juice." From dusk to dawn the walls resounded with merry shouts, foul oaths and laughter. A bunk cost a dollar. Standing room, sitting room, or space on the floor, fifty cents.

Nearby appeared John Newman's stone house,[4] the first permanent structure on the mountain.[5] Terry used it as a rendezvous for Southerners. There he organized the forerunner of "the Knights of the Golden Circle." "We must hold Washoe," Terry thundered, "in the name of the South." Newman developed into the most rabid of his followers. He hated a Yankee "wussen pizen." Came a night when he knifed one—"Sailor Jack." For no other reason than that he despised Northerners and wanted to be ranked among the "killers." [6]

With pick and shovel all the boys were soon at work in hard-rock. For aside from her rich silver sulphurets Washoe had no other asset. As bald and barren as a billiard ball, she had no wood to burn, no water to drink, no fields to plow, no orchards to cultivate, no cattle to breed, no flocks to fold. From the beginning the boys realized that everything, from stay-timbers to strawberries, would have to be imported by pack-train from "below." A mining town on the slopes of Sun Mountain would be as strange a proposition as Nebuchadnezzar's hanging gardens were in Babylon. Worse still, Washoe was far distant from every centre of population. Salt Lake was 700 miles to the east. St. Joseph, Missouri, was more than twice as far. The infantile towns of California were still in their cradles and beyond a mountain range which, for a good part of the year, was impossible to cross.

From the outset the boys realized the strength of the primitive forces pitted against them as, one after the other, Washoe unleashed her weapons in her effort to drive them away. Her stout resistance stimulated rather than discouraged them. The elemental in Washoe challenged the primitive in them. They were transported out of themselves. The worse the obstacle, the greater their daring, the more courageously they sallied forth to accomplish triumphs of ingenuity, which under ordinary circumstances they might not have attempted. In the face of the magnitude of the proposition they were born again, greater than they would have been under milder circumstances. Washoe required giants to overcome her. She found them in Stewart, in Mackay and Sutro. It was to be a war of Titans. Washoe against man's initiative. Flint against steel.

One of Washoe's chief weapons was her hurricane. There never was another wind like that, so diabolical, so malicious. It disdained greatcoats, shirts, and jeans. It twisted upon itself like a corkscrew. It pursued the unfortunate biped wherever he sought cover, pursued him down the back of his neck, up his coat sleeve, down the leg of his pantaloons, into his boots[7]—yanked him out of his brogues!

Once this gale picked up a donkey from where he was grazing on the side of Sun Mountain, lifted him hundreds of feet into the air, then whirled him away toward the desert. As he sailed over the cabin of his erstwhile master the poor brute stretched forth his neck to its greatest extent and brayed in heart-rending tones.

That devilish wind tore the first Catholic church, belonging to the Passionate Fathers, from its foundations, carried it away and smashed it into kindling-wood.[8]

Frequently in the middle of the night, when the boys were wrapt in slumber, dreaming of rich croppings, black sulphurets and wire silver, this hellish wind would come tearing down the mountain, rend their canvas dormitories to tatters, and leave the hapless sleepers exposed to the peltings of the pitiless storm. Howling and swearing, screening their half-naked persons under the fluttering fragments of their disrupted tabernacle, the boys would rush through the storm in search of some mud hole in which to crawl.

But the boys were not discouraged when roof and wall sailed bodily away on the wings of the wind. With invincible humor they shook their fists at the hurricane and called it a damn'd Washoe "zephyr" as if it were a summer-wafting breeze. Like stampeded prairie-dogs, many burrowed into the earth and scooped out tunnels for themselves, running their stove-pipes up through the rocky roof. Before winter Sun Mountain smoked from hundreds of mouths, like so many active volcanoes. "Holes in the wall," the boys called these underground abodes. Some drove coyotes out of their lairs. Others constructed cairns of broken rock, into which they crawled like lizards. Dark, slimy holes, they were, through which the melting snow dripped with monotonous plash.[9] In one of these dugouts twelve boys slept, among them Mackay and O'Brien. They made holiday of it—laughed at discomfort. In another, Father Manogue erected porphyry steps, leading up to a stone altar, where lighted candles, night and day, threw lurid light on white-robed Madonna and kneeling supplicant.

A hermit, who had studied for the ministry, constructed a three-room subterranean apartment. The room nearest the mouth of the tunnel served as a kitchen. Two rooms farther back served as bedroom and library. In the latter the lord of this subterranean castle installed several hundred books. A vein of gold-bearing quartz decorated his roof. Silver quartz tiled his floor. On Sunday, even as St. Paul, the hermit stood at the mouth of his tunnel and preached the Gospel of St. John to the boys squatted before him.[10] In another subterranean vault were installed two billiard tables. In still another, where a floor had been laid, the boys danced the "French-four" to the scrapings of a "yaller-backed" fiddle. Life in the hard-rock was not so bad if you kept laughing.

If the Washoe zephyr did not discourage the boys it looked for a while as if Washoe water would annihilate them. The water in its subterranean peregrinations became impregnated with arsenic, plumbago, and copperas. No man could drink it and live. No man could live and not drink it, so there was no choice. Besides, the dream of alchemists had been attained in Washoe water. It contained gold and silver in potable form. That intrigued them. When the boys, already stark-mad for silver, learned this, they drank it in greater quantity. Drank until it doubled them up with violent cramps and intestinal disorder.

Practically every man fell ill. Hundreds died that fall and were buried in the bitter sage. There was lack of nursing and dearth of medical care. Doctor McMeans and Doctor Bryant did the best they could with drugs rushed over from Downieville. Julia Bulette turned her palace into a hospital. Caldrons of broth and steamers of rice stewed on her stove. Night and day she went from bed to bunk in cabin and tent on her mission of mercy, soothing and comforting, feeding and nursing like a white angel. To those whom the physicians and Julia Bulette could offer no help, Father Manogue and the Reverend Rising brought the Crucifix and the Sacrament of the Church. It mattered not to what faith the boys clung. These brought the message of the Cross! The miners saw and heard, smiled and dreamed. . . .

But if Washoe had any idea that drinking water was going to drive these adventurers any farther away than a grave on her sterile hillside, she was much mistaken. They had come to conquer, not to be conquered by wind and water. A new policy was adopted. They poured out a tumblerful of whiskey. To it they laughingly added a tablespoon of water. "Whiskey neutralizes water," they gasped as they gulped the fiery mixture down. "You can't drink this damned Washoe stuff straight." "Drink all you want, boys," urged *The Territorial Enterprise* with grim humor. "Washoe water with its strong arsenical content, preserves the complexion and saves embalming expenses!"

Along with hurricane and arsenical waters there was a dearth of wood and warmth on Sun Mountain. Aside from scrubby junipers, and palsied pines, there was nothing with which to kindle a blaze, let alone maintain one. Within a month after their arrival the boys had cropped Sun Mountain clean of brush. As far as you could see, up and down its slopes, every vestige of bush, piñon, and juniper was grubbed out.

Piutes were hired to bring in loads of brush. As winter approached the Indians looked at their demolished piñon groves with dismay. "Bad medicine." Not only had the whites burned the brush, destroyed their seed, but worse still, they had cut down their "orchards," as the Piutes called their piñon groves. With coming winter, starvation stared the Indians in the face. Grasshoppers had hopped away. Crickets were silent. Every source of food was gone.

Papooses grew weak. Buck and squaw became sullen and withdrew from the camp. Pah-Ah was offended! Offended because they had let the white men mistreat his red children. But if the Piutes were sullen over their piñons—they striped their chins with red cinnabar when the Williams boys, down at their station on Carson River, captured two of their squaws, manhandled and imprisoned them in a tunnel. It was then that the young bucks donned war feathers and went to their chief. But wise old Winnemucca only shook his head sorrowfully. Too many white faces. "Five moons," threatened the bucks, "five moons."

As winter approached, not an Indian could they find to wash, or to grub sage. The boys shivered with cold, the trail-makers with apprehension!

More and more Sun Mountain's wealth attracted the attention of San Francisco. Before winter Wells Fargo & Company established a bank at the corner of what was afterward "A" Street and Sutton Avenue and installed Charles Forman as manager.[11] Thereupon the Ophir, Mexican, and Gould & Curry mining companies withdrew their sacks of bullion from Lyman Jones' keeping and deposited it in iron safes.

San Francisco stock brokers, anxious for the last word from Sun Mountain's silver ledges, prevailed upon Colonel Bee to construct a telegraph line between Virginia City and Placerville. Wires were strung from tree to tree. When the wind blew, the wires would stretch and lie in loops on the ground, like trailing grape-vine. The "grape-line telegraph," the boys dubbed it. "The long tongue," said the Piutes shaking their heads. More bad medicine. The telegraph had a difficult time. Often Ponies outspeeded the wire. When stage or freighter broke down in the Sierra, the drivers would cut off a convenient length to mend tire or brake. When the telegraph company remonstrated the Jehus responded that they thought the wire was strung there for the purpose for which they used it.

In San Francisco new foundries were springing into existence, reduction-works were multiplying, commercial houses were thriving and expanding to meet the needs of Sun Mountain. Washoe was breathing new life into everything "below."[12] Every community of any importance built a road to Gold Cañon.

By 1859 Sun Mountain had become an ant-hill—with ants hastening towards it from every lane in California. There were 6000 boys on the mountain, and many towns. Besides Virginia City, there were the Divide, Gold Hill, Silver City, American Flat, Devil's Gate, and Dayton strung like beads along Gold Cañon. Down Six Mile, on the north side of Sun Mountain, was the Flowery District. In Seven Mile were numerous mines and arrastras. Along the base of the mountain were Williams' Station, Steam Boat, Dutch Nick's, and Sutro's holdings. At night, from the desert, the mountain looked like a monstrous Christmas tree strung with candles. Within its pyramidal bounds was contained the whole of Washoe.

CHAPTER XIV

MALEVOLENT FORCES

1859–1860

Early in November a foot of snow descended upon Sun Mountain. Before it had melted a white blanket, four feet in thickness, fell on cabin, tent, and hovel. Sleet drifted through chinks and covered those within with icy powder—but the boys were undismayed. They drew their blankets more tightly about their necks and closed their ears to the blasts that howled about their heads.

Sometimes their tunnel lodges were overwhelmed with avalanches. Once, when three of the boys complained of the length of a night, they found they had been buried by an avalanche. It took them two days to dig their way back to daylight. Another time several boys disappeared in an avalanche that swept down Six Mile. Although their pals sought them for weeks, it was not until the following spring that their bodies turned up miles below the Cañon.[1]

Long before Christmas the supplies of Sun Mountain were exhausted. It began to look as if Washoe's unproductiveness would drive them out. There was no game to shoot. Both bird and mammal knew better than to loiter amidst such God-forsaken peaks in winter time. Sugar was exhausted. Flour sold for eighty dollars a sack and but little was to be had. Barley was seventy-five dollars a hundred. Beans were more expensive. Horses and mules died for something more nourishing than shavings mixed with hay. Even whiskey was getting low. Perhaps the supply would stand the pinch of another week. The prospect was gloomy. Messengers were dispatched to Carson. Word came back that that valley was snowbound—the inhabitants slowly starving. Sierra passes were drifted sixty feet deep with snow. No pack animals could make their way across. A few had tried it on blankets placed on the drifts but had foundered. The streets of Placerville were said to be congested with food destined for Washoe. But neither bull-whackers nor muleskinners would tackle the drifts. Snow had made their red-hot anathemas impotent. The boys could not live on prospects. It was a discouraging outlook. It looked as though Washoe had won. They could exist without women, overcome hurricanes, and survive avalanches but they couldn't exist without food. Finally they turned to the Washoe "canaries" and eked out a precarious existence on salt mule.

But they kept up their courage and refused to say "die." Kern River had beaten them. Trinidad had laughed in their faces. The Fraser had flouted them. They wouldn't, they couldn't go back to California conquered again. Appetites were appeased on sinewy Jack, thirst quenched with melted snow, and long wintry nights passed by candle-light with singing and joking. Dawn of every day found them, like flocks of hungry crows, lined up along Six Mile straining their ears to catch the tintinnabulation of a pack-train from Placerville. The situation grew daily more critical. Snow continued falling. The zephyr howled incessantly. Drifts piled higher and higher. Hourly starvation became more imminent. With no signs of opening trails the supply of "Washoe canary" grew alarmingly low. There were plenty of dogs—and once in a while a coyote—but no self-respecting man would entertain that idea. Not yet—at least. If the worst came to the worst, a sleek pine-nut-fed Piute would not be so bad! Christmas came. The New Year dawned. It looked as if Washoe had triumphed. The boys must go back to California ignominiously beaten. February passed on leaden feet. Some of the boys started through the snow-drifts and froze to death on the road to Placerville. Better to die in passes leading to plenty, they had said, than to starve ignominiously on Sun Mountain without making an attempt.

On a day late in March one of the boys came running into camp. "A mule train," he shouted. Adits, tunnels, coyote holes, billiard saloons, groggeries disgorged their starved contents. Through the wintry air came tinkling bells. Cheer after cheer went up. The boys could hear clattering hoofs, rattling packs, the blowing of tired mules. At last the leader, a gaunt gray fellow, staggered over the Divide. The boys yelled and yelled. The mule was heavily laden. The barrels on his back swayed perilously from side to side. A barrel of beef, or pork, or bacon, the boys hoped. Their mouths watered in savory anticipation. The brand heaved into sight. Per Baccho! It was neither beef, pork nor bacon—but whiskey—old Bourbon whiskey! Shouts died on their lips. In utter silence they watched the swaying load.

"Another mule tottered forward, staggered under two half-barrels. Speculation was rife. Every man with a stomach and an appetite for wholesome food was interested. Pigs' feet? Salt mackerel? Perhaps preserved chicken? But there was the mark. Brandy—nothing but brandy.

"There came a third, with a load of five-gallon kegs. The boys took hope. Molasses this time, syrup for pancakes, butter for bread, good sweet butter, yellow firkin butter? Wrong again—gin—nothing but gin. Alas for human expectation! One by one the jaded animals passed groaning and tottering under their loads—rum—bitters—baskets of champagne—pipes of California wine—bar fixtures—Havanas—glasses—tin plates—but nothing nutritious!"[2]

A few days later a load of flour tottered over the Divide and was sold at auction.[3] The hungriest paid five dollars a pound for it. The famished mixed it with snow and ate their batter raw. God they were hungry! That flour broke the back of that malevolent spirit that was starving them out of Washoe.[4] That night 200 of them paid a dollar to sleep on a red carpet and 50 paid a half dollar for a pillow stuffed with shavings.

Spring came—the spring of 1860. Sun Mountain emerged from winter garments, dripping from every point—wind-swept from every quarter. Lead bullets were flying again, gulches running red, graves were filling with bloody shrouds. The shafts of the Ophir, Gould & Curry, and Mexican were baled out and sunk deeper on the inclines—the deeper, the richer became the silver sulphurets. Sandy Bowers was growing fabulously rich. Eilley Orrum, like a bird of rare plumage, flaunted silks, satins, and feathers in the gloomy cañon. There would be more millionaires that year. Dynamite detonated in the bowels of the earth. Concussion rocked Sun Mountain on her foundations. Streets pulsed with excitement. Six Mile and Seven Mile throbbed with life.

Gold Cañon resumed connection with the outside world. "Snowshoe" Thompson brought in mail and papers. The boys read. Their country was distracted—all over the Blacks—all over slaves in the territories. Perhaps they would have slaves on Sun Mountain—hardrock slaves like themselves. "The States" were at cross-purposes—the Southerners were "fire-eaters"—the Northerners were rabid abolitionists—their house was divided against itself—it could not stand—it must fall. Can a territory forbid slavery when Congress cannot? Can water rise above its source? Douglas was a "traitor,"—a "renegade"—a "Judas." John Brown was a fanatic—a murderer. Their countrymen's shoutings came feebly up Six Mile and Seven Mile. How foreign they sounded! Their problems were elemental ones—earth—water—wind—fire. Who cared what Missouri did or how Kansas bled, when you had so lately been cold, thirsty, and hungry?

"Snowshoe" brought in type for a newspaper. With so much happening the boys must have news. They got it from *The Territorial Enterprise*. Once a week, twice a week, the Overland Stage bound for "the States" rattled by the mouth of Gold Cañon.[5] If they only had a "pile"—back they would go—perhaps by summer—latest by fall. The "grape-line" was restrung—but it was always out of order. They could never depend on it.

Mule-driven arrastras commenced grinding on the river—horse-stamped patios smoked and steamed. Bullion was moulded into flat, squat bars. Twice, three times a week Wells Fargo's express picked them up and dashed off to San Francisco—"the City" was getting more opulent and high-handed, and all on Sun Mountain. Silver had given a fresh lease on life to everything "below."

The rush continued—more tramplings echoed through the passes—more freighters and mule teams—more bull-whackers, more mule-skinners—more snaking of whips—curses, groans, and grinding brakes—more shooting—more carving and wringing of necks. The Piutes listened to the rising tumult, watched the swift pageant with sullen eyes. "Bad medicine," they muttered, "bad medicine."

There was more and more talk of secession, slaves, and State's rights. The Federal Government didn't take any interest in Sun Mountain but the Confederacy and Governor Terry would. Sun Mountain was undermined by treason as well as by dynamite. Lawlessness, treachery, calumny, all intermixed with dust. Alkali-laden zephyrs blew stridently down the cañons. The boys must have some kind of law. Their claims—their lives weren't safe. They wouldn't be governed by Utah—wouldn't pay any attention to that Mormon justice-of-the-peace. They got together and organized Washoe County. Anyhow they were all Californians. They petitioned the State legislature for admittance. California would admit them if she could. She took Roop County—but she couldn't take Washoe. No one paid any attention to them—they felt their isolation. They began to listen more ardently to Terry. If the South seceded, why not a Pacific Republic? Terry was as plausible, as tempting as Satan.

If the Federal Government didn't do something to curb these malevolent forces surging about Sun Mountain the boys would believe what Mephistopheles said—that they must do something for themselves.

Sun Mountain's needs reinforced the demand that the last vestiges of remoteness be removed.[6]

CHAPTER XV

THE PHANTOM OF THE DESERT

April 12, 1860

One Thursday morning in April a crowd of the boys went down the mountain to Spafford Hall's Station at the mouth of the cañon. All morning they sat around and waited. But nothing happened. About three o'clock that afternoon, just as they were on the point of giving up and going back to Virginia, they caught the sound they had been waiting for—the winding of a horn out on the desert. That's him, they shouted, as they jumped to their feet, ran down the roadway, and peered out into the sage. Sure enough. A cloud of dust was rolling in from Twelve Mile. Now and then, out of the dust, bobbed a horseman bearing a small flag—their flag!

The horseman was riding furiously toward them. Quickly, the boys lined themselves up on either side of the roadway. Some of them had been looking for him for nine days—ever since April 3, when they knew he must have left "St. Joe."

Simultaneously with their view of the horseman, a nervous heel-and-toe artist among them fell into a clog and jigged madly. A fire-gong on top of the station rang out. Revolvers popped. A cannon up the cañon belched forth its noisy welcome. An anvil chorus over in Six Mile took up the answer. Nine guns were fired—one gun for every day they had waited! Nine days from Missouri. Nine days from ocean to ocean! Nine cheers for Washoe! Gold Cañon! Sun Mountain was within touch of the World.

Amidst firing, shouting, and waving hats, the pony, covered with alkali, came thundering down the road toward them. Nearer and nearer. Foam flew from lathered flanks. Thick clouds of dust rolled over their heads. Buried them. They coughed. Sputtered. Blinked. Rubbed their eyes. Presto! A rider and pony, white with alkali, rattled up to the station. The Pony Express! Nine days out of St. Joseph—1500 miles in nine days! The boys broke into fresh hysteria. Hip, hip, hurrah for the Pony Express! A tiger for the pony that shoved a continent behind his hoofs.[1]

The rider, in picturesque combination of artillery and leather, dismounted and ran to the office. Two hostlers hurried forward a fresh, lively, saddled sorrel. She was skittish. Nervous ears and restless feet. They held her by the head. In a second, the mochila, labelled "Overland Pony Express," was thrown into place.

Bang! went a gun! Hurrah! went the boys! Whiz! went the sorrel! Switch! went her tail—down the road toward the Sierra, out of sight before any of the boys could mention the name of one Jack Robinson!

Such was the excitement in Gold Cañon on the arrival of the Pony Express in mid-afternoon, April 12, 1860.

It was hard for the boys to think of a letter whisked in nine days over the same bleak, lonely land over which they had crept with the wagons back in '48 and '49. The thought was a mingling of wry humor and bitter regret, particularly to those who had left dear ones in nameless graves along that weary way.

Thereafter the homesick boys rode down to Dayton the day the "Pony" was expected, to get the news from "the States" or from "the Bay," as fresh as possible—and just to see the "Pony" pass.

The "Pony" was a triumph of American pluck and energy.[2] Every mount was chosen for speed, heart, stamina; every man for gameness, resource, and knowledge of the country. There were 500 wiry cayuses, and 100 jockeys, man-size in soul, to ride them from San Francisco to "St. Joe," Missouri, 2000 miles through the heart of the Indian country. No weakling ever sought the job. Some were outlaws, for court warrants did not reach into the sage. Many were desperadoes, for bad men have desperate courage. All were men! Few were quitters. They played out the hand that had been dealt them; whether it was a full one or not, made no difference. They played it out to the best of their ability, to the bitterest end.[3]

One courier, westbound, rode into Dry Creek clinging to his saddle-horn, shot through and through by the Indians. But he brought in the mail, safe and sound in its blood-stained mochila— before he died. Another charged pell-mell into his station, his thin fingers clutching the horse's mane like the claws of a bird. They could not break that hold. They had to cut the mane to loosen the grip. He had been dead for hours. But he had brought in the mail, safe and sound in his cantina. He had lived up to his oath—"before the great and living God . . . that . . . I will conduct myself honestly, be faithful to my duties. . . . So help me God!" Faithful unto death—faithful beyond. . . . What more could you ask of any man—good or bad—than that he give up his life for an ideal? And an ideal it was—expressed in blood, bone, sinew, and nerve!

Once a week in the beginning, then as the country began to writhe in the throes of Civil War and State and Nation hung in the balance, twice a week, one of those ponies dashed up the emigrant road from Buckland's Station—thirty-one miles away, and stopped at Dayton. In the twinkling of an eye the messenger changed mounts and was off again down the emigrant road to Carson, Yank's, and so on to Placerville, Sacramento, San Francisco. Once a week, then twice a week, the Pony from the West hammered along the emigrant road, stopped at Dayton with news from California, then disappeared in clouds of dust on the Eastern horizon. The boys couldn't depend on the "grape line" but they could on the "Pony." Those gallopings caused a profound sensation in Gold Cañon. Awake or dreaming, the thud of flying feet was never absent from their thoughts. The "Pony" was bringing Sun Mountain and "the States" into close juxtaposition. He was streak-lightning—a phantom. The boys' spirits, like barometers in changing weather, went up and down with his comings and goings.

News from "back home" had become keen and biting.[4] Stirring things were brewing east and west of them. From the Missouri, the "Pony" brought the first faint rumblings of civil war. Louder and louder they grew. More and more insistent. More and more clamorous. Until the rumble burst into a cannon's roar. Terry was jubilant and held more and more tenaciously to his prediction. "As the South goes, so goes the Lode." He tongued the words again and again as he strengthened the sentries on duty before his walls. To-morrow perhaps! Tomorrow! "As Kentucky goes, so I go," yelled another Rebel.

From San Francisco Bay came more alarming news. California's allegiance was torn to shreds. She was more Southern than the South. Her spokesmen were all rebels. Her Governor, Downey; her political leaders, Gwin and Weller; the commandant of her military department, Albert Sidney Johnston, all—all—were secessionists. "As the South goes, so goes California, so goes Washoe, so goes Sun Mountain," was an understood fact in Gold Cañon. For some unaccountable reason the Yankees were supine. Snowed under. Dumfounded. The only voice heard was that of Johnnie Rebel. Blatant! Vociferous! How exultingly it arose! How supreme it swelled with every bit of news favorable to the Southern cause! Yes! And it was all favorable! Every word of it!

Distance had annihilated allegiance. It was up to the "Pony"! On his swift back was borne more than dispatches. Fates—destinies were riding. Now loyalty was in the saddle. Now treachery. Now wavering fidelity. Now Judas Iscariot! The honor, the dishonor of the Pacific! Those swift little cayuses were breaking their hearts for no other reason than to banish distance, to beat time—to keep California and Washoe in touch with "the States." The Federal authorities knew their psychological value. They must be kept running at all hazards—day and night—summer and winter—at any price! To stop them meant isolation. Isolation meant alienation. Alienation meant treason. No one preached treachery louder than the Southerners. The ponies were riding against their preachings and against the West's secession. Or worse, a Pacific Republic. Then secession!

The Piutes watched the flying feet make streaks through their hunting grounds. "Bad medicine," they muttered as pony and courier clattered by. "Bad medicine."

The first "Pony" had brought news of great import to Sun Mountain. A bill had been introduced in Congress, amendatory of the act organizing the Territory of Utah, by which the seat of government was to be removed from Salt Lake City to Carson Valley and the name of the Territory changed from Utah to Nevada.

That bill took Sun Mountain by storm. Control! Regulations! Administration! The boys were jubilant. Congress after all was paying some attention to their signals of distress. At last they would have some form of law to replace the outlaw and his derringer. They began to feel a little streak of loyalty toward a government that had been apparently ignoring them.[5] Nevertheless they hearkened to Terry. Secession—it was a fascinating, adventurous word! It promised lawful order—protection—State's rights.

CHAPTER XVI

"BENECIA BOY" OR SAYERS?

1860

The "Pony" brought even more important dispatches to Washoe—news of the great fight at Farnborough, England. With the whole sporting world of that time, the boys were anticipating "Benecia Boy" Heenan's fight with the Englishman, Sayers, the British champion pugilist, for the world's pugilistic honors. It was to be the great classic of the ring.

On April 24 the second "Pony" from "the States" came pounding down the emigrant road. What dispatches, this time, of interest to Washoe? Listen. The Chief Constable of Herfordshire, England, had obtained a warrant for the arrest of "Benecia Boy" and Tom Sayers. A howl of protest reached the skies. Both had been "bound over" for a year. The constable wanted to stop the Sayers-Heenan fight for the championship of the world! It couldn't be done—its promoters had gone too far! The boys were indignant at the bare suggestion. What difference what the Herfordshire constable thought?

For days the boys had talked of nothing else. Many of them had known Heenan in California—worked with him. Hadn't the bruiser been a blacksmith with the Pacific Mail Steamship Company at Benecia[1]? Hadn't several of them, in days past, put on gloves with "the Boy"?

He still was—Washoe's idol of manly prowess. Didn't they have a "Heenan Bar," a "Heenan Exchange," and "Heenan Sample Rooms" on Sun Mountain? Didn't their bootblacks pride themselves on their "Heenan licks"? Didn't their barbers advertise a "coiffure à la Heenan"? When it came to "the Boy" no adulation was too extravagant. He was a furore in Gold Cañon.

For weeks every red-blooded man in Washoe had been looking forward to April 16—the red-letter date set for the great match. With the Pony, figured the boys, they ought to have that news by the 6th of May. That British constable couldn't call off the fight! According to schedule the bruisers would meet on April 16—plenty

Courtesy John Newbegin.

"BENECIA BOY" AT FARNBOROUGH, ENGLAND, APRIL 17, 1860.

Many of the boys in Washoe had worked with J. C. Heenan ("Benecia Boy"). He married Adah Isaacs Menken.

MONTE.

From the De Young Memorial Museum Collection.

LADY'S CHAIN!

of time for news of the outcome to catch the transatlantic Vanderbilt Mail Steamer, which was leaving Southampton, April 18. Those
dispatches would be intercepted off Cape Race by the news yacht of
the New York Associated Press. Seven days later the dispatches
would reach New York. By the 27th their contents would be telegraphed to "St. Joe." From Missouri the Pony would bring them
to Washoe. There was no doubt about it. They would have the
news of the fight by the 6th—the 8th at the latest.[2] They waited
with impatience.

Nothing in Washoe was as important as that fight! Not gold nor
silver. Not arastra nor patio. Not Gould & Curry nor Ophir. Not
drift, nor tunnel, nor winze. Not secession nor Union. Not even
the Republican Convention that was to be held at Chicago the middle of May to make nominations.

"Seward is the logical man for the Presidency," said Washoe
Free-soilers in dismissing the subject. "Without a doubt he will be
nominated." Even presidents paled into significance beside "the
Boy."

While conventions agonized themselves and bullets whined and
men died and Piutes dipped their arrow points in rattlesnake venom
and "wildcats" flourished and stocks soared and Ponies came and
went, the Heenan-Sayers fight remained the dominant topic of
speculation and conversation. "Benecia Boy" would win the championship belt.

The Democrats at Charlestown failed to nominate the "Little
Giant," read the dispatch the Pony brought. Alabama and seven
cotton States walked out. The convention adjourned making no
nomination. The delegates were to reconvene at Baltimore on the
18th of June.[3] Within a twelvemonth prophesied Alexander Ste-
phens, the ablest statesman of the South, the nation will be engaged
in a bloody civil war. That was catastrophic. That was the news
Terry was expecting—the Northern and Southern Democrats would
never agree. The party would be divided—the South would secede
—the hour was about to strike. "But how about the fight?" queried
the boys.

With ill-concealed impatience the boys awaited dispatches from
Herfordshire. "Every effort is being made to stop the fight." "Warrants have been issued binding both 'Benecia Boy' and Sayers
to keep the peace for one year." "Heavy sureties are being required."[4] "Hell," said the boys, "that won't stop a championship
fight."

Then it was the 1st of May. The eighth Pony came and went. The next Pony, said the boys, would bring the great news they had so long awaited.

Each Pony as it raced across their hunting grounds left the Piutes in a worse humor than the previous one.

"Bad medicine. Bad medicine. Bad medicine," they reiterated. Winnemucca shook his old gray head. He couldn't hold those hot-blooded bucks much longer.

The ninth Pony would make known the decision, said the boys.

But the ninth Pony was late. Many things could happen in 2000 miles, said the boys philosophically—rain—sheet lightning—ambush. But even thoughts of such things depressed the boys. For a month those news-starved youngsters had come to depend mightily on those galloping cayuses.

The Pony was their only tie with secession, war, conventions, nominations, prize-fights—a tie that kept them in ever-increasing foment. By day they listened for trampings. By night they dreamed of a string of ponies rushing at top-notch speed toward them with news of "Benecia Boy" in the mochila. It was an incubus thrilling while it lasted. Men who had been to Gold Lake and Fraser River, who had fought with Walker in Nicaragua and had filibustered in Sonora, lived on excitement. When they thought of what might befall that chain of blood and muscle and nerve, many a bearded Washoeite actually dropped on his knee and prayed to his God for the safety of the Pony bearing news of the fight.

No Pony on the 6th. None on the 7th.

About dark on May 8, Bob Haslam, the hardest riding of the express jockies, actually tore down the emigrant road with the tidings of the prize-fight tucked safe and sound in his mochila.[5] It had taken place as scheduled. But those who waited were disgusted. Bob went by Gold Cañon like a streak of greased lightning—without stopping. Fight or no fight, the dispatches must go through and "Pony Bob" was making one of the greatest rides of all time[6] —"Before the great and living God . . . I will be faithful. . . ." What matter though his mouth was bleeding! What matter that his jaw was broken in two places! One thing only counted to "Pony Bob." His dispatches must go through. Those who saw him pass Gold Cañon knew that he was riding like grim death.

In "Pony Bob's" wake thundered two expressmen. They, too, were riding like mad. They dashed up Six Mile and down "C" Street. To make way the boys fled to sidewalks. At Wells Fargo and Company's Express Office the Pony riders pulled the foam-lathered mustangs to their heels and stopped.[7]

The boys crowded around. One question on every lip. Who had won the championship of the world? "Benecia Boy" or Sayers? All attention, the boys strained forward to read the messengers' thoughts—mouths agape to catch the great news. "Benecia Boy" or Sayers?

Minutes passed. The riders didn't speak—couldn't speak—they thumped their chests in their effort to recover their breath.

"The Piutes—the Piutes are coming!" one of them finally gasped out. "Yesterday they attacked Williams' Station . . . killed five men . . . a woman . . . a child . . . burned the station to the ground . . . shot an arrow into the ribs of Williams' dog. Five thousand of 'em are riding on Six Mile. Arm yourselves—quick!"[8]

CHAPTER XVII

PIUTE WAR

1860

After that warning, where was the man who cared about the decision in the Heenan-Sayers fight? Who cared whether "the Boy" had won the belt or not? Who cared that the bruisers had fought forty-three bloody rounds? Who cared whether Tom Sayers had drawn "the claret" or "the Boy" had spilt "the ruby"? Who cared that a tremendous "poultice" on Tom's "ivory box" had sent him on an extended "kissing excursion to mother earth"? Who cared that the umpire had been forced out of the ring? That the police had cut the ropes . . . ?

Who cared? Who cared? Certainly not one of those boys who heard the Pony expressman gasp out his warning. "The Boy" was thousands of miles away. The Piutes were riding on Devil's Gate.

The boys were thrown into a frenzy. Sun Mountain swirled with alarm and agitation. The Piutes were well armed—good fighters— deadly marksmen with bow and arrow. Strange—but thoughts of an Indian uprising had been farthest from their thoughts. With the excitement over silver, secession, bad-men and bruisers, who had given the red-men a thought?

But now no one could think of anything else. The Piutes were coming on pounding mustangs—thousands of them with poisoned arrows—tomahawks and shotguns—coming straight up Sun Mountain! The chills ran up and down their spines. All the boys were hoisted out of the Ophir and Gould & Curry, armed with picks and shovels. The Mexican's million-dollar mules were commandeered. Wims stopped their hoisting. Cars were pulled out of inclines. Arrastras ceased their grinding. Patios were left to simmer. Bullwhackers forgot their cursing. Black-snakes ceased their snaking. The Piutes were coming! Who would have thought it? Who had ever thought about those damn'd Indians anyway?

Telegrams were sent to Governor Downey at Sacramento begging for arms. "We have plenty of men," the wires read, "but no arms." There was no use appealing to Utah. Salt Lake was hundreds of miles away through the heart of the Piute country. No courier could get through alive. Not even the "Pony." Sun Mountain was defenseless—unorganized. No authority. No garrison. The boys formed in squads and discussed the prospects of the bloody affair. Some proposed to start out at once and kill every Indian in sight. Others, of more temperate view, advocated mediation, the organization of regular companies to hunt the guilty Indians and chastise them. But it was only the minority that proposed mediation. The majority demanded action. Discussion grew fierce and fiercer until toward evening some 2000 boys were milling about "B" Street, demanding vengeance in a voice that poured from a thousand throats. Maybe the Williams brothers had ravaged Piute squaws. What of it? What right had those red devils to be judges and executioners at one and the same time? Pioneer lynch-law and Piute lynch-law were two different things! They'd teach 'em a lesson . . . to let the white man alone. Instinctively they thought of Bill Stewart. He couldn't be found. He'd gone down Gold Cañon. Calls for a meeting were made. Frank Pixly, editor, took the stand. Mounted messengers were dispatched in every direction to warn prospectors of the danger. A committee of five to manage the situation was appointed. Among them young Henry Meredith, Bill Stewart's partner.

Meredith began to organize a company and to enroll the names of those who would fight, of those who had horses, mules, weapons, powder, balls, provisions, and of those willing to contribute money. He was very systematic—calm—collected. He heartened them. The boys had confidence in him and rallied to his standard. He made a stirring speech. They made him Captain.[1] Soon he had several hundred enlistments and liberal contributions poured in. At one time it looked as if the whole town would be manless by morning. Everybody was going. Whether the darkness, the bad news, or Henry Meredith's courageous speech had most influence in stirring the spirits of so many individuals, it is impossible to say. But enthusiasm was at such fighting heat that many said if Meredith could not organize a company, they would go on their own initiative and fight the savages. If he couldn't muster enough horses they would walk. If he couldn't find enough weapons, they would go empty-handed, unarmed, unmounted, and slay the dastardly redskins, like Sampson of old, with their naked jaw-bone fists. They were mad that night in their mania. Vengeance they wanted! Vengeance they would have. At dawn. Vengeance.

Sentries were stationed at the heads of Six and Seven Mile to

watch the approaches to the city and to give warning of any untoward signs. Terry increased the guards at his fort. Terry feared
that the Indians would attack that night. The women—there were
five or six of them now, including Julia Bulette and Eilley Orrum
—were taken to Peter O'Riley's unfinished stone hotel, the walls of
which were only part way up. The doors and windows were hastily
barricaded and guards were stationed to march back and forth.
Whatever happened the gallant boys were determined to protect
their women. With their blood. With their lives, if necessary!
That's what the boys thought of women. They would have protected
Julia Bulette with their hearts' life!

Meredith made a last inspection. He gave orders that a candle
or lantern must burn in every tent, in every cabin all night. No man
should get out of his clothes. All must go to bed with their boots
on, sleep on their guns, and have rations in their pockets. They must
hold themselves in readiness for any emergency at a moment's
notice. Many did not go to bed at all. In every saloon the click of
dice, the chink of coins, and the shuffling of cards was heard until
dawn. Every time these gamblers heard the cry of a coyote or a
rustle in the brush there was a scramble for shotguns and bowies
. . . then back to the bar. Everything arranged for the next morning, Meredith retired to his cabin, wrote a few letters, and slept.
Slept until the dawn, with its long white fingers, crept through his
door and clutched him awake.

A bugle blew. "To arms! To arms!" Men jumped up from tables,
out of bunks, seized their guns, and hastened to the rendezvous on
"C" Street. But where were all the volunteers of the night before?
Out of the thousands barely a hundred avengers were mounted and
ready to start. Where were the others? And then they learned.
During the "wee-small hours of the morning" the others had suddenly remembered that they had very important business in California. They had left by a back trail, taking their arms with them
—it was important or they wouldn't think of going. But those
avengers were like their mustangs, champing at the bit in their impatience to get started. There was no organization among them.
They were poorly mounted, and wretchedly equipped with rust-
covered muskets and sawed-off shotguns. But what they lacked in
arms they made up in enthusiasm.

Henry Meredith, quiet, collected, sat his charger like a gallant
young Roman. How valiant he looked that morning!

Just then Bill Stewart rode up. He was impatient. Turning to Meredith, Bill begged him not to proceed with such a disorganized company. He told Meredith that his followers had had no discipline; that many of them were toughs; that they wouldn't obey orders; that fighting Indians with such an outfit would prove disastrous.[2]

Meredith promised he would go only as far as Williams' Station, then turn the command over to some one else and come back.

At that, Meredith had plenty of good stuff in his command. There was a boy, hardly sixteen, whom they called "Boston," on account of his pronounced New England accent. No one as yet had gotten the rest of his name. But that didn't make any difference. Names didn't count in Washoe. Only action. If one had plenty of sand, if he was quick on the trigger, no questions were asked. "Boston" had all these qualities and was certainly quick! Out of his gray eyes gazed the soul of a peerless hero. His boyish face did not blanch! Any mother would have blessed him, that morning, with tears of gratitude in her eyes. Any father would have been proud that he had such a son! He might not be an Indian fighter, but he had the spirit to fight.

Then there was Joe Baldwin, a young Southerner, another fearless lad just turned sixteen and son of a supreme court justice of California.[3] "Little Joe" they called him. "Baron" Fairfax stomped about in a pair of borrowed boots. Sutro as correspondent for *The San Francisco Bulletin* was also a volunteer.[4]

Most of these men saw in this affair a chance for adventure and an opportunity to "teach the red devils a lesson!"[5] "The Piutes won't fight," one of them said, "we'll get plenty of haar." The Indians had always been so inoffensive that the idea of their offering any resistance never entered the head of any one of them.[6] Sam Brown pranced about in his clanking spurs with the watchword "an Indian for breakfast and a pony to ride." He contemplated with pleasure the opportunity of sacking Piute villages, capturing a young squaw or two, getting a few man-sized scalps, and running the rest of the Piutes out of the country. But there were more like Meredith and "Boston" and Joe Baldwin, prompted by the loftier sentiments of patriots and heroes.

A drum beat a grim tattoo. Captain Meredith and his ill-assorted cavalcade in slouch hats, boots and jeans, clattered down "C" Street. Julia Bulette, standing at a paneless window of Fort O'Riley, waved a parting handkerchief. And the warriors waved gallantly back.

To the popping of guns and wild hallooing the cavalcade disappeared down Gold Cañon on their way to Williams' Station to administer what they called "even-handed justice" to the Piutes. According to Sam Brown that meant putting to death as many of the tribe, including papooses, as fell into his clutches! As they passed Devil's Gate, those on guard fired a parting salute.

At Silver City they were joined by young Captain R. G. Watkins, a veteran of the Walker filibustering expedition to Nicaragua, where he had lost a leg. Because of his previous experience the boys invited him to take command. But on account of his crippled condition he at first declined. Finally he consented. Mounted on a powerful horse and strapped to his saddle,[7] he fell into line with the company and passed on down the Cañon.

Just outside Dayton the Sun Mountain force was joined by a delegation from Carson, commanded by Major Ormsby and Judge John Cradlebaugh. The latter had recently been appointed by President Buchanan to preside over Washoe jurisprudence and had just arrived. With him was John Blackburn, the Tennesseean, now Marshal of Sun Mountain.

Thus augmented to a hundred and five, the little army skirted the base of the Mountain and pushed rapidly off toward Williams' Station. Within the year those men had hungered, thirsted, starved for Sun Mountain. Now, they were going to fight for her. Kill or be killed for her—perhaps. Verily, the spirit of Washoe was waxing strong within them. It was a blithe, fresh, smiling morn. The hot sun beat down on the sage, filling the air with its stench. They breathed it in—it was as bracing as wine. Their galloping mounts whirled the dust about them. It stalked in their wake.

All that day—the day of the 9th—the hundred and five were gone. No message came back to those on Sun Mountain to tell how they were faring. Not even Henry Meredith—Bill Stewart was disgusted. That night the signal-fires of the Piutes blazed out on every mountain-peak below the city. It was a startling sight to see that line of fires blaze out, now here, now there, in one lurid glare after the other. The boys knew what that fire meant. The Piutes were signalling the position and movement of the cavalcade to their bands out on the desert. That was a night of vigil on Sun Mountain. Wolves howled dolefully. Coyotes yelped. Guards watched the passes. Virginia watched the desert. The sentries about Terry's forts marched back and forth. Safe and sound at Fort O'Riley, Julia Bulette slept.

All the next day—the 10th—the hundred and five were gone. As soon as it was dark the coyotes and wolves began their yappings. The signal-fires burst forth again—but on more distant buttes! That meant that the hundred and five were marching farther into the desert. The boys knew that by this time they must be approaching the mouth of the Truckee down near that narrow, rocky defile that led into the narrow, rocky valley close to the shores of Pyramid Lake.

All the 11th they were gone. No word. No messenger from the desert. At dark those lupine cries and Indian fires burst forth again. The intermittent silence was ominous, out in that vast panorama. There was a feeling that something had gone amiss. What of the hundred and five? That night, when the signal-fires moved here and there in the desert, Virginia was filled with dread and foreboding. The very flames seemed to flicker, die out, then burst furiously forth again. Dark figures, like silhouettes flashed on a screen, seemed to be jumping up and down before the fires.

On the fourth day, Sunday the 13th, the morning of the Sabbath, a frantic, alkali-covered horseman foamed furiously up Six Mile. A crowd gathered around him. He was one of the hundred and five. He had ridden all night, he said. Five score of miles! A marathon! A swifter courier than the Biblical runner who brought to David the news of the death of Absalom. He had outrivalled the speed of "Lexington." They had been ambushed at four o'clock the afternoon before, near Pyramid Lake, he said. They had ridden like rats into a trap, through a narrow pass into a deep valley when suddenly they had found the heights above them alive with painted Piutes. The savages had outnumbered, outmanoeuvred them. They had closed in upon them, and the majority of the boys, with concerted, despairing cry, broke for the river. Captain Watkins, when he saw the rout, dismounted, supported himself on an improvised crutch, and tried to rally them. Failing in that he blazed away at the oncoming Indians and held them at bay until he could reach the entrance to the valley. There, like Leonidas in the Pass of Thermopylæ, Captain Watkins had made a second stand and held the narrow defile until all near him had escaped. Then he himself had fled. "Boston" had given a magnificent account of himself. Refusing to run, he entrenched himself behind a dead horse and fought like a hero. And he died, died gloriously, his face to the foe. Captain Ormsby, pierced by a poisoned arrow, had toppled from his horse and perished. At the most crucial moment Joe Baldwin was wounded. Fell from his mule, but managed to remount. At that same instant Sam Brown clambered up behind him and put spurs to the mule; and when Joe, too dizzy to hold on, swayed in the saddle, Sam had flung him into the bushes and fled.[8] As for Meredith, he had been too proud to run;[9] had held honor more precious than life. Deserted by his company, alone, he faced the oncoming Piutes; and died fighting. Early in the engagement, wounded, he had fallen from his horse. Unable to rise, one of his fleeing companions had ridden up and begged him to mount behind him and flee; but Meredith declined. "No, sir," he had said, "I would endanger your life. Go!" Then as the Indians closed in on him, Meredith pulled himself to his knees and blazed away with his revolver. Two of the Piutes fell. Thus, unquailing, with more than a hundred Indians at his throat, the brave Meredith had perished. Death unsullied was sweeter than life dishonored.[10]

The news was a terrific blow to the boys. Meredith was one of their outstanding men. They were horror-struck at what had befallen him. They couldn't believe it. A cry for vengeance went up. Meredith! In the desert—dead!

Then Sam Brown arrived astride Joe Baldwin's mule. He had spurred the poor brute almost to death but he had made second-best time from the battlefield. What about Joe? Sam didn't know. He had left him in the bushes, probably dead. What difference did it make to Sam? Another notch? "Another man for supper"?

Came slogging "Baron" Fairfax. He blamed the borrowed boots for his flight.

All that night refugees straggled up Sun Mountain. All with the same ghastly tale to tell: of sudden ambush, rout, carnage, flight. The martyrdom of "Boston" and Meredith! Forty-six of the hundred and five were unaccounted for—out there in the sage-brush —dead. One had seen the redskins toss his unconscious comrades, still warm, still breathing, into the coals of the signal-fires. How anxiously the boys had watched those fires flare up—die down— blaze forth! little knowing that their comrades were feeding the flames.

The Comstock was in a panic. Fear gripped the boys by the

throat. The Piutes were reported coming on the heels of the refugees. One refugee reported that he had seen thousands of mounted savages headed toward Six Mile. They were only a few miles away, riding like the wind. This precipitated a stampede. On inquiry, it was found that not more than one hundred men could be armed. The others, to the number of thousands, had already gone over the Sierra. Gone and taken their firearms with them. That night panic-stricken messages poured over the "grape-line" telegraph into California. To Governor Downey, to Downieville, to Nevada City, to San Francisco. All of the same tenor: "Help. We are helpless and unarmed. The Piutes are coming!"

A meeting was called. The city was declared under martial law. Resolutions were adopted that "during the next sixty days, or until the settlement of the present Indian difficulties no claim or mining ground within the territory shall be subject to relocation, or liable to be jumped for non-work." That was the worst thing they could have done. All fear of "jumping" of their claims removed, many who wavered sneaked away during the night. But Major Hungerford, Judge David S. Terry, and a number of other intrepid Southerners stayed behind. They urged Julia Bulette to go. They pointed out that it was no place for women! But Julia stuck. "I will make soup for the boys," she said. "If they stay I will too." All those who remained, enlisted in one company or another.

Captain Edward F. Storey, a young Georgian and a veteran of the Mexican War, organized one—the Virginia Rifles. There was no ammunition so he fed melted-down silver and lead pipes into bullet moulds. He vowed that he would give the Piutes a taste of silver in a spot where they didn't want it. The varmints! The window openings in Fort O'Riley were bricked up. The walls, strongly barricaded. Whatever happened, Julia and Eilley Orrum must be protected. Julia Bulette had never had such tender care bestowed upon her. When they planned to go into the desert she didn't want to stay behind. Not Julia. She wanted to follow the boys and take care of them. She would nurse them. But the boys wouldn't listen.

A fort was hastily constructed above Devil's Gate. A genius in command constructed a home-made cannon. He bored out a pine log, hooped it with iron hands, mounted it on a caisson, filled it with scraps of iron and bits of chain, and trained the muzzle so that it would rake the Cañon to a great distance.[11] "We'll make those damn'd Piutes," said the belligerent Silver Cityites, "eat saltpetre."

Then some one recalled that Major Hungerford, a hero of Cerro Gordo and Chapultepec and the founder and commander of the Sierra Battalion at Downieville, and one of the best tacticians of his time,[12] was on the Lode. It was known that he had trained the Sierra Guards, and that under his control just across the border was plenty of arms and ammunition. A committee waited upon him. They asked him to get arms and ammunition from Downieville and to fit out an expedition to fight the Indians. But the major had some doubts about the propriety of taking California property beyond the State line. In the midst of his quandary a telegram was handed to him:

"San Francisco, May 3, 1860.
"To Major Hungerford:
"*Sir:* You will please collect such arms and ammunition as you can find in Downieville and forward them, by express or otherwise, to the scene of action in Carson Valley.
(Signed) "JOHN G. DOWNEY."[13]

The Governor of California had received the boys' dispatch!

Immediately the major wired his son-in-law, Doctor Edmund G. Bryant, at Downieville, who had lately returned to his family:

"Send me immediately all the arms and ammunition of the National Guard. Telegraph Lieutenant Hall at Forest City to send all the rifles in his possession. Send to Goodyear's Bar, to Captain Kinniff to send me all his rifles. Forward as soon as possible. Big fight with the Indians. The whites defeated. Send me your heavy sabre. I hear Meredith and Baldwin killed.
(Signed) "MAJOR D. E. HUNGERFORD."[14]

At the meeting held that evening the commander-in-chief appointed Hungerford as his adjutant in the defense of Sun Mountain. All that night the adjutant recruited and drilled. The tramp-tramp of hob-nailed boots and hrup! hrup! of quick staccato orders were heard until dawn.

In spite of those comforting sounds no one could relax. "Indian" was the sole topic of conversation. Many retired in various stages of excitement to spend the night in fitful sleep. Among them was an honest Dutchman who slept in a store with four others and awoke to hear one of his comrades shouting in a nightmare, "Indians!

Indians!" The Dutchman bolted for the door, *Gott mit uns!* rushed down "C" Street, and in stentorian tones shattered the night: "Indians! Indians! Turn out everybody!" Everybody did turn out and it was hours before they could breathe in peace again.[15]

There were only two classes now on Sun Mountain. Those who were not frightened at all and those who were scared out of their wits. Among the latter was one young fellow, a Teuton, so overcome with fear, that he prevailed upon his partner to lower him into a shaft fifty feet deep, thinking that would be the safest place that could be found. His pal promised to draw him out when all danger had passed. After the pal had deposited the Teuton at the bottom of the shaft he went down "C" Street. At dawn the guard watching Six Mile pass gave warning that the Indians were sighted. Everybody was aroused. Everybody listened. Everybody could hear the sound of galloping horses coming up the Cañon! There was no doubt about it! The Piutes were falling upon the city! "The Piutes are charging," some one shouted. Many took to the back trails and struck out for California. Among them was the Teuton's pal. In his fright he thought only of himself. Immediately after his departure a drove of mules, which had been stampeded down the Cañon, clattered up the Mountain.

In the meantime the poor Teuton roosted at the bottom of the shaft. For three days and nights he yelled for help before any one came to his assistance. By then he was nearly dead.[16]

One day Major Hungerford received a telegram from Downieville notifying him that his command, the Sierra Battalion, was approaching Sun Mountain.

The major rode down the Cañon and met the battalion eight miles from the city. There he assumed the command. On the following morning, with martial music and flags flying, the battalion marched up the Mountain again, under arms and in full military order.[17] On every hand it was received with cheers.

On May 24 Colonel Jack Hayes, commander-in-chief, with an army of 750 men marched over the Divide. In the advance went 250 horsemen; then came Major Hungerford with the Sierra Guards, flags fluttering, drums beating; next Captain Storey with the Virginia Rifles; while the rear was brought up by Captain Fairfax with the howitzers; Captain Stewart with the United States Infantry from San Francisco Presidio; the commissary with droves of beef and cattle and ordnance with pack-animals loaded down with ammunition.[18] Virginia cheered as they passed. Julia Bulette cheered. Gold Hill cheered. Eilley Orrum cheered. Silver City fired a salvo from Devil's Gate. Dayton saluted with her anvil chorus.

Down the emigrant road trotted the horsemen, down rushed the cattle, pack-animals, and dogs, and disappeared among desert sands.

As soon as it was dark the signal-fires of the Piutes blazed out on a hundred buttes below the city.

Colonel Hayes proceeded toward the Truckee. Not a Piute was seen. Nothing but sand-hills—sage-brush—alkali-pools—whirling dust and oppressive silence. A raven flapped gloomily overhead, mingling his hoarse croak with the wind that whistled across bleak dunes and rustled among dry sage.

On the battle-field, near Pyramid Lake, they came suddenly upon the body of Henry Meredith—stark naked. The only one on the spot where the battle had raged.[19] Around him the savages had held a war-dance as he lay in the centre of a well-trodden circle. The contracted muscles, the clenched fists bespoke a scene of horror that made them shudder to contemplate, suggesting that last moment when bleeding and exhausted he had sunk upon the sand, the war-whoop ringing in his ears, a thousand fingers clutching at his throat. They gazed down upon him—pity in their eyes, anger in their hearts —vengeance in their souls.

He had been scalped! His breast was transfixed by more arrows than ever had stabbed San Sebastian. He had died gloriously—magnificently! Where his life-blood had spilled upon the earth, a wild rose had sprung into life, as if to mark the spot where a gallant soldier had fallen.[20] Thus had Washoe's soil been hallowed.

His comrades picked up the broken body, laid him gently upon a stretcher, and covered him with a military cape. The Indians were sighted. The battle of Pinnacle Mount began. Bearing Meredith's corpse fiercely before them, the boys drove the Piutes pell-mell into the utmost reaches of the waste.[21]

CHAPTER XVIII

BUCK FANSHAW
1860

In the last skirmish of the battle of Pinnacle Mount, Captain Edward F. Storey was shot through the lungs and fell back into the arms of his troopers mortally wounded. The boys vied with one another in their ministrations. One brought water from the river in his hat. Another wiped the bloody ooze from the captain's lips. A third screened him from the burning rays of the sun. While a fourth, with more enthusiasm than consideration, rushed up waving a bloody scalp. "Look! Captain, look!" he exclaimed. "Here's the Injun that shot you; three of us killed him."

"Take it away," said the dying man, his eyes rolling heavily. "Why should I want to see it?"[1] For a moment he lay with his eyes closed. Then: "Tell me about the Rifles," he muttered. "How are my men faring?"

Hayes, Fairfax, and Hungerford rode up and dismounted. When they saw how Storey was faring they took off their hats.

When the Rifles marched back to Virginia, they brought the body of their commander.

Two days later, Sunday, June 10, at two o'clock, the boys accompanied him to a new-made grave on the crown of Cemetery Ridge, northeast of the city.

Colonel John C. Hayes, Captain Stewart with the Regulars, Major Hungerford with the Volunteers, led the procession. There followed Captain Storey's horse—head lowered—empty saddle—boots in reverse—covered with a pall of crape. Then came Masons in blue-satin aprons, and the captain on a beplumed catafalque, drawn by six horses—all the pomp and circumstance that Sun Mountain could muster.

At the cemetery were Masonic farewells, throwing of evergreens, and the firing of a final salute. A short time later when the county was named the boys gave it that of Storey.

On their way back from the cemetery, the boys pressed their

mounts in a race to "C" Street. Life must move fast. Faster. Who knew? Perhaps tomorrow? The next day? What with war, Indians, caving earth, scalding water, premature explosions. Who knew?

Back on "C" Street "Old Gus," one of the Volunteers, marched from saloon to saloon with an Indian arrow stuck in the muzzle of his musket, from which dangled a Piute scalp. Wherever he went it was "Hurrah for Old Gus, he got his Injun." [3] This gave Old Gus all the whiskey he wanted until the officer of his company inadvertently explained to the hangers-on that it was a dead "Injun" that Gus had scalped. Accidentally, he said, he had come upon him at the moment when Gus, a pipe in his mouth, and a long knife in his hand, was obtaining his trophy.

From the funeral, Colonel Hayes marched down Gold Cañon and disbanded his troops. He was on his way back to California and did not want to take that eighty-odd stand of arms with him. There was no arsenal in which to deposit them. Fort Churchill was not yet built. To Terry, who just happened to be on hand, he left their care, little dreaming of the use to which he would put them.[4]

Terry was jubilant. He had forts—men, and now guns. What more could the prospective Governor of Washoe want? The spread of the ordinance of secession? The bells of Charleston? The guns of Sumter? All was going well with the rebel cause along the Lode.

With an ample supply of arms and ammunition Terry's attitude became more threatening. The calls of his sentries more bellicose. Any man that looked over his stone walls saw his followers drilling.

"The separation of the Union is imminent," declared Terry. "California will secede. Washoe will follow. Sun Mountain will surely be a part of the Southern Confederacy. Whoever is in possession of the mines will be allowed to hold them.

"As the South goes, so goes the Lode.

"As Kentucky goes, so I go."

Followed a fight between two of the boys, a big Yankee and a small Southerner, over secession. They agreed to settle the matter in the Heenan-Sayers manner. During the fracas the small one pounced on the big one and pounded him until he was satisfied. As soon as the big one was back on his feet he took out his derringer and fired point-black at his opponent, hitting him in the side. There were cries of crooked deal. Pistols were drawn in the crowd. "Take that," yelled one of the boys as he fired, and the big Yankee fell, fatally wounded.[5]

That very same night, over the very same subject, another man was shot. And a third, who wouldn't give up though he was ill, died of pneumonia in the street.[6] The drama had begun.

A promoter was organizing a company to build a "bulkhead" around Virginia to keep out the Washoe zephyr.[7]

While another, irritated because the sun sank so early behind Sun Mountain, promoted a company and sold stock to cut a tunnel through the mountain, so designed that it would let the western sunlight through. Nothing was too chimerical, too fantastic, too superlative for Sun Mountain.

But they had to think of the silver fleece. So, back the boys went to the Ophir, Gould & Curry, and Mexican. Down they went into dark shaft and murky incline. Millions of tons of black sulphurets were waiting to be taken out. By March forty tons had been disgorged by Ophir alone. Forty tons at $4000 a ton!

Some of the boys, like Tom Peasley, despised the drudgery of underground work in the Ophir, Gould & Curry, or any other mine for that matter. Tom wanted something more exciting than slinging a pick. He found it in fire. Whenever the firebell began to clang he would drop whatever he was doing and bolt for the blaze.

There were fires aplenty—great, terrible conflagrations that swept the mountain with blasting heat. With Washoe zephyrs to fan them, and a chronic lack of water, it didn't take those fiery tongues long to lick up whole areas of paper-lined cabins. Thrilling while they lasted, they called for instant decision and great energy. If the great red-painted mining works caught afire the lives of thousands of men digging in their depths were endangered. Nothing pleased Tom Peasley more than to get one of those on-charging fires under control. The danger of the flames called out every ounce of his ingenuity.

Around him on Sun Mountain, Tom gathered a group of men who had been enrolled in New York fire companies. Although their original training had been with fists and spanners and fire trumpets, they quickly mastered the new kind of fire-fighting demanded by Washoe.

Out of these boys' enthusiasm for fires grew a voluntary fire company. Out of the volunteers developed Virginia Engine Company, No. 1, of which Tom was elected foreman.[8] When Virginia Hook and Ladder Company, No. 1, was organized Tom was likewise chosen foreman. In the course of time when five or six rival companies sprang into existence he became Chief Engineer.[9] Such was Tom Peasley, the genesis of Mark Twain's famous Buck Fanshaw.[10]

At first Virginia Engine Company, No. 1, had the most powerful apparatus on the Pacific Coast. Tom ordered it in New York. It had nine-and-one-quarter-inch cylinders, seven-and-one-half-inch stroke, and twenty-four-foot brakes, with 600 feet of hose. A magnificent machine. Everything Tom was connected with had to be like that—the biggest—the best of its kind, so that when Young Engine Company, No. 2, ordered an engine with ten-inch cylinders and a hose that could throw five streams at the same time, if necessary, there was bad feeling right away.[11]

Tom had sixty-four men under him. Big, powerful, good-natured men, as robust and fearless a set as ever lived—but terrible when aroused, such as Jack Perry, George Birdsall, Pete Larkin, Riff Williams, Ned Ingraham, L. Rawlings, Cap Mathewson, Louis Wardell, Bruce Garvey, Johnny Skae, Ike Brokaw, James Phelan, A. Hirschman, and a host of others. Without exception all strong Union men —every one of them bursting with exuberant energy and aching for any opportunity of exhibiting his prowess or working off excess steam. In any other community than Sun Mountain, that immortal sixty-four would have been leading stock-brokers, merchants or speculators. As it was, all of them were leaders. No other place of its size ever drew more of that element than Sun Mountain.

With his engine companies Tom Peasley began to bring that energetic, restless, sometimes reckless element that milled about Sun Mountain under social and political control. Every man who acted under Tom had to listen to rules and regulations or else he couldn't belong to Virginia Engine Company, No. 1. In this way Tom did more toward harnessing the exuberant spirit of Sun Mountain and directing it along right channels than any other force.[12] After organizing Virginia Engine Company, No. 1, on a firm basis, Tom collected funds to build an engine house on "C" Street, which developed into the most powerful political unit on Sun Mountain. As a symbol of ideal manhood he hung on its walls a portrait of that bright-eyed, smiling Ephraim Ellsworth, whose patriotism was sweeping his old friends into the ranks of the New York Fire Zouaves.[13]

Then Tom divided the city into four wards and built the tall red fire-tower high up on the mountain and installed watchmen there whose business it was to keep an ever vigilant eye on the city day and night and clang the bell when they saw any signs of flame.

Tall, compact, quick as a leopard on his feet, with a tread as soft, Tom was a perfectly co-ordinated specimen of manly strength and grace. His profile would have honored a Roman coin. He would have been superb in a toga! On a forum! The idol of a populace! As a leader his men would have followed him into a furnace and having reached it died with only one regret, that they hadn't more than life to offer. The boys were idolatrous in their devotion to him. But his superb manhood, his intelligence, his fine moral qualities, his leadership were not lost on Sun Mountain.[14] In no time his spirit of mastery asserted itself, and he ruled the rollicking and reckless, among whom his lot was cast, with a firm hand. As occasion demanded he could be as tender as a woman or the roughest of the rough. And he attained on Sun Mountain a distinction that few equalled and none surpassed.

His excess of animal spirits, his exultation in his great strength, his consciousness that something unusual was expected often led to the commission of acts deeply regretted and bitterly atoned. A New England conscience coupled with the playfulness of a panther is a bad combination. Oft Tom had occasion to rue it. Sometimes in joyful salutation Tom would knock over an acquaintance with a slap on the back. Sometimes instead of unlatching the cabin door of a particular crony, he would smash the panel. His impulse to play was as uncontrollable as a pup's. Once in such a mood he met Langford Peel, the bad-man, in front of the International Hotel, and bashed the latter's head against the wall.[15] For no other reason than that he didn't like "Chiefs." How he escaped death or challenge no one ever knew. Except that Tom was an artist with nature's weapons and an expert with acquired ones, and Peel knew it. Thus the roughs learned to fear Tom Peasley. He had brought rules and regulations to the mountain. Rules and regulations were anathema to toughs, and fear engendered hate.[16]

On one national fête-day, Tom staged a celebration that stood out for years as the high-water mark. The day required a queen. Julia Bulette was elected. As the Goddess of Victory—or was it of Flame? —crowned and helmeted she stood in wind-blown splendor amidst the glittering brasses of Fire Engine, No. 1. In her arms was a brass fire-trumpet, its base filled with roses speeded from Sacramento for the occasion. Behind her swung a legion of the red-shirted—red-bound fasces swaying in their hands. Before each engine proceeded a banner with the designation of the company, worked by Julia's own hands.

In everything connected with the Fire Department Julia Bulette took the greatest interest. When a blaze broke out and steam whistles began to shriek, Julia would rush from her palace and down the street in the direction of fire and smoke. Often she mounted the fire-engine as it sped by and lent a hand at the brakes or worked at the pump.[17] If it was one of those terrible conflagrations when Sun Mountain vomited cinders and ashes like an erupting Kilauea, Julia would brew coffee and carry it to the boys. If one of them grew sick from exposure or came down with lung-fever Julia would nurse him back to health. Hands, heart, and money were ever ready to lend assistance to the fire-boys.[18] Out of gratitude the fire-boys elected Julia an honorary member of Virginia Engine Company, No. 1.[19]

CHAPTER XIX

"LINCOLN'S ELECTED"

1860

The Piute War and Washoe's seditious attitude had attracted the attention of Federal authorities. They realized that something must be done to preserve Sun Mountain's loyalty, safeguard "Ponies," and protect the overland mail. As an answer to all three questions, Fort Churchill, at the bend of the Carson, almost at the mountain's base, came into existence. By June, 1860, it was occupied by United States troops. As Washoe became more and more rebellious, these forces were augmented by the Third Regiment of California Volunteers, under command of that supreme patriot Colonel P. Edward Connor, one of the immortals who had faced Santa Ana at Buena Vista.[1]

Colonel Connor lost no time in letting the secessionists feel his iron hand.[2] All persons accused of defaming the Federal government were arrested, put to work, and confined until such time as they took the oath of allegiance. It was a bit ironical to Terry's loud-mouthed adherents to find themselves within three days of the colonel's arrival carrying sand from the river bottom and laying the foundations of a Union stronghold.[3]

The colonel had placed a silencer on the mountain none too soon. Due to war and the disruption of the Pony Express the boys were feeling their isolated condition acutely and Terry had won over many of the doubtful to his side. It was the middle of June before the "Ponies" were re-established and despatches arrived announcing to the boys that on May 17 the Republicans had nominated Abraham Lincoln—a rail-splitter—for the Presidency, at their "Wigwam" convention in Chicago. This piece of astounding news came not by the overland route, but by "Pony" from California and caused considerable disappointment on Sun Mountain.[4]

"Who in the hell is Lincoln?" was heard on all sides. Nothing was known of him. He was a debater was he? A rail-splitter? Why hadn't they nominated Seward? The logical man for precarious times. The boys had set their hearts on him. It choked them to "hurrah" for Lincoln when they had planned a "tiger" for Seward.

"Ponies" from "below" proved that California was equally disappointed. "If Lincoln is elected," declared ex-Governor Weller, "the South will surely withdraw from the Union. They would be less than men if they did not." [5]

Sun Mountain—heart and soul—was against Lincoln. Every newspaper the boys read supported Breckenridge or Douglas. There seemed to be no chance for Lincoln in either California or Washoe.

No chance except with the loyal fire-lads. So discouraged were Tom Peasley and his red-shirted pals that they recruited a "Committee of Safety" from those daring souls who made up the roster of the different fire companies. Every lad took an oath. If the rebels dared to seize Sun Mountain and declare it as seceded it would be accomplished only over their dead bodies.

Then they set to work. Thomas Fitch, a silver-tongued orator, was imported to arouse public sentiment against secession. Fitch gave rousing lectures for Lincoln at Dayton—Silver City—Devil's Gate—Gold Hill—Virginia.

Later, Thomas Starr King, the apostle of Unionism, was engaged to awaken Sun Mountain's loyalty. With all his ardor, King threw himself against that citadel of secession—speaking in Gold Cañon— Six Mile and Seven Mile—everywhere stimulating the boys to the highest pitch of Unionism.

But it was reserved for Colonel E. D. Baker's "Apostrophe to Liberty" to fan the waning love of country on Sun Mountain into flame.[6] The "Apostrophe" was delivered in San Francisco but its text reached Sun Mountain as fast as Pony feet could carry it. Every word thrilled the boys like a shock of electricity—just as its oratorical drama had swept thousands to their feet in the American Theatre. That eleventh-hour speech won the West for the Party of Freedom. At the polls on election day Abraham Lincoln received a tremendous plurality.[7] His victory encouraged Tom Peasley to hope for the best in the East.

What had happened in "the States"? That was the question which agitated Tom and every other loyal lad on the mountain. They couldn't know for a week. It would take a Pony that long or longer to rush the news west. In the meantime their anxiety amounted to agony. Who had been elected? Lincoln—Douglas— or Breckenridge? Lincoln—with secession and war? Or Breckenridge—with slaves on Sun Mountain and Terry for Governor of Washoe?

Only the Pony could tell them—a Pony over a thousand miles

away—a Pony galloping toward the mountain as fast as hoofs shod with steel could fly.

Special arrangements had been made. The election had taken place on the 7th. The Pony with the news should reach Sun Mountain sometime on Monday, November 12. Fort Kearney to Sun Mountain in five days!! [8] That would be lightning speed. Ten miles an hour—in November! Could horseflesh maintain such a pace? Extra ponies were led far out from their stations to rush the message through. The fate of the country—of Washoe—depended on the issue. No expense was being spared. Was it freedom or slavery?

Monday the 12th dawned—waned—no Pony. Tuesday the 13th —midday—no news! Midnight—silence—no clatter of hoofs—no winding horn. All eyes were turned to the desert. All hearts yearned toward the Pony. All ears strained for the faintest sound of pounding feet. A little after midnight the sentinel at Fort Churchill caught the dull thud of approaching hoofs. It was "Pony Bob." [9]

"Lincoln's elected," he shouted as he ran. "Lincoln's elected." [10]

CHAPTER XX

TERRITORIAL ENTERPRISE

1860

In the wake of the swift-footed Pony came a demand for a newspaper on Sun Mountain. Superlative events were happening to the East. The feeling between North and South was stretched taut. Any day might witness its snapping. The passion for news was intense. The boys were impatient to know the latest at the soonest possible moment. A posted dispatch on the bulletin board at Wells Fargo's was no longer satisfactory. The call was urgent. And as practically the whole population of Washoe was centred on Sun Mountain *The Territorial Enterprise,* which had been founded in Genoa in 1858, took up quarters at the corner of "A" Street and Sutton Avenue, then the business section of Virginia. A short time thereafter Joe Goodman bought the concern and took over the editorship.[1]

Before joining the Washoe rush, Joe Goodman had been a contributor and compiler on *The Golden Era* in San Francisco. He was a handsome, reckless dare-devil youth of parts—a poet of imagination, a scholar, a dramatic critic, a playwright, and a writer of leaders. Everything that came from his pen had literary quality.

It was well that Joe was so well fortified, for Washoe demanded editorial ability of the highest order! Above all, her editors must have the courage of their convictions, honesty without bigotry, and talent without stint. Joe brought to *The Enterprise* more than Washoe demanded. Without this, as he soon learned, he wouldn't have lasted a week. For the boys required that their editors must say what they felt, without fear. They must be willing to back up their statements with a gun and if required, in their behalf, to lay down life without a qualm. That was a large order but it conformed to Joe's literary creed. Bullets as well as pi were an integral part of a Washoe reporter's daily régime. And Joe wouldn't countenance any one on his staff who refused to subscribe to his formula.

Joe's paper became the mirror of Washoe's audacious life—the vade mecum of every mining town on the mountain. As Virginia thrived Joe came to occupy a more and more conspicuous part in the community life. Soon it was necessary to have some one to whom he could delegate editorial drudgery. His choice fell upon Rollin M. Daggett, even then famous in coast literary circles for scissors and "seven-up." "Dag" was a gray, obese cynic with more than a dash of Iroquois in his makeup. He had an eye for the picturesqueness of his calling and arranged himself accordingly in red shirt and black top boots. Soon he was hurling vitriolic sentences with the precision of a tomahawk and sneering at the discomfiture he caused. To head the local department Joe installed Dan De Quille—a bright-minded, sweet-spirited, keen-witted, whimsical sprite with a courage more ardent than the bowie he always carried.

The office of *The Territorial Enterprise* was a one-room, rickety shanty with a lean-to. In the room were conglomerated an old-fashioned Washington press, cases of type, desks, and tables. In the lean-to were a dining-table, "bunks" arranged one above the other, a kitchen stove, and "Old Joe," a Celestial cook, who spent his time chasing a pie-eating devil.

The office did well enough in summer when the Washoe "zephyr" was in good humor and played fitfully with dust and cranny, and did no worse than to cause compilers to cough and sneeze and swear in a manner horrible to hear; but in winter when Zephyr grew bold and howled with cold it was another story. Then copy, sleet, and curses flew helter-skelter about the room. Compositors stood at their cases with barley-sacks lashed to their legs, blue breath on their lips, and icicles clinging to their beards.

With spring thaw, conditions grew worse. The roof leaked like a sieve. White-string leaders diverted dripping water from case and table to the sides of the room. At times so many strings were in use that the ceiling took on the appearance of the huge cobweb of a Brobdingnagian spider.

For his news Joe couldn't depend on the grape-line telegraph. Thus the Pony became as necessary an adjunct to his columns as Dan or "Dag." It was the Pony that brought the latest reports from the "plains," of emigrant trains making their way across the wilds, of the movements of Indians, of new discoveries, of the slave question that was convulsing "the States." Of nights that rickety room saw lively times with editor, compositor, pressman, and devil dashing about; expressmen hurrying up from Six and Seven Mile with reports of rich strikes and Ponies dashing in from Forty Mile with tidings of Indian raids and impending war.[2]

The headlines of Joe's sheet partook of this excitement. "By Pony

Express" never failed to give the boys a thrill. Those magic words conjured up an image of a chain of horsemen, extending from "the States" to Sun Mountain, running night and day at break-neck speed toward them with the latest news of national import.[3] It was an image in terms of the superlative—but then the boys lived by the extraordinary.

From the beginning Joe gave *The Enterprise* a spirt of exaggeration, aggressive to an extreme. He allowed his staff to perpetrate hoaxes and assault one another as well as editors of rival sheets in columns of matchless abuse. One editor was "a walking whiskeybottle" and another "a Fenian imp."[4] Over these classic onslaughts the boys would roar their applause. And Joe allowed them to say anything they pleased just as long as they were game enough to back up their statements.

When the throb of presses had ceased for the night, editor and compiler composed their difficulties at the nearest bar and sang songs of comradeship until dawn came up the trail or else stood their ground at twenty paces and filled one another with cold lead. What was considered thrilling in California, what would have excited mirth anywhere "below," passed unnoticed in Washoe, as too tame, too insipid for the feverish brains and throbbing pulses of those who milled about the mountain.

Nothing ordinary would do for them. Their literary palates required the highly seasoned food of a Latin population. But Joe Goodman could not always cull this kind of news from transpiring events. This deficiency had to be supplied by the fertile brain of his reporters. Thus blood-curdling yarns of fictitious massacres, red-hot scalpings of auburn-headed women, fantastic accounts of mythical caves and subterranean grottoes lined with virgin gold found their way into the columns of *The Enterprise*. All these tales had to have a local touch, familiar names and surroundings; otherwise the boys wouldn't read them. In this way Joe and his readers created an unmarked, fabulous frontier which lay somewhere between Washoe and that nebulous realm that poppy-dreamers inhabit.

To be on the staff of *The Enterprise* was no mean accomplishment. Gems of thought, shafts of wit, bits of color, fantasy, travesty, extravaganza, burlesque, satire, irony, phantasmagorial minglings of rhetoric and derision were daily required. In addition both editor and reporter had to know all about geology and mineralogy and had to be able to call a man a liar, a thief, or any other little epithet that entered his head and be able to back up his assertion with stamina, heart and intestinal fortitude. Otherwise so far as Washoe was concerned he might just as well "go over the grade." [5]

For instance—one day Colonel Calhoun Thompson, aspirant for sheriff, perused with indignation what a Washoe editor had to say on his character. "White livered," was he? Arming himself with a huge hickory cane, a bowie-knife, and a pair of derringers, he sallied forth to settle the account. He'd show him! Having taken on a little Dutch courage at the nearest bar, the colonel strode into the newspaper office, at the noon hour. All the staff had departed save an undersized, beardless, fragile-looking youth, who was seated at a table scissoring a pile of exchanges.

"Are you," sputtered Colonel Calhoun Thompson, pounding his cane upon the office floor, "are you the blankety-blank scoundrel who edits this paper?"

Without looking up, the young man at the table snatched a cocked revolver from the table drawer—then levelled it at Colonel Thompson's heart.[6]

"I am," he said, and the flabbergasted colonel found himself gazing down the muzzle of a derringer. "Anything to say about it?"

But that was the end of that.

You had to be quick on the trigger to survive the literary game on Sun Mountain.

CHAPTER XXI

OPHIR

1860

While stocks, firehouses, bars, assay offices, editors, and ponies were multiplying on Sun Mountain the Ophir sank its incline deeper along the ledge. With every foot attained the richer grew the ore, the higher soared dividends and the more luxuriously lived the directors in San Francisco. Everything "below" was booming on the strength of the discoveries on Sun Mountain. Night and day now the Golden Gate city was bathed in the red glare of furnaces that were turning out everything that Washoe needed, from nuts to cages.

At first the Ophir used a windlass and a bucket to lower miners and to hoist out ore. On the surface the ore was assorted into grades. The richest, promising $1000 to the ton or upward, was sacked for shipment to England. The second- and third-class scuff was piled aside for future milling. That which ran fifty dollars a ton or less was utilized in grading "A," "B" and "C" street' Thus the roads leading up Sun Mountain were paved with silvc

When the Ophir shaft reached a depth where windlass and bucket could no longer stand the strain, some one hit upon the plan of a horse and whim and the work went merrily on. Brighter and brighter was the glint of metallic silver and more and more opulent the ideas of directors.

Then the Ophir struck a snag—water!—the bane of all miners. There was hardly any on the surface but when the shaft reached the fifty-foot level, water ran in so rapidly that miners could no longer work on the ledge. Unless something could be devised, and devised swiftly, they would be flooded out. When dividends ceased and the water climbed menacingly up the incline the directors rushed up the mountain.

Sutro was vindicated. "Umph," he said. "Vat could you expect? The vorking of the mines is done vitout any system, vitout an eye to future success. If the Ophir ran a tunnel from low down on the hill, and then sank a shaft to meet it, they vould not have any trouble

vit drainage. Instead vat does the Ophir do? Open a shaft from
above, vich requires timbering and exposes the mine to all sorts of
difficulties."

According to Sutro it was all wrong. Any one with half an eye
could see that. The ledge should be mined by way of a tunnel from
the Carson River.

"Ridiculous," returned the Ophir.

Finally the directors installed a fifteen-horse-power steam-engine
—the most powerful in the West. It was a great occasion, one of the
seven wonders of the camp, when steam was applied against the
sump and water spurted out of the shaft in a stream and poured
down Six Mile. Their new steam-whistle blew a mighty blast. The
boys cheered. Water was conquered by steam! That primitive element had met its match.

But pump as it would, hour after hour, the fifteen-horse-power
engine failed to empty the sump. It would take fifty—a hundred
horses! As fast as the water was pumped out, just as swiftly it seeped
in and flooded the men out. The boys were positive that they had
tapped the underground outlet of Lake Tahoe.

That failure was a disappointment to San Francisco, where the
pump had been designed and made. It was a disappointment, too, to
Ralston. He needed those Ophir dividends to carry on his banking.
Ophir stock began to fluctuate. There was a flurry on the stock
market. The wise men who had gone to sea in their bowl got wet.
They were loud in their denunciation of Sun Mountain.

When it was evident that the pump could not answer the water
question, the directors decided on an adit. Joining forces with the
Mexican and Central, a contract was let to drain the ledge to the
depth of 200 feet. When John Mackay heard about the projected
tunnel he applied for a job as a "mucker." He wanted to learn
something about this drainage business and the best place to learn it
was at the face of the drift with pick and shovel.

Beginning June 8, 1860, at a point below the Ophir outcroppings,
the tunnel was pushed night and day through 1100 feet of hard-
rock and reached the shaft line, 155 feet below the surface, exactly four months later. It had cost $10,000—the eighth wonder of
the camp! Shaft and incline were readily drained to bed-rock.
Stocks went up. Good times came back. The incline burrowed its
way into danker, darker corners of Sun Mountain.

Then the Ophir met another problem. At the fifty-foot level the
vein of sulphurets had been only three to four feet wide and was

easily extracted. As the shaft sank deeper the vein widened. The earth became so friable that a pick was hardly needed. To stay it up, posts and simple lintels were used.

The directors were jubilant. They had had no idea of the extent in richness of their ledge. Stocks soared and soared. With every foot achieved in depth, the broader became the silver ledge, the richer the assays, but the more crumbly the earth. Cave-ins were frequent, and the boys complained more and more about the danger of their surroundings. The miners were now digging considerably below the level of the Union tunnel. The pump handled the water problem satisfactorily but the earth had become harder to handle. Who would have dreamed that silver could be a liability? Certainly not the directors. How were the sulphurets to be removed without endangering the lives of the miners? Finally the boys refused to be lowered into the shaft until something was done to protect them.[1] Engineers from California were stumped. Engineers were brought from the East. They were nonplussed. Engineers were imported from Europe. No one had ever seen a silver vein of such magnitude.

Suddenly, at the 175-foot level the vein broadened to 65 feet in width—the first bonanza. It was beyond the dreams of Aladdin. With each shift of their candles, the walls and roofs of the gallery glistened like stars. But when the boys put a pick into it down would come an avalanche of meteors. Two miners, picking away at the face of the drift, were buried alive and suffocated before they could be rescued.

The directors were perplexed. Engineers were afraid to proceed. Instead of dividends there were assessments. With oceans of drink in sight there was not one drop in the cup. Timbering was tried— posts and lintels—placed so close together that the drifts were sheathed in pine planking. The boys were safe. They could work straight ahead—but not above or below. The output was slackened.

Then the supply of pine in Washoe Valley became exhausted. Any scrubby tree was seized upon, spliced together with iron bolts and bars. But they were no sooner in position than the earth would slack and swell. Too weak to stand the pressure, they were constantly broken and shoved out of place, endangering the lives of all who worked beneath them. Like Sisyphus' boulder, walls were no sooner propped into a desired position than down they would tumble, ready to crush out life. The "blue-stuff" had come into its own. It was master in those dark, dank, disintegrating depths. Surrounded by untold wealth the directors saw themselves lacking the ability to

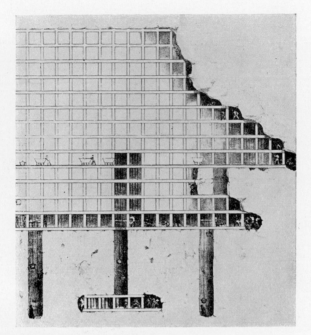

INTERIOR AND PLAN OF WORKING A MINE.
From the author's collection.

MINERS AT WORK UNDER "DEIDESHEIMER SQUARE–SETS."

DROVE of BACTRIAN CAMELS, en route for WABUCE to the BIGTREE-ROUTE, passing through the MAMMOTH GROVE (Sept. 1857).

From the author's collection. CAMELS USED TO CARRY SALT FROM DESERT MARSHES TO WASHOE MILLS.

carry it off. That "damn'd blue-stuff" had become an elephant on their hands; and the elephant had gone "loco."

Thus matters drifted until November, 1860. With millions in sight the mine had produced less than $200,000. More than that had been consumed in getting that amount out. The proverb that it takes gold to get silver was correct. The Ophir bid fair to ruin its owners.

In this emergency, director William F. Babcock of San Francisco sent for Philip Deidesheimer, a native of Darmstadt, Germany, a miner by profession, who was then successfully operating a quartz mine in El Dorado County. From what he had heard about him, Babcock felt he would be just the one to solve the problem of the Ophir and he requested Deidesheimer to meet him in San Francisco.

"What would you do if you had a quartz lode fifty or sixty feet wide?" [2] asked Babcock when Deidesheimer had arrived.

"I've never seen or heard of a vein of ore of such great width," replied Deidesheimer.

"Could you work such a vein?" asked Babcock.

"I couldn't tell what I could do," retorted Deidesheimer, "until I have studied the place."

"Up to this time," said Babcock, "our engineers have failed to properly work the Ophir, and it is a very valuable mine. Unless some way of supporting the earth can be discovered it will be of little value to the directors or owners. Go to the Comstock tomorrow at our expense."

It was November 8. Deidesheimer went up to Washoe, and descended the Ophir to the 50-foot level.[3] What could be done?

Up to November 14 he had arrived at no conclusion. One morning he came to the surface and threw himself down on a log near the Ophir cut. He was discouraged and looked out across the desert; at the bitter waters of those lost rivers; out where the Carson ended ignominiously in a sink. He was like that river—sunk—frustrated.

A bee fluttered across his vision. Deidesheimer watched it nestle in the yellow sage then disappear into its hive. Back and forth it flew—collecting honey—storing it in the cells. A thought dawned upon Deidesheimer. He slapped his knee, jumped to his feet. "I have it. I have it," he sputtered. "Why not support the walls of the Ophir just as the bee supports his honey-comb?"

That day he hit upon the plan of building up square sets of timber similar to the walls in the cell of a honey-comb. He would build cell after cell in the hive of Sun Mountain.[4] The Ophir would become a honey-comb.

At Deidesheimer's direction the Ophir descended on a Sierra forest twenty miles away. Trees were felled, lumber was squared, mule-skinners lashed the timbers to the backs of trusty mules, and the great traffic in lumber commenced.

Deidesheimer then began operations. He opened up the third gallery of the Ophir, a chamber cut in the silver vein some 215 feet below the surface. Under his directions the carpenters had framed a big supply of timbers. The boys were puzzled when they saw them lowered into the mine. They looked insignificant, and some were disposed to laugh at the performance. They had no idea of the manner in which they were to be put together. Even after the first row of sets had been placed in position they did not see what was to happen next. But when the second set had been placed on the first they caught the idea. Deidesheimer was building a bee-hive in the bowels of the earth and they were to be the bees!

By building up and extending these square sets Deidesheimer successfully "stoped out the ore" from wall to wall, across a deposit averaging over sixty-five feet in width, and the ground supported by the wall of timber stood as firmly as did the undisturbed sections of the mountains. In that gallery a whole forest of Sierra pine found a grave.

With this plan the boys could extract ore at any height, or any width, or any length, or any depth. Without it they could do nothing or next to nothing.

When the directors saw the great advantages of Deidesheimer's plan of timbering, they gave him full charge of the mine and, like the kings they were to become, bestowed upon him the title of Mining Engineer—and Deidesheimer owed the whole idea to a bee! Sun Mountain became a Mecca for German, English, and French engineers who came from Europe expressly to report upon the Comstock system of timbering and working large ore-bodies. All declared that it could no more be improved upon than could the cells of a honey-bee.[5]

CHAPTER XXII

MILLS
1860

With pumps keeping the water under control and Deidesheimer's "square sets" holding the earth in abeyance, the boys met with their third problem—a ready method of robbing the matrix of its silver. Hard-rock was as adamant as ever. It held the precious metal entombed in its heart as tenaciously as the tentacle of an octopus holds to its prey. How to break that grip became of master import. How to break that hold was a question as old as Solomon, as hoary as the Incas. Many a priest and layman had gone to his grave leaving the proposition unsolved. Could Sun Mountain solve a riddle older than that of the Sphinx?

Until the Ophir could break that hold cheaply what was the use of expensive water-pumps, tunnels and "square sets"? Not all "blue-stuff" was worth shipping to Swansea, Wales, or Freiburg, Saxony, for reduction. How were they going to break down that second- and third-grade stuff that was piled up in ever-increasing dumps before their works? Unless they could reduce it to a pulp and extract the silver cheaply they might as well stop their pumps.

At first the boys tried the "patios process," that most primitive of methods imported from Mexico. They cleared an immense circular area of brush, paved it with flat stones, spread out their rock and over it urged a drove of mules round and round. In stamping the rock to a pulp, the hoofs of the poor brutes were worn to the quick. At best it was a slow, painful, as well as expensive, process.

Nevertheless "patios" sprang up like weeds on every stretch of level ground. One operator employed a band of white horses to do his crushing. When he added salt and copper sulphate to his amalgam his horses' tails and legs were suddenly dyed a brilliant green and their necks and heads were spotted black with polka-dots. It was amalgamation in terms of the futuristic future and caused considerable amusement on Sun Mountain. "Patios" could not cope with the magnitude of Sun Mountain's output. Some other method had to be devised.

In desperation the boys turned to the Mexican arrastra. Bigger
flat-bottomed basins were excavated, lined and paved with green-
stone and the hard-rock spread out upon them. Into them was
turned loose a group of brawny Thors with hammers. When they
had crushed the rock, a heavy "muller," operated by horse-power,
ground it to dust. This method proved more successful, and the
banks of the Carson were soon dotted with water-driven arrastras.
Mule-driven ore-wagons snaked their way up and down the Cañon
between river-bottom and shaft-head. The race of mule-skinners
and bull-whackers came into being filling the air with dust—curses
—writhing black-snakes and groans. Profits were enormous. Arrastras multiplied like jack-rabbits. Many earned as much as $1000
per day—but it was soon evident that even this method was inadequate to cope with all of Sun Mountain's unprecedented output in
silver-bearing rock.[1] Something better must be devised.

Almarin Paul suggested "iron pans." He had used them in the
gold mines of California. He was convinced that they would van-
quish the obdurate qualities in Sun Mountain's hard-rock. Old-
school metallurgists told him that his plan was absurd. Experts
from Freiburg contended for the Germanic "barrel system." The
Mexican stuck to the mule-driven "patio" of his ancestral pueblos—
a few insisted on smelting.[2]

But Paul stuck to his "pan process" and instituted a series of careful tests that confirmed previous opinions. Satisfied that he was
right he determined to erect a mill at Devil's Gate, on account of
accessibility to water, and equip it with no other apparatus than his
pans.[3] In March, 1860, with the assistance of George Hearst, he
founded the "Washoe Gold and Silver Mining Company No. 1,"
with a capital stock of $500,000, divided into 1000 shares at $500
each.[4] Even with Hearst's backing it was a hazardous undertaking.
Mill-men were averse to innovation. To capitalists it seemed a
foolish venture. Leading assayers of San Francisco, jealous of their
profits, predicted failure. The Ophir with hundreds of tons of rich
gold- and silver-bearing quartz lying idle on their dumps, refused to
make any contracts with him. The Mexican, satisfied with their
slow, sleepy system of centuries past, likewise refused. Paul's resolution was unshaken. He advertised that he would crush and reduce
hard-rock for $25 to $30 per ton. Finally several venturous operators
like Sandy Bowers agreed to let him reduce 9000 tons providing Paul
would pledge the completion of his mill within sixty days from the
date of the signing of the contracts. It was then June 12, 1860. By

August 12, would his mill be ready for operation? Could he begin by crushing Sandy Bowers' ore? Paul said he could. Although at that time foundations were not laid, machinery was not assembled—not even ordered—and the lumber was still growing in Sierra forests, he signed the contracts.

Few men would have undertaken such risks. Machinery had to be made to order in San Francisco and transported across the Sierra. Growing trees had to be felled to get the required lumber. But Paul worked like one inspired. A San Francisco firm, the Howland, Angel & King Company, where he ordered his machinery, rivalled him in dispatch. The completed castings were forwarded by steamboat to Sacramento. From there they were carted by freighters over the old emigrant road. Through snow, rock, and mire, straining mules, urged forward by kicks and blows, dragged the iron freight to the Devil's Gate. There Paul was anxiously waiting, with stone foundations and walls in readiness. Nails were hustled over on mule-back. Lumber landed at the site cost $60 per M. Expenses were enormous. But money was no consideration. The mill must be completed at any cost within sixty days. On August 11, just in time to save his contracts, the first steam-whistle heard in Gold Cañon shrieked his victory as the twenty-four huge stamps rose like one enormous inspired pestle in a Titanic mortar and fell with a thunderous clatter, shaking the building to its foundations, rocking Hosea Grosch in his coffin, reverberating and reverberating among desert hills.

From the pans the pulp was successively run through settling-tanks, amalgamating-pans, agitators, and separators. Refuse material passing away, quicksilver collected the precious metal into a mass of shining amalgam, soft as putty. Into the fire-retort went the amalgam. Quicksilver was left behind. Bars of shining silver emerged and were rushed off to San Francisco.

When Paul fitted steam-chambers to his pan bottoms the Washoe process of pan amalgamation became a pronounced success. Mill-men came from all over the world to study the method. In a few months Paul's company began to build a larger mill of sixty-four stamps. More mechanical improvements were introduced. Three hours after Paul's first mill awakened the echoes of Devil's Gate, a second mill, that of Coover & Harris, came into being with another shrill shriek and the pounding of nine stamps. Other mills followed quickly.[5] The whole complexion of Gold Cañon changed. The blue sky was blackened with soot. The thunder and clatter of stamps was deafening. The shouts of bull-whackers and mule-skinners, the creak of brakes, the groans of ox and mule, merged into one indescribable pandemonium.

Paul's mills were as nothing in comparison to that of the Gould & Curry constructed on a rocky point at the junction of Seven and Six Mile Cañons. Upon an artificial plateau, levelled at enormous expense, was erected a building in the form of a Greek cross, 250 feet long, with arms 75 feet in length and 50 feet in breadth. The foundation and lower storey were constructed of massive blocks of ochre-colored stone.[6] Upon these rested a superstructure of brown-stained wood. Smooth approaches were blasted out of the rocky hillside. Arched culverts of hewn stone spanned ravines. Graded terraces, ascended by flights of broad steps, surrounded all. Near-by, a small lake was excavated in the solid yellow rock, lined with blue tile, and filled with water.

The lake was a gem of engineering beauty. In its centre, dripping with moisture, as if just emerging from a dip in those clear waters, emerged three laughing marble naiads! Between them they supported a fragile pink shell upon which floated a white swan, head thrown back spouting a jet of crystalline waters high into the eternal blue of the mountain sky. The whole ensemble in the sterile waste was pagan!

Twin calves dragged a light cart over smooth lawns. Roosters crowed. Poultry cackled. Swine grunted. Cattle lowed. All contributed to the illusion that this was the country-seat of some mining Crœsus of Washoe. Belshazzar with his hanging-gardens, Cosimo de Medici with his ilex-bordered Boboli paths, never achieved anything more startling!

In such surroundings how importunate the clatter of stamps! How insistent the clouds of dust that arose from pans! When the directors saw those clouds of alkali blighting lake, lawn and hacienda, they arranged for fans to drive it into an especially prepared room. When necessity demanded an addition to the original length of the building, the directors objected. It would ruin the symmetry of the cross![7]

Not to be outdone, the Ophir built a magnificent mill to handle their ore on the pine-clad banks of Washoe Lake at the base of the mountain. The buildings covered an acre. To reach them the lake was spanned by a picturesque brass-mounted bridge—as red as the lacquered one at Nikko. Regularly every Saturday night Ophir Caliphs drove down the mountain, crossed the red bridge, and gathered about a wine-laden table to celebrate. After dinner they occupied the night and sometimes the entire Sabbath in playing the great American game with blue chips, and a sky limit. Stock was selling for $4000 a share. The trustees sniffed at the stars.

The Ophir and Gould & Curry did their amalgamating with quicksilver, salt, and a few ounces of copper sulphate. Most of the other mill-men did not like anything so prosaic. Knowing nothing about the working of silver ores, they tried all manner of experiments with the idea of thorough amalgamation of the silver contained in the hard-rock. This in the opinion of many was to be accomplished by the use of chemicals. A more promiscuous collection of strange drugs and vegetable decoctions was probably never before used for any purpose.[8] In the variety and villainousness of their contents, the amalgamating pans surpassed the caldron of Macbeth's witches. Not content with blue-stone, salt, and one or two other articles of approved efficacy, these men poured into their pans all manner of acids. When the mineral kingdom was exhausted they started in on the vegetable. Bark was peeled from cedar trees, and boiled down until a strong tea was obtained. When this failed a decoction of sage-brush took its place. Being the bitterest, most unsavory, nauseating-tasting stuff to be found in any part of the world, it was dumped into amalgamating pans on the theory that not being good for anything else, therefore, it must be good to reduce silver. Australian sheep-dip was used and an infusion of two-bit cigars. Anything as palatable as tobacco-juice would surely coax even the matrix out of silver! Sutro, with his inventive genius, concocted a special process and built a mill at Dayton to develop it. Like the prudent man that he was, he had it fully insured. So that when it failed to reduce hard-rock to the proper consistency but burst into flames, Sutro was enabled to collect a neat little sum.

Every superintendent had his own secret process of reduction which he operated behind closed doors. In the course of time there were as many quack methods of attacking silver as there were quack doctors dispensing drugs. The object with them all was, by hook or crook, to physic the silver out of the rock. At least to make it so nauseated that it would loosen its hold upon its matrix, come out and be entrapped by the quicksilver which was lying in wait for it at the bottom of the pans.[9] When their inventive genius exhausted itself the mill-men returned to the quicksilver, copper sulphate, and salt of ancient history. That was costly enough. Every one of those ingredients had to be brought over the Sierra at enormous expense.

Quicksilver was mined in California in the hills back of San José, refined, and packed into iron flasks and transported on the backs of trusty mules.

Salt, too, was brought from California. But the folly of transporting it across the Sierra to a territory whose soil differed little from that of Sodom was early seen. Provision was soon made for a supply of this staple from the banks of the "lost" rivers and the beds of "dead" seas about them.

CHAPTER XXIII

SHIPS OF THE DESERT

"My God!" cried an astonished youth as he stood stock-still gazing transfixedly at the oncoming spectacle. "There comes the Resurrection!" [1]

It was a starry night and a crescent moon hung like a scimitar in the blue sky. Fresh from a wine festival, several of the boys had just turned into a side street when one of them saw the sight that took his breath away. The others followed his gaze. They were so overpowered at what they saw advancing that some fell to their knees and began telling their beads while others took to their heels.

Down the street stalking toward them came a caravan of camels. Mounted on the back of the largest, blackest one sat a red turbaned Turk. On the backs of the eight others were white blocks that glistened in the moonlight.

The boys, as they watched the swaying camels, remained motionless as statues and rubbed their eyes. Was it a Bacchanalian dream or a mirage? Presently it would fall to pieces. If you could see ships and sea-gulls in desert air, why not camels seeking a manger? Visions of the Far East—burning sands—holy shrines—minarets trooped through their excited brains. Had a muezzin suddenly appeared on the gallery of Tom Peasley's red fire-tower and called out the hour of prayer: "Allah! Akbar! Allah! Akbar! Allah—Allah—Allah!" the boys could not have been more amazed. Nearer and nearer, toward them, packs swaying, feet padding, stalked the solemn procession. None of them had ever seen anything so startling.[2]

But it was not a miracle, nor a mirage, nor a gift-bearing caravan, but the materialization of Yankee genius—nine Bactrian camels imported from Tartary expressly to bring salt from Teal's Marsh on Walker River to Sun Mountain's mills.[3]

The traffic grew. Subsequently two other camel-companies were organized to feed desert salt to clattering pans.[4] One of them alone furnished sixty tons monthly to the Pioneer Mill.[5] With a glass the boys could often follow those salt-laden caravans making their way across the sands of Forty Mile and Twelve Mile toward Six or Seven Mile Cañon. They never ceased to cause excitement. Thirty-five miles a day with an 800-pound pack was enough to make them gape with astonishment.

The camels took to Sun Mountain. It bore a resemblance to their native habitat. They liked the deep warm sand at its base. They felt it to be as barren and hostile as any in Arabia. When their packs were off they would roll and frolic in it like so many gigantic kittens. But if they liked the sand—they hated the alkali that burned their nostrils, reddened their eyes, and irritated the raw spots on their backs.

Horses and mules were "scared to death." They would catch the strange scent a mile ahead and bolt in terror. As soon as a caravan could be seen coming through Devil's Gate—just as soon would ore-teams, freighters, Concord coaches, and pack-trains bolt over the hills in every direction. On this account the camels were brought up at night, over unfrequented roads and through back streets to a rendezvous above the Piutes' wigwams on Sun Mountain.

There was one grizzly old camel that attained a great reputation in Washoe. The boys called him "Old Brigham" because he was the patriarch of the herd. He had a magnificent mane over four feet long. Upon it more than one of the boys cast envious eyes. It would make a fine lariat for their mustangs.

Came a morning when they rode to where "Old Brigham" was seen feeding with his harem. One of the boys urged his frightened horse near enough to throw his lariat over "Old Brigham's" head before the camel realized what was intended.[6] It happened to be just at that season of the year at which "Old Brigham" felt no inhibitions. He was lord of the range. The king of the trail. The Sam Brown of the caravan. The sultan of the seraglio. As soon as the lariat began to caress his neck, "Old Brigham" did not wait. He turned. Threw back his ears. Opened wide his mouth. Displayed his teeth. Emitted a roar like that of a royal Bengal tiger and charged. Straight for the horse. That animal, wild with fright, turned and sprang into a run. "Old Brigham" thundering after. The rider was in a fair way of being yanked out of the saddle and trampled to his doom. Just in time he snipped his lariat from the pommel and rode for his life. "Brigham" kept up the chase for a mile, then returned to his family, still proud, still haughty, but obviously disappointed that he had not overhauled that creature that had dared to throw the rope on him.

The camels required very little care. They ate greedily all kinds of grasses, thistles, cactus, and were particularly fond of the acrid greasewood. But they disliked the stony path that led skyward through the Devil's Gate to the Lode. The sharp edges of the quartz-filled road was a *via crucis* to the soft pads on their feet. Torn and bruised, they left a path of blood in their wake. The shifting of the packs, on the steep climb, chafed and blistered their humps to the raw. The working-in of alkali dust left them in a pitiable plight.[7] Sometimes they cried with the pain. Bull-whackers and mule-skinners were unsympathetic drivers. They would fondle their mules and caress their "Washoe canaries" like babies— but they had only cuffs and sneers for the weary camel. Cursing them as hunchbacked, misshapen brutes, they flogged them aloft with vicious three-thonged whips. The dislike that sprang up between camel and tender was immediate and mutual. Usually mild and slow-moving beasts, they were aroused by the ill treatment meted out to them and would kick and bite to surpass the worst army mule.[8]

When the camels had climbed to the Divide and could look up Sun Mountain to the great rocky finger that pointed into the blue sky there was gratitude in their gaze. Their heads would go up. Nostrils would dilate. They would sniff the Alpine air with pride. Instinct enabled them to recognize it as a congenial clime. Long-enduring, but sagacious in their apparent listlessness, they noticed everything. They were particularly fond of their eerie perch on the flanks of Sun Mountain with its wide panorama of desert scenery.

When they had reached their destination, they would halt, and patiently kneel until the mule-skinners removed the great burdens of salt from their bleeding backs. Then, fatigued as they were, they would look around for the loftiest spot that commanded the most extensive view. Having located it, they would scramble to their feet and stalk majestically upward. Then with their heads toward that region of bitter waters, dead seas, and lost rivers, they would sink to their knees, like orthodox Mohammedans bowing toward Mecca, and remain seemingly lost in contemplation. If annoyed at these times by their keepers, they would give unmistakable evidence of impatience. Unceremoniously they would spew cuds into the face of an offender. Then turn away with something between a moan and a groan.[9]

CHAPTER XXIV

THE SQUAW AND THE CHIEF
1860

By the fall of 1860 an incredible community clung to the steep slopes of the mountain. The Ophir had burrowed some 200 feet into its depths. Ore was assaying from two to four thousand dollars a ton. Mills were going full tilt. Stamps were making an unearthly clatter. Bullion was pouring into moulds. An endless traffic was moving down the Cañon—a perpetual cavalcade of ore-wagons feeding rock to river mills; and Wells Fargo expresses rushing squat silver bricks off to San Francisco. An equally ceaseless tide was climbing Sun Mountain—lumber-wagons hauling timber up to the mines, bull-whackers snaking freighters through jammed traffic, stages careening on up-grades. Now and anon above the clamor of traffic sang out the staccato tones of a Colt. Life on the surface was played fortissimo; in dark, subterranean drifts, in more subdued tones.

Before winter set in the Piutes in small bands trudged up Six and Seven Mile. Not long since, as the lords of Washoe they trooped aloft, as the devout seek a temple, to offer up thanks to Pah-ah, for piñon and grasshopper. But now they stole back as beggars seeking succor. There was no other place to go. Better to starve on the unfriendly fringe of this so-called civilization than to succumb in the hostile sands of the desert. With piñon groves cut down, sage-brush uprooted, grasshoppers flown—every source of food had vanished.

Forlornly they stumbled upward. They shook their heads sadly as they looked up at that stony finger. The boys paid them scant attention. When they pitched their wickiups in their wonted places about the spring, some ruffian would order them to move on.

"Don't squat there! That property's worth $1500 a foot. Get out."

When they pitched their wigwams on the fringe of "C" Street, they were left unmolested only long enough for the staggering rows of cabins to push them peremptorily down to the outskirts of "D" and "E" Streets. When "E" was built up, down they were shoved to "F." As fast as the whites scrambled up the mountain down went the Piutes.

With their return, a strange figure was remarked among them. A squaw, who stalked like a shadow in the wake of her tribe, but never in its midst—a thin-visaged, solemn-looking squaw, of great height and tremendous stride. Calico skirts, of the meal-bag pattern, flopped disconsolately about her long thin legs and enormous moccasined feet. A red blouse was pulled taut over her drooping shoulders and flat chest. Her arms hung limp. Big brown hands flapped listlessly at her side. It was a well-knit but sinister figure with a hangdog, hopeless air. Over her head was drawn a calico bandana, drawn so low that it hid the gaunt features and lack-luster eyes. No buck looked at her. No "Mahala" spoke to her. Not a word, not a grunt, good, bad, or indifferent, passed between her and any other member of the tribe. When the Piutes walked down "C" Street she walked alone in their wake—neither shunned nor avoided, but rather a shadow that passed unnoted, unheeded. It was evident that so far as the Piutes were concerned no one followed them. So utterly oblivious were they of any presence pursuing them that she might have been a wraith . . . or some mystical being.

Even the small bucks seemed doubtful about the existence of that strange figure that stole furtively behind their tribe. Sometimes, to prove it, they dropped back, and scoffed or barked as a dog might growl.

But there was never any response. The gaunt face wore the same calm—resigned—inexorable look.[1]

Sometimes the urchins picked up rocks—threw them—hit the creature. There was never any outcry. No sign of pain, no wince, no cringe. They might as well have hit a shadow for all the response they elicited. At such times the other Piutes walked stolidly on without making any attempt to frighten her tormenters away. If she were hit, bruised or cut, no one seemed to care.

One day, when one of the boys could withstand his curiosity no longer, he stopped a buck and pointing at the forlorn figure of the squaw asked: "What's the matter with your 'Mahala'?" The buck looked.

"Him's no squaw," he replied without change of expression. "Him's Charley. Charley heap scared battle down Pyramid Lake. Charley no want fight, got no gun, he say, throw 'um away. Charley all time, run, run; all time cry, cry, heap cry, all same papoose. Yeah—Charley heap scare. Charley squaw now. Piutes call 'um 'Squaw Charley'."

For having shown the white feather in battle Charley was condemned to remain a squaw for the rest of his life!

Although Sam Brown's marathon from the Pyramid Lake battlefield would compare favorably in speed with Paul Revere's ride, and although he had left Joe Baldwin to die on the desert, nevertheless those disgraceful acts had placed no white feather in his cap, nor skirts about his legs, nor had they dimmed his reputation as a "bad man" on Sun Mountain. On the contrary Sam was considered a "smart fellow" to have gotten out of a bad trap with his hair on, to say nothing of his boots. The latter was a tender subject, for like all "bad men" Sam had a horror of dying with his boots on.

Back on the mountain he became a bigger "Chief" than ever and proceeded to uphold the only law the mountain knew— the law of the outlaw, fortified by the six-shooter and bowie! Everybody had developed great respect for Sam. The roughs scrambled about when they saw him coming and made way for him along the brass rail of every bar as if he had been an Oriental prince. The boys paid him no less respect than the toughs. Hadn't he sixteen notches on his gun-butt? Didn't he maintain his own private cemetery? Such was the legend. Far be it from them to add to it. Dust was all right in a winze, on your whiskers, between your teeth— but God forbid! Not six feet of it on your chest! Thus, so far as Sun Mountain was concerned, Sam was the "Big Chief."

One night, soon after his return from the battlefield, Sam had occasion to re-prove it. Perhaps he felt that his conduct there had tarnished his reputation as a "bad man," and that he must do something to refurbish it. His opportunity came in a "C" Street saloon, when a weak, pale-faced barroom lounger lurched against him with a remark that Sam chose to consider offensive. Without a word the killer wound his long gorilla-like arm about his victim's neck and drew the pale face toward his own. Holding him as a snake might constrict a bird, Sam sank his sheath-knife twice into the quivering body. The last time he twisted it "Maltese fashion" completely carving his heart out. Then, to show how terrible he was, Sam flung his bleeding victim to the floor, wiped his bloody knife on the barroom towel and, rolling up in his blanket, went to sleep by the corpse. When, a few minutes later, by-standers lifted the pale-faced one from the red pool beneath the bar, Sam Brown was seen sleeping as calmly as a child.[2] After that performance, where was the "Chief" who dared say that Sam Brown was not the uncrowned czar of Sun Mountain? Four more murders, among misfits, followed quickly and consolidated Sam's position in his self-imposed rôle.

From them on, there was an orgie of crime. The nights were punctured with the whine of bullets. Stampedes from gambling-houses were frequent. As innocent parties were as likely to be killed as those engaged in the impromptu duels, those not actively concerned withdrew from the firing-line much as a flock of sheep come through a gap in a fence with a dog at their heels.

The street gained, they would peek back. If the firing had ceased, back they would go, exacting no apologies from the gentlemen who had interrupted them.

"How long, O Lord?" said many who were waiting for some reassuring word from Washington. "In the midst of life we are in uncertainty."[3] The boys were notably cold toward the swaggering bullies who were giving Sun Mountain a tradition of murder. They would have liked to get rid of them—but as long as the toughs confined their murders to one another they did nothing but beseech Washington for official help.

The boys wanted government of the kind they had in "the States." Some were so disgusted that they advocated seceding from Utah and setting up a government in defiance of those about Salt Lake. Others hearkened more closely than ever to what Terry had to say about secession. But government they must have. It began to make no difference whether it was the proposed Confederacy or "the States" who offered it.

The Piute War had demonstrated to the boys the utter inefficiency of the civil authority, vested in a justice of the peace and a constable at Virginia City and a probate judge at Gold Hill. It was a travesty. Who had come to their assistance during the War? Not Utah, but California. They wanted to be joined to that State. They were all Californians. If California seceded—they would too. They weren't going to be isolated on a mountain in the midst of a sea of sand.

President Buchanan had appointed Judge Cradlebaugh to preside over the first judicial court. But he would not sit until September. It was evident that there was no immediate help from the law. In the meantime Sun Mountain was becoming a sanctuary for all the bankrupts, state-prison convicts, roaming thieves, loafers, gamblers, and murderers driven out of California. That State had contributed her best along with her worst, but no means of governing either.[4]

In their desperation the boys posted a notice that they were going to hold a meeting on a certain night for the purpose of appointing delegates to form a provisional government for Sun Mountain.

The boys utterly refused to be governed any longer by Utah. Salt Lake was too far away—too callous of their welfare. Since '57, in spite of all their pleas, Brigham had left them at the mercy of six-shooters and bowies. Now, like all other self-respecting Anglo-Saxons, they intended to have some government.

They sent their appeal to Washington—either the County of Washoe to be joined to California or the state of Carson to be added to the Union. Which?

On the way their appeal fell into the hands of the Mormons and called down upon their heads a bitter denunciation from the hierarch of the Mormon Church. "Since the first organization of the Territory," wrote that churchman, "Washoe has been a most unremunerative burden upon Utah. What is she now? A worthless unaccountable scab." Then he shot out the last vitriolic drops of his invective. "A scab which cannot find a place in any honest vocabulary. So let her remain dried up—buried—forgotten."[6]

Thus vitriol was applied where oil was needed. They wanted decency, an end of czardom, government like their fathers had had —they would have it even if they had to listen to Terry. Six-shooters and bowies were driving them into the camp of the rebels.

Bill Stewart was consulted. He advised patience. Nevertheless he helped them to draw up a petition for a separate territorial government, and sent it to Washington, D. C. *The Territorial Enterprise* was agitating a change of government. The law of the Mormon, said Joe Goodman, was unsuited to Sun Mountain. For one thing, where were the women? They couldn't boast of more than two or three—Julia Bulette—Eilley Orrum. Polygamy would have to be reversed to polyandry to suit such a state of affairs. Moreover Brigham had decreed "Thou shalt not drink." Think of living in Washoe and not drinking! It was only drink that made them forget that God-forsaken country. "Give us whiskey or give us death," was his answer to that decree.

Lawlessness became so rampant that many of the thin-skinned left—they would not live on Sun Mountain for all the silver in Washoe—no, nor for all the women in Salt Lake thrown in to boot.

But the hard-rock men stayed. What ailed Sun Mountain, said

Bill Stewart, was that it was a he-society. What Washoe needed was a few good women and a child or two. Then the story would be different! But with men sleeping in bunks—debauching on whiskey —lounging on gaming tables—fighting fires—what could you expect? In addition the Lode gave off an unhealthy—argentiferous exhalation. Men breathed it in. It made their blood run hot. It excited their passions. It consumed their brains with fever. In their delirium they went wild. They shot and stabbed, minced and maimed. If only Washoe had women or children or trees! Even a gallows-tree! said Bill, under whose shade the hot-headed could cool the fire in their blood. But always the glare of bright light. No wonder lawlessness ruled and Sam Brown reigned. What Washoe needed was Law.

CHAPTER XXV

SECESSION

1860

Finally the managers of the Ophir, Mexican, and Gould & Curry held a meeting. Riches were pouring out of the earth. Rules and regulations must come out of it as well. Something must be done immediately to safeguard life and property in Washoe. Under existing shot-gun conditions their claims were apt to be "jumped" at any moment. In a body they went to Bill Stewart's office.[1]

In a few months Bill's unflagging energy and colossal self-assertion had lifted him above the "muck" to the head of the Washoe bar. He had become its leader—a tyrannical—despotic one. Seemingly nothing resisted his will—neither nature, gods, nor "bad men." Because he was generally successful in everything he attempted, the boys endowed him with supernatural attributes. They needed a "Chief." They found their wants embodied in Bill Stewart. He had all the qualifications that make gods out of men—boldness—strength of will—good judgment—experience—character—and not a sensitive nor sentimental streak in his body. Already he was legendary. He always won his battles. To the boys he was the reincarnation of Cæsar.

So it was natural enough that they should turn to Bill when they wanted their mountain set aright. They wanted something to live by, and they knew that Bill could supply it.

"We want you," said their spokesman, "to drive Terry from his forts. He's on our land."

That was a big order. Sun Mountain was in a chaotic condition. These boys thought he was a healer. They wanted him to touch the mountain and make it whole. Bill smiled. He had an instinctive knowledge of the character of the men before him. It was this accurate sense that had enabled him to become the force he was. If he failed to bring order out of chaos, he would be immediately discredited. His power lay in successes. Let him fail and his feet would be clay. He was not going to make that blunder.

There wasn't a surveyor on Sun Mountain—never had been. Not

one of those men before him knew where the lines of the Ophir began nor where those of the Gould & Curry left off. All their lines were like the threads of a tangled skein—in a snarl. According to their imperfect rules, established at Gold Hill, each location was entitled to 300 feet with all its dips, spurs, and angles. Yet the number of feet claimed by every one of them was twice as much as really existed. Claims overlapped each other throughout the entire length of the vein and it had not been determined in what direction they extended underground.

And the boys wanted him to put Terry off Sun Mountain!

There was likewise no geologist on Sun Mountain and never had been. Did the foot-wall pitch to the east? Did it incline to the west? Where was the hanging-wall? The boys didn't know. No one knew. But every one of them had it inclining in the direction most advantageous to himself. And yet those boys wanted him, Bill Stewart, to drive Terry off their land. Probably with a six-shooter.

But Bill knew only too well that their dips, spurs, and angles were all in conflict with one another; that the Ophir was spurring the California; that the California was spurring the Central; and that the Best & Belcher was spurring the Gould & Curry.

Under those conditions, Bill was too good a tactician to go to Terry and tell him to surrender his forts because he was on forbidden ground. Terry was no fool. He knew that the claim to his forts was as good as the next man's to his mine. Beside, where was the law on Sun Mountain? Terry could shoot as straight or straighter than he could. Hadn't he killed Broderick at twenty paces? As things stood it was not only a foolish but a dangerous thing to interfere with Terry. The boys must first have surveyors and geologists find out where they stood. Then he would help them litigate.

"Your locations are all in conflict with one another," said Stewart, after looking at Sun Mountain from every angle.

"We're all friends, and have no disputes," replied the boys grandiloquently. "But we want Terry put off the mountain and we want you to drive him off."

"As soon as you commence mining, you will find you are all enemies and will become involved with one another," retorted Stewart. "It is not worth while meddling with Terry until your own disputes are settled."

Then Bill pointed out to them that they must first hire geologists and surveyors and locate their end- and hanging-walls and adjust company-lines before they could even think of Terry.

Thus it was that a corps of engineers was imported from San Francisco; that end-lines were established and that the disputes between the Ophir and Mexican, Gould & Curry and Collar were adjusted.

That accomplished, back the boys came to Stewart. "The time has arrived," they reported, "to put Terry off."

"Not yet," said Stewart, after examining their blue-prints. "You must leave him alone until you have bought the lead that 'Old Virginny' located—the Virginia lead. Buy that and divide it among your holdings so that your claims will extend to the foot-wall and then report to me."

The Virginia lead was bought. But in order to avoid any future cloud upon their titles Bill demanded that, before closing the deal, the original notice of location must be produced.[2]

It couldn't be found. Neither could the boys find Finney—"Ole Virginny" who had discovered it. Finally Bill made a search of the barrooms and located him in one, fully "ginned." Stewart shook him to wake him up. "Where is the original location for the Virginia lead?" he shouted.

Finney was too drunk or too cunning, Stewart couldn't tell which, to explain intelligently what he had done with it or where it was to be found. To bring him to his senses Bill had him decoyed into a tunnel belonging to the Ophir Company. As soon as Finney had entered, the iron gate at the mouth of the tunnel was closed and barred behind him. On the following morning Bill appeared before the bars to do some quizzing. But "Ole Virginny" refused to grasp the situation until he was provided with an "eye-opener." When that was supplied he agreed to guide Bill to the spot where he had concealed his notice.

After scrambling about the rocks, "Ole Virginny" finally found the cache he had discovered that day years ago. He lifted off the piece of rock with which he had sealed it and drew out a strip of yellow paper covered with dust and moths' eggs. It was the most precious piece of paper on the Comstock. Upon it was scrawled in still legible characters, "Ole Virginny's" claim, with all its dips, spurs, and angles, to the main silver-ledge of Sun Mountain—now worth millions of dollars![3]

Bill was satisfied.

"How about getting rid of Terry?" said the boys. "Now he must go at all costs."

"First we must litigate," returned Stewart.

By that time it was September 3, 1860, and Judge Cradlebaugh, whom President Buchanan had personally appointed, was holding court at Genoa.[4] Stewart and Terry both agreed to recognize his authority and to try a test-case, known as the McCall case, before him. What was really at stake was whether Terry's claim would hold or not, whether the Comstock should belong to Northern or Southern men. McCall was represented by Judge Terry, while the Ophir retained Bill Stewart. The crux of the case revolved about a geological problem. What constituted the Comstock Lode? Was it one ledge as Bill Stewart claimed? Or was it many ledges as Terry contended?

The trial was held in a hay-loft over a livery stable—a dingy, badly ventilated, poorly lighted place, with an atmosphere redolent of the odors of the stall. Often the proceedings were interrupted by the rich profanity of the hostlers. The loft was reached by a ladder. Both Terry and Stewart ascended into court supported by over a hundred men armed to the teeth to help their respective sides to behave. When all were assembled the ladder was pulled up by the bailiff and deliberations began. There being no tavern, at night the Judge, with Terry on one side and Stewart on the other, slept in the hayloft, while the humbler attendants bivouacked in the sage. Excitement over the one-ledge or many-ledge theory, over North and South, was at fever-heat. More than one shot was fired at an important witness as he galloped down Gold Cañon to attend court.

The trial lasted a week. Every day the courtroom was crowded to capacity with excited partisans. An unguarded expression, at any moment, would have brought on a collision between the adherents of the North and South, which would have covered the floor with bleeding bodies. The rival sentiments of those hailing from north or south of the Mason and Dixon line were more on trial than the merits of the one-ledge theory. Both Bill Stewart and Judge Terry were fully aware of the disposition of their respective supporters. They exercised a judicious courtesy in discussing the writs of rival claims. They were markedly courteous in their personal allusions to one another as well as in the examination of witnesses, while their show of deference for the rulings of the court was extremely flattering to Judge Cradlebaugh.

Before starting the case Stewart caused a tunnel to be run from the Ophir workings through and into the workings of the so-called Middle Lead and found ore all the way, a distance of about thirty feet. So far as Bill was concerned, that settled the contention. All the witnesses that Stewart introduced swore to the effect that the Ophir and the Middle Lead were one and the same body of ore. Proving the one-ledge theory.

Terry introduced an equally large number of witnesses who swore positively that there was a twenty-foot granite "horse" between the two claims. Proving the many-ledge theory.

Thus the case stood when court adjourned that night. Immediately Stewart located a surveyor and sent him to the Comstock, thirty miles away. With him he sent ten men with forty small sacks, instructing them to take a specimen of ore every six inches from the so-called "vein" which Terry and his witnesses had sworn was solid granite. Stewart provided them with relays of horses, at Carson and again on the Comstock Lode. Before court opened the next morning the party returned with their forty sacks full.

Stewart instructed the surveyor that when the jury was called he would attract the attention of Judge Terry and meanwhile, he, the surveyor, was to open the sacks containing the ore, which were marked to show where they came from, and place them before the jury.[5]

When Judge Terry observed what was going on, he objected. It was not rebuttal. But when he saw the jury examining the ore he realized that it was too late and gave in, saying the trick was so smart that he would let it pass.

The jury retired. Bill was jubilant. It looked as if he had won the case. But even with that positive evidence before them the jury disagreed. Terry had succeeded in "hanging" them. He had taken the precaution of including in the panel some of his staunchest secession friends. Not being able to agree, the jury was discharged. Eight stood for the single-ledge theory, four for many ledges. Eight for the North. Four for secession.

Thus Terry and his followers remained in control of their "forts" much to the disgust of Stewart and the chagrin of the Ophir and the Gould & Curry. It was the first time Bill's genius had failed. His prestige was damaged. The "All's Well!" of Terry's sentinels took on an insolent ring.

Bill did not acknowledge defeat. He planned to appeal the case. Before that could be done a pony galloped down the emigrant road with a dispatch from President James Buchanan. Judge Cradlebaugh had been removed from office and a certain Judge H. P. Flenniken, former Minister to The Hague, had been appointed in his stead. Flenniken had not arrived, would not arrive until late fall. Cradlebaugh refused to retire, claiming that the President of the United States, even an ungrateful one, could not remove a territorial judge! He appealed his status to the Supreme Court of Utah and waited.

Under the conditions, Stewart saw the hopelessness of continuing the suit. In the meantime Judge Terry, jubilant over his success, sat entrenched behind his stone walls. Everything was going the way he wanted it. The best part of the Comstock was already in the hands of himself and his friends. There were many ledges on Sun Mountain. "Shot-gun possession" meant possession.[6]

"As the South goes, so goes the Lode," reiterated Terry again and again. "Whoever holds Washoe wins the war!"

CHAPTER XXVI

"FIGHTING SAM BROWN"

1860–1861

Meanwhile an unheard-of event, in Sam Brown's eyes, occurred. One of his gang, who had killed an innocent man, was arrested and taken before Judge Cradlebaugh at Genoa. Worse still, in Sam's mind, Bill Stewart was engaged to assist the district attorney in prosecuting the case. Bill claimed he would hang the "gangster."

Sam Brown was furious over that threat. He made up his mind to go to Genoa and free friend murderer. Before starting down the Cañon he bragged that not only would he clear the killer but that he would make the court accept it.

So he braided his long side-whiskers, tied them under his chin to protect his windpipe, strapped on his spurs, mounted his mustang, and clattered down Sun Mountain.[1]

When he entered court next day, dragging his spurs across the floor, his sudden appearance and clanking heel-irons caused consternation to judge, jury, and spectators. The killer could afford to laugh. Some of the jury jumped out of the windows. Others hid behind benches. At any moment they expected to see Sam "open up" and "shoot up" the place for the fun of it. The only unimpressed man in the courtroom was Bill Stewart. He felt for his derringers. Caressed them. He had an inkling of the import of Sam's visit. Before Sam could pull a weapon, Bill had him "covered."

"Thow up your arms," growled Bill. Brown, taken unawares, stopped dead in his tracks and found himself gazing down the muzzles of Bill's derringers. Slowly but surely up went his arms above his head.

"Disarm him," thundered Stewart.

"Take the witness-stand."

Brown obeyed.

"Swear him."

Brown was sworn.

"Now, Mr. Brown," said Stewart calmly, "you have bragged that you would come down here and swear this defendant free and make this court accept your testimony. I am here to tell you that if you attempt any of your gun-play or give any false testimony I'll blow your fool brains out."

Stewart kept him covered while he examined him. He made Sam admit that he knew nothing of the case whatever. He even made him admit that the defendant had a bad reputation. In the end he succeeded in making a good government witness out of him. When charged by the counsel for the defense with "intimidating the witness," Stewart insisted that he was merely preventing the witness from intimidating other people. Fondling his derringers and smiling confidently, Stewart asked Sam if he felt that he was in any way being intimidated. Any "bad man" would have to disclaim such a suggestion. Having bullied Washoe ever since his arrival, Sam Brown was loath now to admit that he was being "intimidated."

Finally he extricated himself from his dilemma. He was under indictment in Plumas County, California, he told Stewart, for an assault with a deadly weapon. Needing an attorney, he had dropped in to retain Stewart as his counsel.

Rising from the witness-stand he proffered Stewart $500 as a retainer. Still covering him, Stewart blandly accepted the money and stuffed it in his pocket. Then Brown asked the court to adjourn while he treated. It was late in the afternoon. Court was a little shaky anyhow. They repaired to the nearest bar where Brown, apparently in good humor, "set up" the drinks for everybody in sight.

It was a tragic deflation for a "bad man." Rearming himself, Brown rode out of Genoa brooding on the damage to his career.[2] Bill Stewart had worsted him again. This time it had cost him $500. He was in a bad humor. If he was going to maintain his tradition as "Chief" something had to be done to uphold it. He hated Bill. Bill meant the law. Bill wanted to establish a territory on Sun Mountain. He would have liked to shoot Bill, but he couldn't. Bill had too big a following. It looked like Bill would be "King of the Comstock." Looked like he wanted to be. Sam was seeing "red."

As Sam rode away from Genoa he met a chance acquaintance. "Come along," scowled Sam. "This is my thirtieth birthday and I must have a man for supper."[3]

Terrified, the chance acquaintance was compelled to accompany him. On reaching the wayside inn of Henry Van Sickles, Sam dismounted to adjust his spurs. The supper bell was just ringing.[4]

Van Sickles, hearing the clatter of spurs in his courtyard, ran out on the porch.

"Shall I put up your horse, Mr. Brown?" called the affable inn-keeper.[5]

"Hello, Van," came Sam's cheery reply. "How you feeling?"

"Tip-top," was the rejoinder.

"Guess you're feeling too damned good. I'll take a shot at you just for luck." And Brown proceeded to pump lead at Van Sickles, laughing as he did so.[6]

Unarmed, and knowing the character of Sam Brown, Van Sickles ducked into the dining-room, at that hour filled with guests at the supper-table. Brown followed, pistol in hand, cocked. The men at the table jumped to their feet, covering Van Sickles' retreat.

"Where's the . . . .?" demanded Brown.[7]

Seeing so many men, Brown went out of the house, mounted his horse, compelled the acquaintance to follow him, and clattered rapidly away. That was a hornet's nest! But he must have "a man for supper!"

Van Sickles secured his gun—a double-barrelled fowling-piece—mounted his horse, and went in pursuit with only one idea in mind. Brown had "begun" on him. He must "get" Sam. Might as well settle the affair once and for all. No use living in fear for the rest of your life.[8] He purposed to kill Brown.

Van Sickles' gun was loaded with fine shot. He did not take time to draw it, but added a charge of buckshot to each barrel.

About a mile up the road Van Sickles overhauled Brown. Sam fired. His shot went wild. As soon as Van Sickles was within shooting distance he waved the acquaintance aside, raised his gun, discharged both barrels, and blew Brown off his horse. Apparently uninjured Brown picked himself up, fired from the hip and missed. Running for his horse he remounted, and put urgent spurs to his mount and clattered away.

Van Sickles reloaded, whipped up his horse, galloped after Sam, and fired again. Sam's hat fell to the roadway. His face was burnt from the fire. But Van Sickles was disgusted. He had failed to reach what he was after—Sam's head.[9]

Sam ceased firing, spurred his horse to a run, and rode frantically toward Gold Cañon. If only he could reach Sun Mountain he would be safe.

Van Sickles tore after him. His ammunition was almost exhausted. Sam would escape. A sport-loving friend anticipating his wants rushed up, supplied his need. Van reloaded and charged after Sam.

Three miles farther on. Again, Van Sickles came within gun-shot range and "turned loose." Sam returned the fire. Missed. Darkness came on. Van Sickles lost track of him in the gathering dusk. Van left the road to reach an objective-point ahead. He knew Sam must pass that way. If he failed to "get" Sam now, it would be only a matter of time before Sam or one of his hirelings would "get" him.

Van Sickles pushed ahead. He reached his objective-point . . . drew into the bushes . . . dismounted . . . waited. It was pitch black. He could hear nothing, see nothing.[10] But knowing Sam must come that way he bided his time. A half-hour slipped by. He struck a match . . . looked at his watch. It was almost 11 o'clock. Sam must have escaped.

Suddenly through the darkness came the jingle of spurs. Sam's! Now was the time. Van Sickles waited until Brown rode within range. Then he stepped out into the road and covered him. " . . . ." he hissed through closed teeth.

Mortal terror seized Sam. He was cornered. Unutterable fear seized his lips. But the horror of his predicament forced a spasmodic, agonizing scream of despair between them. He begged for his life.[11]

"I've got you," growled his nemesis. "Now I kills you." Van Sickles jammed the muzzle of his gun against Sam's breast and fired both barrels. Without muttering a sound Sam Brown, like a big bundle of old clothes, toppled from his horse and rolled in the dust.[12]

On the 8th of July an inquest was held. Twelve balls had perforated what had been Sam Brown, "bad man." "Samuel Brown," read the verdict of the public-spirited coroner's jury, "has come to his death from a just dispensation of an all-wise Providence." "It served him right."[13]

Thus died "fighting Sam Brown"—died with his "boots on"; an end which all "Chiefs" dread. But Sam was destined to do Western literature and the cinema a real service—providing the silver screen and the lowly Western with their first "bad man."

He had set a tradition that the Southwest would rarely equal. He supplied Mark Twain and many a writer of Western stories with a ready-made coroner's verdict that has become a classic.[14]

CHAPTER XXVII

LANGFORD PEEL

1861

With Sam Brown's death there was considerable excitement among the "bad men" as to who would succeed him as "Chief" of Washoe. Among other candidates were Langford Peel and "El Dorado Johnny." The choice seemed to point to Peel—a noble-looking youth with mild blue eyes and long golden beard. He had already proved his prowess, as the six notches on his gun-butt could testify.

But Peel hadn't intended to be a "bad man." Frontier justice had made him one. He received the first notch in self-defense.[1] But in acquiring it Peel had incurred responsibilities that no red-blooded man could ignore. Up until then Washoe equity had demanded an eye or a tooth in retribution. In defending those accessories he had added five other notches to his gun-butt. For a college man—and Langford was said to be a Cambridge graduate—he was a dead shot.

So every one in Washoe felt rather badly when "El Dorado Johnny," a fresh-faced newcomer, made up his mind to provoke Peel into a fight.

"El Dorado" had unique ideas as to the general appearance of a "Chief" of Washoe. He felt that he should "look nice." So, before he sent out his challenge he went into the nearest barber shop. "Fix me up fit," he said. "I'm going after a 'bad man.'"[2]

The barber gave him a shave, trimmed his whiskers, and marcelled his hair. And the bootblack polished his boots until he could have seen his own reflection in them.

Then "El Dorado" sauntered into Pat Lynch's saloon, where he knew Peel could generally be found, and casually inquired:

"Any 'Chiefs' about?"

"You probably intend that remark for me," said the sensitive-eared Peel, who was standing at the bar.

"Any one can take it up that likes," replied guileless Johnny.

"Very well; we'll settle it right now," rejoined Peel. "Come out into the street."

Out into "C" Street stepped "El Dorado." But Peel hesitated in the doorway. As Johnny wheeled to aim at him, Peel fired a shot that caught him squarely between the eyes and dropped him dead in his tracks.[3]

"I'm sorry," said Langford Peel, almost in tears, as he rejoined his cronies at the bar. "That poor fellow knew no more about handling a gun than an infant. It was like shooting a baby, but what could I do? He had his gun trained on me; had it gone off, my body, instead of his, might be lying out there. I almost wish it was."

"George," he called, turning to the bartender, "run up to Brown's and tell him to come down here and fix up 'El Dorado.' Tell him to spare no expense, but to give him the best he has in the shop and I will pay for everything."[4]

"El Dorado Johnny" made as pleasant a looking corpse as the roughs ever turned out to bury. They laid him out in Pat Lynch's saloon in a magnificent casket, elegantly upholstered, silver-mounted. They smoothed his hair, recurled his whiskers, cleaned and pressed his clothes. From Friday until Sunday Johnny lay in state. During those days, seven bartenders in white coats with diamond-studded shirts were kept constantly busy handing refreshments over the bar to the thirsty hundreds who dropped in to take a last look at "El Dorado." For Johnny was a brave man! And he had died with his "boots on."

On the following Sunday, "El Dorado" was escorted to the cemetery by the largest funeral procession that had ever been seen in Washoe. On the door of every saloon hung a sable emblem. Over the top of every green-baize gambling-table was stretched a shroud of crape. Even the mirrors were veiled in black. An air of sadness pervaded the whole community. A band, playing mournful dirges, led the procession. In their wake came nickeled axes and brass helmets, all swaying in habiliments of woe. Pete Larkin, afterward hanged for murder, was master of ceremonies at the grave. When Johnny's body had been consigned to the earth, the procession reformed, the band struck up "When Johnny Comes Marching Home Again," and back the boys marched to the city.[5]

Peel was not punished for this murder, nor for any of the other five which "El Dorado's" friends forced him to commit soon after. He was not even arrested. The taking off of each one whom he shot or stabbed added to the feeling of general security. Those who were in favor of law felt that Peel was making a greater contribution than any edicts could accomplish. He was "cleaning house" by getting rid of a class better dead than alive. At any rate, neither the marshal, Blackburn, nor any of the self-appointed police were anxious to meddle with "Chief" Peel. And he had such a quiet, gentlemanly way.

One day Peel behaved so outrageously that a unanimous demand went up for his arrest. This was accomplished with difficulty by a party of self-appointed officers and a posse of outraged citizens. By his captors he was taken before the Mormon justice of the peace, Judge Davenport, who sentenced him to a fine of $100 or twenty days in the city jail.

"I haven't any money with which to pay the fine," said Peel, "but if your Honor will let me go out on my own recognizance I will get it and settle up."

Judge Davenport, who was a mild man with an excessively long beard, of which he was excessively proud, readily consented.

Out Peel went and "ginned up" afresh. In about half an hour, with his blue eyes glittering and his blond beard bristling, he returned to the court, which was still in session. Up he walked to Judge Davenport:

"Judge," he interrupted very politely. "I've come to settle that fine."

"Very good of you, Mr. Peel," replied the Judge, stroking his long beard with complacency at the subdued manner of the desperado. Thereupon, quick as a flash, Peel seized Davenport's long chin whiskers in both hands and pounded his head against the wall until he was almost dead. Half a dozen officers were in the room, but made no remonstrance. That gun-butt demanded respect. When he had "wooled" the Judge to his heart's content, Peel walked calmly out of the courtroom. So far as Judge Davenport was concerned that was the last of the affair. Straightening his long beard, he continued his judicial duties. He considered the fine settled.[6]

CHAPTER XXVIII

STRUGGLE FOR CONTROL
1860–1861

R. P. Flenniken, the new judge of Washoe, elderly and pompous, arrived late in the fall of 1860 and made his entry on Sun Mountain as if presenting himself at some foreign court. He had been United States Ambassador to Holland, so that when he rode up the mountain he donned his silk hat and frock-coat. It was the first silk hat Washoe had seen and consequently caused considerable commotion.[1]

Bill Stewart took the new judge's measure. "Flenniken is better adapted to adorn a foreign court," he said, "than to deal with the complications of Washoe jurisprudence." He could take care of Flenniken. Forthwith Bill announced himself as well satisfied with Judge Cradlebaugh's decisions. The judge believed in the single-ledge theory, and was an intense Unionist. That was enough for Bill. So why change?

Judge Cradlebaugh, encouraged by the dynamic Bill Stewart, held his ground, refused to resign, and continued holding court until such time as his appeal should be decided.

Terry became Judge Flenniken's ardent supporter. Flenniken was open to the many-ledge theory and like his patron, Buchanan, had a sympathetic ear turned toward the South. So why support Cradlebaugh? After Flenniken's arrival, Terry notified Stewart that he would not try any more cases before Judge Cradlebaugh. That judge's charges to the jury accorded too closely with Stewart's views of law and evidence. Flenniken was the legally constituted judge of the district. He had been appointed by President Buchanan. He, Terry, intended to recognize Flenniken's authority and his authority alone. Stewart could think what he liked; do what he pleased.[2]

Thus matters stood when some of Terry's secession gang, the Rich Company, "jumped" the Saint Louis properties, Stewart's clients, at Devil's Gate,[3] discovered valuable ore, and began to strip their ledge. As soon as Bill learned that Terry's clients were in possession of the Devil's Gate diggings he brought suit, obtained an injunction in Cradlebaugh's court and ordered it served upon the Rich Company.[4]

163

When John Blackburn, constable of Judge Cradlebaugh's court, climbed the rocky path to the top of Devil's Gate and served the injunction, the Rich Company replied that they recognized orders only from the court of Judge Flenniken, the regularly constituted judge of Washoe.[5] Judge Cradlebaugh was an interloper.

Blackburn withdrew for further instructions.

When Terry heard what had occurred he knew that that would not be the end of the matter—not if Bill Stewart had anything to do with it. He had his clients build a stone fort on top of Devil's Gate, after his own model, and garrison it. Then ·he had turned over to them the eighty-odd stand of rifles that had come over the Sierra at the time of the Piute War. With those guns he instructed his men to resist Stewart's injunction. Terry intended to show Bill Stewart that he couldn't run everything in Washoe to suit himself.[6]

The situation was embarrassing to Bill Stewart. All the arms on Sun Mountain, suitable for battle, were in the hands of the Terry secessionists. It was absolutely certain that if a warrant were placed in the hands of John Blackburn, both warrant and officer would be resisted by the secessionists in the fort. Bill knew Blackburn for a desperate man. If he had to serve the warrant he would serve it or die in the attempt. The inevitable consequences, with feelings running so high, would be the spilling of blood—and a civil war right there at Devil's Gate.

Therefore Stewart proposed to visit Judge Flenniken and arrange a compromise if possible. That evening, with his junior counsel, he called upon the judge.[7]

Bill, in his rugged manner, explained to Flenniken that he was anxious to avoid civil war at Devil's Gate. The controversy between the two judges was not only disgraceful but injurious to the mining interests of Washoe and should be terminated. Judge Cradlebaugh's injunction had been ignored by the men at Terry's Fort. If agreeable to Flenniken he would commence suit in his court. If his showing was sufficient to satisfy the judge that an injunction ought to be issued, he would serve his injunction and make a joint effort with Flenniken's marshal and the marshal of Judge Cradlebaugh to enforce the order of the two courts.

To all of this Flenniken readily consented. It was the right thing to do.

Bill returned to his office. Drew up the papers. Retired. Went to sleep. Bright and early the next morning he called on Flenniken to issue the injunction.

During the night Flenniken had changed his mind. He refused to issue an injunction. He denied ever having had a conversation with Stewart on the subject. He went so far as to say that he had never seen Stewart at all, at any time.

So the evening of February 15, 1861, found Stewart in a quandary what to do next. While he was deliberating, the Pony Express galloped in from Salt Lake City. The Supreme Court of Utah had handed down a decision in favor of the right of Judge Cradlebaugh to hold court, notwithstanding the action of President Buchanan.

Bill Stewart was elated. Terry was thunderstruck. He had not counted on such a decision.[8]

As soon as Judge Flenniken heard the report, he went out on the street and publicly announced to many of the boys that he was no longer judge. Cradlebaugh was their lawful judge. It was the duty of all good citizens to obey his orders.

Stewart joined him. Would Flenniken sustain Judge Cradlebaugh?

Flenniken assured Stewart he would—absolutely.

Stewart immediately procured an order for arrest, for contempt, of the occupants of Terry's Fort, and placed it in the hands of Marshal Blackburn with instructions to collect a posse, set out at dawn, and take possession of the fort at Devil's Gate. Then, worn out with his exertions, Stewart went home.

Before sun-up, there came a pounding on Stewart's door.

"Judge Flenniken's changed his mind during the night," said his junior counsel. "He is out on the street publicly contradicting the report of his resignation."[9]

Stewart's disgust and alarm at this announcement were unspeakable. Bill knew that by that time the fort would be apprised of Flenniken's position and would refuse to surrender. He also knew that Blackburn, resolute and reckless, would execute the order of arrest with his armed posse. A desperate fight would follow. He would be held responsible. If Flenniken persisted in his course, he might even be called to a bitter reckoning for his assumption of authority. The more he thought about it the madder he became. He was in a pretty pickle now. All on account of that four-flushing Flenniken. With such thoughts racing through his mind he jumped into his clothes, belted on his derringers, and went in search of Flenniken. He met him in front of a nearby saloon.

"Good morning," said Flenniken blandly, with a dignified wave of the hand.

"Good morning," replied Stewart curtly.

"What's the news?"

"Bad news," retorted Stewart. "They are slandering you. They say that you are claiming to be judge and defying the authority of Judge Cradlebaugh."

Flenniken cringed.

"I anticipated something might go wrong," went on Stewart. "I took the precaution to be deputized. I, now, summon you, Flenniken, to carry a musket to assist me in arresting the jumpers on the Saint Louis claim. Further, you've got to give the lie to the slander that you are usurping the functions of Judge Cradlebaugh."

Flenniken stepped back astounded.

Stewart grabbed him by the collar. Jerked him off his feet and into the gutter; then to his knees. Holding him at arm's length with one hand, he drew his derringer with the other. "You'll carry a musket in front of me," he commanded in his best "bad man" manner, "or I'll know the reason why."

Flenniken raised his hands imploringly. An ambassador of the United States!

"Is there no way to avert it?"

"Yes, if you do as I say."

He consented, silently, recognizing the fact that he was a prisoner-of-war in a wild camp.

Holding to Flenniken's collar, Stewart jerked him to his feet, down the street and into Aaron Fleishhacker's store, where there was a telegraph-station, surrounded by a railing. Pete Lovell, the telegraph operator, was at his instrument and a clerk named F. A. Tritle was waiting on customers. Holding fast to Flenniken, Stewart commanded Tritle to write as he dictated. Bill then dictated four or five dispatches in Flenniken's name. One was addressed to President Buchanan; one to Blackburn; another to Grice, the marshal appointed by Flenniken; one to the fort and several to prominent men at Silver City.

The telegrams were all alike, announcing Flenniken's resignation and declaring in emphatic terms that he was not judge. Cradlebaugh was. Cradlebaugh's orders must be obeyed.

"Now sign these!" demanded Stewart, loosening his hold long enough for the half-dazed judge to obey.[10] When he had complied, Stewart tossed the parcel of dispatches to the operator. "Send those telegrams," he ordered. "Then keep away from that instrument for two hours."

"Come outside the railing," said Stewart to the operator as soon as the telegrams had been sent. "Stand where you can hear the messages, but don't you touch those wires."

Lovell did as he was ordered. Together the three men stood silently listening, outside the rails. The telegraph instrument kept on ticking. Stewart held to his prisoner until Lovell reported that Judge Flenniken's resignation had been received,[11] and the garrison had surrendered to Marshal Blackburn and were accompanying him to court.

Then Bill released his hold; and the ex-ambassador followed meekly in his wake.[12]

When the crestfallen garrison were brought before Judge Cradlebaugh, Stewart arose. "His Honor knows," said Stewart, addressing the judge, "that there has been a conflict of authority. Doubtless the prisoners supposed themselves to have some sort of legal justification for the mistaken position which they occupy. But they have been misled by a usurper named Flenniken; who falsely pretended to be a judge. They are good citizens, but they have defied the authority of the court, under a mistake. I hope they will be allowed to depart without punishment."

Acting on Stewart's motion, Judge Cradlebaugh discharged the astonished prisoners.[13] Unfortunately Stewart made the mistake of allowing them to depart with those eighty muskets which had already caused enough worry.

During this time Judge Terry was absent in San Francisco; otherwise things might have been quite different. However, Joe Vaughn, who was Terry's partner, came to Stewart on hearing what had happened.

"I want to see the original dispatches signed by Flenniken," said Vaughn.

Stewart took him to the telegraph office. The telegrams were produced. Vaughn read them over carefully and satisfied himself that they were genuine. Flenniken naturally was scarcely willing to make known the full details of his impromptu resignation. It was currently believed that Bill Stewart's persuasion had been too cogent, but the boys had no use for a judge who could not maintain his position on Sun Mountain.

The day following, Judge Terry returned. Stewart was a little uneasy. Who wouldn't be? Everybody supposed that Terry would be indignant and that something sensational would occur. Perhaps a shooting or a duel. Soon after arrival, Judge Terry stomped into Stewart's office. Bill faced him as he came through the door. Bill never forgot what Terry had to say.

"We were beaten deservedly by our own negligence," he said. "For we never should have trusted our general in the camp of the enemy. You had both commanders. It is no wonder that our forces were routed; but it is too late now to grumble. The victory and the spoils are yours."[14]

That very night Terry turned his forts over to his secession friends, mounted his horse and rode down Gold Cañon to join the rebel armies that he knew would soon be forming south of the Rio Grande.[15]

CHAPTER XXIX

REBELS CAPTURE SUN MOUNTAIN
1861

Twelve days after President Lincoln had delivered his momentous Inaugural from the central portico of the Capitol, "Pony Bob," with a copy of it tucked in his mud-stained mochila, pounded through the gates of Fort Churchill. Such had been his speed that he had covered the 120 miles from Smith's Creek in eight hours and ten minutes, an average of almost fifteen miles per hour—record time for flesh and blood, facing cutting winds, blinding snows, and plains made suddenly white and strange. More than one steed had run itself to death rushing the President's message toward Sun Mountain. That speech, outlining as it did President Lincoln's policies on the approaching conflict, was eagerly awaited by every man in Washoe and no effort had been spared in getting it into their hands.[1]

High water on the Platte had rendered parts of the message unintelligible.[2] Where the wording was difficult to understand the operator at Fort Churchill made it plain. Within an hour *The Territorial Enterprise* had an extra out and the boys were eagerly reading what their President had to say.[3]

Tom Peasley read those prophetic words in regard to the awakening of the better angels of our nature. They inspired him, but little he realized how prophetic they would prove. One by one the firemen learned that Ellsworth, their friend, was with President Lincoln! That was enough for them! They turned their attention to the summit of Sun Mountain. Up there was the place for Old Glory! They found a tall pole intended for one of the drifts, lashed it to a camel's back, transported it to the summit, and planted it on the highest point. Up the halyards they ran a banner over thirty feet long. As it went aloft they burst into "John Brown's Body," and an enthusiast pledged Washoe to raise bullion enough to squelch the rebellion.[4]

Pony Expressmen far out on the desert, fighting blizzard and snow-drift with icy fingers, saw the Stars and Stripes floating over

Sun Mountain. It gave them heart to finish their perilous task. All must be well, they reasoned, on the great mountain. Little they knew of the rebel sympathizers who were even then undermining its loyalty and planning at the opportune moment to take Washoe in the name of the Confederacy.

One day a patriotic Yankee ran the Union flag up the pole over the Tahoe House, where he lived. The hotel was kept by one Laura D. Fair, and patronized almost exclusively by Southern chivalry. As soon as Mrs. Fair learned that a Federal flag was floating over her premises, she picked up a revolver, ran to the roof and ordered the Yankee to pull it down. When he refused, she pulled the trigger and the Yankee fell severely wounded. Mrs. Fair was arrested and tried for attempted murder. *The Territorial Enterprise* and the fire boys were against her. But Laura D. Fair, the favorite of A. P. Crittenden, a leader of the Washoe bar[5] and a member of the Crittenden family of Kentucky, had powerful backing. When Mrs. Fair's case came up, Crittenden impanelled a jury to his liking and made an eloquent plea in her defense. The jury, confused by her beauty and swayed by oratory, acquitted her.[6] No matter what you did on Sun Mountain, if you could prove you were a secessionist you were safe from whatever law existed. Even when the notorious gangman, Mayfield, murdered John Blackburn, the territorial marshal, the murderer was permitted to escape because he was a Southerner.[7]

On April 20, 1861, the "Pony" brought astounding news to Washoe. Eight days and fourteen hours before a shell had hurtled from the mortars of Fort Johnson—screamed over the harbor of Charleston—burst above Fort Sumter—the opening shot of the Civil War! The sound of that bursting shell, transmitted by flesh and blood, produced consternation in Gold Cañon.[8] The Flag had been fired upon! The fire boys were tremulous with emotion. They had never dreamed that would happen. Crowds of them swarmed in front of the bulletin-boards of *The Territorial Enterprise*. Deep down in their hearts patriotism smouldered like a glowing coal. The report of that bursting shell fanned it into flame.

That bursting shell and the fort's evacuation gave the forces of chivalry a defiant attitude. They strutted up and down "C" Street as if they ruled the mountain. Their loud exultation was heard in every saloon, at every gambling-table. "If the South doesn't stand up for her rights," said Johnny Rebel, "she doesn't deserve any." In comparison the fire enthusiasts appeared to be a scattered lot of subdued underlings—stunned by startling news. A stranger in

Washoe would have been pardoned for thinking himself in the heart of Dixie instead of thousands of miles away on the outcroppings of a silver lode. But not Tom Peasley. He was listening— biding his time.

With the fall of Sumter the rebels, or "the Knights of the Golden Circle," as they now called themselves, made up their minds that the time had come to seize Fort Churchill and take Washoe in the name of the Confederacy. A day in June was set for the capture. Arms and ammunition were distributed and the Knights drilled daily in the subterranean galleries of the Gould & Curry. News of the plot reached Tom Peasley. The "Committee" dispatched a warning to Fort Churchill. No attention was paid to it.

As the appointed day of attack drew nearer, a Southerner, loyal to his distressed country, notified the "Committee" of the approaching danger. "I deem it my duty to warn my countrymen," he wrote, "that a company of 107 men have been formed here to help Jefferson Davis and the Confederacy, to take this Territory and declare it as seceded from the United States Government. Those men are enrolled by Doctor McMeans. Terry is to join them soon, and John Brown, the man-killer, is on his way here. Prompt action is needed. If not, we are all lost. It is the intention of the party to capture the fort, and take all the arms from it. They boast of having eighty-three stand of arms. Be cautious. I am ready for action—to fight for the Union, for the Constitution, and shoot any traitor I may meet: So help me God!"[10]

Again Fort Churchill was warned.

"The secessionists have completed an organization of over one hundred," wrote the "Committee," "to seize the fort and get possession of the Territory. We are destitute of arms. Can you furnish us from the fort?"[11]

Brigadier-General E. V. Sumner, commander of the Department of the Pacific at San Francisco, was warned the same day:

"The secessionists have organized in this place under Doctor McMeans. He has 125 men—they intend to seize Fort Churchill and take possession of the Territory. Can you furnish the Committee with three or four hundred stand of arms? If you shall conclude to favor the Committee, have them boxed so as to resemble merchandise, long handle shovels, for instance—and direct them to Taylor & Company, Merchants, Virginia City, Nevada Territory."[12]

Immediately Sumner withdrew artillery and infantry from Oregon and dispatched a part to Fort Churchill. By "Pony" he advised the War Department, "There is no law or government in Washoe—the Territory is a place of refuge for disorganizers and other unruly spirits. I would respectfully and earnestly represent the great importance of organizing the civil government in Nevada Territory immediately—if the governor and other officials had been there this difficulty would not have arisen."[13]

On June 5, when the boys awoke, they found the Stars and Bars of the Confederacy proudly floating over rebel quarters in Johnny Newman's saloon.[14] They saw Johnny himself with a rifle over his shoulder, patrolling the sidewalk. Across the street stood Doctor Mc-Means with 200 "Knights of the Golden Circle," armed to the teeth. The doctor declared he was acting under authority of the Montgomery government.[15] The Lode belonged to the Confederate States of America.

"We'll put down any demonstration," he affirmed defiantly, "that the Union may attempt to get up."[16]

The boys' hearts ached on beholding the vile secession flag floating over their mountain. But without arms they felt powerless.[17]

There was not lacking loyalty to resent this affront, but, somehow, it became sicklied o'er with the pale cast of prudence when it ran up against Johnny Newman leisurely patrolling the sidewalk with a rifle on his shoulder and 200 armed abettors standing sullenly by.[18]

Suddenly one of the fire boys, R. M. Waterhouse, jumped upon the roof and planted a Union flag at the other end of the building, then drawing his pistol and standing beneath it, he defied the rebels. "I'll kill any one who tries to take it down,"[19] he shouted. Feeling ran high. Civil War had hit Sun Mountain.

John A. Collins, a Committee man, mounted his horse and rode for Fort Churchill.[20]

Presently the boys caught the strains of martial music coming up Six Mile. Shortly afterward they saw Lieutenant Baker with a detachment of dragoons charging up the cañon. Before the Regulars could reach his store Johnny Newman pulled down the Stars and Bars and ran up the Stars and Stripes.[21]

From that day on Tom Peasley and the Committee men went fully armed.

CHAPTER XXX

BULL RUN
August 1861

From the beginning of the war, two "Ponies" a week brought momentuous dispatches to *The Territorial Enterprise*. With the advent of each one, Joe Goodman got out a "Pony Extra." On reading them the fire boys grew more and more agitated. Thus they learned that their friend Ellsworth had been made a colonel.[1] Ten companies of their old New York comrades—now called "Fire Zouaves"—were marching under his command. They had been ordered to Washington, and then across the Potomac to Alexandria, Virginia.

Tom Peasley devoured those dispatches. He knew every man mentioned. He read them first to himself then to any one who would listen. Those messages brought the conflict close. And his heart marched, in unison with those of his old comrades, to the scene of conflict.[2]

In June a "Pony" came with bad news. Ellsworth had fallen at Alexandria—shot in the act of tearing down a secession flag. Into his heart a rebel had discharged a golden circlet inscribed with the legend: "Non nobis sed pro patria." Ellsworth's death produced a startling image. The fire boys saw him lying dead with a golden circlet embedded in his heart. That image inspired them with fresh ideal of country. They were ready to sacrifice themselves for it. That image filled them for the first time with hate. In every firehouse Ellsworth's picture was draped in mourning—but the boys saw red not black when they looked at it.

Never once that spring or summer did a "Pony" bring any tidings of successes to the loyal forces on Sun Mountain. Every dispatch chronicled disaster and defeat.

Just in proportion as the "Pony" dispirited Washoe's loyal fire boys, it elated the sympathizers with secession. All was going their way. They rejoiced like sons of Philistines. The Lode would yet be a part of the South, they crowed! As each "Pony Extra" appeared recording one rebel success after another one might easily have imagined himself behind rebel lines. Their exultation grew more and more galling to Tom Peasley and the fire boys—who frequented the resorts where the triumphant spirit was most pronounced.

On June 20 came news of the disastrous day at Big Bethel. Another hideous blunder! Yankee had fired upon Yankee! Major Theodore Winthrop, their old California friend, had been shot at the head of his company. One minute erect—glowing—magnificent —waving his sword—in the wild swirl of battle—the next falling forward—dead.[3]

This unintermitting tide of adversity palled upon the spirits of the fire boys and all those who loved the Union. It was like seeing one of whom they had been justly proud dragged through the dust. They were resentful of such abuse. They wanted to fly to their country's assistance. To knock down her assailants. Adversity was bringing them closer to the country they had repudiated. They loved her better for her blunders and panics than they could have for victories. It made her more human.

But the final straw had not yet been laid upon the back of their forbearance.

August came—broiling hot on Sun Mountain—dust drove in clouds through the streets—hung like mist over Sugarloaf—whirled in funnels through the desert—fell like ashes on mine, mill, and cabin. One morning a foam-flecked "Pony" dashed into Fort Churchill with the most disheartening news Washoe had yet received—the panic at Bull Run.

At noon *The Territorial Enterprise* was getting out an extra containing particulars of the disastrous defeat when Tom Peasley stepped softly into the composing-room and asked to see the proofs. He read the dispatches all through. Then he read them again. The Union army had been routed. They had been driven pell-mell back to Washington. The New York Fire Zouaves had been cut to pieces! Without saying a word he stood there, while tears, like two great water-courses, streamed down his cheeks. Then he pulled himself together, and slid his pistol a little more to the front, where it would be handier.

"No damned secesh," he growled as he left the office, "had better crow within my hearing today."

He went straight to the Fire Department, rounded up Jack Perry, John A. Collins, George Birdsall, Pete Larkin, Riff Williams, Ned Ingram, Cap Mathewson, Louis Wardell, Bruce Garvey, and a host of others. To all of them he told the story of Bull Run. All of their old comrades were cut to pieces. Together they recalled that host—name by name. All of them! He infected his comrades with his own feeling. Loyalty blazed within their breasts. Just what he said to them, no one ever knew. But when the firemen sallied out on "C" Street—they were in a fighting mood.

An hour later *The Territorial Enterprise's* extra was on the street. "Disaster at Bull Run!" yelled the newsies. " 'Xtra! 'Xtra!"

Unsuspicious, the Southerners commenced crowing. The next moment you would have thought the battle of Bull Run itself had struck the mountain. Not an exultant "secesh" mouth was opened but it was instantly closed by a massive fist; not a head indicated a secession tendency but it was unmercifully hit; not a disputant appealed to the arbitrament of pistol or knife but he was responded to so quickly and effectively that that style of argument was speedily abandoned. As President Lincoln had prophesied, the better angels of their nature had been aroused. The chorus for the Union had been swelled on Sun Mountain—by disaster—to a shout.

Perhaps the North lost the battle at Manassas Junction but the Virginia firemen won their battle in Washoe. The rout was complete and final. Union spirit had asserted itself. Loyalty might wane but never again would it fail. It took adversity to do it, but it became so loud and insistent, that most of the boys rallied to its standard.[4]

Another "Pony." Another. President Lincoln called for volunteers. A recruiting-office was opened on Sun Mountain. Two drummer-boys, with J. H. Mathewson, one of the firemen, carrying a flag, marched down "C" Street. They had not marched a hundred yards when Johnny Rebel sprang from a crowd of secessionists along the sidewalk and jumped right into one of the drums—destroying it. He was proceeding to demolish the other when Mathewson knocked him down. Tom Peasley came running up with a new drum. Acting as drummer-boy, Peasley led the march in triumph. It grew to a grand procession—a mile in length. It serpentined down "B" Street to the City Hall, where an enthusiastic Union meeting was held. Tom Peasley delivered a rousing patriotic address. Recruiting was resumed. While no violent measures were taken by the secessionists, there were many expressions of disapprobation, but the firemen overcame them with firmness and courage. In an hour there were many volunteers.

Major Daniel E. Hungerford threw himself with all the ardor of his patriotic soul into drilling these boys for the front.

A night came when they marched down Sun Mountain on their way to fight for their country.[5]

CHAPTER XXXI

THE GOVERNOR

July 15, 1861

General Van Bokelen, the marshal of the day, looked at his watch. It was one o'clock. He waved his baton; wheeled his horse toward the Divide. The Metropolitan Band struck up "The Conquering Hero." Troops fell into step and the procession moved up "C" Street.

Behind the boys came Fire Companies—Engine Company No. 1, Hook and Ladder No. 1, The Knickerbocker, Washoe, Eagle, and Young America—walking in open formation preceded by Tom Peasley, stepping magnificently along in his brass helmet and red coat.

Two carriages with driver and coachman brought up the rear. In the first, with the trustees of the city, in silk hats and broadcloth, sat Bill Stewart. The procession proceeded to the Divide, halted and looked down Gold Cañon. Up Gold Cañon was coming a similar procession, a band, regulars from Fort Churchill, and an open carriage in which sat several figures likewise outfitted in silk hats and black cloth. How incongruous such outfittings looked on Sun Mountain! When the upcoming procession reached the steep grade leading to the Divide, the Metropolitan band burst into "Hail to the Chief." Guards lined up on either side of "C" Street and presented arms. The five trustees arose in their carriages with uncovered heads. Onlookers cheered. Those on balconies waved their hats. Down a lane bristling with bayonets, proceeded the carriage that had come up the Cañon. The man in it, hat in hand, bowed right and left. Cheers grew vociferous, the blaring band deafening, cannon boomed. "Three cheers for the Governor of Nevada," yelled one of the boys. Thousands took it up. The air was rent with shouts. James W. Nye, first governor of the Territory, arose in his carriage to acknowledge the acclaim of Sun Mountain.

Down "C" Street, through an immense arch which Julia Bulette had worked night and day to cover with evergreens and artificial flowers, marched the procession. On every hand was enthusiasm.

Nye represented the coming of law to Washoe. Who wouldn't be enthusiastic? Not Langford Peel, the roughs, or the rebels. Liberty and license were doomed.

At Union Square the procession halted. The guards drew up in hollow formation. The orators of the day addressed the Governor in ornate terms. Nye responded amidst such continuous cheering that no one heard a word he said.

The governor was escorted to the International Hotel, where a banquet was in readiness. More speeches were made. More toasts were given. Much champagne was drunken. Virginia admired herself immensely. For a two-year-old without tradition or background she was acquitting herself with honors! Terrapin, champagne, oysters, and smilax, all sent from "below" for the occasion, exactly expressed her feeling. She had only one worry. If only the rowdies wouldn't cut up! That would be all she would ask. But the roughs were strained to the breaking point. The coming of law was almost more than tough fiber could bear. On the least excuse, as the boys knew, off would go guns and "navies," leaving the streets strewn with corpses. But the boys were hopeful that nothing untoward would disgrace Washoe on the governor's first visit.

By 1861, the chaotic state of Sun Mountain was well known in Washington, D. C. Hadn't the boys repudiated Utah? Hadn't they tried to install a governor of their own choosing?[1] Hadn't Jeff Davis appointed Terry to govern Washoe? Wasn't there danger of secession?[2] Hadn't General Sumner warned the War Office? Without Colonel Baker what would have happened? Something had to be done.

To allay this danger and bring order out of chaos, Congress had literally created the mountain—for there was nothing else in Washoe—into a Territory—the Territory of Nevada—and had appropriated $20,000 to pay the bills. And President Lincoln, out of the gratitude of his heart, had appointed his friend James W. Nye, governor, to rule this alpine principality.

By the time he reached the White House, President Lincoln felt very grateful to Nye. In the late campaign Nye had done great things for him. Due in great part to those efforts, Lincoln had carried New York with a majority of 50,000 votes. As these were the days of political preferment, President Lincoln expressed his gratitude by proffering the ex-police-commissioner the first gubernatorial honors of Nevada. And Nye had jumped at the chance. Not that he cared so much about ruling over a wilderness of sage, in-

JAMES W. NYE OF NEW YORK, APPOINTED GOVERNOR OF WASHOE BY
PRESIDENT ABRAHAM LINCOLN.

Nye was the original Bill Nye of Bret Harte's "Heathen Chinee."

THE BONANZA KINGS.

James Graham Fair, father of Mrs. Graham Fair Vanderbilt and Mrs. Herman Oelrichs. At right, John W. Mackay.

RESIDENCE OF JAMES GRAHAM FAIR, VIRGINIA CITY.

Mr. Fair is seated on the porch with his children.

habited by the silver-mad, but he had a far-seeing eye. Even in New
York, Nye could see that there was a door on Sun Mountain—a door
which properly manipulated would allow him to enter upon his
ambitions. For years he had been looking for such an opening. So
he accepted the governorship of Washoe—now called Nevada, but
only with one idea in mind.

Nature had been generous with Nye and had bestowed on him a
face remarkable for manly beauty, a fine figure, and unshakable
poise. These qualities were augmented by a musical voice, a reten-
tive memory, and unusual imitative powers. He was a fine story-
teller; for every occasion he had an appropriate yarn. As an orator
there were none better, as a wit he had few equals,[3] as a debater, he
was as quick as a duelist with a rapier.

His ease of manner, his magnetic voice, his knowledge of men,
drew all classes to him in Washoe.

"He's a jolly old fellow," one said.

"Reminds me of Jackson," said another.

"The man for the country," declared a third.[4]

When the governor in his speech at the banquet said that Nevada
was a solid country because it had a true metallic ring, he had won
the hearts of his hearers. They liked exaggerations, these boys—
and Governor Nye dealt only in superlatives.

Not all of Governor Nye's official family were with him that day
when he rode up the mountain. Orrion Clemens, his secretary of
state, and Sam Clemens, the prospective secretary of the secretary,
were still en route with their tobacco, pipes, and dictionaries; but the
judges were there—Chief-Justice George Turner, Horatio M. Jones,
and Gordon N. Mott, associate justices of the Supreme Court. The
governor was an excellent choice. But all four would serve their
purposes.

If there ever was a time when the President of the United States
should have selected judicial officers with extremest care, it was when
Washoe, begotten by labor and enterprise out of weird deserts and
barren hills, was suddenly thrust into the lap of dazzling affluence.
If there ever was a time when a President was distracted by noise
and tumult, it was during that period. How could President Lincoln,
in the spring of '61, have foretold the great destiny awaiting Sun
Mountain? If he had, he would have sent his most powerful jurists,
his strongest magistrates instead of his weakest lazzaroni. What
could be expected of briefless barristers, broken-down politicians, in
a clime whose pitiless white light stripped every man of mask and

pretense? What could be expected of such men placed in positions supposed to be trifling but suddenly discovered to be of the gravest importance and of the weightiest responsibility? But sometimes weakness manifests strength. And it was through their frailties that the judges would play the powerful role that fate had reserved for Sun Mountain.

Unaware of the fierceness of the Roentgen-ray-like lights that were beating upon them, Governor Nye and his official family did full justice to the champagne and terrapin placed before them.

All went well until 5 P.M.[5] Then one of the boys, named Butler, got into a colloquy with the deputy-sheriff, John Williams, and made himself conspicuous with a pistol. If there was going to be any shooting, said the sheriff, he wanted to be in on it. Governor or no governor, the sheriff had a secret ambition to be "Chief" of Washoe.[6] So when Butler resisted arrest and drew his derringer, Williams whipped out his gun and opened fire. And right there before the Governor of the Territory an impromptu Washoe duel took place.

"Go it, Jack," yelled a trustee, forgetful of silk hat and broadcloth, as Williams opened every chamber. He was a good marksman. In less than a minute Butler received three balls, one in his knee, another in his shoulder and a third scraped his face.[7] Three were too many; Butler threw up his arms. The boys were disgusted at the fiasco. Just because he was seriously wounded was no reason for Butler to quit. There was as yet no stigma attached to murder in Washoe and the code demanded that he should shoot it out like John Blackburn, Joe Goodman, and Tom Peasley, and other real men did. They would have shot it out to the bitter end. Boots or no boots!

When Winnemucca heard that the Great White Father had arrived, he sent word to him that Winnemucca, chief of the Piutes, wished to smoke a pipe with him. A day was set for the Piute chieftain's reception at the executive mansion. At the last moment the scene was shifted. All because of a widow.

When this woman learned that Winnemucca was coming to confer with the governor, she was enraged. Her husband had been scalped in the Piute War. She vowed now that she would kill the chief in revenge.

To avoid a possible catastrophe, Governor Nye gave orders that he would receive Winnemucca on the outskirts of the city.

Thither the governor repaired.

But the old Indian stood upon his dignity and refused to talk.

"Go away," said he to Nye—disdainfully. "Send me Big Chief. Winnemucca make talk only with chief."

"But," said the flabbergasted Nye, "I am governor of Nevada. I am chief of the Whites, Winnemucca, just as you are chief of the Redmen."

"Go away," grunted the Indian, "go away. You no chief of one woman."[8]

Right away the governor began having his troubles. The government appropriation of $20,000 was insufficient to support his official family. Judges began to forage for themselves. How much for a favorable opinion? With decisions bought and sold, the Lode became more speculative than ever. The new judges found the idea of one ledge ridiculous. There were many—many ledges. No one knew how many. But just as many as any man could pay for.

By the time the legislature convened, the governor was in a funk for funds. But he hadn't been a New York politician without learning the ropes. He asked and received an appropriation of $75,000 to build a dam to irrigate the desert for the Piutes and to erect a mill in which to saw lumber for them. That fall, a miserable excuse for a dam made its appearance on the Carson but no mill followed. The dam could have been built with Indian labor at an expenditure of $1000. Month after month went by. Still no mill. Finally a Washoe editor sent absurdity flying to the four quarters of the globe. "Governor Nye," wrote he, "has a dam by a mill-site, but no mill by a damn sight."[9] Bret Harte has preserved the Governor's identity for posterity in his famous "Bill Nye" of the "Heathen Chinee."[10]

Before long every illusion regarding the judges was dissipated. The boys' opinion of them was aptly expressed by the newly appointed bailiff of the Territorial Supreme Court when he first announced to the assembled Bar of the Territory that its highest judicial tribunal was open for business. Without traditional formula to guide him, the bailiff stretched forth his long arm:

"Oyez, oyez, oyez," he cried, "the Honorable the Supreme Court of the Territory of Nevada is now in session. God help the people of the Territory of Nevada!"[11]

Neither had the stage-drivers any illusions regarding the judiciary. One night, when Hank Monk's coach was late in its schedule, Monk drove very hard, to the terror of the self-important judicial personage seated within—who vainly expostulated again and again, and at last with great dignity blurted out:

"I'll have you discharged before the week is out. Do you know who I am, sir?"

"Oh, yes!" replied Monk, "perfectly well. But I'm going to take this coach into Carson City on time if it kills every one-horse judge in the Territory!"

CHAPTER XXXII

LAW

1861

Governor Nye began at once to set the wheels of government in motion. He divided Washoe into twelve elective districts and called for representatives.[1] Among those elected was Bill Stewart. On him more than on any of the others the governor depended for help in moulding the wild, heterogeneous population on the mountain into shape.[2]

His legal skill made Bill the most prominent member of the council. His bold front prevailed over every gathering. He was a member of every important committee. He introduced more bills than any other councilman. What was more, he saw to it that every one of them was adopted.

This assembly whetted Bill's appetite for statesmanship. Before it was over he found himself longing for further worlds to conquer. He espied on Sun Mountain the same door that Governor Nye had set his eyes upon. Bill knew what the governor had in mind. Perhaps the governor had found his inspiration in Washington. Be that as it may, Bill made up his mind to reach the door first—open it and enter upon his own ambitions. Nye was an interloper. Bill had come to Washoe first. And he intended to keep that door for his exclusive use.

As practically the entire population of the new Territory was still centred on Sun Mountain, a movement was started to make Virginia the capital of Washoe.

But Bill wouldn't have it. By this time Bill was the father of numerous progeny. If the arsenical waters on Sun Mountain did not agree with him, neither would they with his offspring. On that account he threw his colossal influence into having the capital of Washoe established on the banks of the Carson River, at the place where it gushed, fresh and sweet, out of the Sierra. There was great opposition to that plan. Sun Mountain had created the Territory. The capital must rise upon it. But Bill had made up his mind—opposition or not—the capital must be on the Carson. As over half the votes had already been pledged to Virginia, the only way Bill could defeat the measure was by creating new counties whose votes he could control. This he did. Among them was Humboldt. Not

183

a living thing within its borders but snakes, lizards, coyotes, and an occasional sheep-herder. But Bill had his way—the capital was built on the Carson—and the young Stewarts had the purest drinking-water in Washoe.[3]

Besides locating the capital, Bill regulated the proceedings in civil cases, defined judicial districts, and fixed the terms of the district and supreme courts. Like Moses, he gave Sun Mountain her laws but he did not reverence the Mountain that had made him, as Moses had Mount Sinai—otherwise the gilded dome of the capitol would have crowned Sun Mountain instead of lying like a sop at her feet.

The legislature remained in session forty-nine days and forty-nine nights. All that period Bill kept the floor. His Act Adapting the Common Law contained 714 articles under seventeen titles. His enactments and joint resolutions covered 518 pages of a royal octavo book, eight of which were devoted to toll-road franchises—only six of which were granted.[4]

Telegraph-poles began to stalk across Gold Cañon and on into the desert beyond. Shining wire was stretched from pole to pole. The Piutes were worried. They went to the governor. Why was the Great White Chief running a fence through their hunting grounds? Which side was intended for his red children?

On October 23, the wire of the Transcontinental Telegraph was connected up, and the dirge of the Pony Express began. Its first use was offered to the Nevada Legislative Assembly. Bill Stewart was delegated to draft the first message to President Lincoln.

"Nevada Territory," wired Bill, "through her first Legislative Assembly, to the President and People of the United States—
"Greeting:—
"Nevada for the Union, ever true and loyal! The last born of the Nation, will be the last to desert the Flag! Our aid, to the extent of our ability, can be relied upon to crush the rebellion.
" Signed WILLIAM M. STEWART (*Chairman*)
Committee from the Council."[5]

The first dispatch from the East brought rage to Gold Cañon. Another blundering Union defeat! Colonel E. D. Baker, the savior of the Pacific, had been killed at Ball's Bluff![6]

Bill Stewart was not satisfied with the idea of a Territory. Territorial laws were inadequate for Washoe. He wanted a State. It was a preposterous idea, said the boys—a mountain becoming a State— but that was what Bill wanted. These were troublous times. He knew what he was talking about. There was that door to think about.

Immediately Bill set the machinery in motion. The Territorial Assembly passed an act authorizing a general election to vote for or against State government. Bill was elected to the convention. Of course Washoe wanted statehood.

Governor Nye was urging more Federal assistance. He was keeping the President cognizant of all that was going on in Washoe. Lo and behold! In his first annual message to Congress, President Lincoln praised the civil government inaugurated in a Territory in which the "leaven of treason" existed.[7] He asked Congress to advertise the natural resources of Sun Mountain in order to encourage settlers in going to Washoe. He hinted at the possibility of organizing Washoe into a State. A State! The boys sat up and took more notice. Why should President Lincoln want to turn their mountain into a State?

CHAPTER XXXIII

THE NEW CHIEF

1861

Having created the Territory of Nevada in forty-nine days and forty-nine nights, Bill Stewart rested.

Then he turned his thoughts to material things. He must have money to match his improved estate. Litigation had not begun in earnest. On credit he acquired a mine in Gold Cañon and a quartz mill on Carson River. In one superb gesture after another he hired a hundred operators, constructed gravel roads to mill and mine, bought ore wagons and freighters, eight teams of six mules each, to haul ore to his mill and California hay and barley to his stables. Everything that Bill touched was done on a colossal scale. Rightly so. Now he was on the point of becoming a millionaire. He had struck a rich mine and his mill turned out thousands every week. In November he was offered half a million for his holdings, but he refused. It was worth millions!

The middle of December brought a terrific snow-storm. A Washoe zephyr howled through the Cañon and laid a white blanket of snow six feet deep on Sun Mountain. Then it grew warm. The snow turned to rain. For ten days and ten nights it poured. The snow melted. A wall of water, eight feet high, arose and surged down Gold Cañon carrying everything before it. Bill Stewart's mine was filled to the shafthead with sand and gravel. His mill was swept away. His quartz, barley, and hay were lost out on the Carson Sink. Overnight Bill lost a potential million. Worse, he had a crowd of men and a drove of horses and mules to house and feed. He owed thousands of dollars. He was utterly broke. He must have money. He could not evade his responsibilities, let his men go unpaid, his animals unfed. No, Bill wasn't that kind. Moreover, he didn't want any one on Sun Mountain to know how badly he was injured. Besides, his own young needed food. Driven by the needs of cattle, men, and babies, he made up his mind to go to San Francisco. He had a wealthy friend there—Chris Reis. He would borrow enough, thirty or forty thousand dollars—to tide him over.

His credit was still good on Sun Mountain. It must stay good. He bought fodder for his mules at two bits a pound. He hired a boarding-house to feed his men. He stocked up his own family larder. Then he turned toward the Sierra to get the money to pay his bills.

He started on his long journey—alone—over the same route that had claimed the life of Allen Grosch. Now there were many passes and stations. It was about Christmas time. His young would have to do without a tree. He must get to San Francisco. Three hundred miles away. As quickly as possible. The Sierra passes were choked with snow. Telegraph poles were completely covered. It was still snowing.

That first night, after a hard tussle, he reached Yanks—an important station a mile and a half south of Lake Tahoe. The tavern was crowded—no bed for him. So, Bill wrapped himself in his blankets, threw himself on the floor, and went to sleep. At dawn he was up. It was still snowing. The drifts had blotted out the tavern windows. His friends tried to keep him from going on. It was foolhardy in such weather. They reminded him of Allen Grosch. Bill listened. Hesitated—his kids—his cattle—his men—his credit. No, he must go on. He must redeem himself. He sat down to a hearty breakfast of coffee, beans, and flapjacks. He buckled on his snowshoes. His friends never expected to see him again as they saw him disappear in blinding snow.

He reached the summit of the Sierra. It was still snowing—wet—heavy—blinding snow. About noon Bill met his friend Salisbury, who had just come from California.

"Turn back," yelled Salisbury. "You can never cross the mountains."[1]

"I must go on," said Bill. "Must."

He sailed ahead. He had gone about 150 yards when he heard a fearful racket behind him. He turned and looked back. An avalanche was coming down the mountain. He saw Salisbury engulfed—saw him struggle—saw him swept over a precipice into the American River, a thousand feet below.

Bill was shaken. The snow was falling so thick that he could scarcely see. He guided his course from tree to tree. He travelled four miles in five hours.

It grew dusky in the forest. Night came on. Bill ploughed ahead. He knew the direction of Strawberry. He saw the lights of the tavern and steered his course by them. He made it.

He ate a hearty dinner. Smoked his pipe by the immense fireplace. Sank back into a restless sleep on the floor. The racket of the storm was terrific. It kept awakening him. Trees were crashing. Torrents were raging in every ravine. Earth was sliding—boulders clattering against the tavern. At dawn he was up and buckling on his snowshoes. The boys told him he was a fool to go on. It was raining and snowing by turns. The mountains were softened. Avalanches were frequent. From all around came fearsome sounds— splintering wood—falling earth—raging waters. He must get on. Like a Viking—he was up and away. Landslides—behind—ahead —below—kept up a continual crash louder than thunder.

He proceeded fifteen miles. He heard a dreadful racket to the right of him. He looked up. Trees—rocks—cliffs—were moving toward him. Water was leaping to meet them. He turned. He ran back. The whole side of a mountain crashed by. He gazed into the ravine below. The south fork of the American River had disappeared. The torrent was dammed. The earth quaked—crumbled —and rocked under him. He dare not go on ahead. He waited. Earth sounds ceased. He took off his snowshoes and ran. He reached the station on the solid ground of the other side. The inmates were paralyzed with fear. Their horses and cattle had been swept away. Bill quieted them, demanded a cup of coffee and bread, and was away.

He ran and walked—walked and ran. That night he reached Placerville—forty-eight miles since morning. He slept a few hours. There was no stage leaving. Too dangerous. He tried to hire a horse. Couldn't. He bought one on credit. He must reach Folsom and catch the train to Sacramento. He rode like mad down the foothills. He had thirty-five miles to cover. He arrived at Folsom. The Valley of the Sacramento was flooded. Stations—railroad—cars —engines—were all swept away.

He waded his horse to a knoll within four miles of Sacramento. The water was too deep. The horse could not go on. He would have to swim. Along came a rowboat. Bill traded his horse for the skiff and rowed himself down a Sacramento street. Houses were under water! Night came on—cold—dark—foggy. He rowed to a friend's home—tied his boat to a shutter—climbed through a second-storey window—found a bed and slept—exhausted.

At dawn he was out drifting about in his boat on the lookout for a steamer to San Francisco. Passenger boats had been taken off to pick up the half-drowned residents of the valley. Bill thought he would have to row to San Francisco. He was equal to it. Then he saw a side-wheeler coming. He signalled with an oar. Clambered aboard. That night he reached Chris Reis' house and borrowed $32,000 on his mine.

The next morning with his pockets stuffed with scrip and certificates of deposit Bill started back to Gold Cañon. Just a week from the day he had left Yanks he was back there. The boys were still beleaguered. Nothing had passed through since Bill left but jack-rabbits and wolves.

Bill immediately proceeded over the Sierra. His kids were all right. He paid the stable-bills for his mules, board-bills for his men, and went to work to dig out his mine. Within the month he sold it for $60,000. The man who bought it took millions out of it.[2] Bill was jubilant. He paid off Chris Reis. He was a free man again. No one knew that he was flat broke that December.

Bill's run over the Sierra in mid-winter appealed to the imagination of the boys. He became a supernatural—miraculous being. They conceded him mysterious power and acclaimed him a hero. They would have followed him anywhere—he would bring them through safely.

The first district court under Judge Gordon N. Mott opened. The calendar was loaded with all sorts of suits, most of them hinging on the question whether Sun Mountain contained one lode or many. Bill still maintained it contained only one. There wasn't a geologist or mining engineer of repute that could make him change his mind. The boys believed him. If Bill said there was only one vein on Sun Mountain—there was only one vein. But in the meantime the Lode had become the mecca for all the brightest lawyers in California. They disputed Bill. The war was on. Did Sun Mountain harbor one lode or many?

There was never a berseker in all the realm of Odin who loved to fight for the fight's sake, for the very joy of combat, more than Bill Stewart.[3] Glorious, incomparable, undismayed, tireless "Old Bill." Though fortune forsake him, though death stare him in the face, though he look down the muzzle of a dozen derringers, though bowies dissect him, though bullets fly like hail, though his clients, or the clients of his opponents, or the judge, or the jury, or both, be bribed, Bill Stewart's steel-blue eyes never lost their glitter; his tawny hair its bristle; his port its erectness. Whatever the menace Bill sprang to the danger-zone, vigorous, virile, alert, ready to parry at a moment's notice the most deadly of his antagonist's thrusts.

Sun Mountain was now plunged into a caldron of litigation.

There was no longer opportunity for mines or mills. All Bill's time was spent in court or in his library. He began to reap princely fees, $100,000 from the Belcher, $30,000 from the Yellow Jacket; $200,-000 a year was nothing. Sun Mountain, Six Mile, Seven Mile, Gold Cañon, the Carson River all paid him tribute. The voice of the young Stewarts grew loud and lusty in the land.

If his rewards were royal, it was well. Bill Stewart worked from dawn to dusk like a galley-slave. The vigor and earnestness with which he carried on the one-ledge theory were colossal. Once enlisted as counsel on a case, he made the cause of his clients his own. He saw no foundation of justice in any claim of any opponent. He left no stone unturned to achieve success. He brow-beat the bribed judges and bribed juries. He exposed them to unmerciful onslaughts of oratory. He left them cowed and trembling in bar and box. His determination to win at any cost—the common belief that he would —that he could match his adversaries with any weapon they could employ exposed him to sharp criticism. But Bill defied his critics to prove their assertions in the courts. They quickly desisted. They were afraid of Bill's wit, wisdom, and lashing tongue. With profligate judges, the Washoe bar was not a nursery for tender consciences. Bill fought fire with fire. He had few imitators, no equals.

Thus by the sheer force of his personality Bill made himself master of judge and jury. Sometimes by his barbed wit he would make the rough jurymen roar with such laughter that his opponents would receive but scant consideration. Sometimes by bitter denunciation of a treacherous witness, such as George D. Whitney proved to be in the suit of the Sierra Nevada Mining Company *versus* the American Mining Company, he kindled jury and spectators to a flame of excitement that swept them with uncontrollable passion.

In the midst of preliminary skirmishing, Bill discovered that Whitney, his principal witness, had "sold out" to the enemy. With Whitney silenced, Bill believed the case was lost—but he had no intention of letting Whitney go scot-free. He painted his act in the darkest colors—the trick of a renegade. "He was false to his duty," he thundered, "false to his friends, false to his honor." He turned angrily upon the defending counsel, Charles H. S. Williams, accounted the ablest lawyer in California. The bribery of the witness was an unpardonable crime, a burning disgrace to the conductors of the defense. It involved Williams in a shameful conspiracy. It would remain an enduring stain upon the profession which he disgraced.

The jury caught Bill's heat and passionate glow. They bent forward, the better to listen. Spectators muttered in sympathy and crowded closely about the bar. As Bill shot out his last fierce sentence an ominous murmur ran through the courtroom. The attempted defense of Williams was a farce. The jury was deaf with passion. They left their seats prejudiced against the witness and the whole case of the American Company. When a bribed juror tried to protest against the action of the majority, the eleven others told him they would hang him if he persisted. Having a well-grounded faith in this assurance the juror instantly yielded and a verdict was rendered at once for Bill Stewart's clients, the Sierra Nevada Company.[4]

Where would Sam Brown or Langford Peel be against such invective? Bill Stewart was now "Chief" of Sun Mountain, the master of her "bad men," judges, juries, mines, rivers, valleys, deserts, as well as the master of his own fate. Never for a minute did he forget that door. He let it be voiced about that the judges whom President Lincoln had appointed were not sufficiently versed in mining law or sufficiently capable to grapple with the great responsibilities they had encountered on Sun Mountain. He represented to the boys that in order to get rid of such a judicial deadfall only one course remained. Sun Mountain must don the robes of statehood. It was the only way. Like Alexander, Bill longed for greater worlds to conquer. A potential Webster; a Clay; a Calhoun. For men of his own mettle.

CHAPTER XXXIV

THE HIDDEN CITY

1861

From then on legal warfare became a continual obligato to all that occurred on Sun Mountain. In no time ten millions of dollars were squandered in litigation. Great strikes were made here, there and yon, but the real fortunes were made and lost at the bar of perjured justice. Bill's voice thundered on and on. Sun Mountain had but one ledge. There was no other ledge than the one Bill Stewart was defending. If other ledges existed or were discovered—they were dips, spurs, and angles of the real ledge. Bill Stewart could prove it, would prove it. The plethoric purse of California's millionaires was being drained in the colossal struggle for Sun Mountain's one ledge. The legitimate costs of this multitude of suits were enormous. The expense of fighting fire with fire was insupportable. The deeper the shafts of the Ophir and Gould & Curry sank, the richer became the yield. The more bitter the court fights. The poorer the owners. The more profligate the territorial judges. The remarkable case of the Chollar Mining Company *versus* the Potosi Mining Company began. . . a contention without parallel in the litigious history of mining claims, in duration, fierceness, and cost. California courts, for the first time in their history, were deserted. Wars had been fought for women, and history made. This fight for the womb of Sun Mountain would yet involve itself in the fratricidal struggle that was wrecking the nation. Strange, that in two years Sun Mountain should become involved in the national maelstrom.

The warfare on the surface was continued in the underground depths of Sun Mountain. Yellow Jacket sappers cut into the Gentry shaft and smoked out their rivals. The Gentrys countermined and blew a stinking smudge into the Yellow Jacket. The surface householder rebelled. Unendurable odors filled every domicile in the city. Gould & Curry stopers broke down the barricade between themselves and the Seneca and cut the latter's windlass and ropes to pieces.

These contests were as nothing compared with the contention between the Ophir and Burning Moscow. That battle literally rocked

Sun Mountain with dynamite, oratory, and judicial resignations. Burning Moscow believed in the many-ledge theory. Theirs was entirely separate from the Ophir. Bill Stewart proved it was not, by running a surreptitious tunnel into Burning Moscow workings. The latter heard Bill Stewart's forces pushing stealthily through the earth. They hired all the toughs on Sun Mountain to greet Bill's miners when the cut was completed. One had had his nose bitten off. Another had lost three fingers. A third was pock-marked with buckshot. Armed with bowies, knives, shotguns, picks, and pitchforks, they proved a vicious reception committee.

Heads were broken. Blood was spilt. The Ophir was driven back to its incline. Burning Moscow's stock skyrocketed while Ophir's fell.

Bill Stewart secured an injunction from Judge Mott. Judge Mott declared that Sun Mountain had only one ledge. That was the ledge that Bill believed in. Burning Moscow was forced to quit work. Their stock fell from $250 to almost nothing. Many were ruined. Hearts were broken. Brokers committed suicide. Judge Mott had been tampered with. It had cost some one $25,000. Every one knew that he believed in only one ledge so he had to resign to make way for Judge North.[1]

Judge North believed that Sun Mountain was entitled to as many ledges as she could pay for. He granted Burning Moscow a temporary injunction. Work resumed. Ophir stock fell from $1700 to a mere pittance. Panic shook the market. Dividends stopped. Stockholders went insane. Suddenly the case was dismissed and the Ophir gobbled all the stock and acquired the disputed property. The fight had lasted, off and on, for two years. It had cost more than a million dollars. A good slice of which went to Bill Stewart's account.[2]

All this time underneath the streets of the city an incredible, invisible, subterranean city of many thoroughfares and cross-streets was building. At every hundred feet, the Ophir and Gould & Curry gave off a gallery—one below the other. Already the Ophir had ten stories underground. And the Gould & Curry had given off an endless maze of drifts, winzes, and passages, the walls and roofs of which were supported by huge timbers.

It was always twilight down there—a soft gloaming pricked by a thousand candles. There was no repose in that mysterious region, neither through long summer days nor short winter nights; no peace, always blasting of dynamite, ringing of picks, clanking of shovels, rumbling of cars, dripping of water, settling of dust; none of the endless changes and renewals of season that sweeten existence on earth; no relapse of day into night or night into day; no summer; no winter; no Sabbath. A land of everlasting night, of continuous menace, where candles in tin sconces threw lurid light over the white, half-naked bodies of men picking at walls and roof.

A trip to San Francisco could not take a traveller nearly as far as he could now journey under Sun Mountain. Miles and miles of dim-lit aisles penetrated it in every direction; a journey to Antarctic regions, during the long night there, could not take a traveller into regions of such pitch blackness; a journey into the most fabulous regions of Aladdin could not take a traveller to a country half so miraculous as that which lay less than half a mile below the parallel of familiar streets above. There were galleries glittering with silver spun as fine as a wire; there were nests of amethyst that glowed with a purple heart; there were clusters of crystal, their prisms flashing like diamonds; there were strips of turquoise, veins of chrysoprase—pale-blue and gray with waxlike luster. There were seams of quartz embedded in dark-red porphyry. There was granular and crystalline diorite.

It was a fabulous country. Like all beautiful things it had embedded in it the elements of cruelty—a hundred-headed earth monster with tentacles—more powerful than those of an octopus—lay always waiting to entrap the unwary miner.

A third of the whole population of Washoe took turns every eight hours going down into those dark depths and peopling that hidden city. Every eight hours a "shift" was belched forth and another took its place. Sun Mountain had become the roof of buildings of five—six—seven and ten stories, centre-of-the-earth-scrapers ever seeking to sink deeper.

Day by day that hidden city was sending surface-ward millions in black-sulphurets and silver chlorides. Comstock, "Old Virginny," and O'Riley would have turned over in their graves could they have seen the output. The wail of their shades would have mingled with the moan of the Washoe Zephyr.

Every hour the boys were facing the menace of cave-ins, of hot water, of noxious gases, of fire. Sometimes they put the point of a pick into a subterranean reservoir and had to run for their lives; sometimes they were caught in blasts and blown to atoms; sometimes they were seared by fire-damp—smothered by gas—but always they died like men.

One day when one of the boys was at work at the bottom of an incline the ground under him suddenly gave way. Down he went, caught in a caving mass of splintering wood and rock. His hands and arms were pinned to his body. Only his head and neck projected above the rock. The earth sucked at his feet. It was pitch black. His lantern went out but he found he could breathe. He drew a long breath—tried out his voice—called loudly for help.

The boys came—running—but . . . the walls of the incline kept cracking—settling and sliding. Flakes of earth, like falling snow, kept dropping upon their comrade's head. No one dared to venture within twenty feet of him. They watched, horrified, as the earth, like a flood of water, crept slowly up his neck. He begged continually to be taken out. He called them by name, first one, then another, to assist him. They forced themselves to laugh and joke that he might not despair. For over an hour they watched as the earth fell about him and he sank slowly deeper.

Once to give him comfort in his black surroundings they set fire to a ball of oakum, saturated with coal-oil, and rolled it toward him. "I see the light," he cried joyfully. "I'm glad you're coming for me, boys." He laughed outright.

At this cry, the boys made a desperate attempt to throw a rope about his body. But in vain—earth—pebbles and rock fell steadily. They could hear him choking—coughing—calling. "Be quick," he muttered in a muffled voice, "I'm smothering." Suddenly a great mass, of clay, rock, and timbers gave way forty feet above. In one grand crash, the earth swallowed him.[3]

CHAPTER XXXV

AMUSEMENTS

1862

The clatter of stamps, thunder of hoists, whirr of machines, shriek of whistles, clanging of bells—mingling into one grand pandemonium—could be heard far out on the desert.

All transalpine roads led up Gold Cañon. Virginia became the centre of mountain trade. Stages, coming and going, found their terminus there. Roads leading to points all over Washoe shot out from there like rays from the sun. Prospectors made it their headquarters. From there explorers left for the Boise, Snake, and Bitter Root country. Daily, pack trains tottered over the Divide with wine, cards, and supplies for the boys; incense, silks, and perfume for the hetaerae; copper and mercury for the mills; horse and ox-driven freighters groaned upward with machinery for mines; provender for markets; wood for furnaces. At night camel trains stalked through quiet streets with salt.

In three years the population of Sun Mountain had outstripped the growth of any Sierra town in the same length of time. Where two years before there had been sage, vaulting jack-rabbits, and slinking coyotes, now all was changed. Sun Mountain was stripped to the dust, not a bush, not a piñon from peak to base. Her breasts were torn with prospect-holes. Her flanks gashed with cuts. Dynamite shook her to her foundations. She had been man-handled more cruelly than Sabines ever had been by Rome. Heaps of yellow sand, like crusted matter, were caked about her cuts and ran in yellow streams from her raw surfaces.

Three terraced streets, "A," "B," and "C," climbed a crazy pathway up the mountain. There were no cross streets. The founders had been in far too much of a hurry. Property was far too valuable. The man who wanted to go from one terrace to another could scramble, as best he could, over the intervening distance.[1]

The streets took on a cosmopolitan appearance. Piutes in picturesque rags; Chinese coolies in pigtails balancing baskets from yokes on their shoulders; Mexican vaqueros on silver-mounted saddles;

196

firemen in red shirts; miners in blue jeans; Frenchmen in tight
clothes; Germans with long pipes—all these, night and day, ranged
up and down the sidewalks. The reputation of Washoe had penetrated to the farthest segment of the globe. Men of every nation, like
buzzards apprised of carrion, flocked to the feast. As early as 1860,
the Frenchmen had set up a "Café de Paris"; the Germans had a
bier-keller, where rotund Teutons mid clouds of smoke sang guttural
songs.

On the eve of Mexican Independence the Mexicans staged a riotous celebration over Spanish Ravine. Around their works they
built a fence, erected a flagpole at the southern end, hoisted their
green-and-red flag, and at regular intervals about their barricade
planted torches. At dusk the torches were lighted to the blare of
music, the crash of anvils, and the accompaniment of rifle-whiskey.
From the streets below, it presented a magnificent tableau—a forti-
fication surrounded by flaming walls such as might have protected
a slumbering Brunhilde. The boys watched the spectacle far into
the night. Sun Mountain had become a back-drop, against which
was staged an ever-changing pageant. Its restless life was likened
to the tumult of Hell. Its turbulence could hardly be exaggerated
but it gave forth a hollow sound. Below surface fanfare, was heard
the deep, solemn beat of the mountain's heart—the muffled boom of
blasting—the stifled sounds of breaking rock.

Wells Fargo moved into a substantial iron-faced structure with
great grim doors and shutters.[2] Alongside stores, saloons, restaurants, lawyers' offices, assay offices multiplied.

In the fall of 1860 the International Hotel made its appearance on
"C" Street—equipped with iron-balustraded balconies, billiard-par-
lors, dining- and smoking-rooms, to say nothing of a sumptuous bar
provided with rows of green-baize tables. The first day the hotel
opened its doors, the office took in over $700 in bullion.[3] Every stick
of wood in that hotel, every plate-glass mirror, every piece of crock-
ery was brought over the Sierra in great Washoe mule-drawn, bell-
ringing freighters.

Down below "C" Street, canvas houses multiplied. The camp appeared as if built of white marble. At night with lamps lit within,
the city glowed like so many alabaster globes.

Below the cabins was the Chinese quarter, reeking of tea, spice,
orange peel, and the sweet sickening odor of red poppies. Over
every door were signs comforting to Virginia's bachelor heart. Chin
Kong did washing. Sam Sing did ironing at the lowest rates with

no extra charge for sewing on buttons. Through open doors John Chinaman could be seen slapping around in loose shoes plying his hot iron back and forth like a shuttle-cock and spraying his clothes from an ever filled mouth of water through yellow, serrated teeth.

The "Chinks" made sad work of the English language. Double e was added to the last syllable of every word, r was changed to l, v to b. "Want washee?" asked John Chinaman. "Washee shirtee bellee goodee. Only two bittee."

Down there in a gilded temple was a golden "Josh" with a hundred uplifted arms surrounded by sweet-smelling punk and dim-lighted lamps. One day a violent quarrel between a Chinaman and a Jew peddler: "Oh, yessee; I knowee you. Hib sabbee. Allee samee. You killee Melican man's Josh!"

There were more women now—rotund Gretchens in hurdy-gurdies, bold-faced, gold-toothed ones at faro tables. Birds of Paradise, decked out in gay dresses, brilliant feathers, and showy jewelry, promenaded slowly up and down "C" Street, proudly displaying vari-colored plumage to rows of ragged, rusty crows who lined the streets with ravenous eyes. But not Julia Bulette. When she "took the air" it was in a lacquered brougham with a painted escutcheon on the panel—a heraldic device that looked like four aces crowned by a lion couchant.

Even to hetaerae the boys gave extravagant homage. Feminine laundry, hanging on a line, filled them with mad longing. About a discarded hoop-skirt they joined hands and staged an ecstatic dance. For a peek through a door-crack at an ancient hag flapping jacks, they paid pokes of gold-dust.

When a white-hatted nun of the Sisters of Mercy walked down the street, some of the boys fell on their knees, and pressed the hem of her robe to their lips as she passed. Once Bob Howland, who could quell a criminal with a glance of his eye, walked forth with his bride of a few months, heavily veiled to ward off the looks of the curious. As they passed a busy corner a total stranger tapped Bob on his arm.

"May I see your lady?" he asked.

Howland scrutinized him carefully. No offense was intended. He lifted his wife's veil. And the youth, who hadn't seen a woman like his mother, for years, gazed into the smiling eyes of Bob Howland's bride.[4] Woman to the average Comstocker was a flame of purity and faith, sweetness and hope. No vestal virgin trimmed her lamp with greater care than was shown for these symbols of home.

Once in a crowded theatre at a fête-day when a band was playing the national anthem, the cry of an infant soared shrill and strong above the fanfare. Instantly the music was quelled so as to give the baby a chance. As the yell arose supreme and free, some of the flannel-shirted cheered while others bowed their heads and wept.

Came a day when the manager of the Melodeon placarded every cliff and signboard on Sun Mountain with posters announcing the coming of one Antoinette Adams, a Boston prima donna.

The boys' enthusiasm was boundless. A real live woman, to say nothing of a songbird, at the mines. On the opening night they filled every bench, corner, and window-sill of the Melodeon.

The very atmosphere was hushed with expectancy. Finally the curtain went up and Antoinette Adams walked down stage to the footlights. She was nearly six feet tall, with a decided stoop to her shoulders, long neck, light blue eyes, a Roman nose, crooked mouth, and faded blond hair that was frizzed into little curls about her forehead. A New England spinster! A horrible disappointment—old enough to be their aunt. Immediately they dubbed her "Aunty."

For her initial song she had chosen "Under the Willow"—a ballad dear to the sentimental heart of the day. Folding her hands in front of her she began:

"Under the willow she's laid with care . . ."

It was a pathetic exhibition—the Washoe "canaries" could sing better than that. The boys looked from one to the other. Consternation, disappointment, chagrin, on every face. They wanted to laugh. They had been taken in. As soon as she had finished the ballad, Hank Blanchard, a good old Yankee himself, jumped to his feet.

"Now, boys, three cheers for 'Aunty,'" he called. The boys arose as one man. Cheer after cheer shook the Melodeon. They fairly raised the roof. Then the boys sat down. Not one of them cracked a smile.

Miss Adams was so flustered with surprise and joy that she could scarcely catch her breath. Her "little" hands clutched her breast. Finally she started again on the Willow.

Again they listened, still as death, until the last cracked note died upon the air. Some thought of rope—others of a gun.

"Look here, fellows," said Hank Blanchard, "I for one think it's time to retire 'Aunty' from the stage. Let's pension her and let her go!"

"Agreed!" from the others.

Then began the applause. The boys hollered and whooped, and stamped and pounded upon the floor with canes and sticks.

There weren't any bouquets, for there wasn't a flower within fifty miles of the camp, but half-dollars fell on the stage like hail.

"Aunty" came back, all smiles and blushes. In an instant there was perfect order. Again she sang "Under the Willow," though her notes began to show weakness. Once more the boys whooped up the applause. Once more half-dollars rained upon the platform.

The third time "Aunty" looked over the coal-oil lamps, that served as footlights, and tried to sing. The exertion was more than she could stand. It was apparent that the applause and the light mountain air were telling on her lungs.

Again thunders of applause greeted her rendition of the song. "Aunty" did not respond quickly enough and the stamping was redoubled. The manager came out and tried to speak.

"Miss Adams thanks her admirers," he began, "for their appreciation of her talent as a vocalist—but . . ."

"Take him off!" yelled the boys, as they might have at a dog that was nipping at their shins. "Gag him!"

"Aunty! Aunty! Give us Aunty!" went up from a thousand throats. "We want to hear Aunty!"

Down the platform came Miss Adams, panting. She looked discomfited but still in the ring. She tried to sing again—but was too short of breath to even breathe. Out she backed—bowing—smiling—throwing kisses—while half-dollars fell like rose-petals about her.

Then there was another storm. The curtain was rung down. The manager came before the curtain and finally made himself heard.

"Miss Adams begs me to say," he began, "that she cannot sing any more tonight, but she thanks you for your courtesy . . ."

"We want to hear 'Aunty' sing," they interrupted. "If we can't have 'Aunty' and 'Under the Willow' we're going home." The manager shook his head. Up they stood. Out they filed.

But the prima donna was a shrewd lady. The next morning's overland stage carried "Aunty" and two sacks full to the brim with the Comstock half-dollars which had been showered upon her—enough to last her the rest of her natural life if she never sang another note.

The boys who saw her go, bowing and smiling, had hoped she never would. "Suppose she got into the hands of a lot of Philistines," said Hank, "who didn't know how to treat a prima donna of the first magnitude."[5]

More than once Lotta Crabtree, with twinkling toes and scintillating ballads, captured their hearts and loose change. Edwin Booth thrilled them with manly drama. "La Somnambula" wooed their ears with melody. The ghost chorus—the haunted libretto—the sleep-walking Armina calling for her bridegroom in touching accents—and crossing a narrow bridge without falling—supplied the necessary thrills.

A Methodist revivalist, the Reverend Adam Bland, standing on a box on the street, captured their attention with exuberant theology and held them as spell-bound as Lotta or the Somnambulist ever had. When the hat was passed it overflowed with gold and silver. Faith without works was unappreciated; still works were by no means lacking. The disorderly camp was fast crystallizing on silver ledges.

The boys may have had a Germanic love of music, a Spanish love of dancing, and an Anglo-Saxon love of institutions—but they were Roman in their amusements. How they would have cheered at chariot-races or bellowed at bull-fights! But they had to content themselves with prize-fights, horse-races, cock-fights, dog-fights, badger contests, or "wildcat" carnivals. Whatever it was, it had to have robust appeal. No milk-and-water exhibitions would have been countenanced. Had it been possible to hang men and afterwards resuscitate them, or blow them from the mouths of cannons as they did in India, and afterwards gather the fragments together and breathe life into them—such extravagant feats would have sufficed. For those excited brains required something exaggerated—superlative—fortissimo.

CHAPTER XXXVI

PROFESSOR PERSONAL PRONOUN

1862

Next to amusements, the boys were devoted to newspapers and magazines. One enterprising editor combined printing-press and bar in the same room so that the boys might read and enjoy themselves at the same time.

Perhaps those boys should plead guilty to extravagance, excitability and recklessness but no one could accuse them of a want of intelligence. No one, unless he had been isolated on a lone mountain in the midst of deserts, could appreciate their hunger for news from the outside world. Their longing for something to read led them to the commitment of a literary abortion. They founded a literary magazine—*The Weekly Occidental*—published on *The Territorial Enterprise* press. In it "The Silver Fiend," the first composite novel, had its genesis. But the venture did not thrive. "Can a lark sing in a cellar? Can summer abide on Mont Blanc? Will flowers blossom in Hell?" asked the most outstanding of Washoe's bards.[1]

Nevertheless, Joe Goodman knew his audience and how to supply its wants. By 1862, his *Enterprise* was sharing honors with *The Sacramento Union* and was read up and down the Coast. Its columns often contained world news before other papers had received their dispatches.

The Enterprise was now installed in a handsome, red-brick, iron-faced structure on "C" Street.

One day Joe Goodman received by stage from Aurora, a mining town 130 dusty miles away, a sketch signed "Josh." It was a humorous little thing, shrewd, graceless, good-humored but cynical. Joe got a good laugh out of it. When it appeared next morning the boys were convulsed. "Josh" did not ask for any pay for his sketch. In fact if Joe Goodman had wanted to pay for it, he could not have, as the author gave no other name than "Josh." He was a miner, soon to be a magnate, and did not want to be known as a camp scribbler. After that one, more sketches came to *The Enterprise*. Whoever "Josh" was, said Joe Goodman, it was evident that he was an artist; that he wrote for the very joy of it. Joe was glad to get whatever he wrote because it had the punch that took with the boys—adolescent, ironic—stuff with a laugh.

One of these was about George Turner, the new chief justice whom President Lincoln had foisted on the new Territory. Already Turner had earned a reputation for being the shallowest, most egotistical and mercenary occupant of the supreme bench. It was known that when he signed his name on a hotel register it was invariably as "Honorable George Turner, Chief Justice of the United States." It was known that when he was about to render a decision he always favored the side that could pay the most for it. It was known that when he delivered a lecture in Carson on some apparently important subject, it turned out to be merely a rehash of his own vainglorious achievements. It was evident, then, that the chief justice was riding for a fall.

"Josh" heard that lecture and burlesqued it in colorful manner, and referred to the chief justice as "Professor Personal Pronoun."[2] The article was a scorching exposition of Turner's vanity, egotism, and emptiness. It closed by saying that it was "impossible to print his lecture in full, as the type-cases had run out of capital I's." Its obvious intent was to discomfit the chief justice and expose him to laughter. Little did "Josh" realize then that this piece of robust horse-play would rebound on his own head. Joe Goodman regarded the skit with favor and published it in the columns of his paper. Immediately it created a sensation throughout the Territory. The man who wrote that, Goodman said, had something in him.[3] Who was this "Josh," anyhow?

Around the 4th of July, 1862, along came another effusion postmarked Aurora. This time it was a burlesque report of a Fourth-of-July oration,[4] purporting to have been delivered near Owen's Lake, near where *The Enterprise's* correspondent was engaged in prospecting.[5] Its opening phrase caught Goodman's attention. "I was sired by the Great American Eagle," it began, "and foaled by a Continental Dam." That was immense! This was followed by a string of stock patriotic phrases absurdly arranged. But it was the beginning which struck the fancy of Joe Goodman. "That man is worth cultivating," he said to "Dag," as he passed the skit along.[6] "That is the sort of thing we want." And he sat down and wrote to "Josh." If he was not making more money mining than he could as local reporter on *The Territorial Enterprise,* he would hold a place for him.[7]

CHAPTER XXXVII

EVOLUTION OF A HUMORIST
August, 1862

"Steve Gillis," shouted Daggett through the window connecting editorial and composing rooms. "You're wanted!" [1]

Steve came running. He gave one glance about *The Enterprise's* editorial room. An unshaven, roughly clad stranger with bushy hair was threatening his friends. Appearances called for action. He was a bantam but he'd show this red-headed fellow . . . !

"There's no trouble, Steve. I called you to make you acquainted with Sam Clemens," drawled Daggett.

Then William Wright, already widely known on the Coast as Dan De Quille, put his head through the window opening. He wanted to see this Sam Clemens who had dared burlesque the mighty George Turner, chief justice of the Territorial Supreme Court, as "Professor Personal Pronoun." That had been great stuff! It had pleased the chief! And the boys had gloated over its extravagant absurdity. He was willing to go back to "the States" if he could leave his local department in such hands. It was to take Dan's place during this absence, that the editor, Joe Goodman, had summoned Clemens from Aurora.

Dan De Quille advanced into the room.

"Hello 'Josh,'" he greeted.

There was little ceremony on *The Enterprise* staff. Proprietor, editor, printer, and devil were social equals. If you could fight and write, or write and fight, no questions were asked. If you couldn't, or wouldn't, it was just as well to quit. From then on Samuel Clemens became "Sam" or "Josh." Just as Wright was already "Dan" and the editor—Goodman—"Joe."

Of course the first thing the staff wanted to know was what "Josh" was doing in Aurora with all those "bad men" and Vigilantes. When Sam told them that before going there he had been a lieutenant in the army of the Confederate States of America, they pricked up their ears and took notice. But he was a little vague as to why he had resigned his command. Sometimes, with great candor, he had been activated by the spirit that had caused the rout at Bull Run. Sometimes he was too fatigued to keep on retreating. Sometimes contradictory orders had so confused his mind that he couldn't tell which side he was fighting on. So he had resigned his commission as lieutenant of Company B, Hannibal Home Guards, to find out.

"I am perfectly willing to fight for either the United States or the Confederacy," he said he had written to the colonel of his regiment, "but this damned uncertainty as to which side I am on is killing me with anxiety." [2]

One of the conditions of enlistment had been that the members of the Guard should not be required to leave their home towns except in cases of invasion of the State by an enemy so that when the Confederate forces invaded Southwest Missouri, Sam saw that, in accordance with the terms of his enlistment, he was required to leave the State at once. [3]

Swearing on his mother's Bible never to throw a card or drink a drop of liquor, he boarded the Overland Stage bound for Washoe. Nineteen days later with an assortment of pipes and tobacco and an immense unabridged dictionary he had arrived and pushed on to Aurora. [4] From which place, during an overwhelming moment of patriotism, he had composed and dispatched to *The Enterprise* that famous Fourth-of-July oration that had so pleased the editors and readers of *The Enterprise* that it had brought him to their staff-room.

The Territorial Enterprise had developed into the most remarkable paper on the frontier. It was the nerve-centre of Washoe, the brainiest sheet on the Coast. It was privy to all of the Mountain's secrets both above and below the earth's crust. It had acquired enormous prestige. It could make or break any man in the Territory. It was honest and fearless. It might fear God—but no puny man. It was the mouthpiece of Sun Mountain—her final tribunal—her judge and advocate. It could be loved; it could be feared like the plague. When it got angry it had claws like those of a mountain cat. It was Comstock to the core—the mirror of her astounding personality—the sounding-board of her buoyant, virile young life.

Joe Goodman—the handsome, reckless editor, could write editorials that would have done credit to a seasoned veteran. [5] In his hand a pen became mockingly alive with the vitriolic impulses of youth. He loved *The Enterprise*. He gave it the best in him and injected into it the fire of his own virile nature. Equally well, and just as courageously, he handled a derringer. Once, when he differed with

Tom Fitch of *The Union* over some trifling journalistic matter, he fought it out with him at twenty paces. He could have killed Fitch. Instead he chose to cripple him. Fitch lost his agility for life, Joe lost a lock of curly black hair. Comstock journalism was satisfied. As for Tom Fitch—he was everlastingly grateful when Joe ran out of bullets and embraced him.[6] Joe insisted that every one in his employ practise the manly art of self defense. He always said you couldn't be a good Comstock newspaper man unless you were fearless and could shoot straight, both with gun and pen. Once a story was published, no apology was permitted. That meant you had to know your way around with a "navy" or a six-shooter. For the reporter who said what he felt was almost certain to find bullets mixed with his pi.

Before starting "Josh" on a reportorial assignment, Joe summoned him and gave him a piece of advice. "Never say we learn so and so," he advised, "or we understand so and so. . . . Get the absolute facts; speak out . . . say it *is* so and so. In the one case you are likely to be shot, in the other you are pretty certain to be; but, dead or alive, you will preserve the public confidence."[7] Poor "Josh!" How he hated rules—regulations—advice! Spontaneity was the thing!

Sam knew nothing about self-defense. Joe had Chauvel instruct him in foils as well as fists. One day Sam's nose was so disrupted that he had to go to Steamboat Springs for repairs while his potential enemy, on *The Union,* made merry at his expense.

Coming to *The Enterprise* was the making of Sam Clemens. Before, he had been with more or less ordinary people. There he found an atmosphere different from any he had ever dreamed of before. The office was filled with bright men.

Rollin M. Daggett was one of his staunchest friends. He would rather be right than President, "Dag" had once said. "We all feel that way about you, Mr. Daggett," replied one of his pals. Whereupon "Dag" looked all over the office for a gun.[8]

Sam first heard about adjectives from "Dag," who specialized in them. From him Sam learned that when it was necessary to call a man names there were no expletives too expressive.

Dan De Quille, too, had the gift of using adjectives. He was no more afraid of hurling them than he was of firing lead.[9] Before long Sam understood that a "navy," adjectives, and how to use them, were absolutely necessary to a berth on *The Enterprise.*

It seemed that adjectives were contagious. There were typesetters who could fling anathemas at bad copy, which would have frightened a Bengal tiger or halted a stampeding elephant. The news editor could damn a mutilated dispatch in twenty-four varieties of expletives. Sam had learned a little about cursing on the Mississippi but he confessed he was a novice when he entered the editorial rooms of *The Enterprise*. For swearing, like murder, had developed into one of the fine arts along the Lode. Even bull-whackers and mule-skinners were vendors of choicest brands.

There was a compositor named Jim Connely. For six days in the week he would do all that he had to do, but on the seventh he went on a protracted spree. Week in, week out, every Sunday found him in his cups. Every Monday found him in such a "twitter" he could hardly handle his composing-stick. One Monday he came into the office and stood gazing out the rear window which looked over Sugar Loaf to Forty Mile beyond. Suddenly he turned around, grabbed Sam Clemens, drew him to the window and pointed an unsteady finger. "Can you see that gray wolf prowling across Forty Mile?" he whispered. "I can see him plain." [10]

"No," said Sam, "but I can hear him scratching his ear."

That was the kind of school in which Sam found himself matriculated that August semester of 1862. The sage-brush school of folk-humor. Nothing, in all our literature, so distinctly savors of the soil and of the folks on it as the books and sketches which emanated from the editorial rooms of *The Territorial Enterprise* and with the authors of which "Josh" was in daily contact. There was something in that region of high altitude, gray alkali, gray sage-brush, gray coyotes, gray rocks, buoyant life, spring freshets, and glorious sunsets that precluded the possibility of writing about anything other than the weird, fascinating, ugly land of the sage. [11] From this palette Sam Clemens was destined to get an imperishable part of his inspiration. If he wrote a good thing, the boys would praise him to the sky and tell him to keep on. If on some nights Pegasus lagged, the boys would hold him up to scorn the next day. Through it all "Josh" noted that nothing was too extravagant, too fantastic, or too fine in the way of description for the vigorous metabolism of his audience.

"Josh" had not been long with *The Enterprise* before he began to develop a vast indifference to news as news. The boys didn't want news. What did they care about murders or accidents? Such horrible stuff was too close to them—too intimate. Daily they were a part of calamity and murder. Hourly they lived a thousand deaths. They wanted to get away from disaster—to laugh and forget. . . . Their palates craved other food, highly seasoned food, wild with the whimsy of rhetoric and strong with the tang of the sage. Thus they turned to *The Enterprise* not for news but for something to amuse them and Dan De Quille and "Josh" gave it to them in allopathic doses. The more absurd, the more fantastic, the more ridiculous, the closer lies simulated truth, the better the boys liked it and the louder they laughed, the more they applauded. Out of this demand developed the humorous school of Sun Mountain. A school designed for men who insisted on looking at life, yes and even death, through humorous eyes.

"Josh" gauged the requirements of his audience. He must make them laugh. Perhaps he didn't relish the rôle he was to play. But he had no choice. The boys had put a cap and bells on his head and a sceptre in his hand. Whether he would or not he must be the buffoon. Soon, "Josh" discovered that they would read only the stuff with a laugh. He must deliver the goods or quit. Perhaps that attitude of the boys had more to do in moulding him into a humorist than any other force.

It was not surprising that the boys obtained their greatest enjoyment from articles that had the tang of the earth. Stories about petrified things were highly entertaining to those who worked all day in hard-rock. They liked to laugh at the force that often flouted them. When fossilized snails, blasted out of hard-rock, came to life and crawled and slobbered down the page of *The Enterprise* they were hugely amused. When an outraged one bored his way back into the rock from which he had been dynamited, they were speechless with laughter.[12] When a vermilion-colored fish, caught in the scalding-hot sump of the Ophir, died of exposure when placed in cold water they were convulsed with the yarn's absurdity. The more exaggerated the specimens of humor, the better the boys liked it. "Josh" made note of the contradictory type of the pattern.

Dan De Quille had already met the requirements of his audience and tickled their palates with many a highly seasoned tale. Witness that pseudo-erudite account of the "Travelling Stones of Pahrangat Valley." That had imagination! It was the cream of Comstock humor. In feigned scientific minuteness Dan showed how these "travelling stones" were by some mysterious power drawn together and then torn asunder, only to be returned in moving, quivering masses to what appeared to be the magnetic centre of the valley. Upon pretended observations he predicated a new doctrine concerning electrical propulsion and repulsion. Dan called this kind of magnetic attraction a "quaint." When a description of this "quaint" reached Germany it caused a great furor among those physicists who were dabbling in electrolysis and electro-magnetic currents.

The secretary of one society wrote to Dan demanding further details. In vain Dan disclaimed any knowledge of electrokinetics. His denial was treated as an unprofessional attempt to keep brother scientists in ignorance of the truth concerning natural laws, the effects of which they were convinced had been first observed and recorded by "Herr Dan De Quille, the eminent physicist of Virginia Stadt."

Barnum, the greatest circus man in America, sent an offer of $10,000 to Dan if he would make those magnetized stones perform under canvas the antics he had described in *The Territorial Enterprise*.

The boys roared their pleasure. Sam Clemens marked time. This was what Sun Mountain demanded? Fabulous—ridiculous—absurd lies. Told without a smile. The fact that Germany treated Dan's burlesque seriously tickled the boys' fancy. That was the best part of it, having the outside world applaud what the Comstock read. That completed the tang. Those same devices were inspiring Sam Clemens.

Dan continued his "quaints" with an immense windmill, a perpetual-motion pump operated by the Washoe zephyr and built on the summit of Sun Mountain. With the zephyr harnessed, the sump in the Ophir and Gould & Curry was drained bone dry. All fear of subterranean floods was removed. A leading Boston engineering journal endorsed the plan as entirely feasible. Its editor actually figured out the exact horse-power engendered.[13] The Comstock roared again. While Dan's reputation spread far beyond Washoe and the world applauded his robust humor, "Josh" was putting finishing touches to his mental notes.

Then Dan manufactured another "quaint"—a Comstock invention called "Solar armor"—a helmet designed for wear while crossing the hot Forty Mile desert. Within, the headpiece was fitted up with an ammonia-tank, the evaporation of which furnished the cold air to neutralize the effects of heat.

One morning when the temperature registered 117° the inventor donned his helmet, set it in action and started across Forty Mile. When he did not arrive at his destination a relief expedition went after him. They found him seated on a boulder in the desert with icicles hanging from eyes, ears, nose, and mouth—frozen solid to the scorching sands. Due to a defect in the mechanism the man had been refrigerated before he could get the helmet off. The story was told minutely in all "seriousness"—while its sheer absurdity convulsed Washoe. Death, in such picturesque form, was excruciatingly funny to men who spent their time dodging it.

The San Francisco papers chided Dan for his trifling.[14] *The London Times* saw promise in the invention and hoped for its early perfection. Her Majesty's government, in a two-column leader, was invited to equip Tommy Atkins with this Yankee armor for service in India and other British tropics.[15] The sage-brush's tall yarning had penetrated the sacred precincts of Piccadilly! That was something for Sam to dream about.

Then there was the "luminous shrub" that flourished in Tuscarora. All day the mountains were monotonously gray with sage. But at night they burst into ghostly, unearthly effulgence. Botanists were "taken in" and flocked into Washoe to investigate this phosporescent shrub. Such splendor of imagination fascinated Sam.

"Josh" had watched long enough. His apprenticeship was drawing to a close. He had mastered the pattern. The mountain had been a good teacher. Sam had had a fight with a Washoe coroner. He must get even. Using the same devices as the bards of Sun Mountain, Sam drenched them in the freshness of his own imagination and gave the boys "The Petrified Man," a burlesque on prehistoric petrification. A solemn earthy yarn with the motif of death, not the solemn death that they despised but wild exhilarating death with the sting removed.

Scholars came from far and near to look at the marvel "Josh" had created. It was the consensus of opinion that the stone man had attained his present condition three hundred years before. At the inquest the sage-brush coroner was completely "taken in" and declared that "deceased came to his death from protracted exposure." That was a priceless line to the boys! The corpse's hands had petrified— one directly in front of the other, thumb to little finger—thumb to nose—in the immemorial posture of derision. In one fell swoop "Josh" had caught the hilarious mood of Washoe and perpetuated it in stone.[16] While the boys made merry at the expense of the grim guest always hovering near them, the story of the petrified man travelled east and west—State after State, land after land, until it culminated in sublime legitimacy in the August *Lancet*.[17] On the strength of it "Josh" acquired a reputation in Washoe for tall yarns. The boys were proud of him. Along with Dan De Quille and

"Dag," Sun Mountain rated him among her bards. And incidentally Sam got even with a coroner he hated.

Thus *The Enterprise* gave "Josh" a reputation far beyond the confines of Forty Mile. After three false apprenticeships it pointed the way to a goal and boundless contentment.

When at dawn the noise of the presses had ceased "Josh" and Joe, Dan and "Dag"—proprietor and devil, would hie themselves to the beer-cellar in the basement of the office.

What matter though the blasted earth shuddered under their feet? What matter though ceaseless files of ore-wagons rumbled overhead? What matter though shifts came and went? Though "zephyrs" blew and sand drifted? Serenely ensconced about a round-table, with foaming tankards in hand they would spin tall yarns and sing war-songs until the sun came up over the desert and the odor of the sage, strong as incense, assaulted their nostrils.

CHAPTER XXXVIII

MARK TWAIN

December, 1862

That winter when the question of statehood came up in the Territorial Legislature, Joe Goodman sent Sam Clemens to report the proceedings. Well he realized that "Josh" knew nothing about political procedure but his reports, at least, would be interesting.

Among those jovial law-givers "Josh" fitted precisely into the picture. He aligned himself particularly with the Humboldt delegation. Bill Claggett and Jack Simmons, the speaker of the house, were especial cronies.[1] They kept him on the inside of the political machine and in touch with Bill Stewart and his ambitions.

As of its predecessor, Bill was the most notable member of this legislature. Bill was still urging a constitution and a ship of state for Washoe. On the bridge he visualized William M. Stewart as captain. Already he had announced himself as a champion of the miner; already he had gained a tremendous following in the camps of Gold Cañon. Already he had coined the phrase "honest miner." Already he knew the value of a picturesque symbol—how it could appeal to the imagination and sweep men off their feet. On every possible occasion he repeated that phrase, "honest miner." It was a bit of imagery, but as a weapon had possibilities. It could break lesser men, sweep away barriers, carry the ship of state and its captain toward his goal.

It didn't take Sam Clemens long to plumb Bill's ambitions. Almost immediately Sam saw the humor of Bill's "honest miner"— and the humor of his intentions. Forthwith he subjected them both in speech and in the columns of *The Enterprise* to some of his unmerciful buffoonery. "If heaven forsakes the 'poor miner'," said the satirist, "he'll be turned over to Bill Stewart."[2] Washoe liked the joke and roared its appreciation. Bill laughed too. But his laughter had reservations.

Sam's reports on the lawmakers were full of glaring absurdities.

As he knew nothing about parliamentary procedure he slipped into many hilarious pitfalls. *The Virginia City Union* poked fun at them. Sam retaliated by dubbing their reporter, who knew legislative work perfectly, "The Unreliable." His reports, wrote "Josh," were festering masses of misstatements. The Comstock applauded. "Unreliable" the reporter remained to the end of his career, while Washoe grew more and more proud of its humorist who could slay an enemy with a stroke of his pen.

Sam was now an acknowledged legislator. Next to Bill Stewart the most influential member of that body. The members themselves laughed immoderately over his burlesque of their efforts. Before long it was evident that they would rather laugh with Sam than legislate with Bill. With his wit Sam could swing more votes than Bill could win with oratory. He could make or break any bill. Laugh any measure into the ash heap. The majority were with him hand and glove. They might refer to him as that "disreputable, lying, characterless, character-smashing, unscrupulous fiend who reports for *The Territorial Enterprise*,"[3] but they laughed. That is, all except Bill. He hadn't feared bad men. Why quail over this buffoon's wit? And he made up his mind all in good time to take care of Sam.

In the meanwhile Sam grew tired of the name "Josh." As his articles and burlesques were read all over the Coast, he wanted to give them some other identity. He went to Joe. "That name's outgrown," he said; it had become meaningless. It belonged to his adolescence. Now, he was man-sized. He must have a cognomen in proportion to his improved estate. He found one to his liking that harked back to those memorable pilot days on the Mississippi. His report to *The Territorial Enterprise* of February 2, 1863, was signed by it—"Mark Twain."[4] With that report the mountain had produced something more enduring than bullion.

Thus it may be said that in Washoe on February 2, 1863, Mark Twain was born. And gave to belles-lettres a name that is better known than any other in our literature.[5]

When the legislature disbanded, Mark Twain returned to the Comstock to receive the plaudits of the boys. He was now one of the most conspicuous figures on the Mountain. As he walked along "C" Street the boys nudged one another, and pointed him out to strangers. "There goes Mark Twain!" Gone were the stogies, Kentucky jeans, hickory shirt, and the roll of blankets. In their stead had blossomed forth a mirror of fashion—the cynosure of all eyes.

What one of them wouldn't have been Mark Twain—the courted
—the applauded? His shuffling gait had become sprightly. His
black eyes burned with a fierce, bright light. He shared honors with
Bill Stewart, the Ophir, Mexican, Gould & Curry, and that hundred-
stamp mill in Gold Cañon. He was no longer Sam Clemens but
Mark Twain of *The Enterprise*—a bard of Washoe.

By way of expressing their appreciation of their new interpreter,
the boys, in traditional Comstock fashion, got up a party and presented Mark with a bogus meerschaum pipe. Being a jester, it was
thought Mark would appreciate the joke. In all seriousness, the
presentation took place before one of the big bars. Charley Pope,
afterward of Pope's Theatre, St. Louis, made the presentation speech.
Mark Twain was tremendously touched.[6] With tears in his eyes he
accepted the pipe and made an ardent reply. His appreciation
brought a lump to more than one throat. Then he spent every dollar
he had saved in treating them to champagne and sparkling Moselle.

When the boys realized that Mark didn't know a real meerschaum
from a bogus one, when they saw how delighted he was with their
dollar-and-a-half gift, they were filled with chagrin. They had not
the heart to disillusion him. Filled with remorse they did their best
to drown the memory of their joke in the potation their victim was
providing.

A couple of days later Mark discovered their treachery—the meerschaum wouldn't stain—the bowl got hot—the bottom fell out.
When "Dag" said any damn'd fool would know the difference between meerschaum and clay, Mark was cut to the quick. The
thought of Charley Pope's speech, his own fervid response, and the
impoverished state of his pocketbook filled him with mortification.
But to the end of his days, among his choicest possessions he kept
the remains of the old pipe to perpetuate the feelings it had once
inspired. On many a night in the after years he would look upon
it and recall those priceless nights of palship with a feeling of per-
ceptible nostalgia. Sometime later, after his first Washoe lecture,
the boys made up for perpetrating that little joke by presenting
Mark Twain with a bar of silver bullion that had been mined and
milled on Sun Mountain.

Upon this bar in great letters was inscribed "Mark Twain—
Matthew V. 41—Pilgrim."

And when Mark Twain looked up the verse in his Bible he read,
"And whosoever shall compel thee to go a mile, go with him
twain."

"A very appropriate present," said *The Gold Hill News* in commenting upon the occasion, "worthily bestowed, and together with Mark himself, may be considered, by the outside world, specimens of Washoe produce."[7]

CHAPTER XXXIX

FLUSH TIMES

1863

By 1863 Sun Mountain was in budding season and the flush times burst into magnificent flower. "Wildcats" flourished without number. Mines worked full blast. Mills clattered. Furnaces roared. The heavens were smutted with smoke. The earth rocked with subterranean detonations. Streets rocked with traffic. Throngs rocked with tumult. Stacks of bullion poured out of mills and were rushed over the old emigrant road into California coffers. San Francisco had nothing worth boasting of but what she owed to Sun Mountain. The Mountain had restored confidence to the Bay. The Mountain had brought ships back to deserted sea-lanes. The Mountain had given life and buoyancy to long dead streets.[1]

On the Lode the boys sniffed the stars and walked about as if pacing the parapet of a fathomless treasure-house. Their heads were constantly in the clouds—clouds of a silvery lining. Beneath their feet they saw a network of silver strands widening into solid wedges. The soberest-minded were dazzled by the vision. The fancy of the imaginative ran wild. No metaphor could exaggerate the prevailing delirium. It would appear that a silver mist enveloped the slopes of Sun Mountain. The boys moved and breathed in this unnatural atmosphere. Drunk with the vapor, all prudent considerations were laughed to scorn. Timid suggestions of the wisdom of thrift, of the possibility of approaching exhaustion of the ore-deposits were unheeded—unheard. Every one of them who was a large stockholder, or even a small one, in a productive mine, counted himself a "nabob" and scattered his money broadcast like a prince bestowing largesses.[2] Everybody was optimistic. The future was unknown. An infinite range of possibility lay ahead. Who could oppose such confident faith? Every stroke of the pick revealed new, undreamed-of riches. A lucky strike, and the poor boy of yesterday became the wealthy capitalist of today. An unlucky move—but who gave thought? Another turn of the wheel. On the morrow he would retrieve. The boys had become inveterate gamblers. One day

"Lucky" Baldwin was pitched out of the International Hotel for an unpaid board-bill. The next, he was a millionaire and the manager was imploring him to return.

With the development of such mines as the Gould & Curry, the Ophir, Savage, and Yellow Jacket, the yield of rich ores near the surface was so enormous that it might well have distracted heads wiser than those of the men who had them in charge. They didn't stop to think what they would do when the cream was skimmed. They didn't stop to consider that they didn't have the machinery to go to the bottom of the can. The cream was going to last forever. Why worry about the milk? Why worry? Why stint? Why save?

Economy in the presence of fabulous fortune became a senseless sham. Mining superintendents went half-crazy on the subject of new developments. They brought forth plans for disembowelling Sun Mountain, for costly improvements, costly machinery, costly mills. Nothing intoxicates like gold and silver. Every superintendent spent money. Life became a spree of spending. Every superintendent lived in a handsome house. Mansions they called them. Stone and brick or brick and stone. No residences of the period handsomer than those of the Gould & Curry, Savage or Collar superintendents could be found on the Coast. Superintendents were paid enormous salaries. The superintendent of the Gould & Curry received $40,000 a year—one of the highest salaries paid in the United States.[3]

The extravagance of the managers was encouraged by the stockholders. They liked to see the managers of such enormously rich mines as the Gould & Curry, Ophir, Mexican, and Savage, live in accordance with the dignity of their positions. It was their due as representatives of million-dollar concerns. One drove a coach and four, with harness of silver. The stock of his whip, the lamps on his carriage were encrusted in gold. Another mountain magnate on his wedding night introduced champagne into the water-tank. At his bridal feast, taps ran with the choicest of French vintages: Mumms, Pommery, Veuve Cliquot.[4]

Jerry Lynch, who had made millions in the Lady Bryan, had his horses shod with silver shoes. In his mansion bedroom was a walnut bed. The head-board was designed to order and extended from floor to fourteen-foot ceiling.

Park's Mansion in Six Mile was the show place of the mountain. Half a million dollars went into its walls. A fresco painter, a modern Vermeer or de Hoagh, was imported at enormous expense from Europe to capture sunshine and imprison it in paint on a bit of dark stair-landing. More than one man stumbled on the threshold of what looked like a sun-room but proved to be only a well-executed painting where lilacs bloomed in the dooryard and aspens quivered at the gate.

Freehanded as private citizens, they delighted in displaying the resources of Washoe, the wealth and liberality of the companies with which they were connected. The display was in part natural, in accord with the prodigal temper of the time, and partly exaggerated. The Comstock had reached its greatest incandescence.

Besides, such display assured stockholders of the unprecedented value of their stock. It dazzled possible investors. Any psychologist knows the advertising value of outward show. Marble fronts, plate-glass windows, glittering signs, and obese porters in purple and fine linen are not lost on the passer-by. High-mettled horses, coaches, silver-mounted harness, brick mansions, gilt, brocade, lilac, and aspen served a similar purpose on the slopes of Sun Mountain.

But the Sun Peak required no other advertising than her vast production of bullion.

Every day Savage cages brought 200 tons of ore to the surface. Every month Wells Fargo & Company carted $300,000 from Savage vaults to San Francisco markets.[5]

The Gould & Curry employed in its underground workings 675 men. With carpenters, blacksmiths, mill-hands, and lumbermen, 2000 were on the payroll. Every month enough money was dispensed to support a population of 7000.[6] The Gould & Curry became a power on the Comstock. The boys who worked there marched together in every parade, with a silk banner, emblazoned "Gould & Curry" in silver letters, preceding them. "As the Gould & Curry goes—so goes the city,"[7] was the common slogan politically.

In spite of expense and waste, the dividends of the Ophir and Gould & Curry were enormous. Their bullion appeared unfailing. The shareholders were well pleased. They did not care for increased profits through a reduction of expenses, but through augmented production. Alpheus Bull, the president of the Gould & Curry Silver Mining Company, in his high-ceilinged, walnut-panelled offices in San Francisco, received daily calls from jovial stockholders. A lackey in broadcloth and gilt braid was always on hand to dispense imported Cuban Beauties to the smokers or pass silver salvers with decanters to the thirsty. The stockholders disdained examining expense accounts and cared little about the methods of extracting

or milling ore. When they visited Sun Mountain they expected the
same luxurious surroundings they enjoyed in San Francisco. A
coach and four were well in keeping! Terrapin or frogs' legs, champagne and sparkling Moselle, nothing unusual!

The idea of extracting only so much ore as could be carefully
and economically reduced in the mill of the company, appeared
preposterous. If the dividends could be temporarily doubled they
did not care how large a proportion of profits was absorbed by
custom mills or how much metal was lost in tailings.

All they wanted was speed. "Snake it out," was their continuous
exhortation to President Bull. "Snake it out," wrote Bull to the
manager on the Comstock. "Snake it out," said the superintendent
to the shift bosses. "Snake it out," the latter ordered the muckers.
With the result that 48,743 tons of ore were "snaked-out" in 1863
and 64,433 tons in 1864[8]—"snaked out" so rapidly that their million-
dollar mill in Six Mile could not cope with the situation. Fifteen
other mills were requisitioned[9] and $1,000,000 was lost in tailings and
slimes by rapacious haste.

At that the Gould & Curry crushed daily $8000 to $10,000 worth
of quartz and moulded four bullion bricks worth $2500 each, the
proceeds of the previous twenty-four hours.[10]

During this fabulous year the stock in Gould & Curry soared to
$6000 per foot; Ophir reached $4000.[11] Empire sold for $20,000 a
share; Kentuck was a bargain at $22,000. That year the Gould &
Curry produced six millions of dollars.[12] In spite of an expense account amounting to $5,940,297.86, dividends aggregating $2,908,000
were declared during two years. So well pleased were the stockholders they scarcely noticed that expenses absorbed two-thirds of
the output. Bullion turned out at such a rate alarmed statesmen.
Financiers feared the value of silver would fall. No wonder President[13] Alpheus Bull was jovial! Or that stockholders believed in
fairies!

There were 25,000 people now on the Comstock Lode[14]—9000
more in Gold Cañon.[15] Everything they ate, wore, and drank; every
machine, mill, stamp, and piston; every stick, log, and timber; every
pin, tack, and button—all had to come over the Sierra from California. Two hundred miles of magnificent, macadamized highways
connected the mountain with California cities. Every pass had its
devotees—via Placerville, via Downieville, via Donner Lake. The
most popular route was the old emigrant one by Lake Tahoe, Strawberry, and Placerville. Alone, over this one highway, passed 5000

freighters, ore wagons, and mountain schooners, each with eight, ten, and twelve span of mules. Fifteen hundred draught animals, 2000 teamsters and hostlers were employed in trafficking freight. Daily 120 tons of freight passed over the line. Every year the Comstock paid out $12,000,000 for freight and $1,500,000 for tolls.[16]

To handle passengers, the Pioneer Stage Company maintained 12 superb Concord Coaches with 6 horses to the stage. Every day they deposited 100 people in Virginia City. In one year they collected $1,000,000 in fares.[17] They had 600 blooded horses in their stables. Fifty-three aristocratic drivers in linen dusters and lemon-colored gloves to hold the reins.[18] One driver was a woman—her sex undiscovered until death claimed her for its own.

Every day Wells Fargo Express wagons, bristling with guards, rattled down Sun Mountain collecting bullion for California. That year the mines dispatched $20,000,000 in bullion. With all this stimulation San Francisco business boomed as it never had before.[19] That year California gave $1,500,000 to the Sanitary Fund for wounded soldiers—a goodly part of which came from Gold Cañon.

All day long from dawn to dusk this Sierran caravan trailed over the mountain passes in long sinuous files. Bells jangled. Whips cracked. Drivers shouted. Swore. Mules tugged. Snorted. Horses shied. Pranced. Lumber carts creaked. Swayed. Mail coaches rattled down the grades at full speed, threading the slow moving lines which parted to give them swift passage. If by chance any freighter got out of line, it was an all-day job to crowd back again. There were no gaps. Every few miles boasted a hotel or lodging-station. Their yards bustled with life three times a day. Drivers, hostlers, hotel-keepers, passengers, mules, horses, jacks, shared the excitement of the animated scene. All was hustle. Bustle. Frenzy.

The same excitable spirit possessed the drivers. Coaches overturned on the precipitous edges of mountain passes. Passengers and freight went rattling down into appalling gulfs hundreds of feet below. The dead were buried where they died. The maimed were picked up when they fell. The safe-and-sound spoke thanks to Providence. No one complained. It was all part of the Washoe pattern.

One California stage rolled down a 150-foot embankment and plunged into the Truckee River. One man was drowned. Another had his clothes torn off. A score were bruised. The driver was held blameless.[20]

A six-horse Johnson Pass coach, going at break-neck speed, toppled over the brink of a 1000-foot precipice. Coach and horses alighted in the topmost boughs of a tough-limbed Sierra pine. The horses fell through the branches and were dashed to pieces on the boulders below. The passengers clambered down, limb by limb, to the ground and congratulated themselves on their escape. No one censured the coachman.

An enormous grizzly bear disputed right-of-way with a Washoe-bound stage and charged. The lead horses, in sudden terror, reared, and crashed backward upon the coach. The passengers, to save themselves, jumped in every direction. Merely an incident of Sierran travel. In eerie spots, masked bandits armed with long-barrelled shotguns held up the stages, lined up passengers, arms above their heads, and looted pockets, boots, and baggage. No one complained. It was all part of the Comstock adventure.

Once, Jack Davis—slickest of all road-agents—spread Buffalo-robes on the ground and served champagne and hors d'œuvres to beleaguered passengers while his confederates were blowing up the safety-box in the boot of the coach and making a getaway with the loot.

Accidents cost the California Stage Company aplenty. Juries were against them on principle. Every claimant who sued was sure to recover. Every time he had an overturn, one driver made a careful examination of his passengers. For those who were dead he closed the eyes—but those that were mutilated he finished with a king-bolt! "Dead folks don't sue," said he, explaining his methods, "they ain't on it; but maimed people do."[21]

Once Ingraham, a Confederate army officer, held up a bullion-laden stage, bound for California, and relieved it of upwards of $30,000. The money was needed by the Confederate army, he said.

Once the guard wounded one of these hold-up bandits and he fell mortally wounded. Rather than fall into the hands of the law he pointed his "navy" at his own head and shouted: "Dead-eye Dick dies but never surrenders." Then he pressed the trigger.

What with horses and coaches, bullets and bandits, the passage of the Sierra had become an adventurous event.

Wood, needed in such prodigal supply in drift and shaft, also had its romance and adventure. Without wood the Comstock could not have endured from sunrise to sunset. It was needed for everything —everywhere—for building, for fuel, for flumes, for timbering shafts, drifts, and winzes. Yearly $2,500,000 went up in smoke and incense to the great god silver. The Gould & Curry alone buried 6,000,000 feet of timber in her "innerds" and then cried for more. The eastern slope of the Sierra was quickly denuded. The tree-lined shores of Lake Tahoe were raped and pillaged. Grand old mountain monarchs, tens of centuries old, stands of pine, fir, and spruce found graves in the insatiable maw of the Lode. Eighty millions of feet yearly slid down those black, slippery jaws to mould and decay. It took 250,000 cords to keep the funeral pyres in mill and mine burning.[22]

Square box flumes, then the famous V-shaped flumes, filled with Tahoe water, floated this holocaust of forests to the very mouth of Gold Cañon. There ox-teams and bull-whackers took up the burden to the mines and mills on Sun Mountain.

Traffic up and down Gold Cañon grew terrific. Powerful teams of horses, mules, and oxen—eight, ten, twenty to the wagon, made frantic efforts to perform this Herculean freighting task. Up through Dayton, Silver City, Devil's Gate, Gold Hill, a 2000-foot climb to the Lode. A *via crucis*—a Gethsemane—for horse—ox—mule and camel—a pitiable sight it was to see them! Enveloped in dust—smoking hot—reeking with sweat—dripping with liquefied dirt, as they pulled, jerked, groaned, fell back, dashed forward, tumbled down, kicked, plunged, and bit. Then buckled to it again—under galling lash and thong. So lived, so struggled these poor brutes for their daily pittance of barley and hay! If they had souls, did they long for death to blot out the sight of greed?—to obliterate the sound of cracking whip, snaking thong, and anathema?—a sliding scale of oaths, to which swearing in all other parts of the world was as the murmur of a gentle brook to the violent rush and thunder of a cataract.[23]

Gold Cañon, from Carson River to Dayton, up through Silver City, Devil's Gate, Gold Hill to "C" Street, was now one continuous line of sawmills, quartz-mills, tunnels, dumps, sluices, water-wheels, frame shanties, and adobes. The whole Cañon had swelled into metropolitan proportions and was practically a continuation of Virginia City. You couldn't tell where one began and the other left off. The main thoroughfare, cleaving to the old emigrant road, was flanked on both sides by brick stores with iron shutters, hotels, express offices, saloons, restaurants, and groggeries. The very walls of the Cañon were riddled and honeycombed with shafts, tunnels, and dumps. Hoisting houses were perched atop every inaccessible mount, stamp mills lined the banks of every trickling creek.

Through this main artery rushed a strident current of sound—mingling of horse, mule, and ox, hissing of steam, clatter of machinery, and the whine of bullets. While above all soared the shouts of bull-whackers, mule-skinners, and the angry shriek of the Washoe zephyr—an uproar continuous in volume. There was no peace about the deserted sage-covered mound of Hosea Grosch.

Over mountain and vale, cañon and ravine, mine and mill, night and day, hung dense clouds of swirling smoke and alkali—from which continually sifted powdered dust. Doors were littered with it. Floors were sanded with it. Everything you touched gritted with it. It was a component part of the atmosphere[24]—of the view that you surveyed, of the sounds that you heard—all your senses were clogged, veiled, muffled by it. No wonder the boys laughed and laughed! After all, what was life but the quintessence of dust?

On Sun Mountain the battle between man and earth never ceased. Assault went on night and day, foul weather and fine, hour after hour. Assailed with crowbars, gutted with picks, blasted by powder, torn by shell, redoubt after redoubt was taken. Yet the grim old Mountain never gave up. Although machines, like tremendous engines of war, were boring, blasting, ripping, and tearing its vitals to fragments and reducing it to a mere shell, yet it never caved in. Battered and badgered by man and machine the mighty earth counter-charged at every opportunity by smiting, crushing, and mangling its assailants. Not a day passed but one of the boys was torn to pieces, mangled or crushed out of all recognition by caving rocks and falling timbers.

"Come on!" the earth might have shouted. "Dig, delve, pierce, and bore with your picks and shovels and your infernal machines! Wring out of my veins a few globules of my gold and silver; hoard it, spend it, gamble for it, bring perdition to your souls with it—do what you will, puny insects! Sooner or later I will win. The death-blow will smite you. The earth will swallow you! From earth you came—to earth you go again![25] Come on, if you must, but remember—victory is mine."

By 1863, the business part of "C" Street presented the distinguishing features of a great metropolis—a bold, black, iron-faced city, doored and shuttered by great sheets of painted iron. Streets were lighted by gas jets on iron standards. The principal stores, saloons, and hotels were ablaze with illumination. Large and substantial brick houses, four and six stories high, lined the main thoroughfares. Every one of them disported a wide balcony, surrounded by black-painted iron balustrades, providing the walks beneath with a continuous, dark, irregular arcade, providing the second-stories with a gallery upon which French windows opened and iron stands filled with red geraniums stood. Scarlet-skirted fuchsias, baskets of oxalis and wandering-jew hung about. In summer, flame-colored nasturtiums cascaded through black railings. Red-flowering oleanders nodded ragged plumes against the walls and morning-glories clambered over the eaves. Amidst such bleakness the boys had an instinctive craving for something beautiful, for color, for rhythm, for anything to banish the memory of those aborted cedars that twisted their limbs like arms in distress. A little water, a little patting, a little attention bestowed on that black earth and it bloomed like a rose.[26] Already piñons were growing back in the ravines. With glad eyes the Piutes saw them thrive unmolested. "Heap good," they said hungrily.

Everywhere shanties were springing up. Carpenters were sawing, hammering, ripping, nailing. Storekeepers were rolling merchandise in and out of crowded doorways. Chinese fruit venders were trotting about with their fruit-baskets. Piutes were scavengering. Auctioneers, surrounded by eager, gaping crowds of speculators, were shouting off the stocks of delinquent holders. Organ-grinders were grinding out music and torturing consumptive monkeys. Hurdy-gurdy girls were singing bacchanalian songs in bacchanalian resorts. Jew clothiers were selling off prodigious assortments of worthless garments at enormous prices. Bill-stickers were posting flamboyant bills of auctions, theatres, and new saloons. Newsboys were crying city papers with the last telegraphic news. Stages were dashing away with passengers for Esmeralda, Como, Pioche, and Humboldt. Stages were rolling in with passengers from San Francisco. Mule trains were trotting with quicksilver from New Almadin. Camels were stalking through back streets with swaying loads of salt from Walker. The inevitable Wells Fargo & Company Express was distributing letters, packages, papers to the news-hungry multitude amidst tempting piles of silver bricks and wonderful complications of scales, letter-boxes, clerks, account-books, and twenty-dollar pieces. Boys were running hither and yon, half mad with excitement. Wind was swirling. Dust spiralling.

Saloons beckoned in every other building. Magnificent saloons, more gorgeous and gold-fretted than any man's club. Bars of mahogany and ebony, inlaid with brass and ivory, ran their length. Murals by the best California artists adorned the walls. White marble figures filled occasional niches. Above the bar in practically every one hung three framed pictures—Lola Montez, Countess of Lansfeld, in dancing skirts—"Benecia Boy" Heenan in sparring tights— and Adah Isaacs Menken strapped to the back of a black stallion.

Before every cigar-store stood a gaudily painted Indian carved out of wood. Pocahontas held out a handful of fine Havanas. Minnehaha distributed "Yellow-leaf." Black Hawk's long blue pipe reached his wampum belt.

The windows of every drug store were hung with immense goldmounted blue, red, and green decanters.

Back of the main streets were the hoisting works—great sprawling, lifelike monsters with tremendous stacks—like so many long black tentacles—drawing their sustenance from the enormous mammillae of Sun Mountain. How wolverine! How gluttonously they suckled! How they clamped their paws—nuzzled—snorted and spat! The air was fetid with their dank breath, smutted with their respirations.

Above the hoisting works every bluff, cliff, and rocky ledge was besmirched with painted advertisements or plastered with flamboyant posters. Gaudy signs drew the boys' attention to pills, syrups, tonics, water cures, magnetic baths, motorpathic exercises. Well might the Piutes raise wondering eyes to those indecipherable hieroglyphics. But they complained no longer. The piñons were growing. Pah-Ah would protect his red children!

Bill-posters told the boys to drink at the Sazerac, to gamble at the El Dorado, to eat at the Howling Wilderness, to dance at the Melodeon. Sometimes they drew the boys' attention to coming events— to lectures by alumni of Brook Farm; to travelogues, "A Trip to Iceland" by J. Ross Browne; or to Arabia with William Burton; to purveyors of the cancan; to Little Eva's celestial ascension; to "Babes in the Wood"; to the "Wild Horse of Tartary." Ah! That was a poster of infinite desire! A white woman—naked to a pitiless storm, strapped to the back of a black snorting stallion, plunging up a dark mountain at a furious speed—that poster made hearts beat faster!

In the middle of the day it was impossible to cross the principal thoroughfares, blocked as they were from dawn to dusk with freighters and pack trains. The embryo of the wild west shows was in those arterials—lassooing, and cavorting mustangs—bareback and trick riding—frequent conflagrations—thrilling rescues—fire-companies spraying one another with high-pressured hose—charging one another in mimic warfare with Roman candles—shooting one another when hose-carts became entangled—threatening to hang one another.

In another ring were prize-fighters, stripped to the waist—mauling—breaking noses—cutting lips. With adverse decisions the firing begins. Five men fall fatally shot. Among them "Muchaco," owner of the Mexican, dies in the street. Two days later at his immense funeral, two bands are playing funeral dirges with tremendous gusto —the procession is boiling over with virility![28] Rank melodrama; slap-stick comedy. Harlequin and Thespis—arm in arm on every balcony—at every corner—waiting—seeking.

Under main city streets, in gloomy candle-lit subterranean galleries the same drama of existence goes on. Rival companies fight for ledges like wolves for a bone. Angry eyes glitter. Lips show their fangs. Throats snarl. Knives flourish. Guns and pick-axes are wielded with deadly intent. Poisonous gases are freed. Dynamite explodes with demoniacal intention. Life on Sun Mountain, like the opera "Aida," was played on two stages, one above the other— played with the gusto and speed of the cinema reel. Swift-moving tableaux of life and death. Increasing tempo—mounting crescendo. It was hard to distinguish tragedy from comedy. The picture was often a blur. It would have had to be a sound-reel to have recorded a moment of Comstock life at the flood—to have caught the shudders and tremors of the earth—the crash of stamps—the thunder of machinery—the hiss of steam—the roll and surge of crowds—their shouts and groans, sobs and laughter. Even then it, too, would have been a confused blur.

CHAPTER XL

THE ROWDY FUND

One night, soon after a real theatre with a drop-curtain had come to Washoe, two of her most prominent citizens, conspicuous for their success in the mining world, swaggered down the main aisle armed with six-shooters and bowie knives. To the terror and consternation of the audience they ordered the curtain dropped. When their command was not instantly obeyed, they made a rush for the stage. The actors fled in dismay. The curtain fell with a bang. Whereupon the "conquerors" proceeded to reduce it to ribbons with their knives. While the audience fled to the exits, the swashbucklers turned their attention to the scenery and stage-setting. In no time at all the place was wrecked.

Right there in the midst of ruin the outraged muse asserted herself. So ashamed were those two boys of this drunken escapade, done on a bar-room wager, that they immediately paid into the town's account a thousand dollars for the benefit of a common school. On the strength of this "Rowdy Fund," as it was called, a teacher was imported. Thus reading, writing, and arithmetic came to Washoe on the blade of a bowie.[1]

A neighboring camp caught the school infection. On a hilarious May night in a crowded bar-room the boys put up a pair of boots of enormous size which belonged to one of their number noted for his big feet. Whatever was raised on those shoes, it was announced, would be devoted to education. The gesture was a huge success. The boots sold and resold until the year's salary of a schoolmaster was guaranteed.

Thus, boys who had never been on the inside of a school-room prepared to wrestle with their A B C's.

And Harry Floty was engaged to be the first teacher. Harry was a university man and had been a schoolmaster in "the States." For two years he had devoted himself to prospecting, only to discover that he was not cut out to be a miner. Se he decided to leave off digging and take advantage of the new opening. He was a pale, slender, scholarly-looking youth. When he presented himself the president of the recently organized board of trustees looked him over sorrowfully.

"You may be book-learned," he said, "but it takes more than books to teach school in Washoe." And he looked over the desolate hills in the direction of that part of town where Sam Brown had maintained his private burial-ground. "The last teacher sleeps in yonder graveyard," he said by way of encouragement. "The last one before him left an eye and one arm to show his incapacity, and the three before him ran away with only four eyes and five legs between them. Our boys don't stand no nonsense. You have to be a man to teach in Washoe."

"Let me try," replied Harry mildly. "I'm weak-looking, I know, but I have a will. I'll open school next Monday at 9 A.M."

At eight, Harry went down to the school-house, with the key in one hand and a valise in the other.

The scholars, many of whom hailed from "Pike" and were bigger than Harry, were loafing around the school-yard in little groups to see what chance the new schoolmaster had of teaching them anything.

"Ready to run if he finds we are too much for him," whispered a big, bow-legged, cross-eyed bully, looking at the valise.

The new teacher, gazing pensively at the adjacent graveyard, opened the valise, took out three navy "sixes" and a long bowie-knife, whetted the latter on the leg of one boot, cocked one of the "sixes," and then said sweetly:

"Ring the bell, boy, and we'll have prayers."

The big bully, whom he addressed, slunk away and pulled the bell-rope.

"Now we'll arrange the classes," said the schoolmaster, as he toyed with the cocked navy-gun and walked down the room.

One after another the boys were examined and assigned to classes. Then the first unit was summoned to recite in geography. A whisper was heard. Quick as light the teacher wheeled and covered the offender with a deadly aim.

"Don't do that again," he said mildly. "I never give a second warning."

Recess time came. The "youngsters" went out on the playground visibly cowed. There was a new "Chief" in Washoe. A schoolmaster was a "Chief"! What was Sun Mountain coming to!

One of the boys threw a ball into the air. Before it started to descend the new teacher raised his revolver. Ping! The bullet pierced the ball.[2] Even a university man could speak the language of the country.

Thus education began in the sage.

CHAPTER XLI

ST. MARY'S SILVER BELL

By the summer of 1860 the Catholics gave up the tunnel chapel and constructed one of wood on the tawny rocks of the Divide—between Virginia and Gold Hill—at the cross roads of the winds. But the good father who built it did not know his Washoe, nor how playful the "zephyr" could be with religious edifices of every denomination. Consequently the chapel fell an early victim of a wayward "zephyr."

With praiseworthy zeal the Catholics went down on the Carson and selected a site along the river. An imposing chapel arose upon its banks. It was no sooner finished than along came another "zephyr" and demolished it. To make bad matters worse, those who had claims for wages against the church carried off the lumber. But the good father, Patrick Manogue, when he arrived, was not discouraged. Find him a rock and he would build the steps and preach the gospel of St. Mark.[1]

On the corner of "E" and Taylor Streets, Father Manogue erected a handsome Gothic structure. The marble altar came from Carrara. The Stations of the Cross were painted in Florence, from money which John Mackay made in Kentuck.

In the lofty belfry swung a silver bell—cast in Spain from bullion from The Lady Bryan in Six Mile—a mine out of which Jerry Lynch took $2,000,000. The good father called the church "Saint Mary of the Mountain." On Sunday the music of that silver-tongued bell brought many of the boys to their knees. They might shoot and kill and gamble for that white metal—but its call from a church tower awakened the better angels of their natures.

Then the Methodist-Episcopalians had a try. Their first revivals were held in a blacksmith shop. Finally at the corner of "D" and Taylor Streets they erected a superb brick edifice costing $45,000. Every brick was hauled over the Sierra from California. The church was no sooner dedicated than another playful "zephyr" demolished it. Not to be discouraged, the Methodists cleared away the debris and reset the brick. Then a fire broke out and the interior was destroyed. Any one of weaker fiber than a curate would have seen plainly enough that Washoe did not want anything to do with churches. But the minister seemed to think the trouble lay in the bricks. They were too fixed in principle for Sun Mountain. So he sold the baked clay and erected a wooden structure—more elastic, he said. Incredible as it may seem, on Christmas Eve the Washoe zephyr worked itself into a fury, burst through the church door, took the walls in its grasp, and shook down every whit of plaster from the laths.

When the Reverend Franklin Rising—"the pale, fragile, fledgling" —arrived he knew all about the zephyr—the enemy of the temple.[2] After leaving his brother's court-room he decided on doing missionary work in a Gold Hill theatre. Now it happened that in another part of the same building a gambling game was in progress night and day. The sports complained. The Reverend Rising's fervid psalms and supplications grossly interfered with the calls of their croupier.

They delivered their ultimatum to the manager: "One of us has to quit. These things don't run together."[3]

So the Reverend Rising was given notice. He decided to give his next Sunday sermon in Chrysopolis Hall near Devil's Gate.

Walls were hung with white muslin. A round table served as altar. Two common candles, inserted in the necks of a couple of empty beer-bottles, shed a dim religious light upon the Sabbath's proceedings. The wind blew through the chinks of the walls. The muslin trimmings ballooned into the room like fluttering wings of angels. The smoke from the flickering candles drifted into the Reverend Rising's face, choking him and halting the services. But so successful were his ministrations right in the very shadow of Devil's Gate, that he soon gathered about him a flock of the faithful. A church was erected. But it was the same old story over again. Came the zephyr—fearful, angry zephyr—wind—rain—snow—howling—moaning—ripping. It was more than a church, even a white-muslin one, could stand. On Saturday night, November the 13th, after severe buffeting, it collapsed.[4] Undismayed, the minister set to work again. He was determined to have a church right there at Devil's Gate. If any place needed redemption it was Devil's Gate. By Christmas Day he had erected a new altar—the Church of the Ascension. The Gate rang with the very fierceness of his Te Deum. Before he left the mountain he laid the foundations of two other churchly edifices upon its slopes, Saint John the Divine in

Gold Hill, Saint Paul's in Virginia. Then came a bishop—O. W. Whitaker from New Jersey——

The mountain might be a difficult place for religion to get a footing; but when it came time for those who directed faro banks or dealt "out of hand" to die, their pals were loud in their demands for the offices of the church and a "good send-off."

They wanted the remains of the backslider taken to church—a hymn or two and a funeral sermon.

Once the pillar of a Washoe community died and his obsequies were posted for the very day the first train was scheduled to go through Washoe. The train was not expected until four o'clock so the funeral was planned for two o'clock.

The bell had tolled. The church was full of the friends of the deceased. The coffin rested on a catafalque before the pulpit. Pall-bearers and pals were grouped about the bier. The choir had just finished singing "Nearer, My God, to Thee." The minister stepped into the pulpit to say a few solemn words of hope and farewell to the pals.

Suddenly the church doors burst open. "Here she comes!" shouted a voice. "The fast train's coming!" There was a general stampede. Everybody left the church, friends, pall-bearers, mourners—even the sexton. No one was left but the corpse in the casket and the minister in the pulpit. As the last mourner bolted through the door the clergyman glanced down at the coffin. For a moment he feared that he detected a movement on the part of the corpse as though it too strove to go.[5]

CHAPTER XLII

REVEREND GROSCH SUES

1863

In the fall of that memorable year, the Reverend A. B. Grosch, the father of the discoverers of silver on Sun Mountain, together with those men who had bought stock in their claims, threw Washoe into consternation by bringing suit to recover their property. Their claims, swore the contestants, embraced the richest portion of the ledge including the holdings of the Gould & Curry, Ophir, and Mexican companies. With a nominal capital of $5,000,000, afterward increased to $10,000,000, they incorporated the Grosch Gold & Silver Mining Company. They hired the best counsel obtainable, and well-known citizens of San Francisco consented to act as trustees.

There were many in Gold Cañon who still remembered the boys and knew exactly where their claims had been. Among them Laura Ellis was subpœnaed as a witness. Hadn't Allen pointed out to her the exact spot where his richest claims lay? Hadn't she seen the book in which he had filed his notices? She was able to point out their locations. The Ophir and Gould & Curry and Mexican had sunk shafts on their ledges. She had promised to loan them $1500 to develop these. She was a valuable witness for the Grosch Company. Eilley Orrum remembered the boys' claims and Sandy Bowers, too. It was no more than right, said Eilley, that their old father should benefit from the rich discoveries of his sons.

But the Grosch suit amused Joe Goodman hugely. He affirmed that no one had any idea where the boys' claims lay. Not even "Old Pancake" had known. That fact was enough for *The Enterprise*. As the boys had been very secretive over their discovery, their father must pay the price of their secretiveness. His was a moral claim not a physical one and moral ones were not collectible.

To Joe Goodman the Grosch suit appeared so absurd that he burst into nursery rhymes over it. It encouraged him to believe, he said, that future generations of Washoe infants would be delighted with ballads just as ridiculous. These nonsensical jingles were printed in

The Enterprise and copied by exchanges up and down the Coast. In them Joe represented Washoe babies singing with infantile joy:

"Who owns the Comstock?
We, say the Grosches,
So loud and ferocious,
We own the Comstock.

"What is your title?
Shameless audacity,
Fraud and rapacity:
That is our title."

With change of meter he continued the metrical argument:

"The Ophir, on the Comstock,
Was rich as bread and honey.
The Gould & Curry further south
Was raking out the money.

"The Savage and the others
Had machinery all complete
When in came the Grosches[1]
And nipped all our feet."

These verses were received hilariously in Washoe. But neither the Gould & Curry nor the Ophir saw any humor in this poetry, no matter how nonsensical. Already they were inundated by suits. Each of them had from nine to seventeen suits to defend. Fifty millions were at stake. Fortunes had been squandered in protecting their titles. Ten millions had been distributed among rapacious lawyers.

But they need not have worried. Moral claims like that of the old father of the Grosch boys had but little chance with a man like Judge Turner on the bench. When he began his suit the Reverend Grosch hadn't the least conception of the devious ways of Washoe jurisprudence—that chicanery won more suits than learning, and corruption more than real merit.[2] He didn't known that George Turner had developed into the most mercenary man in Washoe.[3]

By 1863 Judge Turner was playing the legal game in a regal way. Through his broker, a near relative, he would notify litigants what a favorable decision would cost. In the first skirmish of the famous Challor-Potosi trial he demanded $60,000 and got it.

Occasionaly circumstance would not admit of an intermediary

and Judge Turner had to attend to the business on his own hook. But that was exceptional.

One day, one of the boys, who was interested in a case before the Supreme Court, was notified by Judge Turner that his decision would depend upon $10,000 being delivered to him before the next morning. Ten thousand dollars! And it was already night. The man was in a predicament. Banks were closed—but $10,000 or no decision! He got busy. At that hour such an amount of money could only be obtained in gold coin from some gambling den. As that amount of gold would weigh 40 to 50 pounds, the man brought a thick burlap sack, procured the gold and around midnight, with the sack swung over his back, turned his steps toward the Judge's hotel. The sack was so heavy that he bent under its weight. Around one o'clock in the morning, he staggered with the sack before Judge Turner's bedroom door. He knocked. A light shone through the transom. The door was softly opened. Mrs. Turner, clad only in the sheerest of nightgowns, stood before him.

"Is the Judge in?" he asked.

"Yes, but he's asleep," she whispered.

"I have brought that money."

"I will receive it."

The gentleman produced the ponderous sack. Upon seeing it, Mrs. Turner, woman-like, gathered up her nightgown as she would have gathered up her apron. The gentleman opened up his sack and poured the glittering contents into the improvised receptacle. The weight of the gold tore the nightgown completely off Mrs. Turner and left her standing nude with gold pieces scattered at her feet.[4]

The story got out. It travelled up and down Gold Cañon. *The Enterprise* and Bill Stewart were now in full cry against such a venal official. Joe Goodman scored Judge Turner in scathing editorials but "His Honor" went merrily on.

To accord with these judges—a bar more unscrupulous, had never darkened the portals of any metropolitan Temple of Justice than the one that flocked, like Moslems toward Mecca, to Washoe. Money had become so plentiful that moral restraints were loosened or altogether untied. Unprincipled men were ready to violate, for a consideration, the oath of a witness or the solemn obligations of a juror. The courts became a battle-ground of theft, bribery, and subornation. Thus it was that Washoe developed her second proverb. "An honest man was a ——— who would stay bought."

Under these circumstances the Reverend Grosch saw the futility of trying to recover anything from the discoveries of his sons. On the advice of counsel the suit was given up.

Down in Gold Cañon the sage grew rank over Hosea's deserted grave as if trying to obliterate every trace of the discoverer of all of Washoe's riches. Nor could there have been any quiet in that tomb. With clattering stamps and shrieking whistles on the surface, and dynamiting below ground, what peace could enshroud its tenant?

CHAPTER XLIII

VIRGINIA ORGANIZES

1863

In the meantime, Virginia went about getting her town government in operation. But those petty officials could not remember that they had grown up. They carried out their duties as if they were still boys and only playing at government, instead of really running one.

When the sheriff summoned his first jury he found only those with squint-eyes eligible. The lawyers went almost insane trying to get their attention. The next time the sheriff filled the jury with the fattest men in Storey County. For a whole week the box ran over with oleaginous material. Prospectors came into town from miles around just to see the sight and laugh. Next the sheriff filled the jury with the tallest, thinnest men in the country. The boys called it the "long jury." It gave them another laugh. But when he planned to assemble the handsomest jury Washoe could produce the court interfered.

Then the boys began to note that President Lincoln was taking an interest in Washoe. For what reason? No one guessed. Aside from their bullion what had they to offer a man as worried as Abraham Lincoln? Some suggested that the President needed bullion to carry on the war. That was it! The North and South could give blood and nerve and courage. But they couldn't give the stuff that sustains them. Endurance was going to win this struggle. And Sun Mountain could supply plenty of that stuff. That was why President Lincoln was looking to their mountain. Also they marked that the President had never condemned them for raising that Confederate flag. Rather the President had praised them for inaugurating civil government in a territory in which treason existed. Also they noted that the President kept on urging Congress to advertise the resources of Sun Mountain so as to encourage settlers into going to the new territory. Sometimes he even hinted at the early possibility of organizing Washoe into a State. For what reasons? the boys asked. Aside from her riches not one of them could surmise.

But that interest of President Lincoln appealed to soaring ambitions. Such tall talk went hand in hand with flush times. With robes of state sweeping the desert how magnificent their mountain would be! The boys knew. Every one else knew. Practically the whole population of the territory was centred in Washoe. There were a few mushroom camps off in the Toiyabe Mountains but they were negligible. Most of Bill Stewart's counties were still void of men. Think of a mountain becoming a State! The idea intrigued the boys. Its very unusualness appealed to minds flushed with the times.

Boys, that back in 1859 could speak grandiloquently of a handful of huts as a city, did not have to stretch their imaginations when they began to agitate statehood for Sun Mountain! In four years they had created in Washoe a civilization similar to the one they had left in "the States." Now they wanted statehood to crown their efforts. Besides, the territorial machine could not cope with property of the value of their mines and George Turner and his judiciary were not big enough to fill their niche. Their smallness had made them corrupt. The boys wanted big—honest—men like Washoe's mountains.

At the general election, in the fall of 1863, the boys showed by an overwhelming majority that they were for a State constitution. So strong an indication of popular sentiment inspired Bill Stewart with confidence. It meant that the instrument he had already prepared would be accepted. Accordingly his best efforts went forth to create a constitution which would meet with favor with the boys. One which, at the same time, would serve his own political purposes. For Bill was determined to be Washoe's first United States Senator. He electioneered up and down Gold Cañon, never missing an opportunity to drive home his interest in the "honest miner," in his shafts and drifts and bedrock tunnels. There were any number of the boys who were politically minded and wanted to be State senators. But with the "honest miners" behind him, Bill felt pretty sure of his future. The election would take place in January, 1864. Bill thought he saw his ambition about to be achieved.

CHAPTER XLIV

BULLETS AND POETRY

July 2, 1863

The opening night of Maguire's New Opera House, on "D" Street,[1] was a great occasion in Washoe. The theatre was densely packed to the doors. There was hardly room to move.[2] Even the aisles were jammed with boys. They whistled, shouted, and stamped, so anxious were they for the curtain to go up. There was no doubt about it. Better things were dawning on Sun Mountain—schools—churches—libraries—and now a real theatre! Washoe was taming down. Her wild ways were a part of the past. The frontier was moving eastward into the Snake River and Bitter Root country. Many of the roughs were moving with it. They were complaining about the schools, churches, libraries, and theatres. Always on their heels, they said, came the vigilantes. The boys were jubilant. They sat back in their seats and looked about. Sawdust was gone. There were carpets on the floor.

Maguire's had just been completed—a gorgeous affair for a mining camp. The curtain alone was a work of art—Lake Tahoe from the summit of the Sierra—a glowing sapphire surrounded by emerald trees.

The stage was enormous. And there were footlights, gas ones, in green cabbage-leaf sconces, along its entire length. On either side of the stage were boxes—a double tier of them—elegantly equipped in scarlet brocade, gilt chairs, and velvet railings. The pit was wider and longer than Maguire's in San Francisco.[3] By 1863, next to San Francisco, the Comstock was the most important town on the Coast. So why shouldn't the boys have the best there was to be had? Maguire gave them unstintedly in the new theatre. It was entirely lighted by gas. Glittering crystal chandeliers, dripping with pendants, hung from the ceiling. Off the foyer were billiard parlors, cigar-stand, smoking-rooms, a mahogany bar inlaid with ivory, and green-covered gaming-tables. For the "tiger" must have a sumptuous place to prowl by night as well as by day.[4] The boys were delighted that there was no handsomer theatre in San Francisco—Virginia prided herself on equalling the city.

239

Just as it was time for the curtain to go up, Wasnoe reared her wild head and growled in another frontier gesture. Without prelude, Howard, a notorious gunman, whipped out his big "navy" and began firing at another rough-neck named Jack McNab, who was seated in the same circle but on the opposite side of the house. Howard's bullets were well trained. Instantly the boxes emptied themselves. There was a rush from the vicinity of McNab, who sat with his hands up, signifying he was unarmed.

"An' you call yourself a sport," yelled Howard, "agoin' around without a gun on? Go heel yourself, 'cause I'm goin' to git you on sight." [5]

McNab obeyed the order. He couldn't escape up the aisle, so he vaulted the footlights and disappeared behind the curtain, dropping his knife in the trunk of an astonished actor as he fled! [6]

Except for temporarily emptied boxes and a few damaged seats around where McNab had been sitting there were no other outward signs of the prelusory shooting. As much as they hated it, the boys were used to it. Comedy and tragedy were a part of Washoe's daily life. So intimately were they woven into the pattern that it was often impossible to tell where one began and the other left off.

Excitement over, the boys settled back to enjoy Bulwer's comedy "Money," with Julia Dean Hayne and Walter Leman in the leading rôles. The play was a tender reminiscence for many of them. They knew the lines almost by heart. Hadn't they cut their adolescent teeth on them? It had been a favorite comedy of the good old days in California. Besides, Julia Dean Hayne was the quintessence of a lovely heroine—a symbol of the youth they had left in "the States."

That night she was more legendary than ever as she stepped before the footlights to read the salutation which Walter Leman had composed to celebrate this very night—the opening of a temple of the Muses on Sun Mountain. Her voice was sweet with tender music as it rang out with the opening lines: [7]

> "Where the Sierra's rugged mountains show
> Their peaks aloft—amid the drifted snow,
> Skirting the vale, where Carson's placid stream
> Flows onward to the desert . . . . "

Julia Dean had hardly finished reading the verses before a hellish zephyr swept down the Cañon in all its fury. Stones rattled rat-a-tat-tat upon the tin roof. Pebbles crashed against windows with a noise like the crack of artillery. Maguire's New Opera House rocked and creaked in the tempest like a ship in a typhoon. Julia Dean, transfixed with horror, stood with her hands pressed to her bosom. Even the boys were agitated and jumped to their feet. It looked, for a while, as though the opening and closing of Maguire's would occur on one and the same evening.

Swiftly as it had come the zephyr swirled away. Again the boys quieted down and the play proceeded. Maguire had produced "Money" with a splendor to accord with the flush times.

The play over, the actors turned to gambling-tables but Walter Leman decided to go straight to his room at Wimmer's Virginia Hotel.[9] If Jacob Wimmer had not been an old San Francisco friend, Walter Leman told himself, he never would have gone to such a place. It was continual bedlam there. The room Jake had set aside for him was directly over the ground-floor saloon—noisy—distracting. He could hardly sleep, let alone rest in that room. Far into every night he could hear angry voices below disputing. At times there was scuffling and fighting. It seemed to be a favorite rendezvous for all those with the bitterest antagonisms. By the summer of '63 feelings between Yankees and Secessionists were stretched to the breaking-point.

The rebels were still in the saddle—had been ever since Bull Run. For two years the Yankees had been struggling to take Richmond. McClellan and Rosecrans had been sacrificed in the attempt. Grant was floundering through fever-laden Yazoo swamps. Unless he could do something drastic, he, too, was doomed. "Fighting Joe" Hooker had been defeated at Chancellorsville. The North was at its lowest ebb. After two years of desperate struggle the only trophies Yankeedom had to show were defeat, debt, taxation, and sepulchres.[10] The Comstock Yankees had grown very sensitive over the situation—sensitive as their hair-triggers. The Rebels grew more cocky with every victory. Washoe's spirit of loyalty had never been so faint. Tom Peasley said his back was against the wall. The fireboys wouldn't stand any more "secesh" crowing.

Wimmer's had developed into the battle-ground of these rival factions. Nightly, about Jake's bar the issues of North and South were waged. Indiscreet words were often followed by sharp reports. Dawn never cooled their ardor, nor cold lead their blood. No wonder poor old Walter Leman couldn't sleep, couldn't think in such a room.

One night just as Leman was entering Wimmer's, he met one of his Rebel admirers.

"Leman, old boy," called the Southerner, "I'm sorry to hurt your feelings, but we've got great news from Vicksburg. Pemberton has knocked hell's bells out of Grant's wheel-horses." [10]

Leman, an intense Unionist, went to his room greatly perturbed. That night pandemonium reigned in the bar-room below. Grant was defeated! What next!

Five days later the glorious news of the fall of Vicksburg reached Washoe. Leman was elated. At last, a Yankee victory! That was something to crow about. After the play that night he lay in wait for his Rebel friend. When they met, Leman said quietly, "I'm sorry to hurt your feelings, old boy, but we've got great news from Vicksburg. Grant has knocked hell's bells out of Pemberton's wheel-horses." [11] Then up the stairs he went to his own room. That would be a terrible night in the bar-room—a sleepless night in his bedroom.

He was right. The fall of Vicksburg caused a frightful commotion in Wimmer's bar. The Rebels were unaccustomed to defeat. They didn't like it. Bitterest antagonisms were unleashed. The Yankees gave no quarter—bullying—hectoring.

Leman tried to shut out the noise but no door in his room could subdue the angry voices from below. Might just as well try to sleep in the bar-room, he complained. The commotion was beyond anything he had known before!

He sat down on the edge of his bed, elbows on his knees, chin cupped in his hands, and listened. Scraps of conversation floated up to him: "The flower of the South—," "Picket—Armistead—," "Gettysburg was a great Confederate victory—," "Like hell it was." "Lee was too smart for the Yankee . . . Retreated." "Hell!"

Smiling, Leman leaned forward to untie his shoe. A gun exploded below. He jumped. Back he threw himself on the bed—too late. Up through the floor a bullet had whined—had grazed his ear, carried away a lock of his gray hair, and buried itself in the ceiling above. [12]

CHAPTER XLV

THE FLAG IN THE SKY

July 30, 1863

"A storm is brewing," said the Washoe weather prophet that July morning as he gazed skyward at the thick gray cloud that capped the summit of Sun Mountain. In that benign region a storm in summer-time was practically unknown. The boys gathered in groups on the street corners and gazed upwards.[1] They could not see the granite peak, nor could they espy the flag that always floated, night and day, from the iron flag-staff. It was the only summer day in Washoe that they could recall when they had not been able to discern the flag flying over them. It worried them.

"Is the flag still there?" queried one of another. "Or has some damned traitor pulled it down?"

The thick gray cloud so effectually blotted out everything on the mountain that they were filled with foreboding. Was there bad news? Had Grant met disaster? Had Lee turned retreat into victory?

Like all miners, the boys were a superstitious lot. Signs and portents played dominant rôles in their lives. They had no use for the number "13." They never started anywhere or anything new on Friday! They distrusted opals! Broken mirrors! On a July day, they didn't like to have the flag blotted out. It was a bad omen. Something had gone wrong.

Across the desert, to the east, the boys could see cloud banks massed against the horizon. Off and on, during the day they took note of them. They lay there like a squadron of gray horsemen, ready to be called into action.

At every shift or change, all eyes sought for the flag on the summit. But there was no sign of it—only that column of thick gray cloud. At sunset, when the western sky was generally flooded with crimson splendor, the boys noted that every vestige of color had been drained out of the heavens. Only that massive gray cloud.

The sun went down. The Washoe zephyr swept over the Sierra. Sand drifted in from the desert. Every time the boys gazed heavenward their eyes were blinded with alkali-grit. The heavens grew inkier. The squadron clouds rushed in from the desert. Lightning flashed and thunder crashed over the mountain. Clouds grew thicker and blacker. Suddenly, a bolt of lightning ripped the clouds apart. Through the breach shot a shaft of fire, and struck the granite boulders on the peak a thunderous blow, then burst into dazzling light.

"The flag—the flag!" yelled those who gazed skyward. "See the flag!"

Stores, gambling dens, bars, emptied themselves. All eyes were trained on the summit. Every sign of brilliance had faded out of the surrounding heavens, leaving them blacker than pitch. Through the rent clouds—seemingly suspended in the sky—appeared the flag glorified with light. The wind caught the folds—unfurled them— waved them to and fro—until they leapt as though with flames.

It was an unforgettable tableau—a flaming flag suspended in an inky sky. Before their eyes, some remarkable, unexplainable act of nature was taking place on the apex of Sun Mountain. Awed— mystified—the boys stood watching until the streets were wrapped in darkness. Then suddenly as it had appeared, with a rumble like sliding doors, the clouds closed in with a bang. And the flag was blotted out, leaving the mountain shrouded in darkness, the boys hushed into silence.

What did it mean?

A strong believer in signs interpreted their question in the next morning's *Enterprise*. Undoubtedly it was an omen, he wrote. It recalled the light that had flooded the heights of Mount Sinai. It was reminding the boys that their flag would come through the terrible conflict that then engaged it, provided that all of them remained true and loyal to their distracted country. Sun Mountain was giving the boys a lesson. Were they ready to receive it? [2]

Their flag, went on their interpreter, had been brought to the direst straits through treachery. The vicissitudes through which it had passed recalled the trials of the chosen ones in the desert. Those people, too, had been brought to a serious pass. Until the "Pillar of Fire" had guided them to the foot of Mount Sinai.

"Take courage, then, ye timid-hearted," concluded their spokesman. "And behold 'the Flag in the Sky.' It betokens that our cause is under the protection of the Great I Am. Remember that that protection is coupled with conditions—faith and loyalty to the country." [3]

On the next Sunday, Father Manogue and the Reverend Rising made the glorified flag the subject of their sermons. For days the boys could talk of nothing but the wordless sermon from the summit of Sun Mountain.

Anna Fitch, a member of that little Bohemian group that lived at 25 North "B" Street, had witnessed the glorification of the flag. It had so inspired her that she rushed from the tableau to her rooms and wrote out "The Flag on Fire."

> "Fire! Fire!
> Fire! Fire!
> Who has set the flag on fire?
> What vile traitor,
> By Creator
> Spurned, thus dare defy despair?
> God of prophecy and power,
> Stay the omen of the hour."[4]

CHAPTER XLVI

SATIRE IN WASHOE

1863

In October, when the Gould & Curry declared their usual monthly dividend of $150 a share and distributed some $720,000 to their stockholders, *The San Francisco Bulletin* came out with a query: "Was the Gould & Curry dividend 'cooked'?" In other words, was it a false dividend for the purpose of inflating the value of their stock, so that the directors could sell out at a comfortable figure and then scramble from under a tumbling concern? A *Bulletin* editor had recently been victimized by such a "wildcat" proposition and was correspondingly suspicious.

But the Gould & Curry directors were very much annoyed over the publicity. They believed that *The Bulletin* was endeavoring to throw suspicion on the great Gould & Curry. Why didn't they attend to their own affairs? The Spring Valley Water Company of San Francisco had recently "cooked" a dividend. Even borrowed money to pay it. When the stock soared, the "big fish" sold out, but thousands of "little fish" were ruined. Why didn't *The Bulletin* direct some attention to that crooked deal instead of throwing mud at a legitimate concern like the Gould & Curry?

The Gould & Curry managers appealed to *The Enterprise.* Couldn't something be done to stop *The Bulletin?* For twenty-four hours Mark Twain cogitated on how he could bring *The San Francisco Bulletin* to a realization of their shortcomings. At the end of that time he had mapped out a scheme. He would ridicule them. The boys loved satire.

Accordingly, on the morning of October 28, 1863, an account of an atrocious murder and suicide, set off by startling headlines, appeared in the columns of *The Enterprise.* One P. Hopkins—Philip Hopkins—all the boys knew him as the proprietor of the Magnolia Saloon, Carson Street opposite the Plaza[1]—had gone stark mad in his log cabin in the dense pine woods which stretched along the foot of Sun Mountain, between Empire City and Dutch Nick's. While out of his head Hopkins had murdered a faithful wife and seven children, clubbed them to death with a wooden billet and chopped them to pieces with a hatchet. After scalping his red-headed wife with a bowie, and cutting his own throat from ear to ear the killer had snatched up his wife's scalp, mounted his mustang, and ridden for Carson. Waving aloft the long red hair from which warm, smoking blood was still dripping, he had dashed headlong through the woods and had fallen, dying, in the doorway of the Magnolia Saloon.

Carson was horrified. A number of the boys, headed by Sheriff Gasherie, had mounted at once and ridden back through the dense forest to Hopkins' house, where a ghastly scene met their gaze. The scalpless corpse of Mrs. Hopkins lay across the threshold. Her skull was split open and the right hand dangled by a tendon from the wrist. Near-by lay the ax with which the dastardly deed had been done. In one of the bedrooms, six of the children were found, one in bed and five others scattered about the floor. All dead. Their brains had been bashed out with a blunt instrument. The children had struggled hard for their lives, as evidenced by articles of clothing and broken furniture strewn about the room. The eldest girl, Mary, in her terror had sought refuge in the garret, as her body was found there frightfully mutilated—the knife with which she had been killed still sticking in her side. Two other daughters, Julia and Emma, aged, respectively, fourteen and seventeen, were found in the kitchen, bruised and insensible. When revived, they stated that their father had knocked them down with a piece of wood and then had stamped upon them with hobnail shoes.

It was a frightful description of blood and carnage. *The Enterprise* went on to say that Hopkins had been a heavy investor in Gould & Curry stock but that when *The San Francisco Bulletin* exposed the fact that the company were "cooking" dividends in order to bolster up their stocks, he grew afraid and sold out his entire holding although it was paying well at the time. Shortly after when a family friend, an editor of *The Bulletin,* had advised him to invest all his money in San Francisco Spring Valley Water Company stock, he had done so. But when Spring Valley began to "cook" their dividends and the springs dried up and their stock went down to nothing Hopkins had lost his fortune. This misfortune had driven him mad. In an insane fury he had murdered his wife and seven of his little children, and then committed suicide.

The description of this atrocious crime caused a frightful commotion in Washoe. All the boys knew Hopkins, the genial proprietor of the Magnolia Saloon—one of their favorite resorts. After they had read what he had done they felt nauseated, and left the breakfast-table, food untouched.

In their excitement over the gory details they completely forgot that Hopkins was a bachelor; that there wasn't a red-headed woman in Washoe; nor a family of nine children within miles; that there was no dense forest about bleak, sage-clad Empire; that that city and Dutch Nick's were one and the same place. Everything was forgotten but the bloody details of the murder.

That morning there was no work done. The boys gathered on corners, in the middle of the street, to discuss the matter. The editor of *The Gold Hill News* was shocked into getting out an extra and reprinting the details verbatim. Nothing as cruel had ever occurred in the Territory. As for *The San Francisco Bulletin,* as soon as they had received their dispatches, they, too, got out an extra with startling headlines—"Foul Murder in Washoe." None of the exchanges paid the least attention to the cause of the murders; that Hopkins had lost all his money in Spring Valley, that *The Bulletin* had permitted the water company to go on borrowing and "cooking" dividends, that they had done nothing to expose the villainy of the act. As a result, the cunning ones had slipped out of a tottering concern, leaving men like Hopkins to be caught in the crash.

None of the exchanges paid any attention to the moral Mark Twain had tacked to the end of the gory murder: "We hope the fearful massacre detailed above may prove the saddest result of [*The Bulletin's*] silence." If *The Bulletin* or other exchanges had read that, they had found no satire between the lines. For the editors both in San Francisco and in Washoe had been absorbed by the details alone.

The point was so entirely missed and the story had caused such furor that the next day Mark Twain was forced to explain in *The Enterprise* that the Hopkins murders were a grand hoax. "It took a fearful tragedy," he wrote, "to get any truth into a San Francisco paper." [2]

Having filled their columns with accounts of the killings, *The Gold Hill News* failed to see the humor of the situation. On October 29, 1863, they printed a blistering article entitled "That 'Sell' ":

"The horrible story of a *murder* which was yesterday copied in good faith from *The Enterprise* turns out to be a mere 'witticism' of Mark Twain. In short *a lie*—utterly baseless, and without a shadow of foundation. *The Enterprise* is the pioneer newspaper of the

Territory, more widely read and known than any other, and having been ably and respectably conducted has heretofore been considered a reliable medium of information. The terrible tale related in its columns yesterday, and copied into ours, was believed true, and will be believed elsewhere—wherever *The News* and *Enterprise* are read. It will be read with sickening horror, and the already bloody reputation of our Territory will receive another smear. When the readers of the soul-sickening story are informed that it was a mere bubble of 'wit,' they will feel relieved, although they may utterly fail to see the humor or 'the point'!" [3]

Not a word did *The News* have to say about "cooked dividends." They absolutely refused to see any point to Mark's satire.

As for the editors of *The San Francisco Bulletin,* when they read Mark Twain's signed confession—"I take it all back"—they were furious.[4] They wrote to Editor Goodman and demanded that Mark Twain be discharged. They asserted he was utterly unreliable as a reporter. They threatened never to use *The Enterprise* for an exchange as long as he was on the staff. As for "satire," Mark Twain didn't know what the word meant.

As for the boys, they were provoked. Humorists like them didn't relish being "sold." They liked lies with the verisimilitude of truth, but not damn'd lies that ruined their appetites. No one enjoyed a joke better than they did, but there was no point to Mark's "sell," not even a laugh. Forthwith many of them stopped their *Enterprise* subscriptions and took *The Union* instead.

That was the last blow to Mark Twain. He was crestfallen. His hoax had missed fire. His satire had gone astray. He wished he had let "cooked dividends" alone. He had brought contumely on *The Enterprise,* ridicule on his best friend, Joe Goodman. He was so utterly chagrined at the outcome of his lampoon that all confidence in himself was gone. He was a failure at reporting—just as he had been a failure at prospecting—just as he had been a failure in the composing-room—the old complex of failure seized him. He tossed in its throes. His merry quips were missed from the local column.

For days he sat behind the historic pine table of *The Enterprise,* drinking mean whiskey to drown his misery. His enemies on *The Union* and *News,* finding no jokes among the locals, made merry at his expense.

"Cheer up, friend Mark," wrote *The News,* "the courier brings the welcome news that all is quiet at Dutch Nick's; the 'har' on Mrs.

Hopkins' head is coming out like a new 'red' shoe-brush; the murderer has had that gash in his throat caulked and pitched, and the blood in that pine forest is no longer ankle deep. Awake, Mark! Arise and toot your horn if you don't sell a clam." [5]

But Mark was "melancholy."

"He has got the mulligrubs," said a sympathetic exchange. "Where be his jibes, now? His gambols? His flashes of merriment that were wont to set Virginia in a roar? Not one now to mock his grinning? Quite chop-fallen? 'Bully for Shakespeare!' We haven't had a good square joke out of Mark for four or five days." [6]

In response Mark called the editor of *The Bulletin* a "little parson" and an "oyster-brained idiot." *The News,* he said, "were taking advantage of his folly for the purpose of benefiting themselves at the expense of *The Enterprise."* [7] But his epithets brought him scant comfort. Finally, in despair, he went to Joe Goodman.

"I'm going back to Aurora," he announced, "I've not given value received."

Goodman refused to listen to such a proposition.

"About once a week," Mark Twain continued, "I write something worth reading."

"Admitted," replied Goodman, "but that 'something' keeps the boys hunting the columns of *The Enterprise* every day until you hit it right again."

"I'll never make a writer," Mark Twain insisted.

"You're already one," comforted Goodman.

That was a crucial moment in the world of letters. The world owes a debt of gratitude to Goodman, for his ability to infuse hope and courage into the breast of a humorist whose shaft of wit had missed fire.

So Mark Twain stuck to the local department of *The Enterprise* through the sheer force of a man who believed in him heart and soul.[8] On that frontier sheet he had developed the method and form that were going to make him famous. From out of the depths of the mountain's riotous life he would dip an imperishable part of his fame.[9]

CHAPTER XLVII

KINGS OF BONANZA
1863

John Mackay went to work in Kentuck—not for wages—but for "feet," as that stock was held in "feet," not shares. That fall, Kentuck's owners decided to incorporate, but were unable to do so. One large shareholder could not be found. He had been a Rebel. It was surmised he had gone to war and was fighting for the South. The directors offered a liberal bonus to the man who could get the deed for this part of the ground. That offer appealed to John Mackay. If he could get the deed he would have more "feet." Kentuck was a valuable mine. Mackay could tell from the ore. He hadn't been studying hard-rock for nothing.

Mackay disappeared from Sun Mountain. During the summer and autumn no one could locate him.[1] The war was on full tilt. It was believed he had enlisted. Just before Christmas he was back on Sun Mountain with the deed to Kentuck's missing "feet." He would never tell how he had obtained it. It was said he had gone through the Rebel lines at Chattanooga and found his man fighting in the field. That year Kentuck's stock soared—$5000—$10,000—$20,000—$22,000 a share. John Mackay reaped a fortune. In one foot of Kentuck he had attained his ambition of four years before. Mackay shared his good fortune with his pal, Jack O'Brien, but Jack promptly lost his portion in one riotous night at monte.

Now Mackay had all the gold he wanted. But he found after all it wasn't gold he sought—he wanted power. "I do not want to buy things," he said. "I want to move them. I want a lever that will move mountains." In one flight John Mackay's ambitions had soared into the regions beyond Forty Mile.

Sandy Bowers was literally coining money, $10,000 a month was nothing.[2] Silver and gold, like waves out of the sea, poured from his shaft in such torrents that it was with difficulty he kept above the flood. Backed by the occult powers of Eilley Orrum, which enabled her to foresee future events, Sandy absolutely refused to part with his holdings.[3] Some one offered him $400,000. Sandy only laughed. When Eilley saw signs of his weakening she married him, thus joining their twenty feet on Gold Hill in the holy bonds of matrimony. With some $20,000 a month to spend, Eilley now indulged in more occultism than ever. She consulted her peepstone and saw herself a ruler—the Queen of Washoe!

No law in the sage—plenty of boys reverencing woman—there must be a "queen." Didn't her peepstone disclose her in imperial purple? Didn't it show her regally sitting on a golden throne with a sceptre in her hand and the boys bowing in homage before her? She told the boys of the vision. They were thrilled. After that when they met Eilley on a Cañon trail, they swept the alkali with their hats and called her "Your Majesty." In time Eilley began to feel that she was the anointed Queen of Washoe.

Now the boys told her that if she was going to be their "queen" she must have a castle. They helped her select a beautiful site by the shores of Washoe Lake, close up under the shadows of the towering Sierra. And they spoke of marble baths, conservatories with waving palms, statues, birds, flowers, and ivy climbing stone towers. Who ever heard of a "queen" without such things?

In her dreams, Eilley saw them all—marble baths that would eclipse those of Caracalla—halls to rival those of far-sung Tara[4]—fountains that would outsplash those of Versailles—and ivy that would cling tighter than that of Windsor! There was to be nothing like her castle west of Scotland. It would outshine that baronial one that overtowered her humble girlhood home in the Highlands.

Accordingly, contracts were let for a magnificent stone hall—it should excel anything on the Pacific Coast—not a "nabob" on any one of the seven hills of San Francisco would be able to boast of anything so regal. The plans called for an expenditure of half-a-million dollars. But that was a mere bagatelle to a couple like Sandy and Eilley, whose ledges, like South Sea coral reefs, underpinned Gold Hill.

Bull-whackers freighted the marble over the Sierra. Silver door-knobs and silver hinges were hammered out of bullion from their mill at a San Francisco silversmith's. Skylights were to be of Bohemian glass—richly etched—and the windows of plate-glass. In the place where Eilley was wont to preside over soap-suds, emerged an elaborate natatorium. Hot water, from near-by thermal springs, gushed out of the mouths of silver-headed mountain lions. In the library were morocco-bound books—beautifully tooled—in red,

"BOWERS' MANSION," WASHOE VALLEY.

LEMUEL S. BOWERS (1830–1868).   EILLEY ORRUM BOWERS (1816–1903).

Three of the suspected men still in confinement at Aurora.

MARK TWAIN WITH SIMMONS, SPEAKER OF HOUSE OF REPRESENTA-
TIVES, ON ONE SIDE, AND BILLY CLAGGETT, MEMBER OF LEGIS-
LATURE FROM HUMBOLDT COUNTY, ON THE OTHER.

green, blue, gold—all bought by the yard—all Arabic to Sandy, good old Sandy. To the day of his death he could never tell whether the title was upside down or not!

In the reception rooms were a pair of $3000 mirrors that had once graced the foyer of a Venetian palace. Before them Eilley pirouetted in satin furbelows and feathered fans. Over the plate-glass windows Eilley draped lace curtains, each one of which cost $1200. On the walls hung gold-framed paintings whose inspiration had been dipped from the umber and purple and blues of a desert palette.

In the embrasure of a deep window were a dais and a gilded throne embossed with golden fleur-de-lis. Fountains lined with Spanish tile plashed on the lawns. Tropical plants in marble urns unfolded their fronds in the dank atmosphere of glass-covered conservatories. Real canaries warbled in brass-shuttered cages and a scarlet macaw scolded from a chained stand in the shrubbery. Eilley was here— there—everywhere—in the hall receiving her guests—seated on her "throne" accepting their homage. The peepstone had been right. She didn't see, said good old Queen Eilley, how one could get along on less than $100,000 a year.[5] With Washoe Hall completed, the boys told Eilley that the proper thing to do would be to get acquainted with the Queen of England. That all queens should know one another. Being a British subject and still loyal to the crown, Eilley could see that the boys spoke the truth. She would seek out her Britannic majesty—take her a gift of silver, and ask for a few cuttings of English ivy from the walls of Windsor to climb her own castle. Before her departure the boys inveigled Sandy into giving a farewell banquet at the International Hotel.

"Banquet goes," said Sandy. And the whole hotel was engaged for the occasion.

For the many courses every obtainable luxury had been ordered which Virginia City or San Francisco could boast. Champagne ran as free as water in a spring flood. Toasts were drunk to Eilley—to Sandy—to Sun Mountain. In response to "Our Host," Sandy Bowers, impeccable in black broadcloth and diamond shirt studs, arose to respond.

"I've been in this yer country among the first that came here," he said. "I've had powerful good luck. I've got money to throw at the birds. Thar ain't no chance for a gentleman to spend his coin in this yer country and thar ain't nothin' much to see, so me and Mrs. Bowers is agoin' to Yoorop to take in the sights. One of the great men of this country was in this region a while back. That was

Horace Greeley. I saw him and he didn't look like no great shakes. Outside of him the only great men I've seen in this country is Governor Nye and Old Winnemucca. Now me and Mrs. Bowers is goin' to Yoorop to see the Queen of England and the other great men of them countries and I hope you'll all jine in and drink Mrs. Bowers' health. I have plenty of champagne, and money ain't no object."[6]

The boys drank to the health of the "Queen of Washoe."

When the time for their departure approached, the Bowerses drew from the bank a quarter of a million dollars, and later made further drafts to cover extensive foreign purchases.

When they boarded the stage for San Francisco, Sandy and his Queen took with them a massive oak chest filled to the brim with squat bars of bullion from their mine and mill in Gold Cañon. Its contents were valued at many thousands of dollars. Going over the Sierra a special Wells Fargo & Company armed messenger accompanied them to protect the chest from mountain bandits.

At San Francisco, Shreve & Company, the well-known silversmiths, converted the bullion into a magnificently designed dinner service. When Eilley and Sandy sailed for England along with them went the silver packed in the oaken chest.

On a court night, soon after their arrival, Eilley donned three feathers, a veil, and a long court train, and made her courtesy to the Queen. Shortly afterward she presented her Britannic Majesty with the silver that had come from Sun Mountain[8] and obtained the ivy sprigs that would clamber up her Washoe walls.[9]

Eventually the Bowerses were back in Washoe loaded down with European loot for their mansion. "Sandy was never tired of telling the boys about the fine hogs he had seen in England, and the gorgeous sheep he had seen in Spain, and the fine cattle he had noticed in the vicinity of Rome." No man, he said, could imagine what surprising things there were in the world till he had travelled.[10]

If the Bowers' claim was fabulously wealthy, even more so was Joe Plato's ten feet which adjoined Sandy's on the north.

Plato was a superb athlete—a youth of extraordinary physical prowess. Although not a professional, he could outjump, outrun, outhurdle, outwrestle any Olympian on the Comstock.[11] One morning he awoke to the realization that he was in a fair way of becoming enormously rich. His quartz was worth thousands a ton, and he owned a ten-foot ledge of it. At the time that this fact dawned upon him he discovered to his horror that he had only five feet of his claim left. What had he done with the other five feet? Then he remembered! The previous winter he had been in San Francisco. During one glorious bacchanalian night in a gilded palace on Du Pont Street he had given them to a beautiful woman.

"A token of esteem," he had called them.

"For value received," she had replied.[12]

Five feet in a bonanza! Hundreds and hundreds of thousands of dollars—for a night with a trollop! Royal pay for any courtesan! There was nothing left for Plato to do when the remembrance dawned upon him but go to San Francisco as quickly as possible, find the lady before she became the wiser, reclaim his lost feet and get back to Washoe before some rough jumped the remaining ones.

It was winter—a Herculean task to cross the Sierra, but he was equal to it. He seized a horse. Raced down the cañon and over the Placerville grade to California with only one thought—to locate that woman to whom he had given five feet in a bonanza—before she discovered their real value. Luckily he reached San Francisco and found the lady.

But in the meantime the lady had learned considerable about "feet," and the value of Joe Plato's claim. The only way to regain them, she told him, was by way of the altar. Joe was a gallant! He must regain his feet. So he married her.

On their honeymoon Mr. and Mrs. Plato, mounted on donkeys, floundered through snow-drifts to Washoe. All the way back they were beset by one fear—that some one would jump those ten feet. Up Gold Cañon they raced. What a relief to find those ten precious feet tucked, safe and sound, under a blanket of snow!

CHAPTER XLVIII

BABES IN THE WOOD

December, 1863

On a winter's day the boys found a notice tacked to the door of Maguire's Opera House:

Artemus Ward
Will
Speak his piece
Here
Tonight[1]

Artemus Ward, the great wit of the time, was then at the zenith of his fame as a humorous writer and lecturer. He had come to Washoe from New York in response to the dispatch which Maguire had sent by "Pony" back in 1861. The boys remembered how anxious the showman had been to get the jester for an engagement at his projected New Opera House in Virginia. They were still telling the story of that message: "What will you take for a hundred nights?"[2] Maguire had written. "Brandy and Soda," had been the gist of Artemus' laconic reply. It had become a part of Washoe's folklore. They were still laughing over that yarn.

Artemus dealt in just the commodities that would make a hit with Washoe's youth—lawlessness and audacious exaggeration. A sort of national humor that made itself just as much at home on the railroad and canal-boat as it did in the mining camp and bar-room. Before Maguire brought Artemus up the mountain he had figured all that out. Full of local coloring and life in the raw his eccentric humor would be relished just as keenly in Washoe as it had been in "the States."

When the boys read that message tacked on the theatre door there was a rush for tickets. They all wanted to hear what Artemus had to say on "Babes in the Wood."

That night when the curtain went up Artemus did not look as

256

convivial as his reply had led Maguire to expect. The jester came down-stage in black clothes, a handkerchief with a black border pressed to his eyes, his shoulders shaking with sobs. Grief or not, his appearance was the signal for loud and continuous laughter and applause. Feet shuffled in the gallery. Canes were stumped upon the floor. Between sobs Artemus told them what had happened. He had just received a telegram; "The Boy"—"Benecia Boy"—had been defeated again.[3]

These remarks fell from his lips with such an air of profound melancholy that the boys burst into fresh guffaws. From then on Artemus was welcome to walk on their necks if he chose to. They didn't care whether Heenan was defeated or not so long as they had this tall, gaunt, red-headed individual with a Hamletesque expression—graver than the grave—to make them laugh.[4]

Mark Twain, with parted lips, sat in the "printer's pew"—the row of seats, close to the stage, reserved for newspaper men.[5] Then the jester introduced his "Babes." Without reference to title the Babes were a continuous string of grotesque and absurd witticisms —so keen, dry, and far-fetched that for a moment none of the boys could grasp a point. But each time a laugh was due, Artemus considerately paused. With the first guffaw the boys seemed to catch on—laughs broke forth like corn in a popper—scarcely a minute elapsed at the end of which the sedate Artemus was not forced to wait until the roar of mirth had subsided. But there was not a smile on the face of Artemus. Solemn as a judge he went on with his preposterous nonsense and side-splitting jokes—sense, nonsense, and vice versa. The boys could not contain themselves. They just rolled in their stalls and laughed until tears rained down their cheeks. Not all jokes, either. Here and there were shrewd remarks proving that Artemus Ward was a man of reflection as well as a consummate humorist.

Every time the uproar subsided, a sudden, spasmodic "haw, haw, haw," unreserved as if from a burro-corral, would attract all eyes to the "pew." At each interruption Artemus would glare in mock anger at the seat in which Mark Twain sat. "Has it been watered today?" he would ask. Again, when Mark had caught another point—"You must now all admit the truth of the old saw that 'he who laughs last laughs best'!"

Little did Artemus know that that last laugh convulsed a greater genius than himself and that its tardiness was of a piece with Mark Twain's pokey nature—his deliberate, drawling way of speaking;

his half-skipping, half-shambling gait.[6] Little did Artemus realize that his was the match that was lighting a literary torch more brilliant than his own.

And when it came time for Mark Twain to describe his mentor he did it with that personal touch characteristic of him. "Artemus looked like a glove-stretcher," said Mark, "his hair, red, and brushed forward, reminded him of a divided flame. His nose rambled aggressively before his face with all the determination of a cowcatcher, while his red mustache, to follow out the simile, seemed not unlike the unfortunate cow."

Strange as it may seem, it was Artemus Ward, during his Washoe engagement, who first detected in Mark Twain's writings and conversations the indications of a great humorous power and who strongly advised him to seek a better field for his talents than *The Territorial Enterprise.*[7]

Anyway, Artemus gave Mark Twain a jolt. He had never entertained the idea of writing a book until he listened to the "Babes." From then on there ran a vein of wit through Mark Twain's newspaper output that had not been there before. Many of his brightest hits—although entirely original—seemed to have a familiar cast to those who had listened to Artemus. Without doubt, believed many of his friends, that lecture had awakened Mark Twain to a new train of thought. As a genius, he had been dreaming until Artemus Ward came to Washoe and aroused him to his possibilities.[8]

The boys received Artemus as a brother. They took great pains to give him an elaborate introduction to Washoe's wild ways. Artemus had intended to stay only a few days. But caught in the mad whirl of the Comstock maelstrom he lingered for three orgiastic weeks. *The Enterprise* office became his headquarters. Every time he budged beyond its portals there was a crowd waiting at the door to show him the sights. His rounds became one continuous uproar. Many of the boys laid off work while his visit lasted. As Artemus was anxious to learn the Washoe lingo for future lecture material, the boys made him acquainted with many a Forty-Niner. The half-horse, half-alligator greetings among this fraternity fascinated Artemus. He began passing himself off among them as an old-timer. Once Mark Twain introduced him to his clerical friend, the Reverend Franklin Rising. Mistaking the frail and fragile minister for a pioneer, Artemus hailed him as "Old Two-Pan-One-Color." When the minister's eyes twinkled with mirth, Artemus shouted, "Is the Devil still in your dough pan?" Because he spent all of his time with *The Enterprise* gang, *The Union,* the rival newspaper, referred to Artemus' "dissipated air" and called him a "mercenary clown."

Artemus never tired of life on the mountain—neither on the surface nor down in its drifts. He made a descent into the Gould & Curry. The next morning's *Enterprise* contained a fabulous description of his underground experiences. He seized upon the reckless spirit of the town like a hungry dog upon a bone. The wild character of the scenery, the strange manners of the red-shirted men, and the odd developments of Comstock life never failed to interest him. He even haunted the police courts. And showed himself delighted when an unfortunate horse-thief was sentenced to life imprisonment while a killer got off with three years![10] That was typical of Washoe, he said. One day as he was passing Wells Fargo & Company's office he saw the employees throwing bricks of silver into an express wagon for the transalpine journey. Just as English carters throw cheese from hand to hand, he said to his secretary. Artemus watched spellbound until the wagon was piled with a king's ransom in silver bricks! Then he grew worried. All the silver was leaving Washoe. There would be none left for his "Babes." But that night when he trotted them out they were showered with silver dollars. That astounded him. Washoe's supply must be inexhaustible!

Theatre-bound one night, Artemus passed a gambling den just as two Philistines ran into the street and began pumping lead at one another. A dead man was the result. "Poor devil," said Artemus. "I was hoping my 'Babes' would make these boys better natured." A bit shaken he rushed into the nearest saloon and demanded a glass of water.

Before he had a chance to drink it, a desperado grabbed him. "Well, if it ain't the little boy from New England," shouted the bad-man as he appropriated him. "Shootin' ain't as popular in Washoe as it uster be," he continued. "A few years since we uster have a man for breakfast every mornin'. I've killed men enough to stock a graveyard. Sometimes a feelin' of remorse comes over me! But I'm an altered man now. Hain't killed a man for over two weeks." And he dealt the bar a vicious blow. "Listen—William W. Shakespeare. What'll ye pizen yerself with? Speak up like a man!"

Artemus escaped and hurried on toward Maguire's. What an "outlandish spot" for an "Opera House!" he thought. Gilt—brass—brocade—crystal! He went to his dressing room and looked from the window upon the desert sands far below. On lower slopes he could see Piutes playing poker. Dried scalps dangled from their girdles.[11] For hundreds of miles beyond, nature wore her sternest, roughest garments. Not a shrub! Not even a scrub piñon. Nothing but colorless, dreary sage as far as he could see. Verily, he said, Thalia was a daring lady to loiter in such a cursed spot!

Beyond Virginia, Artemus lectured up and down the mountain. In all the little camps. In Six Mile, Seven Mile, and Gold Cañon, even before Queen Eilley at Washoe. Everywhere he left his listeners laughing. One night Mark Twain arranged to take the "Babes" to Aurora. He hadn't seen anything, said Mark, until he had been to Aurora. But when Artemus learned that a recent lecturer on psychology had been shot by a horse-thief who was "agin literatoore," he postponed the date.

One night when Artemus wanted to visit Virginia's Chinese quarter Mark Twain, Dan De Quille, and Joe Goodman took him down there. It happened to be a night when the Celestials were holding a pow-wow in their joss-house. The boys introduced him to all the leading merchants. He sipped "blandy" with Hop Sing, head of one tong, and a fiery rice drink with old Sam Sing, champion of another. At the height of the celebration a tong war broke out. When fifty shots had been fired and one Celestial had been killed and three had fallen desperately wounded, Joe and Mark, Dan and Artemus bolted. Coming to a string of low frame houses Artemus proposed the tops of the shanties as the safest place of retreat. "Follow your leader!" he shouted as he scaled a low shed and then appeared atop a near-by roof-tree. Mark Twain, Dan De Quille, and Joe came scrambling after.[12]

"Come ahead," shouted Artemus. "We'll go up into town over the roofs of the houses. Follow your leader."

By this time the China "blandy" had made them more venturesome. "No wonder the Celestials fought," said Dan, as he watched Mark, Joe, and Artemus reeling from one ridgepole to another.

Suddenly a sharp command from below—"Halt there or I shoot" —brought them up sharply. Over the eaves they peered. A man in a blue suit and brass buttons had a shotgun trained on them.

"Come down," ordered the policeman. "Quick."

Down they climbed, and marched up to the policeman.

"Right you are," said Artemus. "Take a few of these." And he handed the dazed cop a half dozen complimentary tickets to "Babes in the Wood."

"Well, I'll be damned!" said the vigilant watchman. "You had the closest call you're ever likely to get in your lives."[13]

With the law mollified, on up Sutton Avenue they passed to where they could hear the music of a hurdy-gurdy. Hurdies were something new in Artemus' life. As they entered the dance-hall he announced in stentorian tones, "Here come the 'Babes in the Wood.' "

Artemus was known to all those present. After three cheers had been given for him they went over to the Melodeon to hear the Cornish singers. Here Artemus had an inspiration. He blackened his face, went on the stage, and made a gibbering idiot of himself. Not an actor knew who he was. Neither Joe, nor Mark, nor Dan ever gave him away—for Artemus was as bad as an actor as he was great as a humorist.[14]

Dawn was breaking that morning when the "Babes" found themselves in front of Aaron Hooper's saloon. Artemus was mounted astride a barrel. As the golden disk slid above the desert's rim and Sugar Loaf and Cedar Hill flamed with coming day, he poured out a libation to "Dawn." While Mark Twain atop a near-by packing-case apostrophized Aurora with the contents of a mustard pot.[15]

Last nights come as last nights will. It was New Year's Eve. After a final lecture at Gold Hill, Artemus invited his friends to a farewell party at Chauvel's French Restaurant.[16] Around midnight, Mark, Dan, and Joe Goodman grouped themselves about the table. Artemus filled their glasses with haut sauterne and solemnly lifted his own.

"Gentlemen," he pledged, "I give you Upper Canada."

The company jumped to their feet.

"Upper Canada!" they shouted as they clicked their glasses across the festal board, drank the toast, and resumed their seats.

"Why did you give us Upper Canada?" ventured Goodman.

"Because I don't want it myself," replied Artemus gravely.[17]

Then began a rising tide of humor. Mark Twain had awakened to fuller power. On that occasion he demonstrated his right to rank above the world's acknowledged foremost humorist.[18] Artemus Ward was in his prime. It was a memorable close to one of Washoe's most memorable years—. Through the open window came the steady rhythm of the Comstock—the clatter of stamps—the respirations of great hoists—shrieks of whistles—shouts of bull-whackers. Up from underfoot came the dull thud of subterranean blasts. Those around that festal board vibrated to every impulse of Washoe's virile stride.

"I never, gentlemen, was in a city where I was treated so *well*," said Artemus as they left the table, "nor, I will add, so *often.*"[19] And he did not bat an eye as he paid over to Chauvel $237 for the party![20]

By 2.30 A.M., New Year's Day, Artemus, Joe, Mark Twain, and Dan De Quille were in a private room at Barnum's restaurant still celebrating the New Year.[21]

Scattered over the board were the tell-tale remnants of a chicken and champagne supper. Artemus Ward was standing by his chair thickly reciting the lines from Thomas Bailey Aldrich's "Ballad of Baby Bell." Every few moments he was interrupted by shouts of "Splendid, by Shorzhe!" With a vitreous jangling of applause came the conclusion. And then Artemus:

" 'Let every man 'at loves his fellow man and 'preciates a poet 'at loves his fellow man, stan' up!—Stan' up and drink health and long life—Thomas Bailey Aldrich!—and drink it stanning!' " On all sides fervent, enthusiastic, and sincerely honest efforts to comply.

" 'Well—consider it stanning, and drink it just as ye are!' "

So to a conclusion came Artemus' last night in Washoe. Before he got away his ardent admirer, Governor James W. Nye, presented him with a certificate, duly sealed and signed, wherein it was stated that the Governor reposed "special trust and confidence in the integrity and ability of Artemus Ward" wherefore he appointed the said Ward "for the term of his natural life, 'Speaker of pieces' to the people of Washoe."

From the admiring boys came a massive gold chain so long that it could be wound about the neck but so heavy that Artemus could not wear it comfortably.

With these specimens of good will Artemus fled to Austin, a wild lion-hearted camp in the desert. From which place he penned Mark Twain a letter in which he called him "My Dearest Love," promising to help him reach the light by way of *The Mercury*—the famous New York Sunday newspaper.[23]

And Artemus kept his promise. Through this tie made in Washoe Mark Twain and "The Celebrated Jumping Frog of Calaveras County" hopped into fame. And the world began that laugh that not even three-quarters of a century has served to silence.

CHAPTER XLIX

THE HONEST MINER
January, 1864

When the Constitutional Convention was held early in November, 1863, Bill Stewart was on hand as one of the delegates from Sun Mountain. Bill expected great things to come out of those deliberations. When they were over he anticipated finding himself turning the knob of that door upon which he had fixed eye these many moons—and then—the ambitions of a life-time would be fulfilled.

It was to be a very important convention to decide whether Washoe should don the robes of statehood or not. Bill believed and every one of the boys believed that she should.

As usual Joe Goodman sent Mark Twain to report the deliberations of those embryo statesmen for the columns of *The Territorial Enterprise*.

The session began on November 4, with thirty-four delegates present, most of whom came from the numerous counties that clustered on or about Sun Mountain. The constitution, which Bill Stewart had framed as early as '61, was virtually accepted and scheduled for adoption, when it suddenly hit a snag. Bill had provided a double-action constitution designed to serve both the State and Bill Stewart's ambitions. Bill's constitution provided that when the vote was taken on the instrument itself the officers created by it should be voted on at one and the same time. By that proviso, Bill expected to emerge from that door, upon whose threshold he stood, as United States Senator William M. Stewart of Nevada. The very thought of it made Bill expand his chest.

But by coupling ambition and constitution in the same instrument, Bill made a mistake. Every one of those thirty-four delegates was committed to statehood. Also every one of them was consumed with ambition.[1] Not a one but wanted to be attorney-general, judge, or congressman, but the great majority had their hearts set on becoming a United States senator and going to Washington. All these last balked at Bill Stewart's pretensions. Why should

Bill have the honor of becoming Washoe's first United States senator? Why indeed? Why not one of them? They were so nettled
that they let it be understood they wouldn't help shake the tree
unless they could have the political plums they coveted. Furthermore, they wouldn't vote for Bill Stewart under any conditions.
Among themselves, they decided that the first toga belonged by
right to Judge John Cradlebaugh as the premier judicial official in
the Territory. Hadn't he fought through the Piute War? Wasn't he
a sterling—honest—unassuming man who didn't try to hog everything? In one hour Bill Stewart saw all his plans go awry. With
that convention he didn't have a snowball's chance of becoming a
United States senator. But there was an extremely good chance that
the Territory would be converted into a State—leaving him out in
the cold. That would never do. There was only one thing left for
him. He must defeat the constitutional vote and try again. But
that was a difficult matter.

Up to this moment, Bill had always belonged to the Union
party—the most powerful one on Sun Mountain. Exhibiting the
most intense loyalty to the country—it had always carried everything triumphantly before it. Even now, though hopelessly divided
into factions—it would probably carry the Territory. But not if Bill
Stewart could prevent it. In desperation, Bill bolted his party and
joined the anti-Union Democratic party—whose membership included the secessionists. He bolted with one thought in mind—to
block the adoption of the organic act by which the Territory would
become a State. The Union party retaliated by branding Bill a
rebel. It was a serious charge. To make matters worse Mrs. Stewart
was a Southerner, the daughter of a rabid secessionist, and had
already been accused of rebellious sympathies. But old indomitable
Bill did not let the charges bother him. Charges have no weight,
he said, unless answered. And he proceeded to ignore this one.
The constitution was to be submitted to the voters for ratification
on January 19, 1864. By hook or crook he must defeat it. In the
meantime he wasn't going to waste any energy answering absurd
charges.

The Constitutional Convention was scheduled to remain in session
until December 11. That delighted Bill. It gave him about forty
days to defeat a measure that was bound to ruin his future. And
forty days is a long time when a man is purposeful and determined.

Without awaiting the end of the convention Bill departed and
threw his powerful influence against the adoption of the organic

act upon the grounds that it taxed the "poor honest miner"—his shafts—his drifts—his bedrock tunnels.

That shibboleth—"the honest miner"—caught the boy's fancy—it appealed to their vanity. It was the truth. It carried weight. Bill iterated it—reiterated it—agitated it—exaggerated it. From the frequency and effect with which Bill used that phrase it never failed to provoke a smile wherever heard. It was all right, said Bill, to tax the product of the "poor miner's" shafts—of his drifts and of his bedrock tunnels. Tax his output—his gold—his silver—his bullion if need be; but God forbid! "not the honest fellow's hopes, the aspirations of his soul, the yearnings of his heart of hearts! No! Not those!"

The better to play the part he had outlined for himself Bill donned jeans, boots, a wide hat, and opened his blue-flannel shirt on his hairy chest, and rolled his sleeves well up hairy arms. From then on, Bill might be heard thundering that speech day and night, up and down the mountain. Above the detonation of exploding dynamite; above the anathemas of bull-whackers; above the clatter of a thousand stamps, the protestations of a hundred hoists, and the tumult of the streets, that speech about taxing the "honest miner's" hopes, ambitions, and yearning soul could be heard. It was given ear at the miners' union, at political rallies, on street corners, at banquets, about the blacksmith's forge, at the rail of sumptuous bars, down in dark subterranean galleries. Every nook and cranny of Sun Mountain hearkened to it.

Mark Twain was delegated to follow Bill Stewart wherever he went and report his campaign speeches for *Enterprise* readers. But Mark grew tired of reporting that speech. It was the same old thing —Sam said—rehashed. Day after day. Over and over again. Without variance. Finally with his usual repugnance for news as news, Mark wrote one of his satirical outbursts about it and sent it to *The Enterprise*.[3]

In it Mark Twain reported Bill as making all sorts of ridiculous, illogical statements. Sentences were repeated ad infinitum. Meanings were twisted upon themselves. Heart and soul yearnings were stressed in absurd fashion. No one could make head or tail out of that speech. Its conclusions were ludicrous.

The boys read it—held their sides—and laughed until the tears rolled down their cheeks. Bill read it, and the blue glitter in his eyes grew steely. Making fun of him—eh? Better watch out! Maybe Mark's sketch was humorous to the other fellows but to

Bill Stewart it was not even funny—just personalities. Of late Mark had come to exasperate him to the point that he would have nothing to do with him.[4] In fact he avoided every circle that included him. Mark had become as irritating as a gnat that keeps buzzing about one's ears. However, Bill promised himself that when the campaign was over he would attend to Mark. Now he had something else to do—a goal to reach. But later he would find the opportunity to fix Mark Twain for all this personal abuse.

With renewed energy Bill threw himself into the campaign against the Organic Act—and Mark went on burlesquing him in *The Enterprise.*

"I am not going to sit and listen to that old song over and over again," wrote Mark Twain. "I have been reporting and reporting that infernal speech for the last thirty days. When I want to hear it I will repeat it myself—I know it by heart—bedrock tunnels—blighted miners—blasted hopes. They have gotten to be a sort of nightmare to me, and I won't put up with it any longer. I don't wish to be too hard on that speech, but if Stewart can't add something fresh to it, or say it backwards, or sing it to a new tune, he has simply got to simmer down."[5]

Still Bill was too busy with weighty matters to pay any attention to Mark.

However one day when Mark wrote some characteristic personalities about a distinguished friend of Bill's—an unforgivable lampoon without the slightest foundation in fact, Bill went after him.

"You are getting worse every day," he fumed. "Why can't you be genial, like your brother Orion? You ought to be hung for what you have published this morning."[6]

"I don't mean anything by that," laughed Mark. "I wrote it because it was humorous." Humorous? Well, Bill did not want to argue the point.

"I must make a living," continued Mark, "and so I must write. My employers demand it, and I am helpless."[7]

So Mark remained far from cowed by Bill's growing supremacy in Washoe. He never missed a chance to satirize him. "Why, man," he wrote, "[Stewart] does bestride our narrow range like a Colossus, and we petty men walk under his hind legs and peep about to find ourselves six feet of unclaimed ground."

For the time, Bill let all these shafts of wit pass. But he assured himself that Mark Twain's day of reckoning was coming.

CHAPTER L

GOVERNOR OF THE THIRD HOUSE
1863–1864

While Washoe was responding to the hopes and aspirations of Bill Stewart's "honest miner" and those gentlemen were rallying around their champion, the last day of the Constitutional Convention dawned. So hugely had the lawmakers enjoyed themselves that they were loath to disband.

On the last night, in one final adolescent outburst, they organized a "Third House"—a sort of play House—and elected Mark Twain "Governor."

On the very same night, December 12, 1863, the Third House held its inaugural meeting in the Hall of the Convention. With monstrous ceremonies of convocation Mark Twain was inducted into office.

"Gentlemen," said he, in his acceptance speech, "this is the proudest moment of my life. I shall always think so. I think so still. I shall ponder over it with unspeakable emotion down to the 'last syllable of recorded time.' It shall be my earnest endeavor to give entire satisfaction to the high and bully position to which you have elevated me."[1]

He then suspended all rules and dispensed with the usual prayer, on the ground that it was never listened to by the members of the First House, which was composed chiefly of the same gentlemen which constituted the Third, and was, consequently, merely ornamental and entirely unnecessary.

After "Governor" Mark Twain had appointed the offices of "Secretary," "Official Reporter," and "Chief Page" he had each one come forward and take an oath.

"We do solemnly swear," went the oath, "that we have never seen a duel, never been connected with a duel, never heard of a duel, never sent or received a challenge, never fought a duel, and don't want to. Furthermore, we will support, protect, and defend this constitution which we are about to frame until we can't rest, and will take our pay in scrip."

From beginning to end it was a hilarious session that "Governor" Twain conducted. Every member came in for his share of satire—

no one was spared—some of it was painfully personal—one member lisped—one was an old "granny"—another was a "bump on the log" who appropriated the platitudes of every one else. Every remark had a sting. But if you couldn't give and take like a sport you didn't belong in Washoe. The boys enjoyed their antics to such a degree that Mark was induced to turn one of its jovial sessions into a church benefit. The program so impressed several in the audience that they clubbed together and presented "His Excellency" with a gold watch inscribed, "For the Governor of the Third House."

While the Third House was convulsing itself with laughter over Mark Twain's doings, Bill Stewart was holding rousing meetings on the mountain and explaining to the miners that the proposed tax if it passed would be fatal to the mining industry.[2] "No miner," he said, "who puts his honest work into a shaft without profits is in any shape to pay a tax on what he has done." His furious attack against the movement for statehood produced many animosities among the aspirants for office. But Bill had accomplished something far more important. By his logic and fearlessness he had organized the boys in solid phalanxes behind him.

Election day, January 19, 1864, dawned, Bill rested on his oratory. He had done his best to defeat the measure. When the constitution, which would have sent Judge Cradlebaugh to Washington as Nevada's first United States senator, came up for ratification it was overwhelmingly rejected.[3] From its ashes, like that mythological bird of antiquity, Bill Stewart emerged in all the vigor of immortal youth—the "Political Moloch" of Nevada—as his enemies called him. Bill congratulated himself. He still had a chance to open that door—what a superhuman effort it had required to keep it shut until the propitious time!

With the defeat of the Organic Act, Mark Twain climbed up Sun Mountain and retook his chair on the editorial board of *The Enterprise*. With his gold watch in his vest pocket and the acclaim of the Third House still resounding in his ears he had become a starry-eyed Mark Twain.

Flushed with the success of his own campaign, Bill decided to forgive Mark for his buffoonery and call bygones, bygones. When several of the boys invited him to join them in a welcoming-home party they were getting up for Mark, he did so wholeheartedly.

Great plans were made for that evening's entertainment. It was to

Courtesy Mrs. Robert Howland.

MARK TWAIN'S CABIN AT AURORA.

MARK TWAIN AS GOVERNOR.

Courtesy Harvard College Theatrical Collection.

A. C. SWINBURNE AND
ADAH ISAACS MENKEN.

Courtesy The Library of Congress.

SHOW-BILLS LIKE THIS WERE PASTED OVER THE
CLIFFS AROUND VIRGINIA CITY, TO ADVER-
TISE THE COMING OF THE MENKEN.

Courtesy Fulton Oursler.

ALEXANDRE DUMAS AND
THE MENKEN.

be the finest they had ever engineered. The most beautiful girls in Washoe were invited. The choicest food in San Francisco was provided, the rarest brands of champagne were iced. Mark came. The evening passed royally. Mark enjoyed himself hugely, ate heartily, monopolized the prettiest of the women, and provided the wittiest part of the conversation. To all outward appearances he and Bill were the most jovial of companions.

As soon as the party was over Mark repaired to his *Enterprise* sanctum and wrote up the entertainment in an outrageous manner. Next morning when Bill and the boys read what Mark had to say about their party they were furious. They could hardly believe their eyes. If any of the company was so unfortunate as to lisp, to be awkward, to have big feet or a wart on the nose, Mark did not overlook it—but fairly strained himself in exaggerating the fact.[4]

Perhaps it was humorous. Bill and the boys were not sure. But they were certain of one thing. The time had come to "get even."

Came a night when Mark had to take the stage down the mountain to Carson. Bill and the boys, who had given the party, learned of it in time to don black masks, and lay in wait in a lonely spot off the cañon road. As the stage lumbered by, out they swooped from cover brandishing six-shooters, and held up the driver. Then they dragged Mark and his portmanteau out of the coach, trounced him up and down several times and threw him into a ravine. Ripping open his brief-case, they took out all his papers and tore them to shreds and scattered the fragments over his cringing body.

Although scared out of his wits, Mark did not peep. But the next morning when he crawled back to Virginia City he began to swell a little and to color up the details of the hold-up. He had had a hair's-breadth escape and had been the hero of one of the most desperate stage robberies on the mountain.[5] At every lull in any conversation, Mark might be heard lugging in the story of his heroism.

But now, Mark was distracted with a bill-poster that appeared upon the cliffs above the city. It was a flamboyant thing and represented a beautiful naked woman strapped to the back of a black pawing stallion that was charging pell-mell through a raging storm, up a mountainside. The spectacle made the boys tingle down to their toes.

"The Menken!" gasped Mark. "The circus rider!" He had a few choice shafts reserved for her—she belonged under canvas—not at Maguire's.

CHAPTER LI

MAZEPPA

March 7, 1864

By eight o'clock, that night, Maguire's was packed to the doors. Everybody was there—Julia Bulette, in a stage-box with half-drawn curtains, lay languidly back in a gilt chair. The management wouldn't let her sit out in the audience with the boys, as she used to do in early days. No. Civilization had come up Sun Mountain. A civilization in which Julia was to be exiled to a loge. Great diamonds sparkled in the lobes of her ears. A ruby guled on her breast. Sables nestled about her white-satin shoulders. She looked happy—Julia did—but she was sad and melancholy. She had risen above her calling. She had been of help to man. Now civilization was to exile her to a loge—at the theatre—to a street on the mountain.

It was a gala night—even at Maguire's—with all the boys dressed for the occasion. Those with good taste had black onyx buttons in their white-fronts. Those who didn't care that such a thing existed wore diamonds. Nat Redding's, the gambler, cost $6000 each, and he wore an immense one set in each button of his gorgeous silk-embroidered waistcoats, of which he never donned the same one twice.[1]

Tom Peasley came down the aisle with that soft tiger-like tread of his. He wanted to see the Menken make that perilous ride. All the boys wanted to see her scale that mountain on horseback.

In the newspaper "pew" sat Mark Twain, Dan De Quille, and Joe Goodman. Maguire always gave *The Enterprise* reporters front-row seats, free. In return they were expected to do the right thing by the show as well as for the house. But this time Maguire was going to be fooled. Mark Twain was not kindly disposed toward the Menken. He said she was only a "shape" actress. She didn't have any histrionic ability or deserve any more consideration than a good circus performer. That's what she was—a circus rider! That's where she belonged, in a sawdust ring. He wasn't going to give her a write-up.

Not he. He was going to vivisect her, show her up.[2] *The Enterprise* was considered the best dramatic review on the Coast. They must uphold their reputation. They couldn't afford to write eulogisms on a "shape"—they weren't going to. The actors and actresses who came to the Comstock knew that unless they impressed Joe Goodman, Dan De Quille, or Mark Twain they might just as well take the stage next morning and leave. That these had ridiculed more than one good actor into throwing up his engagement and departing. They knew their power. That night Mark Twain intended to show this far-famed Menken just where she stood.

The Menken came to Sun Mountain enveloped in fable. She had blazed, like a comet, a lurid path across the country. She consummated in melodrama the lust of an era. On the Comstock she found a locality born of it. The papers were full of her exploits—had been for days. The boys told one another what they knew about her, as they awaited the beginning of the play. She was born in New Orleans. Her real name was Dolores McCord. She was the adopted daughter of Sam Houston. But she denied it.

"No, I never lived with Houston," Menken had said. "It was Methuselah and other old men." She had been "Queen of the Plaza" in Havana. In Texas she had been captured by the Indians, tomahawked, rescued by Texas Rangers. There she had learned her circus stunts. Baron Rothschild had called her the inspired Deborah of her race. She had married "Benecia Boy" Heenan. She had borne him a son. One night in an excess of affection the bruiser had stifled his boy. Had broken his mother's heart. After that catastrophe she had never seen "The Boy" again. She was an outrageous rebel. She always kept a Confederate flag in her room. In Baltimore she had decked out the theatre where she was playing, with "The Stars and Bars." She had been promptly arrested by the provost-marshal. In Ohio she had been hailed as the "Darling of Dayton," made an honorary captain of the Light Guard. Her portrait, in sword and epaulettes, hung in their armory. In San Francisco she had been known as the "Frenzy of Frisco." Walt Whitman had taught her how to write poetry. Canova had used her as a model. Or was it Michel Angelo?

Everywhere the Menken had appeared she had caused a furor. Her dress, her talk, her actions had started tongues wagging. She was the chatter of town and country—on the threshold of being the gossip of two continents. She attracted men as a flame attracts moths. She had had many lovers. She would have many more. "Dolores—

Notre Dame de Sept Douleurs," Swinburne, the English poet, would call her. "Adah—of the Seven Husbands," he would really mean to say. But it wouldn't be true. Tired of loving, foiled in love, Swinburne would indite that magnificent lyric—to get even with a woman who had flaunted him.

On the crest of her fame, the Menken came to Sun Mountain—a locality that at the time was literally starved for the sight of woman —a place where any old hag was hailed as a queen—showered with gold and jewels—given attention beyond rhyme or reason. Imagine then the most talked-about woman of her day, the most beautiful siren of her generation, stripped to her beautiful skin—literally riding through their midst strapped to the back of a black stallion. Fancy Godiva riding up Gold Cañon! Picture the superb Menken— a woman with a reputation for "power over men"—doing the same stunt. Imagination alone swept the boys off their feet. Just as it was to sweep all the doddering old fellows in London across Westminster Bridge and into stalls at Astley's to leer at her beautiful body. Just as it would sweep Napoleon the Third and the Duke of Edinburgh into a Paris box to see "this American Venus." Was it any wonder then that Maguire's was packed to see this fabulous woman ride a wild Washoe mustang up a cardboard mountain?

Was it any wonder that a thrill of expectancy ran through the audience as the bell rang for the curtain to go up—and music softened—hub-bub became a whisper—gas-flares dimmed and darkness fell?

The scenery was splendrous—as wild and savage as that of Sun Mountain. The boys found themselves facing the courtyard of the castle of Laurinski. A mass of buttressed masonry. A moat. Drawbridge. Gates. A balcony hanging over a lake. And in the background the river Dnieper at the foot of a lofty mountain that scraped the flies. The moon was setting in a dark sky. The boys fell under its glamor. The scene was as ethereal as one of their own mirages. Would it too, like them, fade into nothingness?

The Menken as Mazeppa, the Tartar Prince, stole across the bridge. She paused beneath the balcony.

In the mystic light drenching the scene the boys could see that the Tartar was lithe, young, and vigorously graceful. Superb in velvet cloak and tights! To some she recalled Lord Byron—the same magnificent dark curly head—the same beautiful full throat—the same great melancholy eyes—the same lips like a flower. But there the resemblance ceased. Her limbs! Such legs Byron had never had. His had been his crucifixion. The Menken's were her glory. Sheer poetry. "Twin melodies," her lover Swinburne would call them—melodies that could move to the rhythm of passionate music.

All was hushed—the boys had never been so quiet—as Mazeppa spoke—Mark Twain and Dan De Quille, who had come to scourge, sat open-eyed, open-eared, open-mouthed, drinking in the beauty of

CARTOON BY SIR EDWARD BURNE-JONES OF THE POET SWINBURNE AND *THE MENKEN*.
From the "Swinburne Library," by T. J. Wise. By permission of Mr. Wise.

that matchless voice. They had never heard a voice like that before! It stilled, thrilled, overwhelmed them with its melody. Tense and immovable as stone images—they sat on the edges of their seats and let that caressing voice break over them in soft musical cadences.

The boys forgot everything. Their bleak surroundings. The barren Sun Peak. Each other. They felt the vibrations of that voice to the uttermost recesses of their souls—in the pit of their stomachs, to the tips of their toes. It overwhelmed them with wellbeing. It invoked fabulous dreams. Beautiful images. It fascinated. Delighted. It was the voice of a siren—Ligea's—the Lorelei's!

They were adrift. Between the Isle of Circe and the rock of Scylla. Straining for gossamer dreams. What was the voice saying? They strained, half-rising in their seats, to listen.

"Olinska!" the voice thrilled. "Dear Olinska! appear, dear life! Raise me to the throne of glory . . ."

Olinska in flowing draperies appeared on the balcony above Mazeppa.

Olinska warned her lover to fly the wrath of her father. He had betrothed her to the Count Palatine.

Instead, the intrepid Mazeppa scaled the buttressed wall.

"Listen, Olinska," he pleaded. "We must fly. The deserts of Tartary where I first drew breath and from which we are separated by only a river . . . offer us an assured retreat. Ah, long since . . ." He poured out a molten torrent of pleading. He dropped upon one knee, kissed her hand.[3] In a trice he was in the courtyard again and disappeared beyond the moat.

The boys sat back, relaxed. That voice still possessed them—stirred them—reverberated among half-forgotten things—breathed life into them. Yes, it was a siren voice—a voice that called to heel. Had it not reduced the handsome Isaac Menken, the Jew, to a kneeling supplicant? Had it not swept their idol—that Titan, "Benecia Boy," off his stance? And Orpheus C. Kerr, the gentle Civil War satirist, what had it done to him? And Jim Barkley the Bret Harte gambler —why did he blow out his brains? What would it do to Swinburne? To Dickens? Charles Reade? Watts-Dunton? Theophile Gautier? Alexandre Dumas? Her friends! Her admirers! Her lovers!

It was one of the great voices of all time. Who that looked at her or heard her voice that night at Maguire's would have doubted her power to inspire the most magnificent lyric poem ever written in the English language? Who would have blamed those Oxford undergraduates for jog-trotting in lock-step around their courts and cloisters, chanting incantations to her?[4] Who would have blamed those feverish devotees of Swinburne for falling on their knees in rapt ecstacy when he read aloud the metrical, truncated lines of that poem?[5] Who would have blamed them, of all that heard the Menken's voice that night?[6]

Certainly not Mark Twain, Dan De Quille, Joe Goodman, or any of the boys who heard her. Now, where was the pen that would be raised against her? Six-shooters and bowies for her defense. Not one drop of ink to vilify. She was splendid! Magnificent! Superb! Such a woman they could understand. The primitive—the pagan—the elemental in her appealed to similar qualities in them. And yet they only dared worship from afar, and called her remote—divine—a goddess—Deity!

As a play, Mazeppa may have been a tawdry affair—an abortive circus performance—a travesty on the genius of Lord Byron,[7] but with the Menken it was reinvested with poetic feeling.[8]

All eyes feasted upon her young beauty—startled—enchanted—magnetized, by the potent charm that burned in her glances, that emanated from her virile young body.[9] In their admiration Mark and Dan forgot to sympathize with her forlorn condition. Her loveliness—artistic perfection of movement—force and beauty of mute eloquence, invested her with an air of inaccessibility from which they recoiled with a humiliating sense of their own inferiority. They were abject, enthralled in their adoration. How could they criticise her?[10]

The curtain went up on the second act. Mazeppa had failed in his plea for flight. It was the eve of Olinska's wedding. Mazeppa entered the chamber of the Count and challenged him to mortal combat. The duel began—at first a perfunctory one,[11] giving the Menken a chance to display those Canovaesque poses for which she was famous.[12] But suddenly and unexpectedly she swung the sword over her head and fell angrily upon the Count. The combat grew desperate. Mazeppa fought like one possessed—stabbed the Count—and blood spilled over his heart.

The boys cried out, as at sight of blood at a prize fight. Excitement breathed hard. The Count reeled—fell, assassinated. Pistols went off. Music grew fast and furious. Guards rushed on. Mazeppa was taken prisoner.

Olinska's father appeared in the door. Pointing an upraised arm and extended hand at Mazeppa, he pronounced his doom.

"Lead the vile Tartar hence. Strip him of that garb he has degraded. Lead out the fiery, untamed steed. Prepare strong hempen lashings round the villain's loins. Let every beacon-fire on the mountain-top be lighted—and torches like a blazing forest cast their glare across the night. This moment let my vengeance be accomplished. Away!"

The boys tensed with excitement. They would have extended their aid. But the dim suggestion was stifled by the thought that any assistance would be scorned by one whose every impulse and action seemed tinged with divinity.[13] Mark Twain and Joe Goodman were enchanted. Menken had cast her spell upon them and caught them in her web. They idealized her! They wished that she would display some imperfection, some flaw by which they might know that she trod the common level of human weakness and fallibility. Such a sign would have placed her in more sympathetic communion with them, miserable wretches that they were. She was far away from their humble vision. She was a goddess—while they were clods. They placed her on a pedestal the better to worship at her shrine.[14]

The boys were all anticipation for the great scene. Would they really strip her? Bare her to their eyes? Lash that lovely body to the back of a wild Washoe mustang? Entrust her to that mountain? It was incredible—blasphemy! Many felt for their bowies.

Lights dimmed. Music softened. Stillness prevailed. The curtain went up. The cold air from the stage swept like a deluge over the boys—cooling their ardor. They lifted their eyes, hardly daring to look. It was scarcely stage-dawn. The sky was dull—gray—a storm brewed over the banks of the Dnieper. The scene was set at the outer terrace of the castle, overlooking a tract of desolate mountain country—as bleak, as forlorn as the flanks of their own Mountain.

Up it, from footlights to flies rose a narrow rocky trail to the proscenium. It made them dizzy to look.

The pathway zigzagged from stage-right to stage-left, going back, forth and up, climbing ever upward until it pierced the very summit beyond the sky curtains. That was no place for a woman lashed, helpless, to a Washoe mustang! Up those barren God-forsaken crags on a runway! A slip meant death. The thought sent tremors through them. It was a perilous undertaking. Once, at Albany, she had fallen and almost broken her neck. Again, her horse had kicked her and broken her ribs. At Sacramento she had slipped and crushed her back. There were those that said that she didn't care what happened—"Benecia Boy" had broken her heart!

The boys shuffled their feet uneasily. They would be glad when she had reached the summit.

Olinska's father and her people were gathered on the terrace to see the execution of Mazeppa's sentence.

The guards led on the mustang—a stallion with champing bit and nervous ears.

Speed was in his limbs. Wildness was in his eye—in the bristle of his mane—in the toss of his tail—in the swelling of his nostrils! He had never known spurs or bridle. He struggled against his leashes.

The boys were aghast. They would never dare tie any woman to that wild untamed stallion!

"They'll use a dummy, you'll see," one whispered comfortingly.

Stillness held them cramped—the stillness and fixity of suspense. They ceased breathing. Mazeppa was led on by the guards. They loosed her. She stood forth—brave—alone. The boys gaped in open-mouthed admiration. She was stripped—a piece of gauze—a mail-lot! That was all! A white wealth of loveliness! Their dulled hearts beat faster. Their adoration concealed nothing of its wantonness. Her body was beautiful. It symbolized infinite desire. Thousands violated her in mimic cruelty.[15] Eyes moistened. Burned.

The boys looked at that girlish figure, the sweet face, uplifted, yearning, divine. She filled them with sadness. They knew her for a thing unattainable. Of unquenchable fire. Of imperishable innocence. Whatever she did or didn't do, nothing could soil such purity! Dim such a vestal-lamp! No, she was eternally virgin!

The oldest, the youngest among them was touched by her divine mystery and responded to her broken smile. The smile of one unafraid of death. They were accustomed to that expression—they saw it in those engulfed in caving earth. They knew its hopeless, helpless quality. The guards lashed her to the mustang—pillowed her head on the mane—bound her legs, stiff and motionless, to the heaving flanks. A sudden lash and they loosed the stallion. Away he dashed —up the narrow runway. Not the most stony wretch among them would have done so dastardly a deed! They leapt to their feet. Cowards! Cowards!

The stallion darted straight up the barren mountain-path. The old Count shouted with raucous laughter. They could have wrung his neck. Back and forth the stallion zigzagged. They were fascinated—leaned forward. They could hear the clank of iron shoes, sharp and metallic, against the cleats of the runway. Faster they fled up the mountain—a white blotch on the back of a wild horse borne upward to the flies.[16] The tempo increased. The storm broke. Wind moaned. Thunder crashed. Lightning flashed. Coyotes cried like a woman in agonized distress. The palms of hard hands grew soft with moisture. The boys jumped upon their seats. Stood on their toes. Craned their necks.

Mazeppa and the stallion were close to the summit now. Far

above them. They reached it. Paused for a fateful second. Disappeared into the murky region beyond the proscenium. It was more than exploit. It was art. Stupenduous. Heroic. Heart-breaking.

As one being, the boys jumped into the air, shouted. Thumped one another upon the back. The applause rolled forth like the tempest that had thundered over the mountain.[17]

CHAPTER LII

ADAH ISAACS MENKEN
1864

Mark Twain, Joe Goodman, and Dan De Quille went back to *The Enterprise* editorial rooms enraptured with the charms of Adah Isaacs Menken. Fallen completely under her spell, they sat down at the pine table and wrote rapturous things about her.[1] They entered into a contest as to which could lavish the most fervid praise.[2] The race of infatuated pens was on.

Next morning's *Enterprise* contained an elaborate symposium, overwhelming in eulogisms of the Menken. Ecstasy was piled on ecstasy.[3] The sky was the limit. The Menken was divine. Remote. Inaccessible! She held the world in contempt! She made them despise themselves.

Such ardent praise excited the jealousy of the remainder of the company. At the next evening's performance, the less favored members of the cast inserted gags at Mark Twain's and *The Enterprise's* expense. Menken was furious over these asides. Freeing herself from the very flanks of the wild horse, she flung herself in a torrent of abuse upon the manager and ordered him to make an immediate and public apology to Goodman. When he declined she refused to go on with her part. The curtain was rung down. A large audience had to be dismissed.[4] Mark and Dan were distraught—their appreciation had proved a boomerang to the Menken. They implored her to resume her rôle.

On the following night she relented and Mark Twain's enraptured critique continued and was copied by papers all over the country.[5]

The excitement and wild whirl of life then in full swing on the Comstock delighted the Menken. She revelled in its syncopated sound. Its rhythm. The ceaseless rumble of ore-wagons—the shrill staccato of steam-whistles, the heavings of hoist—subterranean explosions—the quaking earth—the everlasting roll and surge of titanic stamps. Her whole being vibrated in unison with its vigorous, virile stride. To her the Comstock was a calliope. Upon its keys she played rapturous, strident music. Life on the Mountain, she said, was "in keeping with the wild shrieking of its steam-whistles and the thunder of its quartz mills." [6] She found in its savage exhilaration a rhythm as fantastic and undisciplined as the movement of her own verse. It inspired her to an increased activity of composition. Several of those frantic soul-cries of poetic aspiration, shrieked as they were, out of the darkness into the ear of humanity and God, found their way through Mark Twain into the columns of *The Enterprise.*[7]

The Menken wrote these poems in great scrawling characters of the door-plate order. Mark Twain could scarcely decipher her manuscripts. It was infamous chirography. Once, it inspired him to a bald conundrum:

"Why ought your hand," he asked the Menken, "to retain its present grace and beauty always?"

When she hesitated he retorted, "Because you fool away devilish little of it on your manuscript." [8]

Nevertheless so overcome was Mark with the charms of this Sappho that he held great respect for her literary ability. To her he carried many of his own literary productions, for criticism. "She is a literary cuss herself," he wrote by way of explanation.

Besides the writing of poetry the Menken could show those boys a thing or two along their own lines. "Benecia Boy," the Menken's *"troisième douleur,"* had taught her to box astonishingly well. One night, at the Sazerac, she put on "gloves" with "Joggles" Wright, superintendent of the Sierra Nevada, a Washoe Bohemian, with a keen zest for living.[9] In a couple of rounds she knocked him out of time, winding up the bout by throwing him so heavily that he had to be carried away. She followed up this victory with quick snappy rounds with two more of the boys who had ring aspirations —winning all the laurels.

"Her left," declared the vanquished, "was a thing with which to conjure." [10]

She found only one fault with the city. When Midas touched the Mountain with magic finger, everything green and verdant had withered. Not a tree. Not a shrub. Not a blade of grass. And she smiled wistfully as she gazed across Forty Mile. Frustration, she said, the summation of all lives, was written across the desert.

Nightly after her exposure in the "Tartar Prince" the Menken might be found with Tom Peasley.[11] She delighted in his soft, panther-like step. She liked to waltz with him at the Melodeon, or at the Sazerac to "fight the tiger" until dawn with red and white chips. Tom played a "square game," she said.[12] He was her beau-ideal of Comstock manhood. When the fire-boys elected her a member of American Engine Company No. 2, and voted her a handsome red morocco fire-belt with the insignia of the company embossed in silver bullion Tom Peasley was delegated to make the presentation. On the appointed night the boys serenaded her at the International Hotel. And the Menken, swathed in yellow satins, appeared upon the balcony. While the boys sang of the starry night, Tom buckled the morocco belt about her slender waist and led the cheering which ended with a "tiger." For an *"huitième douleur"* where could the Menken have found a more magnificent candidate than Tom Peasley?

The Menken was in her element with these boys—but then she was in her element with all kinds and conditions of men—from the sublime to the ridiculous. Buffoons. Boilermakers. Kings. Poets. Priests. Prize-fighters. Fire-eaters—all, men of high or low degree—fell under the Menken's potent spell, for her appeal to man was elemental—man stripped of all pretense and power.

Upon the walls of the Sazerac hung three pictures of especial significance to the Menken: Lola Montez, once Countess of Landsfeld, Baroness of the Order of Saint Theresa, mistress of Ludwig the First of Bavaria; "Benecia Boy" Heenan, her one-time husband, in sparring tights, and the Menken herself, "naked to the pitiless storm" in the place of honor directly over the bar.

One night the Menken gazed across the bar at those three pictures, and boasted Lola Montez had begun with a prince and ended with a miner, but she was going to reverse that course. "I began with a prize-fighter," she said, indicating Heenan, "but I'll end with a prince."[13] And she did, with a prince of lyrists.[14]

The Menken took in everything that was going, on the Comstock, bars, gambling tables. Dance halls. Bear-fights, bull-fights, dog-fights, stamp mills. Even boiled an egg in the scalding underground waters of the Ophir.

She haunted the exchange and stock board, gambling like a veteran in all kinds of "wildcat." When she lost, as lose she must, the boys laid never-failing ingots of silver at her feet. Every night when she bared her body to their gaze at Maguire's they showered her with golden eagles. Once they bestowed upon her a bullion bar, handsomely inscribed, valued at $2000.[15]

To her charms the boys responded as they never had to any other actress. A mountain street was named in her honor. A newly discovered mining district was christened "The Menken." "We suppose," boldly commented *The Union,* "the first work done in that district will be to 'strip all the ledges.'" "The Menken Shaft & Tunnel Company" was a veritable fact. Stock certificates engraved with a naked siren strapped to a stallion appeared on all exchanges. A new ledge—the "Mazeppa Mounting Ledge"—was widely heralded throughout the Territory. One mining company presented her with fifty shares of stock worth, at the time, $100 a share. Before she took her departure she disposed of it for $1000 a share.[16] Nothing was too lavish for the Menken. No expression extravagant enough. They were all her bounden slaves.

When she addressed them as "my boys," as she had that night from the International balcony, not only would they have spread their coats upon the ground but they would have thrown themselves headlong in the gutter could they have spared her pretty feet from contamination.

Even with the proud protestations of prize-fighters, the adulation of infatuated miners, even with the huzzahs of great capitals, the applause of princelings, the mimings of lascivious poets—still the Menken was not happy. There was that in her that denied happiness, that could not be appeased with applause, bought with bullion, stifled with wanton cruelties. The Menken was at defiance with her inner self.[17] She had flouted her own æsthetic being. The voice within kept crying and would not be comforted.

In the fantastic life of the Comstock, with its color, surge, and sound, she vainly sought to smother that voice. On the Mountain she actually found a comfort denied her elsewhere. Its wild elemental scenery, its tawny rocks, its golden sunshine, its yellow drifts calmed her. Oft she rode far out on Forty Mile with Tom Peasley. She was mad about its shifting sands—mad about its leonine color —mad about its changing light. "I was born in that yellow sand once, sometime, somewhere," she once said as her horse plunged belly-deep through dunes and, throwing herself from her mount, she buried her face in a mound.[18]

So satisfied was she with her Washoe surroundings that the Menken had half a mind to settle down on the Mountain and write a novel.

One Sunday she invited Mark Twain and Dan to come to her rooms at the International and confer with her regarding the project.

Late in the afternoon Mark and Dan arrived. Wrapped, like a

mummy, in fold after fold of yellow satin, the Menken lay on a tiger's pelt by the fire.

They sat at a little table talking and sipping champagne. Waiters came and went with one savory dish after another. Every now and then, the Menken fed her pet lap-dog cubes of sugar soaked in brandy. Presently the canine took an unwarranted liberty with Mark Twain's leg. In his endeavor to avenge the nip with a surreptitious under-the-table kick, Mark inadvertently hit the Menken, causing her to throw herself in agony on a nearby sofa. The Menken was forgiving but the joy of the day had passed. Feigning a pressing engagement, Mark and Dan excused themselves and the Menken's novel faded into the land of mirage.[19]

And presently the Menken was off to London—to the arms of Swinburne and the caresses of Dumas. Through the "Gates of Paris," she claimed in Washoe, her soul was destined to ascend to heaven.[20]

As soon as the Menken was gone Maguire turned on *The Enterprise* to punish it. He withdrew his printing and advertising and suspended the free list for everybody connected with the paper. It was just what Joe Goodman was always aching for, the chance for an open fight with Maguire, and he made it hot while it lasted.

When a good show came to Virginia, Joe wouldn't mention it. No one would ever have known from *The Enterprise* that there was such a place of amusement in town. But if a vulnerable one made its appearance Goodman or Mark Twain or Dan De Quille would pay his dollar for admission and then take a hundred dollars' worth of fun or satisfaction out of the hides of the poor actors and actresses. Some of these onslaughts were classic in the purity of their abuse.

The situation grew to be a terror to the theatrical profession. Instead of the eagerness with which they formerly sought engagements in Virginia City, companies came with reluctance or refused to come at all. Pauncefoot, an excellent but eccentric actor, was ridiculed so unmercifully that he threw up his engagement. Walter Montgomery, an English tragedian of high repute, who was booked for two weeks, after reading *The Enterprise's* criticism of his Hamlet, boarded the stage and left in disgust, saying he had had enough of Virginia City. Emily Thorne, a beautiful actress, opened an engagement in "Mazeppa," but received such a notice from *The Enterprise* that she refused to appear again and the theatre was finally closed.

Maguire continued making overtures for a reconciliation, but he was informed that in loyalty to the memory of the loyal Menken there could be none without an apology, a restitution of the former patronage, and the dismissal of the stage manager, who had ignored the Menken's plea for an apology to *The Enterprise*. They were harsh terms, but under the stress of circumstances, they were complied with.[21] Thus was the insult offered to the memory of the Menken wiped out.[22]

CHAPTER LIII

ARMY OF THE LORD

1864

"Events are now transpiring," began President Almarin Paul, "which call for immediate aid from our patriotic boys—and the Nevada Sanitary Fund Commissioners have deemed it advisable to make another call upon you."

Drawing closer to the footlights, President Paul explained to those 1600 boys who were seated before him in pit and gallery of Maguire's Theatre how pressing were the needs of the Union Army. Vicksburg had fallen. The Mississippi was free to vex its banks from source to delta. Gettysburg had broken the back of the Confederacy. A hundred thousand soldiers were lying in hospitals, sick—wounded—dying. Grant was in command of the Army of the Potomac. With eyes fixed on the spires of Richmond, he was fighting his way, stubbornly, through the Wilderness. With every step his men were bleeding—bleeding from a thousand wounds—wallowing forward over ground made sodden with blood. Unless those hemorrhages were staunched Grant's army would bleed to death. Would Sun Mountain give of her bullion before their old comrades were exsanguinated? [1]

Boys in blue as well as boys in gray needed lint and bandages, condensed milk and beefstock, spirits and coffee. Would Sun Mountain give and give freely? Thousands of dollars, hundred of thousands, were needed every day. No one had ever turned to Sun Mountain in vain. Now was the time to come forward.

As President Paul drew to the close of his appeal for Sanitary Funds a flushed usher rushed out on the stage. "Reuel Gridley," he said, "with his sack of flour on his back, is in the wings." [2]

"March him on—quick!" replied Paul, taking in the situation at a glance. [3]

"Gentlemen," announced Paul, turning to the audience, "the famous sack of Austin flour, the greatest money-raising flour in the country, and Mr. Gridley, himself, are in the building and will soon appear."

Hardly had the word "appear" passed his lips than down the stage

came Reuel Gridley, a tall, handsome, dark-haired youth with a
sack of flour, decorated with small flags, on his back. Immediately
the boys were on their feet and Maguire's rang with the gusto of
their applause.

It was a psychological moment and must be taken at the flood.
Paul reminded the boys that at that every moment General Grant
was advancing on Richmond. The closer he approached to his ob-
jective—the nearer would be the end of the war. "Every rod of his
victorious advance is paved with bleeding bodies of your comrades,"
he said. "With every step they are falling . . . laying the dust with
their heart's blood." He pointed to the sack of flour. "How much
am I bid? The money goes to those sick and wounded boys."

"An' 'Af! An' 'Af!" he imitated Comstock auctioneers.

At first the bidding was lively. Then the enthusiasm waned . . .
died out. In a half-hour he had sold and resold the sack of flour for
something over $1500 in gold coin,[4] but that was all. Not another
bid. The boys were finished. Paul was disappointed. The boys
"didn't see it," as he had hoped they would.[5] From those madcaps
he had expected much more. He had thought they would rise to
the occasion—as Austin, their great rival on the Reese River, had
risen. With a third of Sun Mountain's population, Austin had given
over $5000 for that sack of flour. He had expected the Comstock to
"raise Austin out of her boots." And the boys had fallen down. He
had counted on their gambling instincts—but most of all on their
sense of humor. He had never doubted their capacity to see the great
humor in paying thousands of dollars for a sack of flour worth only
a few. But he wouldn't let them off. They would have to be worked
up to the flour's significance. Tomorrow. Tomorrow he would
fix them.

The sack of flour had started its spectacular career at a municipal
election over in Austin—the fabulously rich mining town on the
Reese.[6] It had all come about over an election bet. When Charles
Holbrook, an ardent Unionist, ran for mayor against that red-hot
Democrat, David E. Buel,[7] considerable bad blood had been engen-
dered between Yankee and Southerner. Many eccentric bets on the
outcome of the election had been placed. None more startling than
Reuel Gridley's.

If Holbrook was elected, Gridley, a rabid secessionist, had agreed
to carry a sack of flour decorated with Stars and Stripes through the
streets of Austin.

Holbrook was elected and Reuel Gridley was required to shoulder the sack, decorated with the colors he despised, and carry it through the streets preceded by the municipal brass band playing "John Brown's Body." It was a distressing experience for a Southerner, but Gridley was made of good stuff and went through the ordeal unflinchingly.

When the procession was over, Mayor Holbrook gave orders to the band to play "Dixie." That was a tactful gesture. The rebels were pacified. Up went the sack of flour for auction. The proceeds were to be devoted to the Sanitary Fund for sick and wounded soldiers.[8] Over and over again the sack was sold. Now to Copperhead and now to Republican without distinction. In every case the purchaser paid the amount of his bid and donated the sack of flour back to the Sanitary Commission for resale.[9] In this way, with the best of feeling prevailing, the hilarious Austin boys raised some $6000.[10]

Such enthusiasm aroused the patriotic fire that had lain smoldering in the soul of the rebel—Reuel Gridley. It was a glorious cause that could thus win the sympathies of both parties![11]

When the news of the Austin flour-sack reached Sun Mountain it thrilled that erstwhile Southerner—Mark Twain—and that rabid Yankee—Almarin Paul—alike. There was an idea for raising money for the Comstock's share of the Sanitary Fund! Mark Twain had known Reuel Gridley in Hannibal, Missouri. A telegram was sent to Austin.

"Fetch along your flour-sack," it read.[12]

On the strength of that message Reuel Gridley shouldered his flour-sack up Sun Mountain and arrived just at the moment when Almarin Paul was holding a rally at Maguire's to raise funds for wounded soldiers.

So it was a profound disappointment to both Mark Twain and Paul when the sack of flour, upon which they had counted raising thousands of dollars, brought only as many hundreds. Without a struggle, the boys would give thousands and thousands of dollars to the Menken but would give only $1500 for wounded and suffering soldiers! What was the matter with their patriotism? Were they going to let a village like Austin outdo them? No. The boys were not ready for it, that was all. Almarin Paul blamed himself. He had not presented his case correctly. Those madcaps needed a different psychology . . . more light. They would have to turn their pockets inside out, acknowledge themselves "broke," before he would let them off. Tomorrow would be different.

Until a late hour that night Almarin Paul, Reuel Gridley, Mark

Twain, and Rufe Arick, the mayor of Virginia, cudgelled their brains as to how to make the cause of the sack more enticing. Finally a plan was decided upon.[13] When they retired they had no fears for the result. They would fix the boys! Tomorrow!

By eleven o'clock the next morning all was in readiness. Three open barouches, decorated in flags and buntings, and the Metropolitan Brass Band were engaged. In the first wagon went the brass band—ten pieces.[14] In the second carriage sat Mark Twain, as representative of *The Enterprise,* Almarin Paul, and Reuel Gridley with his sack of flour resplendent in fresh paint and wreathed in flags. In the third carriage were more members of the press.[15]

As soon as the band struck up "See, the Conquering Hero Comes," the procession moved up "C" Street, through a lane of wildly huzzahing boys, so jammed about the carriage containing Gridley and the sack of flour that the horses could scarcely move. At the corner of "C" and Taylor the crush increased. It was believed the sale would begin there. What was the boys' astonishment then when the driver whipped up the horses, they were jostled carelessly aside, and away sped the cavalcade, flags flying, band blaring, leaving the boys in open-mouthed astonishment in their wake. The boys were chagrined. The procession acted as if the Comstock had ceased to be of importance to the sack of flour. "The Army of the Lord," as Mark Twain had christened the cavalcade, disappeared in a cloud of dust over the Divide.[16]

Nearing Gold Hill the band played the "Star-Spangled Banner." Main Street was packed,[17] with men, women, children, Chinamen, and Piutes. Flags were flying from every pole. Bunting was waving from every balcony. Bands blared. Boys cheered. A halt was made in front of Maynard's Bank. Tom Fitch, with tongue tipped with honey, fingers touched with birdlime, made a short, stirring speech.[18] Bidding began. A telegram was handed to Paul. General Grant had won a signal victory in the Wilderness.[19] Victory could not have occurred more opportunely. Paul read the news to exulting throngs on every side.[20]

The twelve o'clock whistles blew. Hundreds of boys were brought to the surface. The sale began again, everybody shouting. "Who will make the first bid for the National-Sanitary-Flour Sack?" demanded Gridley.

He was the observed of all observers. Who would not have been the great Gridley at that moment, gazed at as the great man of the age?

What would Grant or Sherman have amounted to, with Gridley in view? What were the Wilderness or Richmond's spires in comparison to Reuel Gridley—the hero of the hour?

Bids went with a bang!

"The Belcher Company bids $500."

Not to be outdone, John B. Winters, president of his company, jumped up. "The Yellow Jacket bids $500."

Enthusiasm mounted. Heavy bids were received with tremendous cheering.

"Austin paid $3500 for that flour," said Fitch. "Can Gold Hill 'see that bet'?" But the most sanguine never expected to see it doubled.

"$5100," said the auctioneer.

"We're beating Virginia all to pieces," said a voice.

"Good, we always do do it," another voice.[22]

"$7052," said the auctioneer.[23]

Amidst continuous cheering Reuel Gridley mounted the rostrum and threw up the sponge to demonstrate to Gold Hill that Austin's bid had been beaten.[24]

In accordance with previous plans, Paul now sent a telegram to Virginia City. His message was posted on the bill-board of the Stock Exchange. The boys gathered around to read it. Gold Hill had raised their ante! Doubled Austin's! That would never do. Every few minutes fresh dispatches came from Paul and were bulletined. Excitement grew. Gold Hill had outstripped the Comstock. Their great rival had worsted them. The boys wired Gridley to bring back the flour; they'd show Gold Hill. Show Austin too! But such was not the plan of the campaigners. The Comstock's hour had not yet struck!

Down Gold Cañon went flour, speakers, music, and carriages, preceded by the Gold Hillers mounted on every available horse in their stables. At Devil's Gate the cavalcade stopped. Tom Fitch held forth again. It was mid-afternoon and commencing to rain. Half the population were at work. Many other things were in the way of a distinguished success. At that, Devil's Gate paid over $1800 for the sack.

That piece of news, too, was wired to Virginia. Even Devil's Gate had outdistanced the Comstock. The latter telegraphed Gridley, beseeching him to return. "Give us another chance," they wired. "We're waiting."

But Almarin Paul proceeded with his program. Down through Devil's Gate went the Gridley cavalcade, with all the buggies in the camp bringing up the rear. The "Army of the Lord" had swelled into a procession of carriages and mounted men.

At the Old Stone Hotel, near Silver City, the procession was hailed by the patriotic proprietress, Mrs. Eliza Elliott. She had $40 for the soldiers and "set-up drinks" for the "Army." With cheers they passed down the Cañon to Dayton.[25]

Flags were flying. Music bleating. It was a quarter to 4 P.M. Raining. Gridley stood up in his carriage and told those around Spafford Hall about the sack. Up went the flour. Out of pouches came $1,847.50.

"Welly good," said John Chinaman.[26]

"Heap good," said Sam Piute listening to the incessant clink of "eagles" falling into Sanitary coffers.

Another telegram went back to the Comstock boys. Notwithstanding rain and an off hour Dayton had paid $1,847.50 for the sack.[27] Virginia was sold out again. Again the Comstock wired for the sack. So excited had they grown that they called out their military companies[28] and sent a hurry call for troops from Fort Churchill.

"Now, for Carson," said Paul.

"No," replied Mark Twain, "emphatically no. The Carson ladies raised $3000 at their Sanitary Fund Ball and then donated the money to a miscegenation society."

And "the Army of the Lord," now augmented into a grand procession, turned about and retraced their steps up Gold Cañon. It was growing dusk, still raining. Passing through Silver City, it was learned that during their absence at Dayton, a large brown bug, which had been caught crawling up a man's leg, had been auctioned for $10; and that Captain Close[29] had soundly thrashed a spectator for using disrespectful language towards the bug and the Sanitary Cause. This madcap humor started the boys bidding all over again. On the strength of that brown bug and its angry champion, over $3000 more was added to the credit of Silver City.[30]

Every move was now telegraphed to the Comstock. Dispatches were arriving fast and furious.[31]

"'Xtray! 'Xtray! Greatest self-rising flour in the country," yelled the newsies. "Army of the Lord marching on the Comstock."

The Comstock wired that their militia had been ordered to go to Gold Hill, capture "The Army of the Lord," take away the sack of flour and bring it back to Virginia.

Sure enough, the telegram had no more than been read before

Gridley could see the Comstock boys, thousands strong, pouring over the Divide with bands playing and flags flying. Up through Devil's Gate were coming another band and more troops—the soldiers from Fort Churchill. The "Army" was caught between two forces.

By half-past eight that night, when the procession crossed the Divide, Virginia was ablaze with color and light. Torches were glaring. Flags flying. Bands playing. Crowds cheering. The three-carriage cavalcade of the morning had swelled to a mighty host over a mile in length—National Guards—Regulars from Fort Churchill —mounted cavalry—multitudes on foot.[32] The streets went wild with excitement as the procession came to a stop in front of Gillig, Mott & Company.[33]

Bidding began. The voice of the auctioneer was drowned in the frantic chorus of bids.[34] Gold slugs, twenties, tens rained upon the sack before Gridley could tell the boys what had happened at Gold Hill, Devil's Gate, Silver City, and Dayton. As soon as the racket subsided he demanded that the Comstock "cover" the entire sum.[35]

When Charles Bonner, superintendent of the Gould & Curry, "raised Austin out of her boots," with one magnificent bid of $3500, the cheers could have been heard above the flag-staff on Sun Mountain. Chollar bid $500. Not to be outdone by their old enemy, the Potosi Silver Mining Company raised their bid to $550. Bill Stewart bid $500. Not only money but county scrip, mining shares, shotguns, bowies, "navies," and money-pouches went to swell the fund. Gridley could not receive the contributions fast enough to satisfy the generosity of the crowd. *The Enterprise* bid $150. Their old enemy, *The Union,* outbid them in one magnificent gesture of $355. "Splurging," said Mark Twain. Tom Peasley bid $100. Booth's Mill paid $50 for permission to drive their wagon through the crowd. Somebody donated $5 for "Andy Johnson of Tennessee." [36] Every bid was greeted with deafening cheers. Julia Bulette bought the sack, for a second. Chinamen gave their savings. Piutes gave their all.[37] At the end of two-and-a-half hours the Comstock had paid in cold cash, for a fifty-pound sack of flour, a sum equal to $40,000 in greenbacks! [38]

"If Grant takes Richmond," yelled Almarin Paul, "$20,000 more goes to the Army of the Potomac." [39]

The generous, charitable character of the boys was never better illustrated than it was that night. They might oppose taxation of their mining interests because they felt it was wrong, but if the sick and wounded of army and navy needed money they would empty their pockets—give everything they owned.[40]

At eleven o'clock on the morning of the 16th of May, Yankees and Southerners were bitter in their partisanship, ready at a moment's notice to fly at each other's throats. By ten o'clock that night sectional and partisan rancor had been forgotten in giving. The call of suffering humanity healed all rancor.

From then on the rebellion was discussed in a different tone from that which had heretofore prevailed. Charity had united them in a kindlier feeling for their distracted country.[41]

Altogether Reuel Gridley raised $275,000 on his sack of flour and turned it over to the Sanitary Commission. All the money collected on the Comstock Lode was melted down into fourteen silver bricks. On each brick was stamped its value in gold and silver and the name of a battle—Gettysburg, Vicksburg, Chattanooga, Chickamauga, Manassas, Chancellorsville, etc. These bricks were forwarded by Wells Fargo & Company's Express to New York to the Reverend Doctor Henry Bellows, president of the National Sanitary Commission.

Word came back of their reception there. A meeting of Sanitary forces was called in a theatre. Doctor Bellows made an opening address. As the band played the Star-Spangled Banner, and the audience jumped to their feet, the curtain went up. Upon the stage stood an immense Christmas tree. Hanging from its branches were the silver bricks which had come from Sun Mountain.[42]

CHAPTER LIV

MARK TWAIN'S LAST HOAX

May, 1864

In the midst of the excitement over Sanitary funds, Joe Goodman was called to San Francisco. During his absence he appointed Mark Twain editor-in-chief of *The Enterprise*.

Mark felt the responsibility very keenly. Not only had he Joe's reputation to uphold but he must make the paper readable to the boys. As such he could not fail in his duty by avoiding any one's sensitive spots. He was so occupied with Sanitary Fund affairs that he had very little time to devote to literary matters, otherwise he might have managed another classic hoax like the petrified man. But being rushed he looked around for something easier. As April was the birth month of Shakespeare and as the tercentenary fell around the 22d, Mark decided to give the boys an editorial on the Bard of Avon. Was he born on the 20th or the 23d? Who knew? There were many things Mark didn't know about the poet. By the time he had written a half-column his knowledge as well as the contents of the only encyclopedia on the Mountain was exhausted. So he completed the column with escapades that no Shakespearian scholar would have recognized. Not facts exactly—but who cared? As usual, Mark was searching for the bard's spirit, not his reality.

On the night of May 17, 1864, Mark came back to the editorial room of *The Enterprise* tired out from another busy Sanitary Fund day. What sort of editorials should he write for the morning's paper? If Joe Goodman had been there the trend of history might have been different. But Joe was far away, Mark was exhausted, and those editorials must be written. When no brilliant idea popped into his head two significant subjects suggested themselves. One was that the employees of *The Virginia Daily Union*—*The Enterprise's* bitter enemy in an editorial way—had failed to pay their recent subscription to the Sanitary Fund. The other was dynamite but good material for an editorial—and Mark was tired.

It was reported that the ladies of Carson, who had just sponsored a successful masquerade ball for the benefit of the Sanitary Fund and had collected some $3000, had decided to use the fund for another purpose. That, thought Mark, would be good for one of those satirical little sketches—women never had the same mind twice—you couldn't depend on them.

Mark entitled his editorial on the failure of *The Virginia Daily Union* to pay their donation to the Sanitary Fund, "How Is It?"

"How is it?" Mark queried editorially. "How is it that *The Union* outbid us for the flour Monday night and now repudiate their bid?[1] How is it that *Union* employees refused to pay their subscriptions when they fell due? Did they pledge themselves for a big amount solely to make a bigger display than *The Enterprise*? Had they any other idea than to splurge?" [2]

With *The Union* thus disposed of, Mark turned his attention to the Carson ladies.

"The reason," wrote he, "that the 'Army of the Lord' did not take the flour-sack to Carson was because it was stated that the money raised at the Sanitary Fancy Dress Ball for sick and wounded soldiers had been diverted from its legitimate course, and was to be sent to aid a miscegenation society somewhere in the East; and it was feared that the proceeds of the sack might be similarly disposed of." Mark labelled this little skit a "hoax"—a little joker—"but not all a hoax"—wrote Mark, "for an effort is being made to divert those funds from their proper course." [3]

Now the Sanitary Fancy Dress Ball was gotten up by the leading ladies of Carson City. When they read what *The Enterprise* had to say about the receipts of their ball, they were furious. It was libellous to accuse ladies of diverting funds from sick and wounded soldiers. Mark Twain had gotten out of his previous lampooning by calling it a "hoax," but not this time. The ladies appealed to their husbands. A committee wrote to *The Enterprise* demanding an immediate public apology. Several days elapsed. When the apology was not forthcoming their president, Mrs. W. K. Cutler, wrote an open letter to *The Virginia Daily Union,* asking redress.

"The whole statement," she complained, "is a tissue of falsehoods, made for malicious purposes, and we demand the name of the author. At a meeting of the ladies, no decision was arrived at as to the proceeds of the ball—but one thing *was decided,* that they should go to the aid of the sick and wounded soldiers, who are fighting the battles of our country, *and for no other purpose.* . . . In conclusion, let us say that the ladies having the matter in charge consider themselves capable of deciding as to what shall be done with the money, without the aid of outsiders, who are probably desirous of acquiring some *glory* by appropriating the efforts of the ladies to themselves." The communication was signed by "Mrs. W. K. Cutler, President, Sanitary Ball."[4]

Mark Twain had not been intentionally discourteous in not answering Mrs. Cutler's letter—he would answer it presently but his "How Is It?" editorial had him fully occupied for the time.

That letter from the ladies of the Sanitary Ball Committee was just the thing that Editor James Laird of *The Union* wanted. He saw in it the chance to humiliate old enemies on *The Enterprise*. He printed the communication in a conspicuous place under the heading—"*The Enterprise's* Libel of the Ladies of Carson." Among his editorials was another entitled "The How Is It Issue," in which the editor flayed the "hoax writer" as a liar, a poltroon, and a puppy.[5]

"Never before in a long period of newspaper intercourse," the editor of *The Union* blazed forth, "never before in any contact with a contemporary, however unprincipled he might have been—have we found an opponent, in statement or in discussion, who had no gentlemanly sense of professional propriety, who conveyed in every word, and in every purpose of all his words, such a grovelling disregard for truth, decency, and courtesy as to seem to court the distinction only of being understood as a vulgar liar. Meeting one who prefers falsehood; whose instincts are all toward falsehood; whose thought is falsification; whose aim is vilification through insincere professions of honesty; one whose only merit is thus described, and who evidently desires to be thus known, the obstacles presented are entirely insurmountable, and whoever would touch them fully should expect to be abominably defiled." [6]

Rollin Daggett and Steve Gillis were delighted with Laird's editorial. They saw in those vitriolic sentences a chance for a duel. Hadn't Joe Goodman crippled Tom Fitch for life for a similar offense? Hadn't Steve Gillis faced three irate men at fifteen paces? Hadn't Dan De Quille faced Langford Peel? They had all faced lead but Mark Twain. Never yet had he received his baptism under fire. Now was his opportunity. Such an insult could not be brooked —it required blood atonement—the best blood Jim Laird could furnish. Mark could really amount to something on Sun Mountain now—he had an opportunity to get his man—to get a notch on his gun-butt. No gentleman could afford to overlook such an opportunity. If he could kill his man in the duel Mark would be more looked up to than if he had killed two men in the ordinary way. It was the chance of a life-time. Steve and "Dag" envied him! Mark was not too enthusiastic over the prospect. The refinements of

Parisian civilization had not yet reached Sun Mountain. You couldn't pink your man and call it quits. A Washoe duel must be fought out. Usually it left but one survivor. Their code required it. The weapons were always Colt navy revolvers; distance fifteen paces; fire and advance; six shots allowed.[7]

Mark Twain was against Washoe duelling. He hated firearms. He was a poor marksman—averse to violence of any kind. But the boys insisted on a duel. They told him there was no way out of it. He wasn't going to allow any man to call him a liar—a poltroon and a puppy, and live—was he? He must challenge Laird at once or he would be disgraced for ever and ever on Sun Mountain. No red-blooded man would countenance such epithets.

Shortly after lunch, with the help of Rollin Daggett, Mark Twain wrote out a vigorous, venomous challenge. He demanded a public retraction of the insults offered that morning in *The Union* or satisfaction on a field of honor. Steve Gillis carried the letter to *The Union* office and delivered it to James Laird in person. Then *The Enterprise* staff sat back—jubilant—but Mark did not join in. As hour after hour slipped by and no reply came from Laird, Mark became more confident. Laird wouldn't fight! The boys took a dismal interest in the matter!

Then a reply came. Mark tore open the envelope, with the boys crowding over his shoulder to read the answer. Mark read:

> Office of *The Virginia Daily Union*
> Virginia, May 21, 1864.
>
> Samuel Clemens: James Laird has just handed me your note of this date. Permit me to say that I am the author of the article appearing in this morning's *Union*. I am responsible for it. I have nothing to retract.   Respectfully,
>
> J. W. Wilmington.[8]

The boys were furious. So was Mark Twain, on the surface. Wilmington was a reporter. Mark must have satisfaction from the responsible party—the editor himself—not a cub reporter.

It was now evening. Shadows were falling fast. Mark wrote out another challenge, hotter than the first:

> *Enterprise* Office,
> Saturday evening, May 21, 1864.
>
> James Laird—Sir: I wrote you a note this afternoon, demanding a published retraction of insults that appeared in two articles in

The Union of this morning, or satisfaction. I have since received what purports to be a reply, written by a person who signs himself "J. W. Wilmington," in which he assumes the authorship and responsibility of one of said infamous articles. Wilmington is a person entirely unknown to me in the matter, and has nothing to do with it. In the columns of your paper you have declared your own responsibility for all articles appearing in it, and any further attempt to make a cats-paw of any other individual, and thus shirk a responsibility that you had previously assumed, will show that you are a cowardly sneak. I now peremptorily demand of you the satisfaction due to a gentleman, without alternative.

SAM L. CLEMENS.

Steve carried it over to Laird's office. Nothing came of it. Mark began to feel quite comfortable.[9] The boys grew more and more exasperated as hour after hour slipped by and no answer appeared.

While anger was at torrid heat in *The Enterprise* office Laird sought out Tom Fitch with Mark's peremptory challenge. Laird's face was white as he handed the challenge over to Fitch.

"I am up against it," he whined. "I must either fight or quit the country. I will sell you my one-third interest in *The Union* for half its value, and sell it on credit, so that you can pay for it out of your share of the profits, and assume the responsibility for my article and fight Sam Clemens."

"Can't I buy you out and then apologize to Sam?" said Fitch.

"My partners wouldn't stand for that. Somebody has got to fight Mark or it will ruin the paper," groaned Laird.

"Sam Clemens and I are personal friends," said Fitch, "although we have been employed on rival papers. I decline to shorten his young and beautiful life, and I know that he would not like to be guilty of the deep damnation of my taking off. I am willing to buy into your paper, but I decline to buy into your fight."[10]

Back to his office went James Laird. There was nothing else to do. He must write a reply. Otherwise he would be disgraced:

Office of *The Virginia Daily Union,*
Virginia, Saturday Evening, May 21, 1864.

Samuel Clemens, Esq.: Your note of this evening is received. To the first portion of it I will briefly reply, that Mr. J. W. Wilmington, the avowed author of the article to which you object, is a gentleman now in the employ of *The Union* office. He formerly was one of the proprietors of *The Cincinnati Enquirer.* He was captain of a company in the Sixth Ohio Regiment, and fought at Shiloh. His responsibility and character can be vouched for to your abundant satisfaction.

For all editorials appearing in *The Union,* the proprietors are personally responsible; for communications, they hold themselves ready, when properly called upon, either to give the name and address of the author, or, failing that, to be themselves responsible.

The editorial in *The Enterprise* headed "How Is It?" out of which this controversy grew, was an attack made upon the printers of *The Union.* It was replied to by a *Union* printer, and a representative of the printers, who in a communication denounced the writer of that article as a liar, a poltroon, and a puppy. You announce yourself as the writer of that article which provoked this communication, and demand "satisfaction"—which satisfaction the writer informs you, over his own signature, he is quite ready to afford. I have no right, under the rulings of the code you have invoked, to step in and assume Wilmington's position, nor would he allow me to do so. You demand of me, in your last letter, the satisfaction due to a gentleman, and couple the demand with offensive remarks. When you have earned the right to the title by complying with the usual custom, I shall be most happy to afford you any satisfaction you desire at any time and in any place. In short, Wilmington has a prior claim upon your attention. When he is through with you, I shall be at your service. If you decline to meet him after challenging him, you will prove yourself to be what he has charged you with being, *"a liar, a poltroon, and a puppy,"* and as such, cannot, of course, be entitled to the consideration of a gentleman.

Respectfully,

James L. Laird.

It was now about 9 o'clock P.M. Mark was getting bloodthirsty and beginning to feel that he wanted to fight a duel. Nothing would satisfy him but a duel. He sat down and wrote another challenge—more vitriolic—more peremptory in tone than the previous one. Laird would have to be a coward to refuse:

Enterprise Office, Virginia City,
May 21, 1864—9 o'clock P.M.

James L. Laird—Sir: Your reply to my note—in which I peremptorily demanded satisfaction of you, without alternative—is just received, and to my utter astonishment you still endeavor to shield your craven carcass behind the person of an individual who in spite of your introduction is entirely unknown to me, and upon whose shoulders you cannot throw the whole responsibility. You acknowledge and reaffirm in this note that, "For all editorials appearing in *The Union* the proprietors are personally responsible." Now, sir, had there appeared no editorial on the subject indorsing and reiterating the slanderous and disgraceful insults heaped upon me in the "communication," I would have simply called upon you and demanded the name of its author, and upon your answer would have depended my further action. But the "editorial" alluded to was equally vile and slanderous as the "communication," and being an "editorial" would naturally have more weight in the minds of readers. It was the following undignified and abominably insulting slander appearing in your "editorial" headed "The 'How Is It' Issue," that occasioned my sending you first an alternative and then a peremptory challenge:

"Never before in a long period of newspaper intercourse—never before in any contact with a contemporary, however unprincipled he might have been—have we found an opponent, in statement or in discussion, who had no gentlemanly sense of professional propriety, who conveyed in every word, and in every purpose of all his words, such a groveling disregard for truth, decency, and courtesy as to seem to court the distinction only of being understood as a vulgar liar. Meeting one who prefers falsehood; whose instincts are all toward falsehood; whose thought is falsification; whose aim is vilification through insincere profession of honesty; one whose only merit is thus described, and who evidently desires to be thus known, the obstacles presented are entirely insurmountable, and whoever would touch them fully should expect to be abominably defiled."— *Union,* May 21st.

You assume in your last note, that I "have challenged Wilmington," and that he has informed me, "over his own signature," that he is quite ready to afford me "satisfaction."

Both assumptions are utterly false. I have twice challenged you, and you have twice attempted to shirk the responsibility. Wilmington's note could not possibly be an answer to my demand for satisfaction from you; and besides, his note simply avowed authorship of a certain "communication" that appeared simultaneously with your libelous "editorial," and stated that its author had "nothing to retract." For your gratification, however, I will remark that Wilmington's case will be attended to in due time by a distant acquaintance of his who is not willing to see him suffer in obscurity. In the meantime, if you do not wish yourself posted as a coward, you will at once accept my peremptory challenge, which I now reiterate.

SAM. L. CLEMENS.

The boys waited. Laird would never stand such insulting language. Midnight came. No answer. They went home to restless sleep. Monday morning the reply arrived:

Office of *The Virginia Daily Union,*
Monday morning, May 23, 1864.

Samuel Clemens: In reply to your lengthy communication, I have only to say that in your note opening this correspondence, you demanded satisfaction for a communication in *The Union* which branded the writer of an article in *The Enterprise* as a liar, a poltroon, and a puppy. You declare yourself to be the writer of *The Enterprise* article, and the avowed author of *The Union* communication stands ready to afford satisfaction. Any attempt to evade a meeting with him and force one upon me will utterly fail, as I have no right under the rulings of the code to meet or hold any communication with you in this connection. The threat of being posted as a coward cannot have the slightest effect upon the position I have assumed in the matter. If you think this correspondence reflects credit upon you I advise you by all means to publish it. In the meantime you must excuse me from receiving any more long epistles from you.

JAMES L. LAIRD.

The man's tone was changing! He appeared to be waking up! He was a man who couldn't be depended upon. The boys exulted. They egged Mark on to a final effort.

In the Tuesday morning *Enterprise,* Mark Twain posted James Laird as a coward.

I denounce Laird as an unmitigated liar, because he says I published an editorial in which I attacked the printers employed on *The Union,* whereas there is nothing in that editorial which can be so construed. Moreover, he is a liar on general principles, and from natural instinct. I denounce him as an abject coward, because it has been stated in his paper that its proprietors are responsible for all articles appearing in its columns, yet he backs down from that position; because he acknowledges the "code," but will not live up to it; because he says himself that he is responsible for all "editorials," and then backs down from that also; and because he insults me in his note marked "IV," and yet refuses to fight me. Finally, he is a fool, because he cannot understand that a publisher is bound to stand responsible for any and all articles printed by him, whether he wants to do it or not.

SAM. L. CLEMENS.

All day the boys waited. Hours dragged on leaden feet—morning—noon—night—midnight—silence.

The Enterprise went to press. In the small hours of the morning the reply came. Laird accepted Mark's challenge. The duel would take place at sunrise in a nearby ravine.[11]

CHAPTER LV

THE DUEL

May, 1864

The staff were delighted. Mark Twain was not, though he tried to appear so. He chose Steve Gillis as his second. Worse still, that morning Mark had received another challenge. W. K. Cutler, husband of the irate president of the Sanitary Ball Committee, wanted satisfaction for the insult offered his wife. In addition, the spouses of the other members of the committee promised Mark horsewhippings for his innuendoes regarding their wives' honesty.

Mark was inundated with threats and challenges. But the duel at sunrise was the pressing matter. Steve and Mark went home. It was long past midnight. Mark looked around his quarters—what priceless nights he had enjoyed there with the gang. Steve, all excited, could talk of nothing but duels; all the ones he had been in and heard of; all the men he had killed and fatally wounded. All the duel fatalities he had ever heard about. In the wee small hours of the night he prevailed upon Mark to make a will. It was better to have a will whether you had anything to will or not. It looked better, if you were killed.

Before dawn Steve rose from his bed and dressed. It wasn't necessary to rout out Mark. He hadn't slept a wink. It was necessary to drill him before he met Laird on the field of honor. They hied themselves into a ravine on the outskirts of the city. It was pitch dark. The groans of the hoists, the rat-a-tat of the compressors never sounded more friendly—ore-wagons were just wheeling into action—what a jovial lot those drivers were! A shift was changing —what glorious fellows those miners! And the sage—how pungent!

On their way to the duelling ground they borrowed a barn-door for a target—borrowed it of a gentleman who was asleep. They propped the barn-door up. Against the middle of it they stood a rail to represent Laird. On top of the rail they stuck a squash to represent his head. He was a tall, lean creature—the poorest sort of material for a duel. Nothing but a line shot could "fetch" him. Even then he might split your bullet. But the squash was all right.

If there was any intellectual difference between the squash and Laird's head it was in favor of the squash![1]

Dawn was breaking. The first faint rays suffused the east. Mark practised and practised. He could not hit the rail, so he tried the squash. He couldn't hit that, so he aimed at the barn-door. Missed it. He was greatly disheartened now. This was to be his last day on earth, and the sage smelt so sweet!

They began to hear pistol-shots in the next ravine. Mark knew what that meant. Jim Laird was out practising, too. Mark was utterly dispirited. Jim would send over spies. They would see that he couldn't hit a barn-door. That he hadn't even nicked it! That would be the end of him.

Just at that agonizing moment a mud-hen—out of the nowhere —flew across his vision and lit on a sage-brush clump thirty paces away.

Steve Gillis, discouraged at Mark Twain's marksmanship, jerked out his own "navy"—aimed—banged—off fell the mud-hen's head, and rolled in the dust.

At that moment Jim Laird's seconds came running up, saw the mud-hen's head in the sand.

"Who did that?" one exclaimed.

"My man—Twain," said Gillis.

"How far off was he?"

"Oh, no great distance. About thirty paces."

"The mischief, he did! Can he do that often?"[2]

"Well—yes. He can do it, about—well—about four times out of five."

Mark Twain knew the cheerful little liar was fabricating. But he never said a word. He never contradicted him. Steve was not of a disposition to invite confidences of that kind. So he let the matter rest. But it was a comfort to see those people look sick, and watch their under-jaws drop. Presently they went away and got Laird and took him home.

The sun came up in a burst of golden glory. It gilded Sugar Loaf—suffused Sun Mountain. The finger flamed! Birds sang! A half-hour later when Mark Twain and Steve reached *The Enterprise* office, they found a note from James Laird—he absolutely refused to fight!

It was a narrow escape. Later, Mark found out that Laird hit his target thirteen times out of eighteen shots![3] If it hadn't been for that mud-hen's head where would the bard's of Sun Mountain have lain?

Of course, after that letter, Laird couldn't hold his head up on Sun Mountain. There was no room for him. He had refused to fight! He was disgraced, and left.[4]

Not for long was Mark the hero of the hour. News of the duel reached the governor and Judge North at one and the same time. Mark hadn't been over-kind to the Territorial Tribunal. Hadn't he burlesqued the chief justice? Hadn't he dubbed him "Professor Personal Pronoun"? A law had been passed, during the last legislature, making duelling an offense with two years' imprisonment. Judge North saw a chance to make an example of Mark Twain. He issued a warrant for his arrest.

The governor—who was fond of Mark—sent him a warning. He would see that the warrant wasn't served for twenty-four hours! And the sage smelt so homey! But—two years in state's prison did not appeal to Mark Twain. He must leave Sun Mountain—Joe Goodman—*The Enterprise*—give up those priceless nights of good-fellowship! But he couldn't leave without attending to Cutler. He was at the International awaiting his turn at fifteen paces. Steve told Sam to go and pack up. He would take care of Cutler. Steve gave Cutler fifteen minutes to leave the city. Within that time Steve was back in Mark's room and Cutler had gone.

Under cover of friendly darkness Mark and Steve took their seats in the west-bound stage and were soon careening down Gold Cañon.

Within two years Washoe had produced Mark Twain and was sending him forth with prestige and a name widely known in literary circles on the Coast but albeit a fugitive from her justice.

BOOK THREE

BORRASCA

CHAPTER LVI

BORRASCA

August 1, 1864

By the summer of 1864, the cream of Comstock croppings had been skimmed. Mines and mills were all in litigation. Thousands and thousands of dollars were being expended for corrupt judicial decisions. Court opinions were for sale to the highest bidder. For adequate compensation one or the other of the judiciary would steal up the mountain and grant an injunction by which hundreds were thrown out of work. The disgraceful struggle over the Chollar-Potosi was raging with unprecedented fury. Bill Stewart still contended that the Potosi was part of the Chollar ledge. Sun Mountain had one ledge and one ledge only. Potosi engineers fought back. They swore theirs was a separate ledge. They caused the resignation of a one-ledge judge and the setting up of an idolator who believed in many. The plethoric purses of California millionaires were drained in the interest of the one-ledge theory. Fortunes were tottering. The speculative structure of Washoe was on the point of collapsing. Something must give or everything would break. There was not money enough to carry on—to buy judges and juries, and pay lawyers' fees and general running expenses. All available funds were being squandered on bribery and corruption, none on legitimate development of Washoe's resources. Not content with a reasonable share of profits—caliphs were destroying one another in the titanic struggle for a lion's portion. The boys were being made to suffer.

In addition the cost of working the mines had increased enormously. Shafts were down as far as known methods could sink them. That was not far enough to continue the exploration of ore bodies. Valuable ledges were disappearing into a muck of steam and scalding water. Seams couldn't be followed until something was done about the water. The pump wasn't made that could control those subterranean floods.

Then Adolph Sutro popped up again. Sutro claimed he could, if given a chance, drain the mines through his tunnel to the Carson

River! But there was no money to finance his construction company. Besides, it was all government land. Sutro would have to get permission from Washington. Due to water all the mines between the Ophir and the Gould & Curry were shut down. Mackay and Fair claimed there was just as valuable ore in that ground, below the water-level, as had been discovered in the Ophir and Gould & Curry. It stood to reason.

It appeared, after all the tremendous expenditure of man-power, horse-power, machine-power, that greed had wrecked Washoe; that the earth was going to win the struggle. Where was the engine, where the pump, where the brains, that could prove that Mackay was right? Sutro claimed he could—but it would take millions to verify it. Where were those millions coming from? The same old proverb confronted them: "It takes gold to mine silver!"

In the meantime mines and mills were closing. Hundreds of boys were thrown out of work. Hundreds more would be. One night Bill Stewart, as the companies' lawyer, called a meeting of the managers of the Sapphire, the Imperial, the Empire, the Comet, the Gould & Curry, the Ophir, and the Mexican, to see what could be done. In the emergency, said Bill, wages must be reduced from four dollars to three and a half dollars a day.

The boys were furious when they heard about this prospective cut. With the high cost of living in Washoe, theirs was hardly a living wage. *The Enterprise* was loud in its denunciation of Bill's plan for wage reduction. Joe Goodman wrote that the magnates should stop their ruinous litigation and pay the boys a wage commensurate with their dangerous occupation. "Cleanse the courts," thundered Joe, "they are filthier than Ægean stables. Turn the Carson into them and get down to legitimate mining. With the millions still in the Gould & Curry and still in the Ophir there is no necessity of reducing wages and ruining business on this mountain."

Then the boys called an indignation meeting in Gold Hill to discuss the reduction of wages. It was reported that Charles Bonner, superintendent of the Gould & Curry; Isaac Requa, superintendent of the Comet Mill; the superintendents of the Sapphire, the Imperial, the Ophir, and Mexican were all determined to reduce wages.[1]

Somebody announced that Bill Stewart had instigated these men.[2] Bill Stewart, with his hundreds of thousands in annual fees! The boys couldn't believe it.

That report about Bill stirred the assemblage into greater fury than anything else. Bill Stewart would grind them under heel! They called him a traitor! And even worse names. He would take food out of their children's mouths—would he? The question was put. It was unanimously agreed to string Bill up the next morning.[3]

Then thousands strong, with music playing, the boys went out into the Cañon and paraded up and down shouting their watchword, "Four Dollars a Day!" Bells rang—whistles tooted—as they marched. They passed Sandy Bowers' mine—he was still paying four dollars a day—with cheers. They went by the Kentuck—a three dollars and fifty cents concern—with unearthly groans.[4] . . .

They agreed to meet en masse in front of the Imperial works at six o'clock the next morning and attend to Bill Stewart, Charley Bonner, Isaac Requa, and the rest.

Before dawn 2000 determined-looking men were milling about the Cañon. In a procession over a mile in length they marched on the Imperial. Without a struggle the superintendent agreed to their demands. Yelling—"Four Dollars a Day!" they turned to the Comet Mill. Isaac Requa, the superintendent, appeared before its doors. When he claimed that he had discharged all his three-dollar-and-fifty men and had only four-dollar men in his employ, the boys were doubtful. A workman was summoned to prove that Requa spoke the truth.[5]

Sinuous as a snake, the procession took up its line of march on Virginia City.[6] Now for Bill Stewart, the arch conspirator! They would swing him from the nearest shaft-head. All that bosh about the "honest miner"! Reduce their wages, would he? A rope was procured. On the Divide, a Virginia City delegation, equally incensed, met them. Four abreast, they turned down "C" Street—straight for Bill's hotel.

Two blocks from the International Hotel, those in the lead saw Bill Stewart calmly smoking his pipe. He looked as though he were waiting for something or somebody. Some one had told him that they were coming. But he couldn't escape! They were ready for him!

"Four Dollars a Day!" shouted the leaders as they came within Bill's hearing.

As they approached still nearer, they saw Bill smile and nod. Saw him run out into the middle of the street and hold out his arms as if to stop them.

They noted the look of confidence on his face. They saw him plant his long legs, like a colossus, apart. They saw him pull his body erect, square his shoulders, as if he would stem that oncoming tide!

"Four Dollars a Day!" shouted the man with the rope, weaving it back and forth, as if he would throw it over Bill's head.

Bill answered. His voice rang out above theirs. They slowed up to listen.

"Appoint a committee," thundered Bill. "Have this matter investigated!"[7]

Bill spoke with a voice of authority. The leaders stopped. That was a good idea—to investigate. They would. They named a committee.

Bill pointed to the balcony of the International Hotel. Let's go up there, he said, where we can be seen by the men below, and arbitrate.

Up the stairs they went. Presently out on the balcony they appeared. All this time the mob, with their eyes fixed on the group on the balcony, kept up a continuous obligato of "Four Dollars a Day!"

Within two hours one of the committee stepped to the balcony railing. They had prepared a resolution, he said. Was it agreeable to the boys? He read it.

Wages should remain at four dollars a day. Those who had plotted to hang Bill Stewart should not be discriminated against. Friendly relations should be restored.

Yes, that was all right, said the boys. But how about Charley Bonner and the superintendents of the Ophir and Mexican? Charley Bonner had been a ring-leader in this reduction business. Some word must come from them, before they would disperse.

Bill Stewart tried to ferret them out. But no luck. They were afraid of being lynched and had run away. Even then Father Manogue was hiding Bonner in the belfry of St. Mary's.

"Adjourn until this evening," admonished Bill. "I'll have Bonner here then."

Night was falling when the mob marched back to "C" Street.[8] As they were passing the balcony of the International a voice accosted them.

They looked up. Their man Frank Tilford—one in whom they had the utmost confidence—was hailing.[9]

Tilford came forward to the railing. In burning words he told his friends the stern hard truth of all the ills that had come upon Washoe. Wealth had brought evil not good upon them.

"There are men," he said, "who, for their own aggrandizement, would coin the blood of a nation into dollars. Such men, and their name is legion, have done all in their power to create a panic, not only in the price of labor but in everything that capital can purchase or poverty can sell. But, beyond all this there is another, and more effective cause at work, potential and active throughout every section of our Territory. You will find it in the deep and universal distrust of our judiciary—Chief Justice George Turner and his satellites, Mott—North—Locke. Among all classes this feeling prevails. Unfortunately this condition rests on a solid foundation of fact and evidence, undisputed, undeniable.

"It is a fact, flagrant and notorious, that thousands and hundreds of thousands of dollars have been expended in obtaining corrupt decisions from these infamous judges. Your judiciary steal into our cities at midnight, grant injunctions by which hundreds are thrown out of employment, and then, like fugitives fleeing from justice, fly before daylight from the indignation of an outraged people.

"Had the thousands of dollars which have been lavished in the bribery and corruption of the judiciary been expended in the legitimate development of our mines, there would at this day be no complaint of hard times and no demand for reduced wages. What is the remedy for the present evils? Is it in lowering the compensation of the toiling miners? Already the price of daily work is hardly sufficient to support you in decency. Everything that you wear, eat, or drink, costs as much now as formerly. To reduce wages is to drive to death and despair the miner and his family. It cannot—it must not be. By the law of ancient Rome, a convicted traitor was hurled from the Tarpian rock. Let the man who, in this crisis, advocates a reduction of miners' wages be girdled and encircled with burning faggots, and pitched from the summit of Sun Mountain headlong into the desert.

"Fellow citizens, where then shall we find the cure for evils which have grown intolerable? No moderate measures will suffice. The diseases under which we suffer are desperate. They require desperate remedies. First, meet in your primary assemblies and petition our present judges to resign. The voice of the people is the voice of God. Speak up. Even these wicked and profligate men, who disgrace the ermine they wear and pervert the power they possess, may harken unto and obey it. If that fails, then let us humbly and fervently supplicate Abraham Lincoln—President of these United States—to remove from us these magistrates, who are more terrible and intolerable curses than the plagues of Egypt."

A cry went up against the judiciary—George Turner—Mott—Locke, and North. They would hang the judges with their ermine.

The boys repaired to an armory and formed themselves into a union—the better to deal with their judiciary. When one of their own number had fashioned a transparency, another shouldered it and together they marched down "C" Street. As it was borne by crowded corners there came an ominous growl such as sweeps tree-tops just before a cyclone breaks. A magic formula was printed on the transparency: "Equal Rights—Laws—Justice." A few words whose philosophy had already reared a pyramid of bones far loftier than that of Old Cheops. What rights? said the boys as it passed, what laws had they in Washoe? Justice trailed her ermine through the gutter.[10]

As the procession passed beneath the balcony of the International Hotel, Bill Stewart might have been seen to lean far over the railing, wave his hat, and shout—"Three cheers for the honest miner!"

CHAPTER LVII

THE THIRTEENTH AMENDMENT

1864-65

When Joe Goodman printed a telegram in *The Enterprise* announcing that Senator Doolittle of Wisconsin had introduced a bill in the United States Senate[1] authorizing a second enabling act to permit Washoe to draw up another constitution and submit it to President Lincoln, the boys could hardly believe eyes or ears. Bill Stewart was dumfounded. Here was something of which he knew nothing. What was happening in Washington? What did Senator Doolittle know of the scandalous state of affairs in Washoe?[2]

From then on, dispatches came fast and furious to *The Enterprise*. From these the boys learned that when the question of permitting Nevada to organize a State government came up in the House of Representatives at Washington, there was plenty of strong opposition against the act. Could some of them have heard what was said of Washoe they would have reached for their bowies. One member declared that Washoe was a wild place. Another that it was petty. It was not big enough to become a State. It was only a mountain.

Then word came that President Lincoln was behind Senator Doolittle's bill. It seemed the President needed Washoe, just as a politician needs a pawn on a political chess-board. Long ago he had figured out that of all available pieces Washoe was the one he required to help him. But to make it of proper utility Washoe must be created into a State.

The boys recalled the interest the President had always manifested in Sun Mountain. Hadn't the President sent them a governor who could be relied upon to be in accord with his policies? Hadn't the President in his first message to Congress congratulated them on setting up a civil government in a territory where treason existed?[3] Hadn't he fostered immigration to Washoe?[4] Hadn't he even hinted at statehood? Hadn't he argued that the mountain's wealth would be an asset in paying war debts?[5] The boys recalled all these facts when they heard that the President was behind the enabling act. It appeared that the President from his position as Captain on the

Ship of State had been guiding his course by Sun Mountain. It appeared that aside from her mere money value their mountain had a moral one. The President would offer Washoe as a God-given tribute at the shrine of Liberty.

During the winter of 1863–64, President Lincoln had made up his mind that slavery must be abolished by Constitutional amendment and that Washoe should cast the deciding vote. Such an amendment, the President had reasoned, would be equivalent to new armies in the field; it would be worth at least a million men; it would be an intellectual army that would tend to paralyze the enemy and break the continuity of his ideas.[6]

In order to amend the Constitution, it was necessary first to have the proposed amendment approved by three-fourths of the States. When he came to examine that question the President saw the issue was so close that three more votes—the votes from one more State— were necessary. It was then that President Lincoln's thoughts turned definitely to Sun Mountain for help.[7] Washoe should be dedicated to the passing of the Thirteenth Amendment and the freeing of the slaves. What greater destiny could the boys have asked for their mountain?

Thus Senator Doolittle's bill[8] to allow Washoe to write another constitution, enabling her to be admitted to the Union, was urged in Senate and House, as the most effectual means of ridding the country of slavery in such a way that it could never be resuscitated.[9] But the opposition to the act was bitter. There were two members in the House and one in the Senate absolutely against it.[10]

The President was greatly perturbed by their opposition. He canvassed the situation carefully. He determined to bargain for those three votes that would permit Washoe to be admitted; that would amend the Constitution and free the slaves.

Thus while Washoe was in a stew over her judiciary the President was making his demands in Washington.

Late one March afternoon, to accomplish his purpose, the President left the White House and walked to the War Office to confer with Charles A. Dana, his Assistant Secretary of War. There was too much disturbance in the White House, and the President wanted to talk quietly to his secretary regarding the importance of the coming vote on Nevada and the Thirteenth Amendment,[11] and the opposition to his plans, of three members. He didn't want to be interrupted. So, as the President entered Secretary Dana's office he shut the door behind him.[12]

"Dana," he said, "I am very anxious about this vote. It has got to be taken next week. The time is very short. It is going to be a great deal closer than I wish it was."[13]

"There are plenty of Democrats who will vote for it," Dana replied. "There is James E. English of Connecticut; I think he is sure, isn't he?"

"Oh, yes; he is sure on the merits of the question."

"Then," said Dana, "there's 'Sunset' Cox of Ohio. How is he?"

"He is sure and fearless. But there are some others that I am not clear about. There are three that you can deal with better than anybody else, perhaps, as you know them all. I wish you would send for them."

The President told him who they were. One man was from New Jersey and two from New York.

"What will they be likely to want?" asked Dana.

"I don't know," said the President, "I don't know. It makes no difference, though, what they want. Here is the alternative: that we carry this vote, or be compelled to raise another million, and I don't know how many more men, and fight, no one knows how long. It is a question of three votes or new armies."

"Well, sir," said Dana, "what shall I say to these gentlemen?"

"I don't know," said the President, "but whatever promise you make to them I will perform."[14]

The next time the bill regarding the admission of Nevada came up in the House the three men who had opposed it voted for the Enabling Act to permit Nevada to draw up a State constitution.

On March 21 President Lincoln signed the bill. Immediately a wire was sent to Governor Nye. At once Governor Nye issued a proclamation calling for an election on June 6, to choose another set of delegates to frame another State constitution.

President Lincoln waited happily. It looked to him as though the admittance of Nevada was a foregone conclusion—and that it would settle the question of the Thirteenth Amendment and of the banishment of slavery, forever. But it all depended on the reception of the act in Washoe.

CHAPTER LVIII

THE THIRTY–SIXTH STAR

October 31, 1864

Unfortunately for President Lincoln's schemes, the boys did not know what was going on in his mind. But when *The Enterprise* published telegrams announcing that the President had signed another enabling act they were ready to meet his plans more than half way. No matter what the price, they must get rid of their judges and deliver Washoe and themselves from borrasca. And Tilford had said the best way to get rid of these was to appeal to President Lincoln. Here was President Lincoln appealing to *them*. He needed three more votes, it was said, to free the slaves. He wanted Washoe to supply them.

Word of President Lincoln's need arrived on Sun Mountain just at the time that the Savage and the Potosi had their horns locked in the last great struggle between the advocates of the one-ledge theory and those of parallel ones.

Bill Stewart was the lawyer for the Savage and Judge North was sitting on the bench. In the thick of the battle Stewart discovered that the Potosi people had corrupted one of his chief witnesses and bribed eight of the jurors. He suspected that the deputy, an ex-jockey, had been the intermediary.

To cope with the situation, Bill bought a celebrated race-horse, had him saddled and bridled, and led to a post in front of his law offices. Then on some pretext he enticed the jockey to his rooms and locked the door.

"If you tell me what pay each juror has received, the conversation which has passed, and the kind of money paid, I will give you as much money as you paid the whole jury," tempted Stewart.

"Don't ask me such a question. I would be killed if I told," replied the tout.[1]

"Look down there; do you see what horse that is? If you were on that horse do you think any one could catch you?"

The jockey looked out of the window.

"Not on your life!" said the jockey.

When the jockey finished his story and had given proof, Bill handed him $14,000. The tout grabbed the greenbacks, stuffed them into his pocket, bolted down the stairs, and without changing his clothes, or packing up his traps, clattered down the mountain.

As the hoof-beats died away in the distance Bill closed his office, went to court, and exposed the whole Potosi plot. The jury was discharged. Potosi stock fell. Bill telegraphed the Savage people to buy it up.

Then Bill reflected on the judges. They had dared to corrupt one of his own men. If the boys lost faith in his honesty the door to his future would be closed forever—his life would be in jeopardy.[2]

Bill rose to his feet. With passionate invective he denounced North as a dishonest judge. When he came to Chief Justice George Turner, he almost exploded in his wrathful denunciation. He did not mention Judge Locke. Locke was too ignorant for consideration, said Bill afterward. He painted the acts of the other judges in the darkest colors. They were false to their duty—to their friends—to their honor—to Washoe. The boys caught his passionate glow and began to mutter, pressing close about the rostrum to catch his every word. As he hurled the last furious sentence from his lips an ominous sound, like a Washoe "zephyr" tearing down the mountain, swept the throng. There was talk of tar and feathers—of rope and hanging.

While he had the boys at white heat Stewart passed out among them a petition requesting the resignation of all three judges. He asked every man to sign it.

This just suited Joe Goodman. For years he had been after that triumvirate. As soon as the signing of the petition was completed Joe gave up a whole issue of *The Territorial Enterprise* to its publication. To it were signed the names of 4000 men—among them the flower of Washoe.[3] In his editorials, Goodman represented Washoe's Temple of Justice as a den of iniquity from which the ermine seldom escaped unsullied and justice never unscathed. At the same time he urged the boys to adopt the State constitution which Bill Stewart had prepared, and deliver themselves from the deadfall of their Territorial Courts.[4]

Partisans of the judges countercharged. The Supreme Court met and announced that on the following Monday they would strike the name of William M. Stewart from the bar.

A man unafraid of mobs, bullets, and bad-men was not the one to be cowed by the threats of a puny court. And Bill laughed in their

faces. On that following Monday, Bill strode into court with absolute proof of the judges' perfidy in his pockets. By his side as
witnesses were a score of men whom the justices had bribed. While
waiting for court to open, Stewart would pull out his documental
proofs, look them over, one by one, and then gaze at the court.

As soon as the judges were seated on the bench Judge North arose
and announced his resignation. Judge Turner had been watching
Bill Stewart. Filled with apprehension, he declared court would take
a recess until evening. While Bill accompanied Judge North down
to the telegraph office and stood over him until he wired his resignation to President Lincoln,[5] the chief justice was in a funk.

Finally Turner sent word to Bill that if he would let up on him
he would resign. Bill sent word back that unless Judge Turner
wrote out his resignation immediately both in a letter and in a telegraphic dispatch addressed to President Lincoln he would swear out
a warrant before the justice of the peace and have him arrested for
bribery. Turner sent the resignations as demanded. While Stewart
was mailing one and telegraphing the other, Chief Justice Turner
made his final self-glorifying personal-pronoun speech and retired
from the realm of Washoe jurisprudence.[6]

Then, as everybody was thirsty and excited, Stewart invited the
court, over 100, to Pete Hopkins' Saloon, the Magnolia. While they
were sipping their champagne Bill told the boys that the occasion
was ripe to accept the resignation of the one surviving judge—Judge
Locke—from the territorial bench. He sent two husky lawyers to
fetch him.

"If he is locked in his room," said Bill, "locks can be broken." [7]

The boys found Locke in his room, dressed him, and led him back
to Bill Stewart.

"What ought I to do?" asked Judge Locke apologetically.

"Do?" thundered Bill Stewart. "Resign, and do it quick."

That very night while President Lincoln was reading the third
telegram of resignation from Washoe, Bill was advocating the new
constitution to his adherents. Heart and soul he threw himself into
its adoption. Bill explained to them that it was the same one he had
written some time since except that the new one was minus the clause
that concerned the taxing of the honest miners' hopes and yearnings.
With this modification, Bill worked as vigorously for its adoption as
he had before for its defeat. Once again in Gold Cañon Stewart
could be heard extolling the "honest miner" and the new constitution which was going to make a State out of Washoe and deliver

them from the curse of unscrupulous territorial judges. And everywhere Bill Stewart went, the voice of the "honest miner" followed him.

"All aboard!" they were shouting, "for the old ship 'Constitution,' Captain Stewart, master." [8]

When the general territorial election came off on the seventh of September there was a majority of over 9000 votes in favor of the constitution. As soon as the votes were counted the news of the success of the measure as well as the entire provisions of the State contitution were telegraphed to President Lincoln who was anxiously awaiting returns. The telegram cost $3,416.77, the largest toll up to that time ever paid for a single dispatch.[9] Stage-coach and Pony Express were regarded as too slow when a nation's life and the freedom of the slaves hung in the balance.

On October 31, 1864, the President proclaimed Nevada a State and wired Governor Nye; and Governor Nye wired Joe Goodman and other friends on the Comstock Lode: "Nevada was this day admitted into the Union. The pain is over. The child is born. Let us see that Nevada is not only *in* the Union but *for* the Union." [10]

The news reached *The Enterprise* the night of the very day on which President Lincoln had appended his name to the parchment that made Nevada a State,[11] and Joe Goodman got out an extra. There was no flag with thirty-six stars but the boys had a banner, forty feet long, with thirty-five. Taking that, and procuring a large silver star, the boys loaded them on a camel and clambered up Sun Mountain. While one of them climbed the flag pole, hand over hand, and placed the star on its tip, others piled all the sage-brush in the vicinity into a huge bonfire, sixteen feet high, on the western slope. As the flag ran up the halyards, the bonfire burst into flame, silhouetting it against the glow. Thirty-six guns were fired from the mouth of old Frémont, the cannon which the pathfinder had dragged across the plains and which had been planted on the mountain these many moons for this very purpose.

Those in the streets of the city, those in Gold Hill, those in Silver City, even those at Fort Churchill and far out in the desert could see the flag floating over the mountain and the thirty-sixth star glowing like a brand in the firelight.

It had taken youth—courage—high humor and invincible laughter to put that star in the Flag. There was the fortitude of the Grosches in that star. The valor of Meredith. The stumbling efforts of "Old Virginny," Comstock, Laughlin, and O'Riley. In it was some of the intrepid soul of Manogue, of Rising, of Whitaker. Plenty of the cool fearlessness of those who worked hundreds of feet below the earth's surface—some of the dauntless qualities of Bill Stewart, as well as a dash of the audacity of the knights of the quill.

Every man who watched the star that night was determined that Washoe should give every vote, on election day, to the re-election of Abraham Lincoln to the Presidency of the United States.

CHAPTER LIX

WASHOE'S GODFATHER

1864

On the night of November 5 Sun Mountain staged a grand celebration to promote the re-election of Abraham Lincoln to the Presidency. Every mountain peak, cañon, and ravine in Washoe blazed with bonfires, red lights, skyrockets, and Roman candles.

Thousands of the boys were in the parade that swept up the Cañon and marched down "C" Street. Transparencies, floats, flaming torches, banners, and brass bands galore were in the line of march. On one transparency "Uncle Abe" was represented as being on the home stretch, with the little Grave-Digger-McClellan far in the rear. There was another with a Rebel cat, poor as a skeleton and tailless, marked "C. S. of A." On the reverse side was shown a Union cat, plump and bushy-tailed. One that brought wild acclaim from sidewalks and balconies displayed a portrait of Abraham Lincoln inscribed with the legend, "Washoe's Godfather."

Then came the floats. One supported a pyramid of thirty-six stars, the apical one being made of silver. On another was a huge wooden cannon, a regular Manassas Quaker, with caisson, etc. Jammed into the muzzle was a broom with a fluttering white flag attached, inscribed: "The Quaker gun captured by Little Mac."[1]

Then came a superb Ship of State, rigged-out completely, manned by a crew of white-clad boys. One of them impersonating Captain Abraham Lincoln walked slowly back and forth on the bridge.

Every store and mine building along the line of march was aglow with lights. In every window blazed a lone silver star.

There was pounding of cannon, fireworks, and blaring of bands. Astride a powerful black stallion Tom Peasley made a rousing speech. "We have fully made up our minds," said Tom, "that Washoe shall be loyal to the Union; that traitors shall not befoul her fair name and future glory by casting her upon the world as a prostitute member of a 'secesh' family. Her Silver Star must not, shall not be dimmed." Whereupon the broom of Democracy was snatched from the mouth of old Manassas and presented to him. Laying it about royally, Tom cleared a passage for his horse and galloped triumphantly away.[2]

Then Governor Nye took the stand. Washoe, he said, must cast every vote for Abraham Lincoln on the following Tuesday. The President's re-election meant the surrender of the South. "Let every patriot," he concluded, "see that the defeat of the Rebels' candidate is so overwhelming as to crush out the last faint spark of hope in the breasts of those at Richmond."

Washoe's enthusiasm for Abraham Lincoln's re-election was well exemplified in the spirit shown by Como, a mushroom mining camp, just off Gold Cañon.

There were 200 boys in Como. Every one of them had pledged his vote to "Uncle Abe." It would be a lasting disgrace to the camp if they did not, said their spokesman. "There are 200 votes in this camp. Como demands a hundred per cent vote for Abraham Lincoln." It was a matter of pride with every one of the boys that such should be the case.

On the day after the procession, one of the Como boys came down with pneumonia. But that wouldn't prevent him from voting, said the sick man.

"Certainly not," said the boys. "If necessary, we'll carry you to the polls."

The sick man grew rapidly worse. The doctor, summoned from Virginia, found that the poor fellow had both lungs consolidated and that he was doomed. He'll never see Tuesday, he said as he left.

But the sick man and the boys were determined, pneumonia or no pneumonia, that Como should cast 200 votes for Abraham Lincoln.

On Monday night, when the sick man's pulse grew weak, his friends plied him with stimulants. At dawn, Tuesday, when his lips began to turn blue they fanned him with newspapers.

At sunrise the polls were opened. When the boys came with a stretcher for their pal they found him breathing heavily, delirious, with his eyes rolling. But he motioned them that he was ready to start.

The bearers hurried him to the voting booth, put a ballot and a pencil in his hand and propped him up in their arms. And the sick man made the sign of a cross on the ticket, and fell back. Some claimed, afterward, that the boy was dead when he made his mark; others that he was alive at the time but died immediately afterward.[3]

At any rate the honor of Como was preserved. Forever after, the camp boasted a hundred per cent loyalty to Abraham Lincoln. As for Washoe, it gave the President a wide majority, as well as the three votes needed to abolish slavery.

CHAPTER LX

THE DOOR

1864

With the aid of Washoe's three votes, the Thirteenth Amendment was passed. Nevada, among the first States to ratify it, was now definitely aligned against slavery.[1]

Nevada's first State Legislature convened December 12, 1864. Before listening to their governor's[2] message, congratulatory resolutions were offered the country on the re-election of President Lincoln[3] and the lives, honor, and fortunes of Nevada pledged in support of the Union.[4] Even General Sherman was felicitated on his "march to the sea."[5]

Then the boys turned themselves to political matters. Two branches of the legislature must be organized. Two United States senators must be elected. Among the five candidates to be considered were Bill Stewart, Governor James W. Nye, and Judge John Cradlebaugh.[6] As the time for election approached, Bill sat back. He, as well as his friends, felt confident that his election was assured. Then a bombshell fell into their midst.

An accusation of secessionism had suddenly been brought against Bill. So bitter were the feelings aroused against him that his constituents became doubtful of his election.

Bill Stewart was flabbergasted at the unexpected turn of events. To accuse a rabid unionist like him of secession tendencies was rank heresy. What had happened? All too quickly he discovered, to his chagrin, that the change of front was due to Mrs. Stewart. His opponents were using the fact that Mrs. Stewart was a Southerner, the daughter of ex-Governor Henry S. Foote of Mississippi, a member of the first and second Confederate Congress, to defeat him. Worse still, Bill learned that Mrs. Stewart had never missed an opportunity to make indiscreet remarks regarding Yankeedom. Her outspoken Southern sympathies had alienated more than one of Bill's staunch supporters.

As he made his way home the night of that discovery, Bill was beside himself. He was almost afraid to face Mrs. Stewart—afraid of what he might say or do. After all his planning and campaigning he was to be defeated by his wife's imprudent talk.

They sat down to dinner. All during the repast one thought hammered its way uppermost in Bill's brain, defeat—and defeat due to the fact that Mrs. Stewart was a Southerner. And yet he could not bring himself to upbraid her—born and bred in the South as she was.

"Annie," he said as they concluded the evening meal, "you need some nice new winter clothes. Carson is going to be very lively this winter." He handed Mrs. Stewart a check for $40,000. "Go to San Francisco tomorrow, fix yourself up fine, and have a good time."

And among the trans-alpine passengers on the next morning's stage sat Mrs. Stewart bound for a shopping trip "below," proud and happy in a husband who could be so generous. On one pretext or another Bill managed to keep his wife in California during the rest of the campaign.

Then Bill and his cohorts got busy. It was a brave man who dared accuse him of Southern sympathies. The "honest miner" was again requisitioned.

When the legislature took up the matter of senators Bill was elected on the first ballot. Through his manipulation of the phrase "honest miner," said newspapers, Bill Stewart had worked himself into the United States Senate. But the plaints of his detractors were drowned out by the voices of the honest miners shouting, "Hurrah, for the State of Nevada and for William M. Stewart, the first chosen senator." [7]

There followed a number of ballotings for a second senator from among the remaining candidates. Nye received, on every one, the greatest number of votes, but not enough to elect him. Judge Cradlebaugh among the least. There seeming to be a deadlock, the convention adjourned. During the interim, Bill Stewart sent a message to Judge Cradlebaugh. If the judge would yield to him all government patronage which would be due by courtesy to both of Nevada's senators, his election would be assured.

"Tell Stewart," replied Judge Cradlebaugh with considerable asperity, "that I had rather be a dog and bay the moon than such a senator." [8]

Next day, with his own election, Governor Nye saw the ambitions of a lifetime fulfilled. Whatever President Lincoln's purpose had been in sending him to Nevada, the main thing that the astute governor had hoped to find in Washoe was a door through which he might enter the United States Senate. In the end it took Bill Stewart to open it for him. [9]

A few days later, Bill went down Sun Mountain en route to Washington. On January 5, 1865, he sailed out of the Golden Gate.[10] A man who had not been afraid to face bad-men, corrupt judges, infuriated mobs, and lead bullets would not be over-impressed by an elegant Cabot Lodge, a bushy-haired Sumner, or an inebriated Johnson when they would attempt to embarrass him. In one withering interview after another he demonstrated to those statesmen that they were dealing with a man among men.

On February 1, 1865, Bill arrived at Washington, D. C. Almost at once he was sworn in and drew lots with Nye to decide which should have the long term. And the gods decreed that it should fall to that master of judges, juries, and opponents; to that creator of a territory; to that moulder of a State; to that glorious, incomparable, indomitable, undismayed, tireless "Old Bill—"[11] William Morris Stewart, first senator from the State he had created and that had created him.

Emanuel Leutze, the artist, caught the inspiration of his life when he immortalized Bill Stewart in that rugged figure surmounting the loftiest pinnacle of his magnificent mural painting, "Westward the Course of Empire Takes Its Way," which graces the gallery-walls above the landing of the grand marble staircase of the House of Representatives in the Capitol at Washington.[12]

Shortly after his arrival at the capital, word came to *The Territorial Enterprise* of the cordial manner in which President Lincoln had received Bill Stewart at the White House.[13]

"I am glad to see you here," President Lincoln had said, as he took both of Senator Stewart's hands in his. "We need as many loyal States as we can get, and, in addition to that, the gold and silver in the region you represent has made it possible for the Government to maintain sufficient credit to continue this terrible war for the Union. I have observed such manifestations of the patriotism of your people as assure me that the Government can rely on your State for such support as is in your power." [14]

Before long, word reached Washoe of the splendid mansion Senator Stewart was building on Dupont Circle. Because of its magnificence, official Washington spoke of it as "Stewart's Castle." The Senator's detractors called it "Stewart's Folly." But *The Territorial Enterprise* referred to it loyally as the "Honest Miner's Camp."[15]

CHAPTER LXI

LEE'S SURRENDER
April 11, 1865

On April 11, *The Enterprise* received the dispatches the boys had so long awaited. General Lee and the Confederate Army had surrendered at Appomattox. The news threw the boys into a frantic state of excitement.[1] Throughout the city were to be seen the wildest demonstrations of joy. Flags were displayed from every window, balcony, and housetop. Huge banners were suspended across every street. At noon the fire-bell rang out with a wild clamorous clash. The bells of Saint Paul's, the bells of Saint Mary's, the bells of the churches of the Methodists, the Presbyterians, the Baptists, the bells of the schools, all the bells in Washoe chimed in.

At the same moment burst forth the fierce scream of every steam-whistle on the Mountain. Washoe trembled with sound. The tremendous shrieks of the sirens, the clank and clangor of iron tongues, filled the air with such thunder that nothing else could be heard. Pandemonium was let loose. Hell reigned in the cañons. Everywhere they met, the boys embraced. Taking each other in their arms they danced up and down like lunatics. Women, on balconies, pelted them with confetti and serpentine. Gamblers showered them with playing-cards. As each new banner was strung across the street, and opened its folds to the breeze, ear-splitting yells filled the air.

The National Guard, without notice of call, took to their armory and were soon upon the streets with two pieces of cannon. But the thunder of those big guns did not content the boys. They must have greater din. Every anvil on the Mountain was pressed into service.

In main thoroughfares, upon housetops, to the north, to the east, south, and west, were groups of boys firing muskets, rifles, and pistols.[2] Bands paraded up and down. Cheers rent the air. Never in the history of Washoe were so many toasts drunk in so brief a time. Over one bar went 4000 drinks as the boys pledged, now one popular hero, now another—the "Old Flag," "Old Abe," "Old everybody." The night grew old as they drank. No such drinking had ever been known in Washoe before or since. In less than three hours the majority of the boys were crazy drunk, including many who had never touched liquor before. Scores were to be seen lying in heaps in the streets. Business was utterly paralyzed. Hoists stopped. Stamps were silenced. Ore-wagons were deserted. Printers, editors, reporters and proprietors all being drunk, no newspapers were issued. Miners, bull-whackers, mule-skinners were far too busy pledging their "Uncle Abe" in one cup after another to think of anything so foolish as the sulphurets of silver.[3] Before the end of the day not a man in the city, except the saloonkeepers, had a cent of money.[4]

Not all, however, were drunk. One man, an old desert rat known as "Uncle Van," who had not been sober since the oldest Comstocker could remember, was awakened by the frantic noise and rushed into the street to learn the cause. When the great news was told to him, and Bob, Tom, Dick, and Harry were trying to drag him toward the nearest bar, "Uncle Van" suddenly pulled back and violently resisted their efforts. All wondered what could have come over "Uncle Van" as he stood pressing his hands to his brow as though trying to remember something.

"No, boys, no," he cried, in answer to eager solicitations. "No, this news is too good to get drunk over; damn'd if I don't get sober and enjoy it." [5]

Without having taken a drop, "Uncle Van" turned desertward. "Damn'd," he said to the boys in parting, "if I don't have one good time over this news!"[6]

That night huge bonfires were kindled. Sun Mountain blazed like an active volcano. Cañons were suffused in the red glow. Skyrockets skidded across the heavens. Roman-candles vied with stars.

All night the National Guards and Emmet Guards paraded. All night bands blared and bullets flew. Everywhere marching flags were received with frantic cheers.

The boys had simple temperaments—any stirring appeal awakened their slumbering emotions. The news of Lee's surrender, completely upsetting their equilibrium, swayed their ranks as a wind sweeps reeds. Knowing no mean between stolidity and delirium, their celebration beggars description.

Two days later when the boys had quieted down and began to clamor for the latest news from Richmond, *The Enterprise* and *Union* got together and issued a peace extra. For hours before it was ready to appear mobs were milling about *The Enterprise* office. The pressure of the throng against the glass doors became so great that they crashed in. Before it could be prevented the extras were snatched from the printing press. Before they could be read eager hands tore them to shreds and the presses had to go to work again. Never did the newsboy reap such a harvest of halves and quarters. Nobody waited for change.

"News. News," was all that the boys wanted. "News from the front." What of Grant? What of Richmond? What of "Uncle Abe"? There came a lull. Dearth of fact gave birth to rumor. Rumor begot anxiety. All sorts of wild reports were circulated. One said there was news from Washington of the most startling nature. The military authorities in San Francisco had suppressed it. The wires had been cut.[7]

CHAPTER LXII

"NOT ENOUGH FOREVER"

7:00 A.M., April 15, 1865

Washoe had scarcely recovered from her carnival of whiskey when early one morning the fire-bell on Sun Mountain began to toll—softly—slowly—solemnly. The boys listened. What was that? The Vigilantes?[1] Too soft. A fire? Too slow. Peace? Too solemn. It sounded like a knell.

They rushed out into the streets. Strange time of day for the fire-bell to toll.

The thoroughfares were still decked out in bunting and flags. Confetti clogged the gutters. Banners spanned the streets. Serpentine hung from balconies. Playing-cards littered the dust. The bell should be pealing with joy—rolling out, clanging out sound. There was Peace! Richmond had fallen. What was the matter with Tom Peasley? What hideous joke were the fire-boys playing? Had Tom so far forgotten himself as to indulge in humor at a time like this? Or was it a scurvy "secesh" prank? Or an *Enterprise* hoax?

Solemnly—the fire-bell rang on. It seemed incongruous for a bell to be tolling, with streets strung with bunting.

That tolling bell gave the boys their first intimation of what had befallen their President the night before at Ford's Theatre, Washington.[2] That bell was telling Washoe that Abraham Lincoln was dead. Assassinated!

The bells of the churches, the school-bells, chimed in.[3] From over the Divide came the muffled monotone of the big bell of Saint John and the chimes of Saint Patrick in Gold Hill; from the Devil's Gate ascended the whispering cadence of the bells in the Church of the Ascension. Hour after hour the dirge continued. Reverberating through cañon, ravine, and gorge. Washoe's godfather was dead!

At first the boys refused to believe their ears. But when later dispatches confirmed earlier ones they were overwhelmed with indignation. They gathered on street corners—spoke in subdued tones—clasped each other mournfuly by the hand. Many eyes, unused to tears, were suffused.[4]

Since Washoe had become a State the boys felt very close to "Uncle Abe." Closer perhaps, 3000 miles away, than they would have felt in "the States." For President Lincoln had turned their mountain into a State. And the President had used the State to free the slaves and had given them a star to float in the flag overhead.

The boys thought of President Lincoln as they had last seen one of their number impersonate him on the bridge of their Ship of State. He had brought that ship safely into port. The exultant shores were ringing with shouts of praise and rejoicing. But in the hour of victory the captain lay upon the deck—"fallen, cold, and dead." [5]

There was no drunkenness, no bluster, no shouting, no horseplay. Every word the boys expressed was a mingling of grief and wrath. They felt themselves in no humor to listen to a disloyal word. When rumors became rife that such and such a Rebel had been heard to rejoice at the ill tidings, there were wild rushes on "C" Street. Loyal hands and loyal hearts were determined to stifle the least hint of traitorous breath. Luckily for the accused, in each case the rumor had arisen from some trivial error. Save for their ceaseless coming and going and the incessant murmur of their voices—the streets were silent.

Newspaper offices, all the engine houses and public buildings were draped in mourning. Balconies and windows were festooned in black and white. Upon the door of even the humblest bootblack hung a strip of crape. Every store was closed. Banks were barred. Courts adjourned. The entrance to every saloon was bolted. Quartz mills were shut down. The clatter of stamps ceased. The heavings of hoists were hushed. The hammering of compressors silenced. There was no subterranean dynamiting. No ore-wagons. No freighters to rock the streets. Maguire's, hurdy-gurdies, and the Melodeon were silent behind draped portals. The quiet throughout the city was oppressive. No Washoe Sabbath had ever known such suspension of sound. Silence after such volume of noise was almost unbearable. During the afternoon, a furious "zephyr" raged. Clouds of dust drove down the streets, overwhelming crowds wherever they stood. But not a man moved nor seemed to heed the dust that bit at eyes and ears.[6]

With the first announcement flags were suspended at half mast. Streamers of black were shot across the street to intertwine their folds with those of the National Colors. Notice was served upon those who did not outwardly conform to this token of respect, that crape was preferable to hemp. Forbearance had ceased to be a virtue. There was no choice. Crape! or rope! Which? About *The Enterprise* large crowds were assembled clamoring for news. There was a frantic rush for every extra Joe Goodman turned out. Hundreds of reports were circulated telling about the assassin. Thousands of tortures were suggested, of which roasting alive was the mildest and the least prolonged.

Trouble broke out in Silver City. Elgin, a Rebel, rejoiced over the assassination. Charles McNair, a Yankee, in chastising him was shot and killed and the murderer escaped, leaving the boys wrought up to the highest pitch of vengeance.[7]

So that when Posey Coxey in Gold Hill, one of the five who had hoisted the stars and bars on Sun Mountain, upon hearing of the death of President Lincoln exclaimed—"I'm damn'd glad of it. It's a pity he wasn't killed years ago," [8] the high point of their endurance was passed.

The boys saw red. They determined to teach Coxey a lesson. A Vigilance Committee was formed. Coxey was seized. Hemp was considered too good for him. But a gallows was prepared. A noose placed about his neck. And the boys were about to string him up when Father Manogue rushed upon the scene. At a glance he took in the situation. Without saying a word he mounted a rock, took out his crucifix and held it up for all to see. His eyes went from boy to boy in a wordless struggle. While they hesitated, the police arrived.[9]

Still enraged, the boys fought off the officers. It looked like more trouble, until a trial was suggested. Posey was tried without benefit of law—found guilty—sentenced to receive thirty lashes upon the bare back.[10]

Coxey was borne to Fort Homestead, a fortified point on the heights overlooking Gold Hill—stripped to the waist and bound to the cannon called "Kearsarge." Then the boys laid on a heavy black-snake whip. When Coxey was more dead than alive, the boys cut him loose, put a card—"A Traitor to his Country," upon his back and thrust the National Flag into his arms. The band struck up "Hail Columbia," and they marched him over the Divide to the guard-house of the provost marshal in Virginia.

On the same day and at the same hour that funeral services were being conducted in Washington over President Lincoln's flag-draped casket, obsequies were held on Sun Mountain. Every half-hour cannon, "Young Sheridan" at Silver, "Kearsarge" at Fort Homestead, and "Frémont" at Virginia, boomed forth in solemn salute. The bells never ceased their tolling. Gold Cañon fluttered in black mantle. Flags floated drearily from mine and mill. All places of public amusement were closed.

In the show-window of every store was a portrait of the President, surrounded with evergreens. Before the banking house of Almarin B. Paul stood a statue of President Lincoln. Above, was poised an immense American Eagle with outstretched wings as though affrighted at some untoward sound.[11] On the base, Paul had inscribed:

> "O thou Recording Angel! turn to that page whereon
> Is traced in undimmed brightness the name of Washington,
> And with thy pen immortal, in characters of fame,
> To stand henceforth and ever, write also Lincoln's name."

The funeral exercises began at Fort Homestead with Bishop Whitaker of Saint Paul's Episcopal church reading the Litany. "Remember not, Lord, our offences . . . be not angry with us, forever . . ." he intoned. While thousands of boys kneeling in the dust before him took up the response.[12]

Then the procession moved through the streets of Virginia. Tom Peasley was among those who walked beside the flag-draped casket.[13]

Hundreds jammed their way into Maguire's to hear Joe Goodman read a poem on "Abraham Lincoln," which he had written to commemorate the honored dead.

> "A nation lay at rest. The mighty storm
> That threatened their good ship with direful harm
> Had spent its fury; and the tired and worn
> Sank in sweet slumber, as the spring-time morn
> Dawned with a promise that the strife should cease;
> And war's grim face smiled in a dream of peace."

A poem that was copied and recopied in exchanges all over the country and subsequently found an abiding place in many a collection of verse.

For days afterward *The Enterprise* devoted a column to verses that were sent in from all over Washoe. Among them was one, entitled "The Martyr," whose refrain had taken the fancy of Mark Twain. He had set it off to suit himself:

> "Gone, gone, gone,
> Gone to his endeavor;
> Gone, gone, gone,
> Forever and forever."

"There is a very nice refrain to this little poem," wrote Mark Twain. "But if there is any criticism to make upon it, I should say that there was a little too much 'gone' and not enough 'forever.'"

CHAPTER LXIII

PRESIDENT LINCOLN'S LAST MESSAGE TO THE BOYS
June 24, 1865

At six o'clock on the morning of a perfect June day, the Overland Stage—from Austin—bounded over the Divide with Schuyler Colfax in the seat of honor with the driver.[1] Streets were silent and deserted. As the coach dashed along, saloon-doors popped open permitting the Speaker momentary glimpses within—mahogany bars with shining rails—gilt-framed pictures on walls—Adah Isaacs Menken—Lola Montez—"Benecia Boy" Heenan—Abraham Lincoln— all shrouded in mourning. The stage stopped before the doors of the International Hotel. Schuyler Colfax, covered with alkali— eyes—nose—lips burning and smarting, alighted, and stood aside while the porters removed a long, heavy, burlap-covered box, and carried it into the lobby. Then he followed. "Careful, boys," he admonished, "careful"—as they laid the box gently on the office floor. When he had given the night clerks directions for its care he went to his room.

In spite of the early hour it was not long before some of the boys— all in uniform—National Guards—Emmet Guards—cavalry—firemen—were at the hotel.

They eyed the long burlap-covered box.

"What's in it?"

"Belongs to Mr. Colfax," said the clerk. "When he went to his room he told us to let nothing happen to it."

"Schuyler Colfax here?"

They were astounded.[2] The Speaker of the House of Representatives at Washington had already arrived. Gone to his room and fallen asleep. They could hardly believe their ears. They had prepared a regular Sun Mountain celebration in his honor—with the Metropolitan Band—mounted troops—firemen—speeches. They had intended to meet him at Devil's Gate and escort him royally up the mountain. The Overland Stage had arrived ahead of schedule. Two hundred miles in twenty-two hours—fourteen less than the mail coach! Pony Express time! That had been a ride! Why hadn't the stage company let them know? The boys were disgusted. Schuyler

Colfax was one of the most distinguished men in the country—third officer in the United States Government. Presidential timber. Now that Johnson had succeeded President Lincoln at the White House, he was heir apparent!

As Schuyler Colfax had arrived Sunday morning—hours before he was expected—the public welcome was postponed until the night following.

Through dispatches the boys had learned that the Speaker brought them word direct from Abraham Lincoln. The last message the President had given was for them. As so many were anxious to hear it the idea of using Maguire's Opera House was abandoned. A bigger place was required. Finally an open-air mass-meeting on "C" Street was decided on. The balcony of the International Hotel would be used as a tribune.

After music, the Honorable Schuyler Colfax stepped to the flag-draped railing and looked down into the street below. A sea of silent, intent faces met his gaze. The Speaker was stirred. From as far as he could see, up and down the street, from roofs, windows, neighboring balconies—eager faces. Waiting. What message had President Lincoln sent to them through Schuyler Colfax?

There was a long pause. The Speaker seemed lost in sad memories.

"You know, my friends," he began, "I was in Washington with Abraham Lincoln on the last day of his life. Upon that occasion he gave me a message to communicate to you.

"On the morning of the fourteenth of April, I went to the White House to bid our President farewell and to receive from him such messages as he desired to send to you. It was the pleasantest and most cheerful visit I had enjoyed with the President for a long time. For the President, satisfied that the Union was finally saved, and full of the most generous intentions toward the South, was free from the load of care which had weighed him down during the war.

"I shall always rejoice, sad as the memory now is, that I was to have the last interview with him on public affairs, and to bring to you the last message of his life.

"After conversing on matters of public interest, President Lincoln suddenly turned to me and asked if I was not going to the Pacific. I told him that I was if there was no danger of an extra session of Congress this summer. He assured me there was none. Then rising and with much more than his usual emphasis he made what seemed to be a speech, which he had previously thought over, in regard to the miners. He impressed upon me that I should communicate it to you."

All attention—eyes on the Speaker—the boys listened, with bated breath.

" 'I want you to take a message from me to the miners whom you visit,' the President said. 'I have very large ideas of the mineral wealth of our nation. I believe it is practically inexhaustible. Its development has scarcely commenced. During the war, when we were adding a couple of millions of dollars every day to our national debt, I did not care about encouraging the increase in the volume of our precious metals. We had the country to save first. But now that the rebellion is overthrown and we know pretty nearly the amount of our national debt, the gold and silver we mine makes the payment of that debt so much the easier.'

" 'Now,' continued the President, speaking with much emphasis, 'I am going to encourage that in every possible way. . . .'[3]

" 'We shall have hundreds of thousands of disbanded soldiers, and many have feared that their return home in such great numbers might paralyze industry by furnishing suddenly a greater supply of labor than there will be demand for. I am going to try to attract them to the hidden wealth of our mountain ranges, where there is room enough for all. . . . I intend to point them to the gold and silver that waits for them in the west. *Tell the miners from me that I shall promote their interests to the utmost of my ability; because their prosperity is the prosperity of the nation, and'* said he, his eyes kindling with enthusiasm, *'we shall prove in a very few years that we are indeed the treasury of the world.'* "[4]

"Three cheers to the memory of Abraham Lincoln," called Tom Peasley. Sun Mountain, Cedar Hill, Sugar Loaf, verberated and reverberated.

"I told him," continued the Speaker, "that I was happy to be his messenger and to bear such a message as this."

" 'Come again in the evening,' urged the President. 'I am going to the theatre. I would like you to accompany me.'

" 'It will be impossible,' I returned. 'I have engagements for the whole evening and I leave the city early tomorrow morning.'[5]

"But that evening—still unwilling to depart without another farewell, I called on the President.

"Again the President urged me to accompany him to Ford's Theatre.

"Again I declined, pleading the many last things to be attended to by a traveller.[6]

"For three-quarters of an hour, we sat and conversed.[7]

"While we were talking, an usher brought in a card. The President read it! 'Senator William M. Stewart of Nevada.' The senator had brought a friend. He begged an opportunity to present him. The President demurred. There was no time for callers. He was going to the theatre. The President wrote out a note on the back of a card—the last words he would ever write—and gave it to the usher for Senator Stewart."[8]

Bill Stewart!

"Finding that the time had arrived when he must leave for the theatre, the President arose. Mrs. Lincoln took the arm of Mr. Ashmun and proceeded toward the door, the President slipped his arm into that of mine. Together we took the last steps that President Lincoln was ever to take in the White House.

"As we reached the doorway the President turned to me and repeated substantially, though somewhat abbreviated, the message he had given me earlier in the day.

"Down the steps, the President went. On one of the lower rounds, again he turned.

"'Don't forget, Colfax, to tell the miners what I told you this morning. I will telegraph you at San Francisco. Good-bye.'

"As the President handed Mrs. Lincoln into their carriage, Senator Stewart stood before him.[9]

"Cordially, the President extended his hand. The senator introduced his friend. 'Come back in the morning,' called Mr. Lincoln as he entered the carriage and drove rapidly away."[10]

Dauntless, indomitable Bill. Had he only known!

"It was his last good-bye on earth," went on Colfax, looking earnestly down into that pale sea of white, upturned faces—"I bring these recollections to you, that you may see and feel and realize that even amid the shock and conflict of war, even amid the triumphs of assured peace, your interests were the last subjects that occupied President Lincoln's thoughts in the last hours of his life."[11]

The sea stirred—uneasily—Bill Stewart's had been the last hand that had pressed the President's in farewell—their interests had been the last to occupy his thoughts. How close it brought Abraham Lincoln to Sun Mountain!

CHAPTER LXIV

AMENDS

June 27, 1865

The next afternoon a carriage drew up in front of the International.[1] The porters carried out the long, burlap-covered box which Schuyler Colfax had brought west with him, and deposited it in his carriage.

A procession formed—led off by the Reverend H. D. Lathrop—Schuyler Colfax, Samuel Bowles of *The Springfield Republican* and several hundreds of the boys, mounted and in carriages.[2]

Over the Divide they drove, rapidly, down through Gold Hill to Chrysopolis Hall, Silver City, where cavalry and troops from Fort Churchill were in waiting. Flags flying, drums beating, the procession passed through Devil's Gate to the neglected sage-brush-covered mound of Hosea B. Grosch.

Standing by the grave was E. D. Tansley, one of Hosea's old Cañon comrades, the only one in the throng who had known him back in '57. Tramping down the sage, the troopers grouped about the mound. The Episcopal burial service was read—a solemn and impressive prayer followed—then Schuyler Colfax stepped forward.[3]

They were there, said the Speaker, to bestow upon Hosea Grosch the last sad rites of remembrance. So that those who came after, in the far-off future, might identify the spot where reposed the remains of one of Sun Mountain's earliest pioneers.[4]

Neither Allen nor Hosea had died in vain. Forty thousand people had followed up Sun Mountain in their wake. Its slopes—its depths teemed with their discovery. Its cañons and ravines were lined with mines and mills—the smoke from whose stacks blackened the heavens—the clatter of whose stamps filled the air and rocked the earth. Their output in bullion had gone forth to swell the coffers of the world—to alleviate suffering on the battlefield—to play a part in national politics—to aid in freeing the slaves—to sustain the failing credit of the country—to provide the national armies with the endurance needed to win the war of rebellion. What more could the Grosches have asked of their discovery than that it had been of help to man? Last, but not least, their discovery had made it possible for President Lincoln to add a much needed star to the galaxy floating over Sun Mountain.

The burlap was removed from the long box. Two marble slabs were uncovered. One was set on a granite block at the head of the mound. One at the foot. Those about the grave read the inscription:

"Hosea B.
Second Son of
Rev. A. B. Grosh,
Born in Marietta, Pa., April 23d, 1826
Died, at Gold Cañon, Nevada, Sept. 2d, 1857." [5]

Taps sounded. A final salute was fired. The troopers wheeled and marched down Gold Cañon. The boys trudged up Sun Mountain. The trampled sage gave forth a pungent smell.[6]

CHAPTER LXV

IRONICAL WASHOE
1865

By 1865, barren borrasca had succeeded argent bonanza. Surface deposits were exhausted. All stocks were practically worthless. Every productive mine was knee-deep in injunctions. About every shaft-head, suits of one kind or another were piled thick as drifted autumn leaves. Mills were rusting for want of work. Their clatter grew less and less. Crushing-pans, gaping like so many open mouths waiting to be fed, went hungry for the ore that was not forthcoming. Respirations of hoists grew hoarse and feeble. Steam from exhausts waxed fainter than breath from departing life. Smoke no longer smudged the heavens with black soot. What there was, hung thin and wispy as crape against the hot, blue sky.

Every shaft of six- to seven-hundred feet depth was wallowing in a sump of dark, boiling liquid, whose breath, thick and fetid from water-logged drifts, polluted the air.

Down in those dank, dreary depths were hundreds of deserted levels—whose timbers were wrapped in muffling mould—whose walls dribbled with monotonous plash—whose roofs were smothered in monstrous dew-distilling growth. Fungi of uncanny form clung with moist fingers to distorted posts, and depended with sticky, slimy tails from beam and lintel. Up from the oozy, miry flooring sprung mineral fungi, efflorescent with earthy crystals.

At times phosphureted gases, the dreaded fire-damp, bathed those moist walls in unearthly, corpse-like pallor. Myriads of small particles of floss-like texture, like motes in a moonbeam, darted here and there in ghostly splendor. Tongues of flame licked the walls and dripped with fiery spume.

To reclaim the priceless treasure in those œdematous walls more horse-power, greater pumps, higher hoists, more air-compressors, more steam, more forests were needed. Where was the pump that could relieve such dropsy? Where was the engineer who could contend with such muffling mould? With all her mineralized alkalis where was the one to purge Sun Mountain? More gold was needed —more stockholders were needed—more assessments—more drains —before work could be resumed in those dismal, dripping depths.

Where was Adolph Sutro? Adolph Sutro, who had boasted he could lead them to their Promised Land through his tunnel. Let him drive his tunnel that he had guaranteed would drain every sump on Sun Mountain. Let him suck out this damp destruction! Below the water were riches that would stagger Crœsus. World-renowned engineers had accorded approval of his plan. Let him run the water into the Carson—let that river reach the Gulf—fulfill its destiny—give them an opening to the sea!

But only echo came back to mock them with closing mine and silencing mill. A five-mile tunnel—it was still fantastical!

In the flooded mines the boys had met their master. With all their iron, dynamite, drills, and powder, Washoe had beaten them—flouted them. And her winning weapon had been water. Now Washoe's "zephyr" could afford to laugh—that hard, sardonic laugh. Water was their Waterloo. Water drowned their ledges—flooded them out—water in the land of drought—ironical Washoe!

Now the conviction became fixed in many minds that the Comstock—the great Comstock—was a "played-out" camp. Like a brilliant meteor, it had blazed across a silver horizon to disappear ignominiously in an ill-smelling sump. That was the case with all camps—with all meteors—they blazed a trail—then faded out. Why not the Comstock? Range after range of desolate surrounding hills had supplied the graveyard of ghostly mining-camps. Even like the Sahara, the tawny desert was an endless tomb of abortive enterprise.

Where now was ancient Memphis—hundred-throated Thebes? Where now Pahrangat? Where Panamint on the edge of the terrible Death Valley? Where that Washoe Golgotha—the emerald-eyed Esmeralda? Where Aurora—that Goddess of Morn? Where were they now? Each had sprung up—and been cut down. Each had had but a short time to live and was full of misery. Each in its death-throes had betrayed homes—destroyed hearths—broken hearts and left suicides in shallow shale. How many of the boys were already enriching the sand they had come to conquer—dust and ash of the whirlwind that swirled toward those cenotaphs in the Funereal Mountains? It was the history of all mining-camps—rise—bloom—decay. Here today—gone tomorrow. Who knew—whither? But the Comstock! The greatest camp of them all! It couldn't be possible! Beneath the sumps? Beyond the mould? Few ever came back—but there was always the hope—of resurrection.

The directors of the Bank of California began to regret the organization of their branch in Virginia City. They became more despondent than the boys. In no time, twenty great mills were turned over to the bank to satisfy obligations.

"What right," said D. O. Mills, "has a bank gambling in mines and mills?" [1] Conservative, that he was, he would have gotten rid of them—gotten rid of that poker-playing William Sharon, too,—if Ralston would have let him. But that fantastic prince of finance silenced him with a sentence—"I will be personally responsible for William Sharon." [2] Responsible for a gambler in the unfriendly game of draw-poker!

In one day, 500 titanic stamps fell, never to rise again. Ore-wagons were unharnessed—brakes given up to rust—mules left on barren range to starve—mule-skinners—bull-whackers consigned to curseless silence. Camels were turned into the waste to shift for themselves[3]—derelicts of the desert—like the black hulk of "Der Fliegende Hollander"—with no soul to care—without port—without course—condemned forever to cruise back and forth—hated—despised—outcast.

Sometimes on moonlit nights to come, a wakeful miner would roll over in his blanket, stare across uncharted seas of sand and there in the distance see what would cause him to rub his eyes and look again. Sometimes it would be a huge white ship followed by a caravel of lesser ones—less often a black ship with a red saddle.[4]

With all these omens of failure about them the boys might well be depressed—but they were not discouraged. Was General Grant disheartened by repeated repulses at Vicksburg? What did he do? He attacked that Yazoo stronghold on other salients. That was what they, too, would do. Washoe was not exhausted. There were just as good ledges in those tawny hills as ever had been explored—they would seek them out—find them—discover a greater Comstock.

Kern River, Gold Bluff, Gold Lake, Trinidad, had taught their lessons. They were ready for the next gamble. The next adventure when it came. Those hoaxes had not worn down their mettle—but rather had edged their wits. Hadn't they found Washoe after the colossal fiasco of Fraser River? The greatest discovery of the century! The greatest adventure! The greatest romance of them all!

In this frame of mind there broke upon their ears an old familiar call—"Silver!" "Silver on the Snake!" "Silver on the Boise!" "Silver in the Cœur d'Ailene!" "Copper in the Bitter Root Country!" "Gold on the Gila!" "Gold beyond the Sangre de Christo!" "Silver on the Reese!" A medley of calls. None so clear as Washoe's. But the call of El Dorado—of the unknown—romance—adventure!

Whither should they go? Where lay El Dorado? Over which mountains? In what direction? Hadn't Gridley come out of Austin? Hadn't Austin sprung from the Pony Ledge? A ledge discovered by a stallion! Didn't the ledge abut on the Reese! Ho, then for Reese River! The Toiyabe Mountains! Austin! Reveille! The Reese would never be exhausted. In two years—barely nicked! Where were the mines that could compete with Panamint—Paxton—King Alfred—the Magnolia—the Mohawk—Diana—Lone Star? To the Reese then! That was the place for them! To the Reese—to those inexhaustible ledges first!

As a river, the Reese was not so long, nor so tortuous, as the Missouri, nor as majestic as the Mississippi, but it was deep—swift—frolicsome—audacious. Its banks were palisaded with bullion—its bed was paved with gold and silver. All one needed was a pick, shovel, and freighter to make his "pile." The strength of that current was driving 500 stamps in twenty-nine mills!

They must see that ledge, said the boys. They must all go to Reese River! The ledge ran six- and seven-thousand to the ton! In one year Wells Fargo had carted away $6,000,000.[5] The best specimens were found with granite casings showing silver chloride—fahlertz—antimonial and ruby silver. Specimens found their way to assay offices on Sun Mountain—ran thousands to the ton—extraordinary! Nothing like it had ever been seen or heard of—not even on the Comstock! The Golden Dome of Quivira had been pierced! The vaults of Cibola's treasure-house! The seven treasure-chests of the seven golden cities! News flew on the wings of Washoe's "zephyr" —up Taylor Street—up Sutton Avenue—down "A"—down "B"—down "C"—down "D"—down to joss-house and wickiups!

"Have you a gold mine? Sell it out and go to Reese!" "Have you a copper mine? Throw it away and go to Reese!" "Do you own dry-goods? Pack them up for Reese!" "Are you the proprietor of lots? Wish them on your worst enemy and go to Reese!" "Are you a doctor, merchant, lawyer, gambler, thief? Buckle on your blankets, and off with you to Reese! For there is the land of promise—of glittering bullion! There lies the pay-streak! There is Oriental magnificence! Trains of camels! Rebekahs! Wells! Knights of Pythias —Redmen—Ancient Order of Hibernians! There!"

Most wonderful of all, the quartz was blue—"blue-stuff"—blue as the stuff the boys had thrown away back in '56—'57—even '59.

The International Hotel—whose balcony was the tribune of the boys—heard the call of the Reese. The International must go to

Austin! Boys were sleeping in bushes—they needed green baise tables—mirrors—lights—swinging lamps! The owners pulled down the building and loaded it on a freighter and joined the exodus.

Mill-owners tore up their stamps by the roots. They would plant them again on the Reese!

John Mackay heard that call. He was already one of the richest men on the Lode. He had made a fortune in "Kentuck." But Sun Mountain had not yet satisfied his ambitions. He did not want more money. He wanted the thing that only money could buy. He wanted to win a name as master and manager of the greatest mines in the world.[6] Those mines were not on the banks of the Reese! He scorned such puny things! He had an idea that they lay in the earth between the Ophir and Gould & Curry. It wasn't possible that, with $15,000,000 to the credit of the Gould & Curry and $12,000,000 to the Ophir, nothing lay in between. He meant to buy up that stock of the Central, White & Sides, the California, and other claims on that 1200 feet. They were under water, he knew. But beneath the water? Beyond the mould? It was worth the gamble—perhaps another bonanza—a greater bonanza lay there! His "pard," Jack O'Brien, heard the Reese call. He was going to Austin. He had been on the Comstock six years. He had had a "good time." Spent his earnings in rollicking nights. Now he must be on his way. He would make his "pile" in the Toiyabe Mountains and go back to "the States."

"Don't go," said Mackay. "I'll 'stake' you. I have enough for us both."

But Jack gave him a deaf ear. The Reese was bulging with bullion. A great thundering stream flushing gold out of the mountains. A Yuba! A Sacramento! El Dorado!

"The Reese is a ditch," returned Mackay in disgust. "A six-foot ditch in the desert. The man who called that creek a river was a humorist."

But Jack was adamant. The thunder of cataracts assaulted his tympana—the rhythm of trampings was in his soul—they were washing mountains of rubies out of the Ruby Mountains—auriferous nuggets out of the golden Toiyabe.

Tom Peasley heard the call of the Reese and rejoiced. But Tom had killed his man—"Sugar-Foot Jack"—a wax-faced youth with aspirations to become a manslayer. The memory of that killing wracked Tom with remorse. In a moment of jovial greeting, at a masquerade ball, Tom had slapped "Sugar-Foot" playfully on the

back. But so hard that "Sugar-Foot" had fallen over on the floor.
In the laugh that followed, "Sugar-Foot" pulled himself to his feet
muttering dire threats. A duel was arranged, and Tom punctured
his man with bullets. It was clearly a case of self-defense, and Tom
was acquitted. But unfortunately Tom's conscience would not ac-
quit him so readily. It granted him no rest. Tormented. Tortured
him. He could not sleep. All night ghastly fingers pointed him out
in his dreams. He was a "killer"—a "bad man"! He had committed
murder. Repentance wore him to the bone. Tom became a changed
man. The old boisterousness gave place to a restrained and gentle
manner. There was a noticeable unbending and softening in his
nature. He withdrew from the Sazerac—from the conclaves of the
firemen—from political rallies. From being one of the most prominent and conspicuous figures on the Mountain he had become a
reticent, brooding murderer. He could not reconcile himself to
what he had done—to the depths to which he had fallen. After
all he had been no better than Sam Brown. He, too, now was
a "chief." He tried a legislative position for a while—but he gave it
up to answer the call of the desert. He would go into the waste—
that region of bitter waters and dead seas, and find peace.[8]

Just then the call of the Reese broke over Sun Mountain. Tom
never reached the Reese. He had involved himself in a Washoe
vendetta. He was a "chief." Whether he would or not he must
defend the title. The code demanded it. One night his nemesis
came upon him suddenly at the Ormsby House—beat him upon the
head with the butt of a gun and discharged a bullet into his breast.
Tom felt the icy hand of death clutching at his heart. By superhuman effort, vengeance burning in his eyes, Tom pulled himself
to his feet, pursued his murderer, grabbed him, crashed him through
a plate-glass door, drew his revolver, took deadly aim through the
opening, fired, and fell back in the arms of his friends, and was
laid on a billiard table.

"Is he dead?" whispered Tom, as life was ebbing.

"Dead as a door-nail," was the ready answer. Tom smiled grimly
and held out his gun-butt. "Make another notch."

That done, came the final injunction.

"Take off my boots."

As his boots came off, Tom Peasley in the spirit, fearlessly and
barefooted, stepped softly across the threshold of the Unknown.

Langford Peel heard the call of El Dorado from the direction of the Bitter Root country. He must go there. They were having lively times in Montana. They were needing some good red blood on which to lay the foundations of that commonwealth. He had a rendezvous there—a rendezvous with the arch-enemy of all "chiefs." As he was dying he admonished his Helena pals to carve on his tombstone, "I know that my redeemer liveth." His redeemer meaning not the Man who would forgive, but the pal who would avenge his death with blood.

Rollin Daggett heard the call. He, too, was going to be a congressman—then a bare-footed minister to Hawaii.

Father Manogue and Bishop Whitaker heard El Dorado's call. They would be needing the Cross on the Reese—in the Ruby Mountains—on the farthest rim of the desert. The good Father had many a new altar to raise and bless before a Bishop's miter crowned his efforts.

Doctor Edmund Bryant heard that call. They would be needing physicians and surgeons in the new camps. In one of them he would find an early grave. In the course of time his widow would lay aside her weeds to become Mrs. John Mackay, and his daughter Eva—was destined to be the Princess Colonna of Rome.

Joe Goodman heard the call of the Mayas. He would make his million and devote his life to translating their hieroglyphics and to writing a book on their civilization that is still a classic.

Jim Fair heard the call of El Dorado. It came from the earth beneath his feet—from the submerged ledge between Ophir and Gould & Curry. There was richer ore there than had ever been discovered. He could catch its aroma.

Marcus Daly's call came from the Bitter Root country. Sun Mountain had been a good teacher. Its finished pupil, he would become a great community-builder—copper king of Montana.

Tritle heard the call of the Gila. Within its carnelian embrace he would become a governor. Billy Claggett heard the call of the Boise—and would fritter away his life on the foundations of Idaho.

And "Baron" Fairfax when it came time to die heard the call of his blood and died for an ideal. When his angered clerk pulled a poniard from the cane he was carrying and drove it into the "Baron's" breast, Fairfax, who was a dead shot, drew a derringer from his vest pocket, cocked it, and aimed the muzzle at his antagonist, then dropped his arm. "You're a cowardly murderer," he said. "You have killed me, but you have a wife and children. I spare your life for their sake."[9]

But Julia Bulette did not answer the call. Strangled one wintry night for the solitaires which sparkled in her ears, for the ruby that coruscated on her breast, for the sables that nestled about her throat, she lay in her grave on Sun Mountain, and the man who killed her was hanged. And the tribute the red-shirted paid her at the grave was when the band played "The Girl I Left Behind Me."

CHAPTER LXVI

QUEST OF EL DORADO

Over the Divide thousands of boys poured in clouds of dust. Down Gold Hill, singing and laughing, through Devil's Gate, by great mills, boarded up and silent, their lights out, their stacks cold. It was time to go. The feast was over. Through Silver City they passed. Houses were half-deserted—windows broken—inmates fled—coyotes slinking through open doors. Out of Dayton they went by the great highway over which they had trudged away back there in the spring of '49. The ebb tide was as swift as the flood. Flight as rapid as the rush. "Heap good," said the Piutes as they gave praise to Pah-Ah that the pale-face was moving east.

Caravans—freighters—stages bound for the Reese were sweeping by the mouth of Gold Cañon in a flood of moving humanity. The boys set themselves adrift on its tide-rip, passing deserted Pony stations—Bucklands—Williams—Millers. The frontier was flowing eastward—170 miles nearer whence they had sprung. One hundred and seventy miles back they trekked over the same route that had tormented them less than twenty years ago—with pockets just as empty—hopes just as full—courage just as high—the only change was the direction in which El Dorado lay.

Some passed Sandy Bowers' mansion. There on the shores of Washoe Lake! What a magnificent pile it had become, with the ivy from Windsor clambering up its tawny walls! The roots of old England's ivy acclimated in that shaley soil! They could see fountains splashing in marble basins; potted palms in plate-glass windows.

Forty miles along the Emigrant Road and they could still discern the bold front of Sun Mountain arising in mysterious power and undefiled splendor from the slimy banks of the Carson into the eternal blue of the sky. How majestically the Mountain swept up from the desert to that rocky finger! How sad and alone—how cruel and indifferent to their fate! Omnipotence—infinity—the endlessness of time, in that uplifted finger! Its very presence—awe-inspiring—divine. From subterranean fires at the Mountain's foot columns of yellow smoke like incense smoldering before gods,

348

spiralled heavenward. Against the hot blue sky the Flag fluttered on the summit—the Flag they had helped to place there. Those with glasses could perceive the silver star on the flag-pole—the thirty-sixth star—that had cheated Death of a million men—that had helped to free more than 3,000,000 slaves. From summit to foothill, in cañon, ravine, and flank, they could follow the straggling lanes of the city they had built and were now deserting. To that rugged Mountain they had brought the traditions of "the States"—of New England— of the South—of their municipal and political institutions—their churches—their schools—their libraries—their communities. They had bestowed on that Mountain the strength of their flesh, the calibre of their nerve, the color of their blood, the homage of their intellects.

Those six years had not been wasted. Every one there had left his lasting imprint. They had given gladly. What had they taken from Sun Mountain? Not gold—nor silver—nor riches! But superb manhood and sterling citizenship. They had not taken blows—nor wrestled with elemental forces, nor overcome them, in vain. Like Jacob in his wrestle with the Lord, labor had strengthened them. They had come away with new titles among men. In hard-rock they had found steadfast courage—iron resolution—contentment— grim humor—capacity for laughter—the gift of friendship.

On leaving Washoe each still had dreams of making his "pile," and going back to "the States." But that very seldom happened. A deep-rooted atavism held them, like Prometheus on the rock, fast-chained to Washoe. They had tasted of her pomegranates. Few would ever break the bonds. Nostalgic longing would always call them back. As long as they lived, they were condemned to surge back and forth over that desert region seeking El Dorado. Now to the Reese. Now back to Sun Mountain. Now to the Bitter Root country. Now to the Cœur d'Ailene. Now to the Nez Percé region. Now to the Sangre de Christo. Now to Tonopah. Goldfield. Rawhide. An endless quest.

There was work for strong men to do in those outposts of civilization. Their lives were dedicated to it. There were torches to be carried—institutions to be founded, speeches to be made, speeches to be listened to. There was voting to be done—pageants to be staged, hats to be waved. The traditions of Plymouth and Jamestown to be implanted out there! They could no more live without doing those things than they could live without life. It was part and parcel of their being to carry the image to El Dorado.

Now the boys had a hundred and seventy miles to cover—a hundred and seventy miles through the most barren, desolate, scorched, waterless, alkali-smitten patch on the North American Continent. A series of horrible deserts to cross—each one more horrible than the last. But there would be compensations—the splendor of blue sky—the balm of sunshine—broad expanses of sage, mournfully grand in desolation—the benediction of sunset—the friendliness of night. Besides, they were an instrument. They had an image to plant on the farthermost rim of the horizon.

On they trudged, or drove, or rode. Through waste after waste. Clouds of dust rolled out to meet them. Into them stepped men such as the world has rarely seen. Men who had been tried in the furnace and freed of coward and weakling. Men with stubble beards. Men with splendor and sheen. Whole-souled—great-hearted —confident men. In twos and fours—mule-back—horseback—high in prairie-schooners. With them they bore an image—an image bequeathed them by their mothers—by their fathers—by their mothers' mothers—by their fathers' fathers. An image that was old that December day on the shingle of Plymouth. They were seeking El Dorado.

With every step those clouds of white, choking alkali clutched at their throats. Thick—constant—penetrating. Beyond experience. Beyond comparison. Dust filled the air—it *was* the air. It covered their bodies. It penetrated them. It soared to almighty altitudes. It became omnipresent—omnipotent. In spite of everything men could do to the contrary it seeped through canvas curtains; seeped under lids of half-closed eyes; crept up nostrils; gritted between teeth; filled mouths with its salty taste. Choked. Stifled. Smelt acrid. Tasted bitter.

And into this acrid dust they went—seeking El Dorado.

APPENDIX

ACKNOWLEDGMENTS

"The life of the Comstock in the old days never has been written so that those who did not share it can understand; it never can be so written, for to be like, all would have to be set down, and that is a feat beyond mortal pen," so wrote Arthur McEwen, outstanding California newspaper man, in *The San Francisco Examiner,* upon reports of the suspension of *The Virginia City Territorial Enterprise.*

That sentence proved a stimulus to these pages. It seemed to me, that having been saturated from infancy on the folklore of Washoe, I could recapture the spirit behind it.

Accordingly I set to work to pick out those facts which, to me, fully expressed Washoe and the Comstock, and to verify them in the prints of the period. The writings of Tom Fitch, Adolph Sutro, Henry de Groot, Frank Pixley, Joe Goodman, Arthur McEwen, Rollin Daggett, Wells Drury, Dan De Quille, Almarin Paul, Fremont Older, and Mark Twain (all noted Washoe newspaper men), in *The Sacramento Union; The San Francisco Alta; Call; Argonaut* and *Bulletin; The Gold Hill News; Lyon County Sentinel; Virginia City Territorial Enterprise,* and *Daily Union* were particularly sought out.

Yellowed files, partial or complete, of these papers were found in the State Library at Sacramento; the Bancroft Library at the University of California, Berkeley; the Library of the Mackay School of Mines at Reno, Nevada; and the Library of Congress, to say nothing of the private collections of Virginia City papers in the hands of Edwin Grabhorn and Paul Elder of San Francisco. From the latter collection, with the permission of Mr. Elder, photostats were obtained of the hitherto unrecorded Mark Twain items in them.

For their researches in these old newspaper files, in my behalf, I am indebted to John L. Fulton, Director of the Mackay School of Mines; Miss Edna Rodden Martin at the Bancroft; and Miss Mabel Gillis, Miss Eudora Garoutte, and Miss Caroline Wenzel at the State Library. Particularly I wish to acknowledge my large debt of gratitude to Miss Wenzel.

Wherever material has been quoted or referred to from these newspaper pages, credit has been given, in the bibliography, to those to whom credit is due.

I also wish to acknowledge assistance from Mr. Clarence Mackay of New York; Doctor Herbert E. Bolton, Professor of History, University of California, for permission to quote from the Ph.D. thesis of Miss Effie Mona Mack on "The Life and Letters of William M. Stewart"; Robert Ray, Librarian of the San Francisco Public Library; Thomas J. Wise of London, for permission to reproduce the line drawing of Swinburne and the Menken; George Barron of the De Young Memorial Museum, San Francisco; Grant Smith, Washoe Historian; John Howell, for pictures; Alfred Sutro, for timely advice; Charles R. Boden and L. H. Hardaker, for painstaking photography; Herbert L. Rothschild, for the loan of his Mark Twain collection; Mrs. Robert Howland of Sausalito, widow of Sam Clemens' old friend of Aurora days, for use of her Mark Twain papers; Francis Farquhar, for Vischer pictures of Washoe; Miss Grove and G. E. Dawson of the Wells Fargo Bank; John Newbegin and Frederick Clift of San Francisco, for copies of pictures in their possession; to Doctor E. Seaborn of London, Canada, for biographical data regarding her father, Doctor Richard M. Bucke; to the Harvard Library Theatrical Collection, for stage settings and directions from their prompt-copy of *Mazeppa,* as well as photographs of Adah Isaacs Menken, Walter Leman, etc.; Fulton Oursler, author of *The World's Delight,* for copies of pictures in his Menken collection, and to Edwin Grabhorn, for use of his comprehensive Washoe collection of books, plays, diaries, account books, and photographs.

Grateful acknowledgment is due to all writers and publishers who have permitted reference to their copyrighted works in these pages. In particular, for the publications of the following firms: D. Appleton & Company: Charles A. Dana, *Recollections of the Civil War;* Charles Howard Shinn, *The Story of the Mine.* Albert & Charles Boni, Inc., publishers: William R. Gillis, *Gold Rush Days with Mark Twain.* Harcourt, Brace and Company: Constance Rourke, *Troupers of the Gold Coast,* and *American Humor.* Harper & Brothers: J. Ross Brown, *A Peep at Washoe* and *Washoe Revisited;* Fulton Oursler, *The World's Delight;* Albert Bigelow Paine, *Mark Twain: a Biography; Mark Twain's Letters;* Don. C. Seitz, *Artemus Ward;* Mark Twain, *Roughing It* and *Autobiography.* Harvard University Press: Lewis B. Lesley, *Uncle Sam's Camels.* Houghton Mifflin Company: Elijah R. Kennedy, *The Contest for California in*

1861; Frederick L. Paxson, *History of the American Frontier.* Little, Brown & Company: Samuel C. Chew, *Swinburne;* Bernard De Voto, *Mark Twain's America.* A. C. McClurg & Co.: Glenn D. Bradley, *The Story of the Pony Express.* Walter Neale (Neale Publishing Company): George Rothwell Brown, *Reminiscences of Senator William M. Stewart of Nevada.* G. P. Putnam's Sons: Arthur Chapman, *The Pony Express;* Ethel Colburn Mayne, *Enchanters of Men.* Yale University Press: Francis P. Farquhar, *Up and Down California.*

To Miss Katharine Cusick, my painstaking secretary, I desire to express my greatest appreciation for compiling, sorting, and arranging notes, for copying and recopying of manuscript, and for unsparing devotion to the needs of "The Saga of the Comstock Lode."

GEORGE D. LYMAN.

NOTES

CHAPTER I

At Devil's Gate, 1849–1850

1. Stansbury, Milton M., *North Pacific Review*, No. 4, Jan., 1863. Central Silverland. The Humboldt—from the scenes of starvation and massacre which had occurred so frequently upon its banks—had been called "the River of Death." The barrenness of the region watered by this stream was utterly unredeemed, so much so that a belt of cottonwood would have made a comparative Eden.

Here the most frightful acts of carnage had been perpetrated by the fiendish banditti who were once the terror of these territories. Here a party of seven young adventurerers were burned at the stake by a party of prowling Shoshonies —the Arabs of the American desert. Several entire parties of emigrants had likewise been massacred here in cold blood. Numerous times those scourges, "the Destroying Angels of the Mormons," were implicated in these outrages; also see Ridge, John R., *Humboldt River*, p. 23, beginning "The River of Death, as it rolls With a sound like the wailing of Souls!"

2. "Nevada's First Nugget," *San Francisco Alta*, 5–17–'80, p. 1, col. 5. There is evidence to prove that gold was discovered in this cañon as early as 1849. See Angel's *Nevada*. Also see Beatie, H. S., *The First in Nevada*, p. 4, Bancroft Collection. "Our party were the first to discover gold in Nevada. This Mr. Abner Blackburn [one of Beatie's party] was the first to discover it. He made the discovery in July while I was gone over the mountains with his brother for supplies. When Abner Blackburn first went over the mountains it seems he had an idea that there was gold in the vicinity of what is now Virginia City; and while his brother and myself had gone over the mountains it appears that he went out prospecting and discovered gold, but got only a small quantity. No other mining was done by our party at that time."

3. De Quille, Dan, *The Big Bonanza*, p. 18.

4. *San Francisco Alta*, 5–17–'80, p. 1, col. 5.

5. "The First Gold Found in Nevada," *Daily Elko Independent*, Thursday, 5–20–'80.

6. "Discovery of Gold in Nevada," *San Francisco Call*, 2–16–'80. *Gold Hill News*, Feb. 24, '80, p. 3, col. 2. "Nevada's First Nugget," *San Francisco Alta*, 5–17–'80. *Gold Hill News*, 5–18–'80.

7. Orr settled on a farm at Duncan's Mills, Sonoma County, Calif. His prized possession to the end of his career was the nugget he had discovered that May day. Prouse returned to the land about Salt Lake City.

8. *Gazley's Pacific Monthly*, Jan., 1865, pp. 34–40.

9. "Virginia City Occidental" in *The San Jose Mercury*, 4–14–'64, p. 1, col. 4.

10. Phelps, Alonzo, *Contemporary Biography of California's Representative Men*, p. 40. Bancroft, *Chronicles of the Builders*, pp. 214–216.

11. Bancroft's *Chronicles*, Vol. IV, pp. 32–38.

12. Phelps, *Contemporary Biography*, p. 9. Hearst was born in Franklin County, Mo., Sept. 3, 1820.

13. Older, Mr. and Mrs. Fremont, *The Life of George Hearst*, privately printed for William Randolph Hearst by John Henry Nash, 1933, pp. 56–84.

14. *California Daily Courier*, July 8, 1850, Brown, J. Ross, "Crusoe's Island, California and Washoe," pp. 401–402.

15. For a description of the Gold Cañon country see Fanny G. Hazlett's "Historical Sketches and Reminiscences of Dayton, Nevada." (Spafford Hall's Station became Dayton.) *Nevada Historical Society Papers*, 1921–22, pp. 3–93.

CHAPTER II

"Blue-Stuff" in Gold Cañon

1. There is another story that he hailed from the state of Virginia.

2. "Early Times," in *Gold Hill News*, 5–16–'73, p. 3, col. 2.

3. Shinn, *The Story of the Mine*, pp. 24–25.

4. Angel, Myron, *History of Nevada*, pp. 50–51.

5. Bancroft's *Nevada*, Vol. XXV, p. 171.

6. De Quille, p. 39.

7. Kelley, J. Wells, *Directory of Nevada Territory*, pp. 378–379.

8. By this time the community about the Station was known as Chinatown because the Celestials had settled along the river. In rotation Chinatown became Mineral Rapids, then Nevada City, and finally Dayton, after a man named Day, an early surveyor. See Shinn, p. 233.

9. Sarah was an educated squaw. For a second husband she took an United States Army officer. She was the authoress of *Life Among the Piutes*.

10. De Quille, *The Big Bonanza*, pp. 29–30.

11. *Sacramento Union*, 9–8–'57.

12. Angel's *Nevada*, p. 50. At his trial Snow snarled oaths and denials of any knowledge of murder at his accusers. As he cursed they dropped a noose over his head and hoisted him off the ground. When he had strangled a bit, the rope was eased and the wretch given a further chance to confess. When Snow commenced cursing afresh he was strung up again. On the third suspension the vigilantes "kept him up a little too long." Thus Snow died by inches.

13. Angel's *Nevada*, pp. 50–51. See "The Story of Lucky Bill," pp. 215–221. Ritchie, Robert Wells, "Hell-Roarin' Forty-Niners." Ritchie says Thorrington's last words were "If they want to hang me, hang me. I'm no hog." Also see *Sacramento Union*, 6–22–'58, p. 2, col. 3; 6–17–'58, p. 2, col. 3; 6–25–'58, p. 3, col. 2. It is interesting to note that the news of this people's court, hanging of Lucky Bill, etc., was brought over the mountains by Snow-shoe Thompson. See *Sacramento Union*, 6–22–'58, p. 2, col. 3.

CHAPTER III

Secret of the Grosches, 1851–1857

1. Annual Report Surveyor-General, 1865, pp. 19–22. The Grosch brothers left Reading, Pennsylvania, in the spring of 1849 with a company bound for

California by way of Tampico and Mazetlan. They engaged in gold mining at or near Mud Springs, now El Dorado (El Dorado County), with varying fortunes. Grosch to Doctor Winslow, in Angel's *Nevada,* p. 52.

2. Davis, Vol. I, p. 383.

3. Angel's *Nevada,* p. 52.

4. As the Spanish proverb says, "Para trabajar una mina de plata se necesita una mina de oro": it takes a gold mine to develop a silver one.

5. Grosch to Winslow, Angel's *Nevada,* p. 52; other authorities, notably T. A. Rickard in his *American Mining* (McGraw-Hill Book Company, Inc., 1932), p. 87, questions whether the Grosch boys ever penetrated "The Comstock Lode" proper, claiming that their "buttons" came from veins and stringers that abounded in the hillside above Johntown—notably the shaft back of their cabin, from which they extracted "blue-stuff." Frank, their Mexican workman, first drew their attention to the possibilities of the "blue-stuff." At one time they developed a company known as the "Frank Mining Company."

6. Angel's *Nevada,* p. 52.

7. *San Francisco Bulletin,* Nov. 11, 1889, p. 2, cols. 3–4; Rickard, *A History of American Mining,* p. 86.

8. Kelly's *Directory of Nevada,* p. 356.

9. *North Pacific Review,* Vol. I, No. 4, Jan. 1863, pp. 149–151.

10. Angel's *Nevada,* p. 51. See letter of Laura Ellis (Dettenrieder) to editor.

11. See Laura Ellis' letter, Angel's *Nevada,* p. 51.

12. Angel's *Nevada,* p. 52.

13. Angel's *Nevada,* pp. 51–52.

14. Lord, Eliot, "Comstock Mining and Miners," *United States Geological Survey,* Washington Government Printing Office. House Miscellaneous, 1st Sess., 47th Cong., 1881–82, Vol. 16.

15. "The Grosch Brothers in Washoe," *Sacramento Union,* 8-17-'65, p. 5, col. 5.

CHAPTER IV

THE CLEW LOST, 1858

1. Shinn, p. 30.

2. Davis' *Nevada,* Vol. I, p. 386.

3. Bucke, Richard M., "Twenty-five Years Ago," *Overland Monthly,* Vol. I, 6-'83, p. 560.

4. Davis' *Nevada,* Vol. I, p. 386.

5. Davis' *Nevada,* Vol. I, p. 385.

6. Davis' *Nevada,* Vol. I, p. 386.

7. Bucke, Richard M., *ibid.,* Davis' account is probably based on Bucke's.

8. See the letter of A. B. Grosch, their father, to Doctor C. B. Winslow, printed in Angel's *Nevada,* p. 52–53; Davis' *Nevada,* Vol. I, p. 386.

9. *Sacramento Union,* 8-17-'63, p. 5, col. 5. Grosch's death occurred at the house of M. Harrison, late of the Assembly from Placer County (now of Healdsburg).

10. Bucke, Richard M., Twenty-five Years Ago," *Overland Monthly,* Vol. I, 6-'83, p. 560.

11. On the headstone of Hosea at Silver City, the name is spelt Grosh. The father uses the same spelling in signing his letter in Angel's *Nevada*, pp. 52-53.

CHAPTER V

FOOLS OF FORTUNE, 1858–1859

1. Years later Dan De Quille was present when these fragments were unearthed. De Quille, *Big Bonanza*, p. 34.

2. *North Pacific Review*, Jan., 1863, Vol. I, No. 4, pp. 149–151.

3. Lord, p. 34; "Comstock Papers," No. 1, *Mining & Scientific Press*, 7-22-'76, pp. 64–65.

4. In the first book of locations made in Virginia and Gold Hill mining districts. See "Relics of the Past," *Virginia Evening Chronicle*, Aug. 30, 1878, p. 3, cols. 3–5. "I, the undersigned, claim this ground for ranching purposes, commencing at this notice and running south half a mile—; east three-quarters of a mile; thence north one-half a mile; thence back to the beginning. H. Comstock, June 27, 1859." Comstock afterward in claiming the property said of the spring, "This was Old Man Caldwell's spring—Manny Penrod and me bought the claim offen him last winter——."

5. *North Pacific Review*, Vol. I, No. 4, Jan., 1863, pp. 149–151; De Quille, p. 35. One day Comstock found back of the Grosch cabin a shaft, partially covered over with logs. He had himself lowered. At its bottom was the skeleton of a squaw. Stones constantly dropped out of the side—"without cause." After that, Comstock refused to be lowered again. Neither would his Piute braves work there. The shaft was abandoned and became known as the "lost shaft." See J. M. Hunter's letter on "Lost Shaft"—Angel's *Nevada*, p. 54.

6. "A Sketch of Early Times," *Territorial Enterprise*, 6-6-'75, p. 3, col. 2. It has never been clear which assay was made first, the one in Sacramento or the one in Nevada City. See Goodwin, C. C., *As I Remember Them*, pp. 192–193. Compare these accounts with Angel's, pp. 59–60, *History of Nevada*.

7. J. Wells Kelley says that Gold Hill was discovered March, 1859. See *Directory*, p. 306.

8. Bancroft, Vol. XXV, p. 100; Shinn, p. 36.

9. *Territorial Enterprise*, June 20, 1875, p. 3, col. 2; Bancroft XXV, p. 109; Bishop's *Directory of Virginia City and Gold Hill*, p. 258; De Quille, *Big Bonanza*, p. 45; also see "Comstock Papers," No. 2, *Mining & Scientific Press*, 7-29-'76.

10. Lord, p. 36; "Early Times," in *Gold Hill News*, 5-16-'73, p. 3, col. 2; Bishop's *Directory of Virginia City and Gold Hill*, 1878–79, p. 258.

11. Wrenn's *History of Nevada*, p. 40.

12. It is probable that Jessup made the first discovery of the Ophir. In the spring of 1859, Jessup left the Ophir to help a man named Sides put up a shop where Gold Hill stands. After the shop was built, Sides and Jessup sat down to play a game of cards for the drinks. A dispute arose and Sides killed Jessup with his bowie knife, stabbing him twice. Sides was taken to Eagle Valley for trial. While the trial was going on, McLaughlin and O'Riley jumped the claim. *Territorial Enterprise*, Sunday, June 20, 1875, p. 3, col.

2. The Lode was probably discovered on either June 12 or 13, 1859. See also Emanuel Penrod's letter in Angel's *Nevada,* p. 56.

13. Shinn, p. 40; Bancroft, Vol. XXV, p. 101; Lord, p. 39; Rickard, p. 95.

14. In the first book of locations made in Virginia and Gold Hill Mining Districts, under June 27, 1859. "Relics of the Past," *Virginia Evening Chronicle,* 8–30–'78, p. 3, cols. 3–5.

15. Shinn, pp. 40–41; De Quille, p. 52.

16. Shinn, p. 41. This account does not agree with that of De Quille, p. 54. But see Bancroft, Vol. XXV, p. 101.

17. Mark Twain, "Early Days in Nevada—Silver-Land Nabobs," *San Francisco Chronicle,* Jan. 30, 1870, p. 3, col. 1. Bancroft Library.

18. Bancroft, Vol. XXV, p. 103. Also consult "The Comstock Lode," in *The New York Herald,* Monday, 12–30–'78. "Virginia City was first called Silver City. I named it at the time I gave the Ophir claim its name."

19. "The Comstock Lode," in *The New York Herald,* 12–30–'78. Hale, a Jack Mormon, came from Carson Valley and with Norcross, a son of Neptune, took up the claim during the summer of 1859. See *Mining and Scientific Press,* "Comstock Papers," No. 40 and No. 45.

20. Lord, pp. 411–412. De Quille, *Big Bonanza,* pp. 77–80.

CHAPTER VI

THE CHRISTENING

1. "The Comstock Lode," in *The New York Herald,* Dec. 30, 1878.

2. The description of the christening of Virginia City is given at length in "Old Virginny's" own words in "The Comstock Lode," *New York Herald,* Dec. 30, 1878.

3. *Western Monthly,* Vol. I, No. 4, Apr., 1869, pp. 235–241.

4. Angel, *Nevada,* p. 60, says the rancher's name was W. P. Morrison— but other authorities agree on Harrison. "Comstock Papers," No. 3, *Mining and Scientific Press,* Aug. 12, 1876. This ore had been given to Harrison by a man named Stone, with directions to take it to Grass Valley and have it tested, its weight leading him to believe that it contained a good deal of metal of some kind. Stone, who resided at Stone and Gates' Crossing on the Truckee River, had been to the mines and having a notion like others that it might be valuable, availed himself of the first opportunity that offered of having its character determined. This is undoubtedly exactly what occurred, as the name of Stone had always been associated with this event and no one seems to have known exactly in what capacity. These facts were obtained from Judge Walsh himself.

5. Lord, p. 58.

6. Figures differ on these assays: some run as high as $6356 per ton. Atwood's assay was made June 27, 1859. According to *The Mining and Scientific Press* of Dec. 16, 1886, p. 392, col. 4, it was as follows:

Silver	3000
Gold	876
Total	3876

Compare this with "Comstock Papers," No. 3, *Mining and Scientific Press,* Sept. 12, 1876. On July 28, 1859, the "blue-stuff" was examined by J. J. Ott of Nevada City, showing:

Silver	1975.75
Gold	964.97
Total	2940.72

This does not agree with Angel's account, p. 60. See also, Davis' *Nevada,* Vol. I, p. 388.

7. *San Francisco Alta,* Nov. 16, 1859.
8. Lord, p. 55.

CHAPTER VII

CALL OF WASHOE, 1859

1. Davis, *Nevada,* Vol. I, p. 389.
2. Hittell, J. S., *Mining in the Pacific States,* p. 26.
3. *Ibid.,* pp. 22–24.
4. Hittell, p. 30.
5. Brown, J. Ross, *Washoe,* p. 318.
6. *Ibid., Washoe,* p. 319.
7. Hittell, *Mining,* p. 35.
8. Lord, p. 65.
9. Angel's *Nevada,* p. 567.

CHAPTER VIII

BILL STEWART, 1859

1. Wells, Harry L., *History of Nevada County, California, Thompson and West Oakland,* 1880, pp. 98–99. To save himself, the wretch who had done the accusing ran for the Yuba River, hoping to make an escape, jumped in and was drowned in the raging current. Wells gives the date 1851—Stewart 1852.
2. Goodwin, C. C., *As I Remember Them,* Salt Lake City, 1913, p. 140.
3. Goodwin, C. C., *As I Remember Them,* Salt Lake City, Utah, 1913, pp. 141–142.
4. Goodwin, C. C., *As I Remember Them,* p. 142.
5. *Ibid.*
6. *Ibid.*
7. The other lady married the man of her choice and the pair answered the Call of Washoe at the same time Mr. and Mrs. Stewart moved to Virginia. The two men were rivals politically and professionally for years, Stewart winning half the honors professionally and all the honors politically. But the other was the abler lawyer. Goodwin, *ibid.,* p. 142.
8. Brown, George R., *Reminiscences of Senator William M. Stewart of Nevada,* Neale Publishing Company, New York, 1908, p. 117.
9. Mack, Effie Mona, "William Morris Stewart" in *Proceedings of the Pacific Coast Branch of the American Historical Association,* p. 185. Stewart was born on a New York farm, Wayne County, near Lyons, reared in Ohio, educated at Yale.

10. Shuck, Oscar T., *Representative Men of the Pacific Coast,* p. 636. Mack, Effie Mona, "Life and Letters of William Morris Stewart," a thesis, Bancroft Library, p. 25.

CHAPTER IX

THE BOYS,. 1859–1862

1. Rickard, T. A., *American Mining,* etc., p. 98; Older, *Life of George Hearst,* p. 81.
2. Older, Fremont, *Life,* p 81.
3. Older, p. 82.
4. Phelps' *California Biography,* p. 11.
5. Rickard's *Comstock Lode,* p. 98; Older, pp. 80–82.
6. So says Gillis, in *Gold Rush Days with Mark Twain,* but there is no such name in the Harvard Quinquennial. Other authorities claim that Peel came originally from Liverpool. See Langford, N. P., *Vigilante Days and Ways,* pp. 429–440.
7. De Quille, Dan, *The Big Bonanza,* pp. 130–131; Angel's *Nevada,* p. 356.
8. "Closing Argument of Adolph Sutro, on the Sutro Tunnel," Washington, D. C., 1872, p. 4. See also Goodwin, *As I Remember Them,* p. 240.
9. Phelps' *California Biography,* p. 38.
10. Phelps' *California Biography,* pp. 195–196. Angel's *Nevada,* p. 590.
11. Murphy, I. I., *Life of Colonel Daniel E. Hungerford,* pp. 166–167.
12. Dr. Bryant did not stay in Washoe the first trip over. He had returned to Downieville by the time the Piute War broke out. His name is listed among the Sierra Guards sent by the Governor of California to assist the Washoe whites. His father-in-law wrote him to bring his sabre. See Murphy's *Hungerford.*
13. Stewart, *Reminiscences,* p. 60; Farish, T. E., *Gold Hunters of California,* pp. 111–113. While a clerk in the Supreme Court at Sacramento, Fairfax had an altercation with one Harvey Lee during which Lee drew a sword from his cane and ran Fairfax through the body. The wounded Fairfax levelled his derringer at his enemy; then, hesitating, said, "You have a wife and small children, Lee. On their account I will spare your life." The wound that Fairfax received that day resulted in untimely death.
14. *Sacramento Union,* 5-30-'60, p. 2, col. 4.
15. Kennedy, *Contest for California,* p. 193.
16. *History of Sacramento County,* 1890, pp. 251–253.
17. *Sacramento Bee,* 2-27-'95, pp. 1–2. Father Manogue was born in County Kilkenny, Ireland, Mar. 15, 1831. He emigrated to the United States in 1848. After residing two years in Connecticut, he spent four years at the University of St. Mary's of the Lake, Chicago, Ill. In 1854 he came to California. For the next three years he earned his daily bread by hard work in the mines near Moore's Flat. Having saved enough money to defray the cost of a more advanced ecclesiastical education, he left for France, entered the Seminary of Saint Sulpice at Paris. On Christmas, 1861, he was ordained a priest of the Church by Cardinal Marlot. In 1862 he left Paris for Virginia City, where he arrived in June of that year.
18. Davis, Vol. I, p. 544.

19. She was born in Liverpool, according to *The Territorial Enterprise,* 1–22–'67, and her real name was Smith; *Gold Hill Daily News,* 1–21–'67.

CHAPTER X
RUSH TO WASHOE, 1859–1863

1. Almarin Paul, correspondent of *The San Francisco Bulletin,* has bequeathed us an extensive account of this route. See *San Francisco Bulletin* for 3–28–'61; 4–3–'61; 5–7–'61.

2. The Rush to Washoe began in the fall of 1859 and continued all winter. Even when the passes were choked with snow, men made their way over them. A few were lost in avalanches. A few had frost-bitten arms and legs; but the great majority made the grade. Population of Virginia increased at the rate of 150 a day. *San Francisco Bulletin,* 5–12–'60, p. 1. The Piute War in the spring of 1860 put a quietus on the rush. When the Indian trouble was over, the rush continued with unabated fury, through 1861–62, and '63. During the winter of 1860 there were 10,000 people on the Comstock Lode.

3. During two days in April a correspondent of *The Sacramento Union* passed 1000 loaded mules; 3500 head of cattle; 800 to 1000 head of sheep, all bound for Washoe. *Sacramento Union,* 4–25–'60, p. 2, col. 2.

4. Sutro, Adolph, *San Francisco Alta,* 4–13–'60, p. 1, col. 9.

5. Paul, Almarin B., "On the Road to Washoe," *San Francisco Bulletin,* 4–28–'60.

6. "Comstock Papers," No. 3, 8–12–'76, *Mining and Scientific Press.*

7. Older, Mr. and Mrs. Fremont, *Life of George Hearst,* p. 82.

8. Sutro, Adolph, in *San Francisco Alta,* 4–13–'60, p. 1, col. 9, dated Virginia City, 3–20–'60; *San Francisco Alta,* 4–14–'60, p. 1, col. 8.

9. Wagstaff, A. E., *Life of David S. Terry,* pp. 221–222.

10. "Nevada Socially," *Gold Hill News,* 10–14–'63, p. 1, cols. 1–2.

11. Once they called Tahoe, Lake Bigler after a California Governor but why they ever chose to call such a magnificent body of water after one who absolutely despised the taste of all water, is a question. But when he had disgraced himself, the community at large changed the name to the sweeter-sounding Tahoe. Rideing, Wm. H., *The Wheeler Survey in Nevada,* p. 70, June, 1877.

12. Bancroft, Vol. XXV, p. 11; Lord, *Comstock Lode,* p. 2.

13. "Cosmos," pseudonym for Almarin B. Paul, correspondent for *The San Francisco Bulletin,* 5–16–'60, p. 1, cols. 1–2.

14. Sutro, A., *San Francisco Alta,* 4–14–'60, p. 1. col. 8.

15. Bancroft, XXV, pp. 7–18. One of these springs reaches a temperature of 109.5°.

16. Sutro Adolph, in *San Francisco Alta,* 4–13–'60, p. 1, col. 9.

17. J. Ross Browne, *A Peep at Washoe,* p. 374. Also see *San Francisco Bulletin,* 5–12–'60, p. 3. A lot 15 x 50 feet in business section cannot be bought for less than $800–$1500. Lumber $150 per M; stores, 12 x 30 feet, rent for $200–$250. Freight 18 cents from Placerville; 2000 mules employed in hauling freight. Riding animals $30 to $35 one way. See *San Francisco Bulletin,* 5–12–'60, p. 1.

18. *Reminiscences,* James Walsh, San Francisco.

CHAPTER XI

ARRIVAL, 1859

1. The date on which Lord says Walsh and Woodworth arrived at Gold Hill, 7–1–'59, p. 55.

2. Soon after arrival, Judge Walsh and Comstock accompanied, muleback, 3150 pounds of selected ore to San Francisco. The ore was worked by Mosheimer and Kustel and netted $4871. This induced the owners to send some 38 tons of rich sulphide ore to the same place for reduction. It yielded about $114,000. The cost of freight and reduction on this last was $552 per ton. See "Comstock Papers," No. 3, *Mining and Scientific Press*, 8–12–'76, p. 112.

3. This sixth interest eventually came into possession of the Maldonado brothers. Hence the various names the property bore, first the Spanish then the Mexican Mine. The brothers took a fortune out of the mine and eventually sold it to Alsop & Company, and Duncan, Sherman & Company for $200,-000. Subsequently it fell into the hands of Ophir for $30,000. "Comstock Papers," No. 3, *ibid*.

4. "Comstock Papers," No. 8, *Mining and Scientific Press*, 11–4–'76, p. 305.

5. In the end, Camp ended his Washoe career where he had begun—dead broke. "Comstock Papers," No. 8, *ibid*.

6. "Comstock Papers," No. 3, *Mining and Scientific Press*, 8–12–'76, p. 112.

7. "Comstock Papers," No. 2, *Mining and Scientific Press*, 7–29–'76.

8. Older, Fremont, *Life of George Hearst*, p. 87; Phelps, *California Biography*, p. 11.

9. Older, *Life of George Hearst*, p. 90.

10. *Ibid*.

11. Phelps, *Biography*, p. 12. In June, 1860, Hearst, having learned that his mother was desperately ill in Missouri, sold out a part of his Washoe interests, took the steamer for home, and made the closing days of his parent luxuriously happy. When he returned to the coast he brought with him his bride, a Missouri schoolma'am, Miss Phœbe E. Apperson.

12. During 1860 Walsh parted with most of his interests, but not at great figures. Woodworth held on to his too long and retired with only a fraction of his once great fortune. Walsh lost most of the money he had made in Washoe in White Pine, Nev., and went out of Nevada poorer than when he arrived. See "Comstock Papers," No. 8, *Mining and Scientific Press*, 11–4–'76.

13. Penrod sold out to Walsh for $6200, removed to Elko County and engaged in hydraulic mining. Penrod enjoyed an excellent reputation for honesty, courage, good sense, and superior business ability. "Comstock Papers," No. 12, *Mining and Scientific Press*, 12–16–'76.

14. O'Reilly was a man of good appearance and more than ordinary intelligence though visionary and flighty. "Comstock Papers," No. 6, *Mining and Scientific Press*, 9–30–'76.

15. There is a MS. of Gould's in the Bancroft Library, Berkeley. In it he writes that he had been in Gold Cañon since '58 and took Comstock and Walsh over the Sierra with the first shipment of ore.

CHAPTER XII

THE IMAGE, 1860

1. Davis' *Nevada,* p. 247. Stewart in his *Reminiscences,* p. 132, says that by 1860 Sam Brown had already killed 16 men. The name of the man whose heart he cut out was McKenzie, in the year 1861, Angel, p. 344. Angel, pp. 343–344, gives Brown credit for 3 murders during '59 and '60 but says he had committed many others before going to Washoe, notably one in Texas, his first; 3 Chilenos at Fiddletown in about 1854 in defending his "bank," and wounded another for which he was sent to San Quentin for two years. See Angel's *Nevada,* p. 356.

2. Angel's *Nevada,* pp. 343–344.

3. Stewart's *Reminiscences,* p. 132.

4. Lord's *Comstock Lode,* pp. 75–76.

5. Stewart's *Reminiscences,* p. 133.

6. Wagstaff, *Life of David S. Terry,* pp. 222–223. See "Comstock Papers," No. 14, *Mining and Scientific Press,* Jan. 27, 1877, for a description of Tom Andrews and similarly bred roughs of desperate courage.

7. Farish, T. E., *Gold Hunters of California,* pp. 171–172.

8. *San Francisco Alta,* Feb. 14, 1875, "The Late Donald Davidson."

9. *Sacramento Bee,* 2–27–'95, pp. 1–2.

10. *Sacramento Union,* 6–21–'60, p. 1, col. 4.

11. Father Manogue built the second Roman Catholic Church on the Comstock in 1862, it was enlarged in 1868, burned to the ground in 1875 and rebuilt in 1876 at a cost of $100,000 and was called St. Mary's of the Mountains. It was a monument to Father Manogue. *Nevada Historical Society Papers,* Vol. I, 1913–1916, p. 157.

12. Lord's *Comstock Lode,* pp. 301–302.

13. "Closing Argument of Adolph Sutro," pp. 4–5.

14. *San Francisco Alta,* 4–13–'60, p. 1, col. 9; *San Francisco Bulletin,* 11–11–'59, p. 2, cols. 3–4. The ore was shipped by Donald Davidson, via Placerville route, at rate of five cents per pound.

15. *San Francisco Alta,* Apr. 20. The Ophir had eleven directors, among them Alpheus Bull, William Babcock, and William C. Ralston. Among Gould & Curry directors were John O. Earl, Ralston, A. B. McCreery, Alpheus Bull, and George Hearst. *San Francisco Bulletin,* 11–11–'59, p. 2, cols. 3–4.

16. Davis' *Nevada,* Vol. I, p. 401.

17. Davis' *Nevada,* Vol. I, p. 401.

CHAPTER XIII

VIRGINIA, 1859–1860

1. Strowbridge, Ida M., *In Miners' Mirage Land,* pp. 3–11.

2. Virginia City has an elevation above the sea of 6205 feet and above the Carson plains 2000 feet. Mount Davidson rises above the city 1662 feet, having a total height above the sea of 7827 feet. Some of the Pine Nut Mountains in the same range are still higher.

3. De Groot, Henry, "Early Times," *Territorial Enterprise*, June 20, 1875; Angel's *Nevada*, p. 571.

4. Lord, p. 64.

5. "Comstock Papers," No. 9, *Mining and Scientific Press*, 11-25-'76.

6. *Ibid.*; also see Angel's *Nevada*, under Sept. 13, p. 344.

7. Brown, J. Ross, *A Peek at Washoe*, p. 376.

8. Shinn, p. 65; see also Angel's *Nevada*, "Roman Catholic Church," p. 205.

9. Lord, pp. 62–64.

10. "The Hermit of Washoe," *The Territorial Enterprise* of July 24, 1870, copied in *Grass Valley Union*, July 28, 1870, p. 2, col. 1.

11. Angel's *Nevada*, p. 571.

12. Angel's *Nevada*, p. 568.

CHAPTER XIV

MALEVOLENT FORCES, 1859–1860

1. De Quille, Dan, *History of the Big Bonanza*, p. 107.

2. Browne, J. Ross, *A Peek at Washoe*, p. 368.

3. Lord, pp. 66–67.

4. John L. Moore, the man who owned this supply of liquor, left San Francisco on the 9th of March. His supply cost some $1600 and consisted of tin plates, blankets, 10 gallons of brandy, 10 gallons gin, 30 gallons whiskey, 10 gallons of rum, 70 gallons of assorted wines and liquors. The total weight of the invoice was 2100 pounds. It cost 50 cents a pound to transport. Moore reached Virginia, Mar. 31, 1860. The day before he reached Virginia he refused a cash offer of $8000. Lord, pp. 66–67.

5. Cleland, R. G., *History of California*, p. 366; Paxson, Frederick L., *History of the American Frontier*, p. 465.

6. Paxson, Frederick L., *History of the American Frontier*, pp. 465–466.

CHAPTER XV

THE PHANTOM OF THE DESERT, APRIL 12, 1860

1. *San Francisco Bulletin*, April 13, 1860.

2. The Pony Express was established by Russell, Majors, and Waddell. The enterprise included 500 superb horses, nearly 200 stations, a hundred riders. The men in the racing saddles were stripped to the last ounce. For protection they carried a knife and a revolver. The mail bags never weighed more than twenty pounds. Every letter was written on tissue paper. The postage on the smallest was five dollars.

3. Raine, William MacLeod, *Bonanza*, pp. 2–5.

4. *Quarterly of the Society of California Pioneers*, Sept. 30, 1925.

5. St. Joseph, Mo., *Gazette*, Apr. 3, 1860. Congress at this time was "at outs" with Utah on account of the Mormon outbreak and the troubles of 1857–1858 and there was much ill feeling in Congress in consequence. Bradley's *Pony Express*, pp. 43–44.

CHAPTER XVI

"BENECIA BOY" OR SAYERS? 1860

1. *Sacramento Union,* Apr. 24, 1860, p. 2, col. 4; *History of El Dorado County,* 1883, p. 83.
2. *Sacramento Union,* 4–16–'60, p. 4, col. 1.
3. Angel's *Nevada,* p. 105; *San Francisco Alta,* 5–8–'60, p. 1, cols. 3–5. "The Pony Express at Carson," dated Carson City, U. T., May 7, 1860.
4. *Sacramento Union,* Apr. 29, 1860.
5. *San Francisco Alta,* May 8, 1860, p. 1, cols. 3–5.
6. *The California Farmer,* May 11, 1860. For a description of Haslam's ride see Chapman, pp. 218–219; Bradley, pp. 120–127.
7. *Sacramento Union,* 5–19–'60, p. 4, col. 5, says the pony expressmen who brought the news from Buckland's Station on the Carson River, whither one of the other Williams brothers had brought the tidings of the tragedy, were J. B. Bartoles and J. H. Smith. Bob Haslam carried the dispatches through to Friday's Station. See also account, *Nevada National,* 5–19–'60, p. 2, col. 3.
8. For the account of the Heenan-Sayers fight, which the Pony Express brought, see *San Francisco Herald,* 5–16–'60, p. 1, cols. 1–5, "Particulars of the Fight." On receipt of the news Benecia fired a hundred guns in honor of the great bruiser and ten cannons rolled their smoke over the hills of Solano. *San Francisco Herald,* 5–19–'60, p. 3, col. 4; 5–21–'60, p. 1, col. 2.

CHAPTER XVII

PIUTE WAR, 1860

1. Sutro, Adolph, "Letter from Washoe, May 9, 1860," in *Bulletin,* May 16, 1860, p. 4, col. 5. See also Almarin B. Paul's correspondence in the *Bulletin,* 5–16–'60, p. 1, cols. 1–2, under pseudonym "Cosmos." See also Sutro's correspondence in *Bulletin* for May 16, and 19, 1860, p. 1, cols. 1–2; *California Farmer,* 5–11–'60.
2. *Reminiscences of William M. Stewart* (Neale Publishing Co.), p. 124.
3. "Little Joe" was a son of Alex Baldwin, who wrote *Flush Times in Alabama;* see Goodwin, *As I Remember Them,* p. 231.
4. Shinn, *Story of the Mine* (Appleton), p. 194. Irrespective of this evidence it is doubtful whether Sutro took any part in either the first or second battles of Pyramid Lake. That he wrote the accounts of them, there is no doubt.
5. *Sacramento Union,* May 14–15, 1860.
6. Lord, p. 68.
7. Angel's *Nevada,* p. 153.
8. By some miracle, both Captain Watkins and Joe Baldwin were ultimately saved. See account Frank Soule, *San Francisco Alta,* 5–25–'60, p. 1, cols. 6–7.
9. De Quille, *Big Bonanza,* p. 120.
10. Sutro, *Bulletin,* 5–19–'60, p. 1, cols. 1–2; *Sacramento Union,* 5–19–'60, p. 2, cols. 3–4; and 5–30–'60, p. 2, col. 4. Meredith was the third son of Dr. Reuben Meredith of Hanover County, Virginia. He was born Aug. 14, 1826. Graduated at College of Columbia, Mo., then returned to Virginia. Studied law under Samuel Taylor of Richmond. Came to California in 1850. Had cholera

on the plains. Commenced practice of law in Nevada City, rose to front rank. Especially distinguished for his skill and ability in the management of mining cases. Ambitious of political distinction. Died when objects of ambition were within his grasp, when the prospects of wealth, political preferment, and professional success seemed to open for him an inviting future. His remains were carried to Nevada City by the Masons. He was buried there 6-15-'60, accompanied to the grave by the largest and most solemn procession ever witnessed in the mountains of California. *San Francisco Alta,* 6-17-'60, p. 1, col. 5.

11. After the war was over, the cannon was carried into the hills and a slow fuse applied. It exploded with a terrible detonation. The air was filled with chunks of iron and wood. Had it been fired in the fort, every one would have been killed. De Quille, *Big Bonanza,* p. 121.

12. Vischer, *Pony Express,* pp. 41-42.

13. Murphy, I. I., *Life of Colonel Hungerford,* pp. 173-175.

14. Edmund Goodwin Bryant, son-in-law of Major Hungerford, died at La Porte, Cal., 1867. Buried, Lone Mountain, San Francisco. Mrs. Bryant subsequently married John Mackay and became the mother of Clarence Hungerford Mackay of New York.

15. *Sacramento Union,* 5-14-'60, p. 2.

16. De Quille, *Big Bonanza,* pp. 121-122.

17. Murphy, *Hungerford,* pp. 176-178. Hungerford, as adjutant, was in charge of the infantry. Colonel Hayes was in command of the allied forces, government and volunteer. Altogether there were two companies of infantry, numbering 144, rank and file, and a detachment of artillery in charge of two mountain howitzers. In addition there were 550 volunteers. See Sen. Ex. Doc. No. 1, pp. 89-92; *Nevada National,* 5-19-'60, p. 2, col. 3.

18. *San Francisco Alta,* 5-25-'60, p. 1, cols. 6-7. "The Army in Washoe," *Bulletin,* 6-16-'60, p. 1, cols. 2-4.

19. *San Francisco Bulletin,* 6-16-'60, p. 1, cols. 2-4.

20. "Closing Campaign of the Indian War," in *Territorial Enterprise,* Friday, June 21, 1872, p. 3, cols. 2-3.

21. In the second battle the whites lost 11 killed. The Piutes 40 to 50. Figures differ with different accounts. See government reports, Senate Ex. Doc. No. 1, pp. 89-92; *San Francisco Alta,* June 11, 1860, p. 1, col. 3. In the first battle also, casualty figures differ. Some say 43; some say 60. See Bancroft's *Nevada,* p. 212.

CHAPTER XVIII

Buck Fanshaw

1. *San Francisco Bulletin,* 6-16-'60, p. 1, cols. 2-4. Edward Faris Storey was born in Georgia, July 1, 1828, a son of Colonel John Storey who commanded a regiment during the Georgia Indian Wars. The colonel afterward removed to Texas. With his three sons, enlisted in Mexican War. Of the sons, only Edward F. Storey survived the war. In 1849 Edward married Adelia Calhoun Johnson of Texas by whom he had a daughter, later Mrs. J. W. Williams of Visalia, Calif. Storey came to California overland through Mexico, bringing with him Edward's orphaned daughter, then two years old. In stock business in

Tulare County before coming to Nevada before the Piute War. See Bancroft, XXV, p. 215; see "H. C. J." letter from Washoe, *San Francisco Alta,* 6–14-'60, p. 3, col. 4. A younger brother was Lieutenant-Governor of Texas, p. 569, Angel's *Nevada.*

2. *Territorial Enteprise,* 6–21-'72, p. 3, cols. 2–3. "Closing Campaign Indian War of 1860. Death of Captain Storey, Masonic Honors Paid to his Memory."

3. De Quille, *Big Bonanza,* p. 127.

4. *San Francisco Alta,* 6–11-'60, p. 1, col. 3.

5. *San Francisco Alta,* 6–11-'60, p. 1, col. 3. See telegram dated Virginia City, June 10, 9 A.M.

6. *San Francisco Bulletin,* 6–14-'60, p. 3, col. 4.

7. *Ibid.*

8. Angel's *Nevada,* p. 588.

9. Goodman, Joseph T., *San Francisco Chronicle,* 2–21-'92, p. 1, col. 1.

10. Langford, N. P., *Vigilante Days and Ways* (McClurg, 1923), p. 438.

11. The membership of these organizations can be found in *Kelly's Directory for 1863,* pp. 299–301.

12. Angel's *Nevada,* p. 578.

13. Ephraim Elmer Ellsworth was born at Mechanicsville, N. Y., Apr. 23, 1837. He was educated for the law but a career of arms was that for which he had the greatest predilection. At the beginning of the war, realizing that our military system was little better than a farce, he had an ambition to train militia for the suppression of rebellion. The light infantry corps of France, under the name of Zouave, seemed to him a model. When Sumter fell he sprang to action and raised a regiment among the hordes of adventurous firemen of New York City, in whom he beheld excellent material.

14. "Comstock Papers," No. 14, Jan. 27, 1877.

15. Goodman, J. T., *Chronicle,* 2–21-'92, p. 1, col. 1.

16. Tom ran the Sazerac Saloon on South "C" Street. See *Kelly's Directory of Nevada Territory,* p. 278. He was sheriff from 1862 to 1864. At one session of the Territorial Legislature he was doorkeeper of the House, and Sergeant-at-arms of the State Senate in 1865. For further data on Peasley see J. B. Levison's *Memories for My Family,* John Henry Nash, 1933, pp. 5–12.

17. *Sacramento Union,* 1–24-'67, p. 2, col. 4.

18. *Gold Hill News,* Jan. 21, 1867.

19. *Sacramento Union,* 1–24-'67, p. 2, col. 4.

CHAPTER XIX

"LINCOLN'S ELECTED," 1860

1. Colonel Connor was wounded early in the engagement. Bleeding from his wounds he fought all day. By night he was practically exsanguinated. Throughout the night two of his comrades lay close to him on either side to keep him from dying of cold and exhaustion. After the war he settled in California and married Johanna Connor of Redwood City. Connor always courted rather than avoided danger. Born in Ireland, he arose by his own merits until the stars of a major-general glittered on his shoulders. Goodwin, *As I Remember Them,* pp. 265–268.

2. Angel's *Nevada,* p. 266.

3. There were six fine brick buildings constituting Fort Churchill. See Angel's *Nevada,* p. 501. The Fort was named for Sylvester Churchill, brigadier-general, U. S. A., a Vermonter who arose from a first lieutenant to a brevetted brigadier-general, Feb. 23, 1847, for gallant and meritorious conduct in the battle of Buena Vista, Mexico. He died Dec. 7, 1862. War Department Communication of 7-12-'32.

4. Delano of Ohio, in seconding the nomination, referred to Abraham Lincoln as a "rail-splitter." See *San Francisco Alta,* June 11, 1860, p. 1, col. 3. The convention met on May 16 in the "Wigwam," Chicago. Owing to the Piute War, disruption of the Pony service, etc., the message had come by overland mail from St. Louis and had then been wired from King's River, Telegraphic Camp No. 21, near Visalia, June 10, 1860, to San Francisco. It is possible that Dr. John De La Montagne brought the first news of Lincoln's nomination to San Francisco two days earlier. He arrived on the Overland Stage, June 8, 1860, and brought the report of May 18, 1860, from St. Louis. *San Francisco Alta,* June 9, 1860, p. 1, col. 1.

5. Eldridge, *History of California,* Vol. IV, pp. 184-187. *San Francisco Alta,* 7-16-'60, p. 1, cols. 2-5.

6. MacDonald, C. G., "Colonel Baker's Oratory," *Sacramento Bee,* 6-19-'94, p. 8, col. 1; Kennedy, *Contest,* p. 158.

7. Baker, E. D., born in London, Feb., 1811. Arrived in America aet. four years. Senator Oregon. Introduced the President at his inaugural, Mar. 4, 1861, in these words: "Fellow citizens, I introduce to you Abraham Lincoln, the President of the United States of America." Killed battle Ball's Bluff. Buried San Francisco, Lone Mountain; see Kennedy, *Contest* (Houghton Mifflin), p. 193.

8. *Sacramento Union,* Nov. 13, 1860, p. 1, col. 4.

9. Robert Haslam was born in 1840, London, Eng.; died Chicago, Ill., at the age of seventy-two. "He was the daring express rider who carried the news of the election of Abraham Lincoln." See *Chicago Record Herald,* Mar. 1, 1912, Chicago Department of Health, Registered No. 6192-5.

10. The Pony Express left St. Joseph, Mo., the afternoon of Nov. 7, 1860, with the dispatches of Lincoln's election. They arrived at Fort Churchill, 11-14-'60, at one o'clock in the morning. See *San Francisco Alta,* 11-15-'60, p. 1, col. 6, with flaring headlines, "Only Seven Days from the East. New York State goes fifty thousand majority to Lincoln." It is about 1120 miles from St. Joseph to Fort Churchill. Traversed in six days, twenty hours. About seven miles an hour, and the month, November. *The Union* editor says the Pony reached Fort Churchill at midnight the 13th. *Sacramento Union,* 11-15-'60, p. 2, cols. 1-5.

CHAPTER XX

TERRITORIAL ENTERPRISE, 1860

1. McEwen, Arthur, *San Francisco Examiner,* 1-22-'93, p. 15. *The Enterprise* was founded at Genoa, Douglass County, Dec., 1858. Removed to Carson, Nov. 5, 1859. In Oct., 1860, moved to Virginia City. On Mar. 2, 1861, Joseph T. Goodman and Dennis E. McCarthy became partners in the publication.

Sept. 24, 1861, weekly ceased, daily began. Angel's *Nevada*, p. 317. *Daily Union* established Nov. 4, 1862. Had the largest circulation and was the paper of the town. *The Daily Old Piute,* an evening paper, was established in 1865 and *The Nevada Pioneer,* a German sheet and the ablest in that tongue on the coast.

2. De Quille, Dan, "The Passing of a Pioneer," *San Francisco Examiner,* Jan. 22, 1893.

3. Chapman, Arthur, *Pony Express* (Putnam), p. 307.

4. Dilke, C. W., *Greater Britain,* p. 148.

5. Angel's *Nevada,* p. 292.

6. Fitch, Thomas, "The Silver State," *San Francisco Sunday Call,* 9–20–'03, p. 14.

CHAPTER XXI

OPHIR, 1860

1. The Mexican could not be bought at this time for $1,000,000, according to the owners. They employed about fifteen men, mostly Mexicans. Quantity of ore already taken out estimated at 750 tons. Adolph Sutro, *San Francisco Alta,* 4–11–'60, p. 1, col. 7.

2. MS. Deidesheimer, Philipp. Bancroft Library, Berkeley, Calif.

3. Angel's *Nevada,* p. 573.

4. "Square-sets" consist of short, square timbers, four to six feet long, mortised and tenoned at the ends so that they can be put together in a series of interlocked cribs and built up in a continuous row or block to any height or width, fitting the whole chamber as the ore is removed.

5. Shinn, *Story of the Mine* (Appleton), p. 97.

CHAPTER XXII

MILLS, 1860

1. Davis' *Nevada,* Vol. I, p. 413.

2. "Comstock Papers," No. 5, *Mining and Scientific Press,* "Pioneer Mills and Millmen," 2–3–'77.

3. *Ibid.*

4. *San Francisco Bulletin,* Aug. 16, 1860, p. 2, col. 1.

5. For a description of "the Washoe process" see Davis' *Nevada,* p. 370.

6. *San Francisco Bulletin,* 6–3–'61, p. 3, col. 5.

7. Baskett, A. G., "Nevada and the Silver Mines," *Western Monthly,* Vol. I, No. 55, 4–'69, pp. 235–241.

8. Goodwin, *As I Remember Them,* p. 241.

9. De Quille, p. 139.

CHAPTER XXIII

SHIPS OF THE DESERT

1. De Quille, Dan, *Big Bonanza,* pp. 369–370. The first camels were brought to the Comstock as early as 1861, see *San Francisco Bulletin,* 11–1–'61, p. 1, col. 4.

2. Lewis, W. S., *Washington Historical Quarterly*, Vol. XIX, 10–'28.

3. *Gazley's Pacific Monthly*, Vol. I, No. 1, 1–'65, pp. 34–40.

4. Report of Edward Fitzgerald Beale to the Secretary of War, April 26, 1856. 35th Congress, 1st Session, House of Representatives, Ex. Doc., No. 124; also Document No. 24, May 30, 1855; Paxson, Frederic L., *History of the American Frontier*, Houghton Mifflin Co., p. 459. For extensive bibliography on this subject see compilation of Gray, Farquhar, and Lewis, *Quarterly, California Historical Society*, 1930.

5. Lord's *Comstock Lode*, p. 201. The substitution of camels for mules was not a pronounced success. They could hardly be urged over the stony trails by blows and curses.

6. Goodwin, C. C., *As I Remember Them*, p. 301.

7. *Territorial Enterprise*, Sept. 3, 1864.

8. Lewis, William S., *Washington Historical Quarterly*, Vol. XIX, No. 4, October, 1928.

9. Farquhar, Francis P., "Camels in the Sketches of Edward Vischer," *Quarterly, California Historical Society*, San Francisco, 1930.

CHAPTER XXIV

The Squaw and the Chief, 1860

1. De Quille, *Big Bonanza*, p. 290.

2. Angel's *Nevada*, p. 344, says this event occurred in 1861. Lord in his *Comstock Lode* gives references to support the date of May 25, 1860. See p. 76.

3. *San Francisco Alta*, 5–17–'60, p. 1, col. 3.

4. *San Francisco Alta*, 5–7–'60, p. 1, col. 3.

5. Thomas D. John's, "Commanding," *San Francisco Bulletin*, 5–19–'60. This was made in accordance with a suggestion of Judge Cradlebaugh, whom Buchanan had appointed.

6. *Sacramento Union*, Dec. 22, 1860; "Historical Reminiscences," in *Territorial Enterprise*, June 13, 1872. The most complete sketch of this period is to be found in J. Wells Kelly's *Second Historical Directory of Nevada*, pp. 33–57, "Historical Sketch of Nevada Territory." It was written by the versatile Henry de Groot. Carson County was actually organized and an attempt was made to elect county officials but the bitterness toward anything that came from Salt Lake produced two political factions and the elections were farcical. The Anti-Mormons refused to recognize the officials elected and they proceeded to organize a territorial form of government with governor, territorial delegates to Congress, and other officials. A constitution was adopted and a legislature was chosen. This provisional government asked California for co-operation, and Senator Wm. M. Gwin, an ardent Southern sympathizer, then California's United States Senator, made an appeal to Congress for a new territory in western Utah. Gwin then had ambitions to see Nevada a part of the Southern Confederacy. The citizens of Virginia absolutely refused to recognize the Utah authorities, thus ending any hope of reorganizing Carson County under Utah supervision. See Mack, Effie Mona, *Life & Letters of Wm. M. Stewart*, 1827–1909, pp. 27–28.

CHAPTER XXV

SECESSION, 1860

1. Stewart, *Reminiscences,* Neale Publishing Company, p. 130.
2. Lord, *Comstock Lode,* p. 141.
3. This was Finney's last public appearance on the Lode which he had discovered. On June 20, 1861, while happily inebriated, he fell from his horse (maybe the one he had received from Comstock in exchange for his share of the Lode), and fractured his skull. Lord, p. 411; *Big Bonanza,* p. 87.
4. Judge Cradlebaugh had assisted Buchanan in his election for the presidency and in return the President appointed him Judge of the Second Judicial District, Utah Territory.
5. Brown, *Stewart's Reminiscences,* Neale Publishing Co., p. 135.
6. The Act of Congress organizing the Territory of Utah provided for its judiciary but made no provision for their removal by the opposition power. See Lord, p. 140.

CHAPTER XXVI

FIGHTING SAM BROWN, 1860

1. Davis' *Nevada,* p. 247.
2. Davis' *Nevada,* p. 248.
3. Angel's *Nevada,* p. 356.
4. See Van Sickles' Statement, *Nevada Historical Papers,* Vol. I, pp. 192–193. This account does not quite agree with the newspaper account of the time. See *Sacramento Union,* 7–8–'61, p. 2, col. 4.
5. Angel's *Nevada, ibid.*
6. Davis' *Nevada,* p. 248.
7. Van Sickles, H., in *Nevada Historical Society Papers,* Vol. I, pp. 192–193.
8. Angel's *Nevada,* p. 356.
9. Van Sickles' Statement, *ibid.*
10. Davis' *Nevada,* p. 249.
11. Davis' *ibid.*
12. See *Stewart's Reminiscences,* p. 133. See Van Sickles' Statement, *Nevada Historical Papers,* p. 193. Van Sickles was a German rancher and lived to a ripe old age, in the Carson Valley.
13. *Sacramento Union,* July 8, 1861, p. 2, col. 4.
14. Sam Davis, Vol. I, p. 249, gives the verdict that has been quoted; but the *Sacramento Union,* 7–8–'61, p. 2, col. 4, says "The verdict of the jury was 'They served him right.'" See also De Voto, *Mark Twain's America,* Little Brown & Co., p. 128; and "Brave Days in Washoe," *Mercury,* 6–'29, p. 233.

CHAPTER XXVII

LANGFORD PEEL, 1861

1. Angel's *Nevada,* p. 357; Gillis, Wm. R., *Gold Rush Days with Mark Twain,* p. 42.
2. *Ibid.*

3. Davis' *Nevada*, p. 245–246. Gillis, Wm. R., in *Gold Rush Days with Mark Twain*, Albert & Charles Boni, Inc., writes that this quarrel took place in Ben Irwin's saloon, p. 43. Gillis' description of this event does not "square-up" with other contemporary ones.

4. Gillis, Albert and Chas. Boni, Inc., p. 46.

5. Gillis, Albert and Chas. Boni, Inc., p. 47.

6. Davis' *Nevada*, pp. 246–247.

CHAPTER XXVIII

Struggle for Control, 1860–1861

1. Lord, *Comstock Lode*, p. 105.

2. Lord, *Comstock Lode*, p. 105.

3. *San Francisco Bulletin*, 1–10–'61, p. 2, col. 3.

4. *San Francisco Bulletin*, 1–17–'61, p. 2, col. 3.

5. *Sacramento Union*, 3–6–'61, p. 1, col. 7.

6. *Sacramento Union*, 2–21–'61, p. 2, col. 4.

7. *Stewart's Reminiscences*, Neale Publishing Co., pp. 133–135.

8. Lord, *Comstock Lode*, p. 106.

9. Lord, *Comstock Lode*, p. 107.

10. Lord, *Comstock Lode*, p. 107. A. Fleishhacker's store was in Virginia City. From Stewart's description one would believe it was in Carson. See picture on end-papers of this book.

11. *Sacramento Union*, 3–6–'61, p. 1, col. 7.

12. Lord, *Comstock Lode*, p. 108.

13. *Sacramento Union*, 3–6–'61, p. 1, col. 7.

14. Lord, *Comstock Lode*, p. 108.

15. *Stewart's Reminiscences*, Neale Publishing Co., p. 139.

CHAPTER XXIX

Rebels Capture Sun Mountain, 1861

1. Bradley, Glenn D., *Story of the Pony Express*, McClurg, pp. 69–70. Chapman, Arthur, *The Pony Express*, G. P. Putnam's Sons, p. 221.

2. *Sacramento Union*, 3–19–'61, p. 4, col. 1. Due to damage to wires between St. Joe and Fort Kearney.

3. Inspired by the urgency of the situation the Pony Express Company determined to surpass all previous performances. Horses were led out, in many cases two or three miles from the Stations, in order to meet the incoming riders and to secure the supreme limit of speed and endurance on this momentous trip. See Bradley's *Pony Express*, McClurg, pp. 66–69.

4. Angel's *Nevada*, p. 578 and p. 265.

5. When Andrew Jackson was President he appointed Crittenden to the West Point Military School, where he graduated in the same class with Beauregard and Sherman in 1835. Soon after the discovery of gold he came to California and entered the law.

6. This was the beginning of a tie that was ultimately to supply California

jurisprudence with one of the most celebrated murder trials that ever rocked her courts. Following this trial Mrs. Fair became the mistress of A. P. Crittenden and bore him a daughter. As the years went by Crittenden became one of the leading lawyers of the Pacific, but failed to discard his mistress. When he refused to divorce his own wife and marry her, she shot him. This event occurred on November 3, 1870, on the deck of a ferry-boat plying between Oakland and San Francisco. The steamer, *El Capitan,* had just left the former's slip, when Mrs. Fair, closely veiled, stepped up to Crittenden, drew a pistol, and exclaiming, "You have ruined me and my child!" fired at Mr. Crittenden. He fell back into his wife's arms, mortally wounded, and died a few days later. See *Fair, Laura D., Trial of, for the Murder of Alex. P. Crittenden,* p. 2, cols. 1–2.

7. Goodman, Joseph, "Early Nevada Days," *San Francisco Chronicle,* 1–24–'92.

8. Bradley's *Pony Express,* McClurg, p. 70. Fort Sumter was fired upon 4–12–'61.

9. Goodman, Joseph T., "A Battle-Born State," *San Francisco Chronicle,* 2–14–'92, p. 1, cols. 1–3.

10. The writer's name was Charles Duval, who was afraid to attach his name. He was approached by the McMeans party because he was a Southerner, a Creole of Louisiana. *Rebellion Records,* Series I, Vol. I, Part I, p. 500.

11. Collins, John A., Capt. T. Hendrickson, Fort Churchill. *War of the Rebellion,* Series I, Vol. L, Part I, p. 490. Collins, John A., to Brigadier-General E. V. Sumner, dated Virginia City, 5–26–'61; for picture of Collins' residence, see end-papers of this book.

12. *Rebellion Records,* Series I, Vol. L, Part I, pp. 490–491.

13. Sumner, E. V., to Colonel L. Thomas, *The War of the Rebellion,* Series I, Vol. L, Part I, pp. 506–507.

14. Goodman, Joseph T., *San Francisco Chronicle,* 2–14–'92, p. 1, cols. 1–3; Angel's *Nevada,* p. 266, says Newman's store was at the corner of "A" and Sutton Sts.

15. See Blake to Buell, *Rebellion Records,* p. 500; also Sumner to Thomas, pp. 506–507.

16. *Rebellion Records,* Series I, Vol. L, pp. 499–500. Doctor Selden A. McMeans, born Danbridge, Tenn., July, 1806, arrived California, 1849. At one time State Treasurer of California, died July 31, 1876, Reno, Nev., *Sacramento Union,* 2–4–'76, p. 3, col. 3.

17. Atwill, Joseph F., to Sumner, E. V., Virginia City, June 5, 1861, *War of Rebellion,* Series I, Vol. L, Part I.

18. Goodman, Joseph T., *ibid.*

19. Angel's *Nevada,* p. 266, col. 1; Wren's *History of Nevada,* pp. 225–226.

20. Davis' *Nevada,* p. 270.

21. Moore to Blake, *Rebellion Records,* Vol. L, Part I, pp. 510–511.

CHAPTER XXX

BULL RUN, AUGUST, 1861

1. When Sumter fell, President Lincoln called for 75,000 volunteers; 1,200 New York firemen at once responded. Ellsworth drilled ten companies of them

at Fort Hamilton. He labored night and day, won their hearts, acquired perfect control over them. They were called Zouaves on account of their uniforms. New York was enthusiastic over her Fire Zouaves and presented three stands of colors to them. On May 2, Ellsworth landed in Washington with his troops and received an ovation equalling that which had attended his New York departure. E. E. Ellsworth was born at Mechanicsville, N. Y., April 23, 1837, and was killed before Alexandria, the latter part of May, 1861. See Shea, J. G., *The Fallen Brave*, pp. 18–23.

2. Goodman, Joseph T., "A Battle-Born State," *San Francisco Chronicle*, 2-14-'92, p. 1, cols 1–3.

3. Winthrop was a Yale man. As early as 1853 he was in California and Oregon. Wrote the *Canoe and Saddle* as well as several novels.

4. Goodman, Joseph T., *ibid*.

5. Angel's *Nevada*, pp. 265–268. Murphy, I. I., *Life of Colonel Daniel E. Hungerford*, pp. 175–200, Hartford, Conn., 1891, privately printed. The Colonel had a distinguished record in the war but never came back to Sun Mountain to live. His daughters were Mrs. John Mackay and the Countess Telfener.

CHAPTER XXXI

THE GOVERNOR, JULY 15, 1861

1. Once already the people in convention at Genoa had seceded from Utah, framed and adopted a state constitution of their own, even installed a governor, and in all sincerity listened to his message.

2. Lord, *Comstock Lode*, p. 109.

3. *San Francisco Post*, 1-13-'77, p. 2, col. 6.

4. *San Francisco Bulletin*, letter dated Washoe, July 21, 1861, Paul Scraps.

5. *Sacramento Union*, 7-16-'61, p. 2, col. 5.

6. Goodman, Joe, *Chronicle*, 2-14-'92, p. 1, cols. 1–3.

7. *Sacramento Union*, 7-16-'61, p. 2, col. 5.

8. Fitch, Thomas, "Some Old Friends," *San Francisco Call*, 10-4-'03, p. 14.

9. Angel's *Nevada*, p. 302.

10. Seitz, Don C., *Artemus Ward*, Harper Bros., p. 142.

11. Fitch, Tom, *San Francisco Sunday Call*, 9-20-'03.

CHAPTER XXXII

LAW, 1861

1. Angel's *Nevada*, p. 78.

2. *Sacramento Union*, 12-3-'61, p. 3, col. 3. Mack, Effie M., *Life and Letters of Wm. M. Stewart*, p. 29.

3. Angel's *Nevada*, pp. 77–80.

4. *Laws of Nevada Territory*, 1861, p. 1.

5. Mack, Effie M., *Life and Letters of Wm. M. Stewart*, pp. 30–31.

6. Bancroft, Vol. VII, p. 293, says this was the first through dispatch, but presumably another had preceded it which was read from the stage of a San

Francisco theatre by J. Wilkes Booth. Kennedy, *Contest,* Houghton Mifflin Co., p. 286, says Edwin Booth, but it was J. Wilkes Booth who was performing there at the time.

7. Richardson, J. D., *Messages and Papers of the Presidents,* pp. 53–129.

CHAPTER XXXIII

THE NEW CHIEF, 1861

1. Brown, *Reminiscences of William M. Stewart,* Neale Publishing Co., p. 143.
2. Brown, *Reminiscences,* Neale Publishing Co., p. 145.
3. Fitch, Thomas, *San Francisco Sunday Call,* 9–20–'03.
4. Lord, Eliot, *Comstock Lode,* pp. 146–152; Vol. IV, of Clarence King's *United States Geological Survey* contains a complete history of the Comstock Mines and the litigation to settle titles.

CHAPTER XXXIV

THE HIDDEN CITY, 1861

1. *Gold Hill News,* 7–26–'64, p. 2, col. 2.
2. Shinn, C. H., *Story of the Mine,* Appleton Publishing Co., p. 133.
3. *Gold Hill Evening News,* Oct. 7, 1867, p. 3, col. 1. Patrick Price, a native of Ireland, 28 years of age. He had worked in the mine for 18 months, was faithful, sober, honest, industrious, beloved by all who knew him and the foreman of the mine. See *Sacramento Union,* 10–8–'67, p. 2, col. 3.

CHAPTER XXXV

AMUSEMENTS, 1862

1. *Sacramento Union,* 10–8–'60, p. 4, col. 2.
2. Lewis McLaine contracted on the 17th of September for the building of a brick and fire-proof house for the use of Wells, Fargo & Company to be completed by October 15 of that year. *Sacramento Union,* 10–8–'60, p. 4, col. 2.
3. *San Francisco Bulletin,* Oct. 17, 1860.
4. Howland, Mrs. Robert, *Reminiscences of.* Told to Author.
5. Drury, Wells, "Aunty's Big Pension," *San Francisco Examiner,* 1–28–'89, p. 9, cols. 3–4. Based on an unsigned newspaper article in *The Examiner.* Presumably the work of Wells Drury, State Library.

CHAPTER XXXVI

PROFESSOR PERSONAL PRONOUN, 1862

1. Paine, Albert B., *Mark Twain: A Biography,* Harper & Brothers, Vol. I, p. 236. Fitch, Thomas, *San Francisco Call,* 10–4–'03.
2. Davis' *Nevada,* Vol. I, p. 393.
3. Paine, *Mark Twain: A Biography,* Harper & Brothers, Vol. I, p. 203.
4. Goodwin, C. C., *As I Remember Them,* p. 253.

5. Daggett, Rollin M., "Recollections," *San Francisco Examiner*, 1–22–'93.
6. *Ibid.*
7. Goodwin, *As I Remember Them*, p. 253. A. B. Paine gives a little different version, see *Biography*, Harper & Brothers, Vol. I, p. 203.

CHAPTER XXXVII

Evolution of a Humorist, August, 1862

1. Goodwin, *As I Remember Them*, p. 253; Gillis, Wm. R., *Gold Rush Days with Mark Twain*, pp. 49–50. Van Wyck Brooks: *Ordeal of Mark Twain*, Dutton, p. 82, sees in the beginning of Sam Clemens' literary career a surrender of his inner self.
2. Fitch, Thomas, "Mark Twain in Bonanza Times," *San Francisco Chronicle*, 3–30–'19, p. 50, col. 1.
3. *Ibid.*
4. Clemens, Will, *Mark Twain, His Life and Work*, pp. 39–41.
5. Graham, J. B., *Handset Reminiscences*, p. 145.
6. De Voto, Bernard, p. 136.
7. Paine, A. B., Vol. I, p. 206. Sam Clemens took rooms with Dan De Quille in the Myers and Daggett Building, 25 North "B" St. Joe Goodman furnished the rooms but sent bill to Dan and Sam. Across hall lived Tom Fitch and his wife Anna, joint authors of *A Millionaire of Tomorrow*, etc.
8. Goodwin, *As I Remember Them*, p. 186.
9. Davis' *Nevada*, pp. 462–463.
10. Goodwin, C. C., *As I Remember Them*, p. 255.
11. For a further dissertation on the Sagebrush School see Ella Sterling Cummins, *Story of the Files*, p. 102.
12. Hart, Fred, *Sazerac Lying Club*, p. 39.
13. Davis' *Nevada*, Vol. I, p. 464.
14. *Ibid.*
15. De Voto, Bernard, *Mark Twain's America*, Little Brown, p. 154.
16. De Voto, p. 134.
17. "The Petrified Man" was first printed in *The Territorial Enterprise*, Oct. 5, 1862. Reprinted in *The San Francisco Bulletin*, Oct. 15, 1862, p. 1, col. 4, as follows:
"A Washoe Joke.—*The Territorial Enterprise* has a joke of a 'petrified man' having been found on the plains, which the interior journals seem to be copying in good faith. Our authority gravely says:
"'A petrified man was found some time ago in the mountains south of Gravelly Ford. Every limb and feature of the stony mummy was perfect, not even excepting the left leg, which had evidently been a wooden one during the lifetime of the owner—which lifetime, by the way, came to a close about a century ago, in the opinion of a savant who has examined the defunct. The body was in a sitting posture and leaning against a huge mass of croppings; the attitude was pensive, the right thumb resting against the side of the nose; the left thumb partially supported the chin, the forefinger pressing the inner corner of the left eye and drawing it partly open; the right eye was closed, and the fingers of the right hand spread apart.(!) This strange freak of nature created a pro-

found sensation in the vicinity, and our informant states that, by request, Justice Sewell or Sowell of Humboldt City at once proceeded to the spot and held an inquest on the body. The verdict of the jury was that "deceased came to his death from protracted exposure," etc. The people of the neighborhood volunteered to bury the poor unfortunate, and were even anxious to do so; but it was discovered, when they attempted to remove him, that the water which had dripped upon him for ages from the crag above, had coursed down his back and deposited a limestone sediment under him which had glued him to the bed rock upon which he sat, as with a cement of adamant, and Judge S. refused to allow the charitable citizens to blast him from his position. The opinion expressed by his Honor that such a course would be little less than sacrilege was eminently just and proper. Everybody goes to see the stone man, as many as 300 persons having visited the hardened creature during the past five or six weeks.'"

The extended story was first published in *Galaxy* June, 1870; in *Memoranda,* 1871; *Sketches New and Old,* 1875, with illustrations by T. W. Williams; *Collected Works,* Vol. XIX, p. 316.

CHAPTER XXXVIII

Mark Twain, December, 1862

1. Claggett was one of Sam Clemens' old friends. See sketch of him in Goodwin's *As I Remember Them.*
2. Angel's *Nevada,* p. 81.
3. Goodwin's *As I Remember Them,* p. 253. *Golden Era,* San Francisco, Feb. 28, 1864, refers to Mark Twain as the "Wild Humorist of the Sage Brush Hills"; *Golden Era* of June 26, 1864, refers to him as "The Sage-Brush Humorist from Silver Land."
4. The reason Mark Twain took this nom de plume may be found in a letter he wrote June 24, 1874. *The Eighteenth Year Book,* 1919, Bibliophile Society, Boston, Mass., 1919, p. 123, *et seq.*
5. De Voto, Bernard, *Mark Twain's America,* Little Brown, p. 133.
6. Goodwin's *As I Remember Them,* p. 255.
7. *Gold Hill Evening News,* April 29, 1868. At the time of his second course of western lectures on "Pilgrim Life."

CHAPTER XXXIX

Flush Times, 1863

1. Goodman, Joseph T., "What We Owe Nevada," *San Francisco Chronicle,* 1-31-'92, p. 4, col. 1.
2. Lord's *Comstock Lode,* p. 125.
3. *Brewer, William H., Journal of* (Farquhar), Yale University Press, p. 559.
4. "J. B. S." (Jerome B. Stillson), *New York World,* 9-7-'65.
5. Brewer letters, p. 556 of Farquhar, *Up and Down California.*
6. "Bancroft Scraps," *Nevada Miscellany,* July 16, 1863, p. 105, col. 1.
7. Twain, Mark, *Roughing It,* Harper and Brothers, pp. 24-25.

8. Lord's *Comstock Lode*, p. 128.

9. "Bancroft Scraps," *Nevada Miscellany*, July 16, 1863, p. 105, col. 1.

10. *Ibid.*

11. At that time stock was sold in feet, not shares. See *Brewer, William H., Journal of, Up and Down California* (edited by Francis P. Farquhar), Yale University Press, pp. 551–559; Fulton, R. L., *Nevada Historical Papers*, p. 911.

12. *Nevada Historical Papers*, p. 557.

13. Farquhar, *Brewer Letters*, p. 554.

14. *Nevada Historical Papers*, 1911, p. 43.

15. Fulton, R. L., *Nevada Historical Papers*, 1909, p. 83.

16. *Sacramento Union*, 9–25–'63, p. 2, col. 2.

17. *Sacramento Union, ibid.*

18. Lord's *Comstock Lode*, p. 195.

19. *Brewer, William H., Journal of* (edited by Francis P. Farquhar), Yale University Press, p. 557.

20. *Marysville Appeal*, 7–25–'63, p. 2, col. 3.

21. *Artemus Ward, Complete Works of*, A. L. Burt and Company, New York, p. 267.

22. Shinn, *Story of the Mine*, Appleton, pp. 116–118.

23. Brown, J. Ross, "Washoe Revisited," *Harper's Magazine*, June, 1865.

24. J. B. S., *New York Herald*, 9–7–'65.

25. Brown, J. Ross, "Washoe Revisited," *Harper's Magazine*, June, 1865, pp. 2–3.

26. Lord's *Comstock Lode*, p. 215.

27. Brown, J. Ross, *Harper's Magazine*, June, 1865.

28. *San Francisco Bulletin*, 9–26–'63, p. 3, col. 4.

CHAPTER XL

THE ROWDY FUND

1. Angel's *Nevada*, p. 220.

2. *San Francisco Argonaut*, "The Nevada Schoolmaster," 12–21–'78, p. 19.

CHAPTER XLI

ST. MARY'S SILVER BELL

1. Angel's *Nevada*, p. 205.

2. Fitch, Thomas, "Sage-Brush Sketches," *San Francisco Argonaut*, 3–2–'78, p. 7. Rising was a New Yorker, sent out by the American Church Missionary Society. A brother of Judge Rising, one of the most prominent lawyers in Virginia City. The minister in Twain's (*Roughing It*) Buck Fanshaw episode. He left the mountains on account of health. Died in a collision between boats on the Ohio River in 1868. See Angel's *Nevada*, p. 199, *et seq.*

3. Angel's *Nevada*, p. 200.

4. Angel's *Nevada*, p. 201.

5. *Ibid.*

CHAPTER XLII

Reverend Grosch Sues, 1863

1. *Sacramento Union,* 9–2–'63, p. 5, col. 5.
2. The Attorney-General of Nevada in one of his State reports referring to this period.
3. Davis' *Nevada,* Vol. I, p. 393.
4. Davis' *Nevada,* Vol. I, pp. 394–395.

CHAPTER XLIV

Bullets and Poetry, July 2, 1863

1. *Kelly's Second Directory,* pp. 481–482.
2. *Enterprise,* July 3, 1863.
3. *Virginia Evening Bulletin,* July 6, 1863.
4. Leman, *Memories of an Old Actor,* p. 297.
5. Graham, J. B., *Handset Reminiscences,* Salt Lake City, 1915, pp. 159–160. Howard, a few days later, trying to keep his word, died with his boots on. He had seven nicks in his gun.
6. Taylor, J. H., *Joe Taylor, Barn-Stormer,* New York, 1913, pp. 69–70.
7. Rourke, Constance, *Troupers of the Gold Coast,* Harcourt, Brace, p. 120.
8. Leman, *Memories of an Old Actor,* pp. 296–297.
9. Wimmer's Hotel was at 38 and 40, North "B" Street. See *Kelly's Directory,* p. 200.
10. See speech of Clement L. Vallandigham, Ohio Copperhead, in the House of Representatives early in 1863. President Lincoln as a grim joke for his treasonous utterances banished him into the lines of the Confederacy. Edward Everett Hale's "The Man Without a Country," appearing in *The Atlantic Monthly* for Dec., 1863, was written around such unpatriotic conduct.
11. The struggle for Vicksburg was one of the bitterest of the war. It was a turning point of the conflict. It meant the opening of the Mississippi from source to mouth. On July 4, a few days after events chronicled here, the great fortress fell into the hands of Grant and Sherman. General Pemberton had defended it valiantly for six bitter months.
12. Leman, *Memories of an Old Actor,* p. 299. Wimmer dashed into the room exclaiming, "My God, Leman, are you alive?"

CHAPTER XLV

The Flag in the Sky, July 30, 1863

1. Angel's *Nevada,* p. 578.
2. *Nevada Historical Papers,* Vol. I, pp. 97–98.
3. *Virginia Evening Bulletin,* July 31, 1863.
4. There are many verses to this poem. See *Poetry of the Pacific,* pp. 322–325. In early days Anna Fitch was connnected with *The San Francisco Hesperian.* She was among the first California women to write a novel, *Bound*

Down; a Book of Fate. She also wrote *The Loves of Paul Fenly* (Putnam), and collaborated with her husband in writing *Better Days, or a Millionaire of Tomorrow.* For further sketch see Cummings' *Story of the Files,* pp. 290–300.

CHAPTER XLVI

SATIRE IN WASHOE, 1863

1. *Kelly's Directory,* Peter Hopkins, Magnolia Saloon, pp. 105–106.
2. Clemens, Will M., *Mark Twain, Life and Work,* San Francisco, 1892, p. 48.
3. "Bancroft Scraps," *Nevada Miscellany,* I, p. 1.
4. *Territorial Enterprise,* 10–29–'63; *San Francisco Bulletin,* 10–31–'63, p. 3, col. 4.
5. "Mark Twain," *Gold Hill News,* 11–2–'63, p. 3, cols. 1–2. *San Francisco Bulletin,* 11–3–'63, p. 3, col. 5.
6. *Ibid.*
7. *Gold Hill News,* 10–30–'63.
8. Davis, Sam R., "Mark Twain," *Nevada Historical Society Papers,* 1911, pp. 40–41.
9. Mark Twain's "Empire City Hoax" may be found in its entirety in *The Territorial Enterprise,* 10–29–'63; in *The San Francisco Daily Evening Bulletin,* 10–31–'63, p. 5, col. 4, under the title of "The Latest Sensation"; "My Famous 'Bloody Massacre,'" *Galaxy,* June, 1870, p. 860; Paine's *Biography,* Harper, 1912, p. 1597. In his *Bulletin* article, Mark Twain has the Hopkins family living in an old log-house. In the *Galaxy* he speaks of Hopkins murdering his family "in his splendid dressed-stone mansion." "Even the very pickled oysters that came on our tables," wrote Mark, "knew that there was not a 'dressed-stone mansion' in all Nevada Territory."

CHAPTER XLVII

KINGS OF BONANZA, 1863

1. Fulton, R. L., "Reminiscences," *Nevada Historical Papers,* 1907–1908, p. 85.
2. Sandy came from Scotland by way of Missouri—a rough, honest, well-liked fellow, though not so canny as he might have been. He owned, originally, ten feet and so did Eilley Orrum. Eilley's ten feet came to her by way of John Rodgers' unpaid board bill, although some authorities claim she bought it for $100. One morning in the spring of 1860, Rodgers was found dead in bed with a pistol by his side. Whether suicide or murder, no one ever knew, although it smacked of crime. Rodgers left a valuable estate. When no heirs laid claim it vanished completely. "Comstock Papers," No. 9, *Mining and Scientific Press,* Nov. 25, 1876; *Brewer, William H., Journal of* (edited by Francis P. Farquhar), under title of *Up and Down California,* pp. 557–558.
3. In the exercise of her occult powers Eilley foretold some events which were verified by subsequent happenings. "Comstock Papers," No. 9, *ibid.*
4. The Bowers' claim made much money at first. When Sandy's mill failed he died, in the late '60's, greatly reduced in circumstances.

5. *Brewer Journal, ibid.*
6. Angel's *Nevada,* p. 622.
7. Welles, A. M., *Reminiscent Ramblings,* Denver, Col., 1903, p. 343.
8. Welles, A. M., *ibid.,* p. 343. In spite of the legend there seems to be some discussion as to whether Eilley was really presented at Court or not, although Mrs. Bowers always inferred that she had been. For a full-length portrait of Mrs. Samuel Bowers, see Swift Paine's *Eilley Orrum,* Bobbs Merrill.
9. Sandy and Eilley spent several years abroad. Although they still had "money to throw at the birds," vultures and other birds of prey had gotten the greater portion. Without any good missionary to instruct them in the art of being rich, the Bowerses continued to dispense their gold while the flatterers, sycophants, and robbers surrounding them applauded.
10. Mark Twain, "Early Days in Nevada," *San Francisco Chronicle,* Jan. 30, 1870, p. 3, col. 1. In telling this story Mark Twain camouflages the identity of Sandy Bowers under the name of "John Smith."
11. Plato was one of the few people who not only made money but had the faculty of keeping it and employing it to the best advantage. He died in San Francisco in the '70's, leaving his wife a considerable fortune. After her widowhood Mrs. Plato married•one of the richest and most prominent business men of San Francisco and became an ancestress of note. "Comstock Papers," No. 9, Nov. 25, 1876.
12. *Brewer, William H., the Journal of (Up and Down California),* p. 558. Only an Irish apple woman by day, Mrs. Plato had been a courtesan by night.

CHAPTER XLVIII

BABES IN THE WOOD, DECEMBER, 1863

1. Graham, J. B., *Handset Reminiscences,* pp. 141–142.
2. Vischer, Wm. Lightfoot, *The Pony Express,* 1908, p. 43; Farish, *Gold Hunters of California,* 1904, pp. 98–99.
3. Goodman, Joseph T., "Artemus Ward," in *San Francisco Chronicle,* 1–10–'92, p. 1, cols. 6–7. This must have been the second defeat, as the international match was long since a thing of the past. Subsequently there was a secondary meeting of little importance.
4. Charles Farrar Browne. Born, Waterford, Me., 1834. Died, Liverpool, consumption, 1867. Began life as compositor on *Cleveland Plain Dealer.* The first of his droll misspelled articles appeared in the columns of that paper. Barrett Wendell in his *Literary History of America,* p. 511, deals harshly with Artemus Ward. In his lectures Ward often assumed the character of a travelling showman closely resembling Mr. Barnum, his fun lying chiefly in the grotesque incongruity between the persons concerned and what they said. His *Panorama* contained pictures of Virginia City and the desert round about. These he took to London. As an example of his method he would point to the desert picture: "The great desert at night—a wild moor—like Othello. A dreary waste of sand. The sand isn't worth saving. Little Injuns seen trundling their war-hoops." *Panorama,* p. 255.
5. Graham, J. B., *Handset Reminiscences,* pp. 142–143.
6. Goodman, Joseph T., "Artemus Ward," *San Francisco Chronicle,* 1–10–'92; Davis, *Nevada,* p. 707.

7. Artemus Ward's *Panorama*, 1869, p. 87.
8. Graham, *Handset Reminiscences*, pp. 142–143. Albert Bigelow Paine shares this same impression. *Biography*, Vol. I, pp. 239–240.
9. De Quille, Dan, *San Francisco Examiner*, March 19, 1893.
10. Artemus Ward's *Travels*, p. 148.
11. *Panorama*, p. 89.
12. De Quille, *San Francisco Examiner*, March 19, 1893.
13. Goodman, *ibid*.
14. Graham, *Reminiscences*, pp. 144–145.
15. Dan De Quille, *ibid*.
16. 12 North "C" Street. *Kelly's Directory*, p. 182. Goodman says Chaumond's, but there was no such place on the Lode.
17. Goodman's "Artemus Ward," *San Francisco Chronicle*, 1–10–'92.
18. Goodman, Joseph T., *San Francisco Chronicle*, 1–10–'92, p. 1, cols. 6–7.
19. Dilke, Charles Wentworth, Great Britain, *A Record of Travel*, p. 148.
20. Seitz, Don C., *Artemus Ward*, Harper Bros., p. 143.
21. Corner North "B" Street and Sutton, see *Kelly's Directory*, p. 172.
22. Paine, *Mark Twain's Letters*, Harper and Brothers, Vol. I, p. 183.
23. Seitz, Don C., *Artemus Ward*, Harpers, pp. 143–144. It was for Artemus Ward's book of *Travels* that Mark Twain wrote "The Celebrated Jumping Frog of Calaveras"—the story that fulfilled Twain's claim to fame.

CHAPTER XLIX

The Honest Miner, January, 1864

1. Bancroft, Vol. XXV, pp. 178–179.
2. Mack, Effie Mona, Thesis, pp. 34–37.
3. Mark Twain, *Territorial Enterprise*, reprinted in Angel's *Nevada*, pp. 82–83. For obvious reasons not repeated here.
4. Brown, G. R., *Reminiscences of William M. Stewart*, Neale Publishing Co., p. 220.
5. Mark Twain in Angel's *Nevada*, p. 82.
6. Brown, G. R., *Reminiscences of William M. Stewart*, Neale Publishing Co., p. 220.
7. *Ibid*.
8. Mack, Effie Mona, *William Morris Stewart, Empire Builder*, 1827–1909. Reprint from the *Proceedings of the Pacific Coast Branch of the American Historical Association*, 1930, p. 188. *Stewart Scraps*, VIII, p. 96. *Nevada Historical Papers, Reno*. Later Mark Twain was private secretary to Senator Stewart at Washington, Brown, *op. cit.*, 224.

CHAPTER L

Governor of the Third House, 1863–1864

1. Angel's *History of Nevada*, 1881. The minutes of the Third House as reported by Mark Twain for *The Territorial Enterprise*, pp. 82–84. In these minutes Mark Twain displays his triple personality "which so distressed his mentors and still intrigues his biographers. Here he is scathing satirist, delightful boy, and crude comedian, simultaneously or in inexplicably swift succes-

sion." See Van Wyck Brooks, *The Ordeal of Mark Twain,* Dutton, 1920, for insight into Sam Clemens' personality. In becoming a sage-brush humorist Brooks claims that Mark Twain sold out rather than fulfilled his soul's high destiny; see p. 84.

2. Mack, Effie Mona, Thesis, p. 37, Bancroft Library.

3. Bancroft, XXV, p. 179.

4. The write-up on the Stewart party is not yet located but, perhaps, some idea of its tenor may be gathered from Mark Twain's notes of the costumes worn by belles of "The Pioneer's Ball." *Golden Era,* 11–26–'65. "The queenly Mrs. L. B. was attractively attired in her new and beautiful false teeth, and the *bon jour* effect they naturally produced was heightened by her enchanting and well sustained smile—her troops of admirers desired no greater happiness than to get on the scent of her sozodont-sweetened sighs and track her through her sinuous course," etc. "Miss C. L. B. had her fine nose elegantly enamelled, and the easy grace with which she blew it from time to time, marked her as a cultivated and accomplished woman of the world; its exquisitely modulated tone excited the admiration of all who had the happiness to hear it." "Being offended with Miss X, I will take this opportunity of observing . . . that it is of no use for her to be slopping off to every ball that takes place, and flourishing around with a brass oyster-knife skewered through her waterfall, and smiling her sickly smile through her decayed teeth, with her dismal pug nose in the air," etc. In the *Golden Era,* 9–27–'63, we find this effusive description of costumes worn at a recent ball: "Miss C. wore an elegant *cheveux de la Reine* and a mohair Garibaldi Shirt; her unique head-dress was crowned with a graceful *pomme de terre* (Limerick French), and she had her hair done up in papers—greenbacks. The effect was very rich, partly owing to the market value of the material." "Miss A. H. wore a splendid *Lucia di Lammermoor* with a deep gore in the neck, embellished with a wide *grecque* of taffetas and garnished with *ruches,* and radishes and things. Her *coiffure* was a simple wreath of sardines on a string." Much abridged, these notes appear in Twain's *Works,* Vol. 19, pp. 338, entitled "After Jenkins."

5. *Reminiscences of William M. Stewart,* p. 222.

CHAPTER LI

MAZEPPA, MARCH 7, 1864

1. Older, Fremont, "Glitter of a Mining Town," *San Francisco Call,* 1932. Davis, Sam, *Nevada,* Vol. II, pp. 719–720. The Menken arrived on the Comstock, 2–9–'64, *Virginia Daily Union,* 2–20–'64, p. 3, col. 1 (Bancroft Library).

2. Mayne, Ethel Colburn, *Enchanters of Men,* "Adah Isaacs Menken," Putnam, p. 333.

3. Payne, John Howard, *Mazeppa,* copy in Harvard College Theatre Collection.

4. Gosse, Sir Edmund, *The Life of Algernon Charles Swinburne,* Macmillan and Co., London, 1917, pp. 160–161.

5. Gosse, *ibid.,* p. 133; also see Chew, Samuel C., *Swinburne,* Boston, 1929, Little, Brown and Co., pp. 35, 50, and 72.

6. Chew, Samuel C., *Swinburne,* Little, Brown and Co., pp. 79–80.

7. Rourke, Constance, *Troupers of the Gold Coast,* Harcourt, Brace, p. 176.

8. The play did not follow in any particular the autobiographical story told in Lord Byron's *Mazeppa.* It is impossible not to suspect that Byron had the circumstances of his own personal history in mind, when he portrayed the fair Polish Theresa, her youthful lover, and the jealous rage of Old Count Palatine. *Byron, Lord, Works of,* London, 1832, Vol. XI, p. 178. Neither does the play follow the historic facts upon which the poem of Lord Byron was based. The story of the young Pole who, bound naked on the back of a wild horse on account of a court intrigue, was carried by his steed into the heart of the Ukraine and being there picked up by the Cossacks, lived to become a prince of the nation and hetman to Peter the Great.

9. Samuel C. Chew in his *Swinburne,* Little, Brown and Co., pp. 79–80, writes, "It is likely that there is a faint glimmering of autobiography in 'Dolores.'" Adah Isaacs Menken was the only woman to whom Swinburne referred as his "mistress." She often called herself "Dolores." In a copy of her little volume of poems, *Infelicia,* he wrote a line from another poem, "Lo, this is she who was the World's Delight." It is possible she may have inspired the poem which Swinburne described as a reverie upon "the transmigration of a single soul—clad always in the same type of fleshly beauty."

10. Perhaps the criticism of Mark Twain that was copied from *The Territorial Enterprise,* perhaps that of Joe Goodman. See *Golden Era,* 3–13–'64, second part.

11. Fulton Oursler, *The World's Delight,* Harper & Brothers, p. 300.

12. Mayne, *Enchanters of Men,* Putnam, p. 336. The Menken had also worked in the studio of one Jones in Cincinnati.

13. *Golden Era,* 3–13–'64.

14. *Ibid.*

15. De Voto, Bernard, *Mark Twain's America,* Little, Brown and Co., p. 126.

16. *Ibid.*

17. For a full-length portrait of The Menken, read Fulton Oursler's *The World's Delight,* Harpers, 1929. Harper & Bros. have kindly given permission to reprint certain passages here.

CHAPTER LII

ADAH ISAACS MENKEN, 1864

1. Davis, Sam, *Nevada,* Vol. II, pp. 719–720.

2. Paine, A. B., *Mark Twain, a Biography,* Harper & Brothers, Vol. I, p. 248.

3. Rourke, Constance, *Troupers of the Gold Coast,* Harcourt, Brace, pp. 181–183.

4. Davis, *Nevada, ibid.*

5. Davis, *Ibid.*

6. De Quille, *San Francisco Examiner,* 3–19–'93.

7. *Ibid.;* Cummins, Ella Sterling, *Story of the Files,* p. 26.

8. Paine, A. B., *Mark Twain,* Harper & Brothers, Vol. I, p. 248.

9. For sketch of life of "Joggles" Wright, see Goodwin's sketch, pp. 299–303, *As I Remember Them.* No one knew his real first name but he was an outstanding character among "the boys."

10. Davis, Sam, "Dramatic Recollections," *Nevada Monthly,* July, 1880, pp. 227–230.

11. No. 9, South "C" Street, see J. Wells Kelley's *Second Directory,* p. 278.

12. Leman, *Memories of an Old Actor,* pp. 301–302.

13. Leman, *ibid.*

14. In this boast, the Menken was ignoring the clown, and Isaacs Menken the Jew, who converted her to Judaism and with whom she enjoyed a spiritual tie denied to all others of her "Sept Douleurs." Lola Montez was probably born in Limerick, Ireland, in 1824, although Scotland and India have been likewise suggested as birth-places. Following the Bavarian revolution of 1848 she came to America (1852) and subsequently to San Francisco (1853), where she married P. P. Hull, editor of *Town Talk.* Her relationship with him terminated within twenty-four hours on account of halitosis, Lola explaining that she couldn't stand his breath (Hull was the miner to whom the Menken referred). The Montez died on Long Island, June 30, 1861, and was buried in Greenwood Cemetery. "Brilliant and Erratic Women," *The Wednesday Press,* 10–15–'02, pp. 1–8; *Themis,* 12–6–'90, p. 4.

15. *Nevada Historical Society Papers,* Vol. III, p. 119.

16. *Gold Hill Daily News,* 3–24–'64, p. 2, col. 2; *Virginia Daily Union,* 3–23–'64, p. 3, col. 1, Bancroft Library; Mayne, *Enchanters of Men,* Putnam, p. 333.

17. Menken, Adah Isaacs, "My Heritage," *Infelicia,* Philadelphia, J. B. Lippincott Co., 1868, pp. 17–19. *Infelicia* contained some of the poems that were earlier published in *The Territorial Enterprise.* No less a person than Charles Dickens wrote the introduction preceding the poems. The Menken herself never saw the finished book. She died with the proof sheet clutched to her heart. And was so buried with her poetical aspirations. Rossetti included four of her pieces in his *Anthology of American Verse.*

18. Miller, Joaquin, "Adah Isaacs Menken," *San Francisco Call,* 7–31–'92, p. 15, cols. 1–2.

19. De Quille, *San Francisco Examiner,* 3–19–'93.

20. Direct from Virginia and San Francisco, the Menken went to London. On the Isthmus she parted with her husband, Orpheus Kerr, forever. En route to London, she met Jim Barkley, a Bret Harte gambler who was mad about her and eventually built her a New York residence called "Bleak House." When she died, he, the last of the "Sept Douleurs," helped to defray the cost of the monument in Montparnasse, Paris, which is inscribed with a line as inscrutable in meaning as the mournful threnody of her own life had been—"Thou Knowest," a phrase from the exquisite "Ilicet" of Swinburne:

"No soul shall tell nor lip shall number
The names and tribes of you that slumber;
      No memory, no memorial.
'Thou knowest'—who shall say thou knowest?
There is none highest and none lowest:
      An end, an end, an end of all."

Strange that she should die in Paris as she claimed she would in Washoe. See Leman, Walter, *Memories of an Old Actor,* pp. 301–302.

21. Davis, Sam, *History of Nevada,* Vol. II, pp. 719–720.

22. *Believest Thou This,* a book of poetic messages received clair-audiently by "A. P. D.," were given to the world in 1913. The poems, some nineteen in number, claim to be the sequelæ to *Infelicia.* The name of the amanuensis and the place of publication are not given. The sentiments in *Believest* are clothed in the same weird, fantastic diction as those of *Infelicia.* A second edition of *Infelicia* was published by J. B. Lippincott Co. in 1888. It contains the best Menken biography extant. (See also Richard Northcott's *Adah Isaacs Menken,* an illustrated biography, the Press Printers, Ltd., Long Acre, London, 1921, p. 53.) Contains, "Infelix," "One Year Ago," "Aspiration," and "Answer Me," the Menken poems included in W. M. Rossetti's *Anthology of American Verse.* Rossetti found in them touches of genius, aspiration expressing a sense of bewildering loss mixed with a wail of humiliation and indignation "like the remnants of a defeated army hotly pursued."

CHAPTER LIII

Army of the Lord, 1864

1. In this hour of imperative necessity, California gave $100,000 to the Sanitary Commission. That year alone, California gave $750,000, three-quarters of the total subscription received by the United States Sanitary Commission from all over the country. Frank B. Goodrich, *The Tribute Book,* Bancroft, 1867, p. 93.

2. Paul, Almarin B., "Gridley and His Sack of Flour," dated San Francisco, 1887, *Scrap Book,* p. 190.

3. *Ibid.*

4. Paul, Almarin B., *Scrap Book, ibid.*

5. Gambling expression of the time, see "Cosmos," pseudonym for Paul, *San Francisco Bulletin,* 5–25–'64, p. 1, col. 1.

6. Charles Holbrook. Born New Hampshire, Aug. 31, 1830, descendant of Puritan ancestors who came to Massachusetts in 1643. In 1850, when nineteen years old, Holbrook migrated to California. Went into hardware business at Sacramento. In 1863 branch established at Austin, Mr. Holbrook made manager. Firm afterward became the well-known Holbrook, Merrill & Stetson of San Francisco, whose business ran into seven figures annually. Phelps, *California Biography,* pp. 141–142.

7. For a sketch of Buel's life see Goodwin's *As I Remember Them,* pp. 132–136.

8. Angel's *Nevada,* pp. 268–269.

9. "A Tribute to the Memory of Reuel Colt Gridley, Stockton, Apr. 9, 1883," State Library, Sacramento. This novel custom of conducting auction sales of this kind was, like many local customs of the Coast, peculiar to mining camps. Auctions where only the winner pays are quite spiritless in comparison.

10. The figure given in the Tribute corresponds with this one but does not agree with Mark Twain's in *Roughing It*—he gives "eight thousand dollars in gold" as the figure, p. 316; J. Ross Browne, *Harpers,* June, 1866, says $3000.

11. Browne, J. Ross, *Harpers,* June, 1866, p. 55.

12. Twain, Mark, *Roughing It*—Harper & Brothers, p. 316.

13. Paul, Almarin B., "Gridley and His Sack of Four," Paul's *Scrap Book*, p. 190.

14. *Territorial Enterprise*, May 17, 1864.

15. Paul, Almarin, *Scrap Book*, p. 190. The carriage personnel does not agree with Mark Twain's description. Mark Twain and Reuel Gridley were schoolmates in Hannibal, Mo. After Gridley went to the Mexican War, Mark did not see him again until that day when Mark got into a fight with an editor on a Carson City street. The editor was a man much bigger than Twain. Suddenly Twain heard an encouraging voice behind him. Gridley had recognized Mark by his drawling speech. See Paine's *Mark Twain's Autobiography*, Harper & Brothers, Vol. II, pp. 216–217.

16. "Cosmos"—Paul, Almarin, *San Francisco Bulletin*, 5-25-'64, p. 1, col. 1. "Our 'Army of the Lord' as a well known local reporter here, Mark Twain, called it."

17. Paul's *Scrap Book*, p. 190.

18. *Enterprise*, May 17, 1864.

19. Angel's *Nevada*, p. 270. The Wilderness Campaign began May 3, 1864, when the Army of the Potomac crossed the Rapidan.

20. Paul to Samuel Copp, Jr., Treasurer Mississippi Valley Fair, dated May 17, 1864, "Bancroft Newspaper Scraps," *Nevada Miscellany*, I, p. 110. In response to that telegram, Almarin Paul wired, "Storey County, Nevada Territory, receives the glorious news of Grant's successes with shouts of joy, and in response will send $20,000 in gold and silver bars. Six thousand five hundred and forty-eight dollars in bars left San Francisco on the steamer of the third of May by Wells Fargo and Company. Go on with the good work. We are with you, heart, hand and purse."

21. Gambling expression, see *Enterprise*, May 17, 1864.

22. *Territorial Enterprise*, May 17, 1864.

23. Angel's figures are as follows:

Virginia City	$13,990
Gold Hill	7,052
Silver City	2,000
Dayton	2,000
Total	25,042

A sum equal to $40,000 in United States currency. Angel's *Nevada*, p. 270. Figures all differ. Several given here with authority.

24. *Enterprise*, May 17, 1864.

25. See *Kelly's Directory*—Silver City, pp. 366–371.

26. *Enterprise, ibid*. This article has the hall-marks of some of Mark Twain's reportorial work.

27. "Tribute to Gridley," *ibid*.

28. Paul, Almarin, *Scrap Book*, op. p. 190.

29. Perhaps A. J. Close, *Kelly's Directory*, p. 367.

30. Paul, Almarin, *Scrap Book*, p. 190. This does not agree with *Territorial Enterprise*, 5-17-'64, $1524 or *Tribute* figures $1375.

31. "Cosmos," *San Francisco Bulletin*, 5-25-'64, p. 1, col. 1.

32. "Cosmos," *ibid*.

33. *Kelly's Directory*.

34. Lord, *Comstock Lode*, p. 209.

35. "Cosmos," *ibid.*
36. *Evening Bulletin,* 5-19-'64, p. 5, col. 5; and 5-20-'64, p. 1, col. 2.
37. Lord, *Comstock Lode,* p. 207.
38. Committees were also appointed to solicit subscriptions. Among them Baldwin, Mark Twain, and the "old Piute," to call on lawyers; to call on brewers, John Donle and Sam Clemens; to call on the ladies, Dan De Quille, *San Francisco Bulletin,* May 20, 1864, p. 1, col. 2; copied from *Territorial Enterprise,* 5-18-'64.
39. "Cosmos," *San Francisco Bulletin,* 5-20-'64, p. 1, col. 1.
40. *Ibid.*
41. Angel's *Nevada,* p. 270.
42. Almarin Paul's *Scrap Book,* p. 190. Reuel Gridley was born in Hannibal, Mo., Jan. 23, 1829. He was a veteran of the Mexican War, came to California, 1852, conducted a newspaper, was a merchant and banker. In 1861 settled in Austin, engaged in merchandising as the senior member of the firm of Gridley, Hobart & Jacobs. He was an ardent Democrat and a wealthy man, but becoming enthused in his "sack of flour," neglected his business and expended his fortune and he died in Stockton, Nov. 24, 1870, penniless—ruined by his love of humanity. He possessed the stuff that heroes are made of, endeared all men to him. His grave was unmarked until one of his friends wrote the booklet "A Tribute to the Memory of Reuel Colt Gridley," which was compiled and published for the purpose of raising money to aid in building a monument to his memory, and establishing a fund for his family. Stockton, 4-9-'83. On the success of that book a monument has been erected to his memory in the Stockton Cemetery.

The annexed is a copy of the dispatch forwarded to Reverend Henry W. Bellows, President United States Sanitary Commission, New York City:

"Place to the credit of Storey County, Nevada Territory, $20,000 in eight bars, making 7,597 ounces of silver bullion, which leaves San Francisco this day through Wells, Fargo & Co., transportation free. Balance of the account by her patriotism, and distribute to the sick and wounded of the army and navy. We are distant, but our hearts beat in unison. Union forever!

ALMARIN B. PAUL,
President Storey County Fund Association."

And Bellows responded to Gridley that the Austin Sack of Flour was the greatest since the sack of Troy. See Almarin B. Paul, *Scraps,* p. 81.

CHAPTER LIV

MARK TWAIN'S LAST HOAX, MAY, 1864

1. *Virginia Daily Union,* 5-19-'64.
2. *Ibid.*
3. *Virginia Daily Union,* 5-26-'64, p. 2, col. 6.
4. *Ibid.*
5. *Sacramento Union,* 5-26-'64, p. 2, col. 4.
6. *Virginia Daily Union,* May 21, 1864.

7. Mark Twain, "A Biographical Sketch," in *How to Tell a Story and Other Essays,* Harper & Brothers, p. 324.

8. *Sacramento Union,* 5–26–'64, p. 2, col. 4.

9. Mark Twain's *Autobiography,* Harper & Brothers, Vol. I, p. 356.

10. Fitch, Thomas, "Fitch Recalls Mark Twain in Bonanza Times," *San Francisco Chronicle,* 3–30–'19, p. 50, col. 1.

11. Paine, A. B., *Biography,* Harper & Brothers, p. 250.

CHAPTER LV

The Duel, May, 1864

1. This account of the duel, entitled "Mark Twain's Last. How I Escaped being killed in a duel," was published in Tom Hood's *Comic Annual* and was reprinted in *The Daily Territorial Enterprise,* Vol. XXV, 1865. It is not included in any of his collected works, although several versions of it exist. One very similar was published in *The North American Review.* In the autobiography there is also another account. From *Territorial Enterprise* in possession of Paul Elder of San Francisco.

2. "Mark Twain's Last," *ibid.*

3. *Ibid.*

4. Laird is said to have returned to Illinois, where he was shot to death by an irate husband for invading his home.

CHAPTER LVI

Borrasca, August 1, 1864

1. *Gold Hill News,* 8–1–'64, p. 2, cols. 1–2.

2. Brown, G. R., *Reminiscences of William M. Stewart,* Neale Publishing Co., p. 164.

3. *Ibid.*

4. *Gold Hill Daily News,* 8–1–'64, p. 3, cols. 1–2.

5. *Ibid.*

6. Brown, G. R., *Reminiscences of William M. Stewart,* Neale Publishing Co., p. 164.

7. *Ibid.*

8. Bill Stewart says that Bonner hid in the attic of Chauvel's, where there was not more than two feet between ceiling and roof. "There was an enormous range beneath, cooking for several hundred people. He was nearly dead with heat and fear when rescued by Bill Stewart." *Reminiscences,* p. 165.

9. *Gold Hill Daily News,* 8–2–'64, p. 2, col. 2. Frank Tilford was afterward United States senator from West Virginia.

10. *Virginia Daily Union,* 8–7–'64, p. 3, col. 1; *Gold Hill Daily News,* 8–8–'64, p. 2, col. 4.

CHAPTER LVII

The Thirteenth Amendment, October 31, 1864

1. Angel's *Nevada,* p. 85.

2. Paul, Almarin, dated Gold Hill, Mar. 28, 1864, p. 101, *Scrap Book.*

3. *Cong. Globe,* 37 Cong., 2 sess., 486; Sen. Ex. Doc. 36 Cong., 2 sess., 28.

NOTES

4. Richardson, J. D., *Messages and Papers of the Presidents*, pp. 53, 129.

5. Donaldson, *The Public Domain*, p. 311.

6. Dana, Charles A., *Recollections of the Civil War*, Appleton, 1898, p. 174.

7. Dana, *Recollections of the Civil War*, Appleton, p. 175.

8. In the Senate the bill to admit Nevada was urged as an effectual way of ridding the country of slavery so that it could not be resuscitated. *Cong. Globe*, 38 Cong., 1 session, 2993.

9. *Cong. Globe*, 38 Cong., 1 sess., 2993. Effie Mona Mack, *Life and Letters of William M. Stewart*. Thesis for Ph.D., Library University of California.

10. Dana, *Recollections*, Appleton, p. 176.

11. Dana, Charles A., *Recollections*, Appleton, p. 174. Dana was Assistant Secretary of War from 1863 to 1865. Born in New Hampshire on Aug. 8, 1819, he had passed by way of western New York, Harvard College, and Brook Farm into the office of *The New York Tribune*—the journal most powerful at that time in solidifying Northern sentiment at the crisis of the Civil War.

12. *Ibid.*

13. *Ibid.*

14. Dana sent for the three men and saw them one by one. They were afraid of their party. Two of them wanted internal revenue collector's appointments. The third a very important berth about the New York Custom House, Dana, p. 176.

CHAPTER LVIII

The Thirty-sixth Star, October 31, 1864

1. Brown, G. R., *Reminiscences of William M. Stewart*, Neale Publishing Co., p. 156 *et seq.*

2. Both Shinn, p. 131, and Lord, pp. 162–163, give long accounts of this disgraceful piece of litigation.

3. These names may be found in *The Territorial Enterprise* for Aug. 10, 11, 12, 17, 18, 19, 1864; see also *Gold Hill News*, Aug. 6, 1864.

4. Angel's *Nevada*, p. 85.

5. Mack, Effie Mona, *Stewart*, p. 110.

6. Brown, *Reminiscences of William M. Stewart*, Neale Publishing Co., p. 161.

7. Brown, *Reminiscences*, Neale Publishing Co., p. 162.

8. *Territorial Enterprise*, Jan. 16, 1864.

9. Mack, Effie Mona, *Life and Letters of William Morris Stewart*. Thesis submitted in partial satisfaction of the requirements for the degree of Doctor of Philosophy in History. Graduate Division of the University of California, 1930, p. 43.

10. *Sacramento Union*, Nov. 3, 1864, p. 2, col. 3.

11. *Evening News*, Oct. 31, 1864.

CHAPTER LIX

Washoe's Godfather, 1864

1. *Gold Hill News*, 11-5-'64, p. 3, col. 1.

2. *Gold Hill News*, 11-2-'64, p. 2, col. 2–3.

3. Angel's *Nevada*, p. 499.

CHAPTER LX

The Door, 1864

1. The famous Emancipation Proclamation was issued New Year's Day, 1863. But the proclamation was only a war measure confiscating "property" in rebellious States. It did not free a single slave in the loyal States of Kentucky, Missouri, Delaware, and Maryland. On the conclusion of the war there was nothing to prevent the South from re-enslaving the Negroes. To prevent this and for reasons aforementioned it was the President's desire to pass the Thirteenth Amendment, to accomplish which required ratification by three-fourths of the States. The President admitted Nevada for that purpose. The amendment was passed through Congress on Jan. 31, 1865, and ratified by Nevada sixteen days later.

2. H. M. Bien of Storey Co., Bancroft, Vol. XXV, pp. 185 and 186.

3. *Ibid.*

4. Bancroft, Vol. XXV, p. 185.

5. Sherman reached the Georgia coast in December and easily broke through the weak defenses of Savannah. On Christmas evening President Lincoln read a telegram from him, announcing "As a Christmas gift the city of Savannah, with 150 heavy guns, plenty of ammunition, and about 25,000 bales of cotton."

6. Mack, E. M., *Stewart,* p. 39.

7. Bancroft's *Nevada,* Vol. XXV, p. 187.

8. Angel's *Nevada,* p. 88.

9. "That Stewart brought his great influence to bear there can be no doubt." Bancroft, Vol. XXV, p. 187.

10. *Daily Evening Bulletin,* Jan. 5, 1865.

11. Fitch, Thomas, *San Francisco Sunday Call,* 9-20-'03.

12. The artist went to the frontier and made his sketches from life in 1861. See George C. Hazleton, *The National Capital,* 195–196. See also, Mack, Effie M., Thesis, University of California, p. 111. Stewart, *Scraps,* III, 29. W. M. Stewart, *Empire Builder,* Pacific Coast Branch American Historical Association, 1930, p. 192.

13. *Ibid.,* Mack, *Stewart,* p. 44.

14. Brown, George Rothwell, *Reminiscences of Senator William M. Stewart, of Nevada,* p. 168.

15. Mack, E. M., *Stewart,* p. 37.

CHAPTER LXI

Lee's Surrender

1. General Grant and General Lee met in a farmhouse at Appomattox on the ninth of April. After a few minutes of courteous conversation recalling the days of their old comradeship in arms in the Mexican War, Grant wrote out the terms of surrender. Lee accepted the terms with sorrowing gratitude. The news reached Virginia City the morning of Tuesday, Apr. 11, 1865. See *Daily Territorial Enterprise,* 4-12-'65.

2. *Ibid.*

3. *Enterprise,* 4–15–'65, p. 5, col. 1.
4. Lord, *Comstock Lode,* p. 209.
5. *Virginia Union,* 4–12–'65.
6. *Virginia Territorial Enterprise,* 4–15–'65, p. 5, col. 1.
7. *Enterprise,* 4–18–'65.
8. *Ibid.*
9. *Ibid.*

CHAPTER LXII

"Not Enough Forever," 7:00 a.m., April 15, 1865

1. The Vigilantes was an organization of men formed to help enforce law. When they were going to hold a meeting or hang a "killer" they rang their bell; tradition started in San Francisco in 1857.
2. Washington, Apr. 14, "President Lincoln and his wife . . . this evening visited Ford's Theatre for the purpose of witnessing the performance of the play of the 'American Cousin.' The theatre was densely crowded. Everybody seemed delighted with the scene being enacted before them. During the third act . . . a sharp report of a pistol was heard, which merely attracted attention, but suggested nothing serious, until a man rushed to the front of the President's box, waving a long dagger in his right hand, and exclaiming 'Sic semper Tyrannis'! He immediately leaped from the box, which was in the second tier, to the stage beneath (catching his spur in the flag which draped the President's box he fell, breaking his leg), and ran across to the opposite side of the stage, making his escape." Dispatch in *Gold Hill Evening News,* Apr. 15, 1865, p. 2, col. 1.
3. *Enterprise,* Apr. 18, 1865. *Gold Hill News,* "Mourning in Gold Hill and Virginia," 4–17–'65, p. 3, col. 1.
4. Muzzy, D. S., *History of the American People,* p. 385.
5. *Territorial Enterprise,* Apr. 18, 1865.
6. Angel's *Nevada,* p. 346. McNair's sister, Mary McNair Mathews, wrote *Ten Years in Nevada,* a book that commemorates a woman's struggle to run down her brother's murderer.
7. "Lashed," in *Gold Hill News,* Apr. 17, 1865, p. 2, cols. 1–2.
8. Angel's *Nevada,* p. 271.
9. *Gold Hill Evening News,* 4–17–'65, p. 3, col. 1.
10. *Enterprise,* 4–18–'65. The prisoner had been locked up in the Station House. When the committee went to inflict the punishment the marshal refused to open the doors. But the committee knew how to unlock locked doors without a key—the job being done with a sledge hammer. "Lashed," in *Gold Hill Evening News,* 4–17–'65, p. 2, cols. 1–2.
11. Writings of Almarin B. Paul, Gold Hill, Nevada, Thursday evening, Apr. 20, 1865, "A Beautiful Tribute."
12. *Gold Hill Evening News,* 4–20–'65, p. 3, col. 1.
13. *Ibid.*
14. *Ibid.*
15. This poem was destined to go down in the annals of the West as one of the great poetical outbursts of the Pacific. Cummins, Ella Sterling, *The Story of the Files,* p. 59. Only a part printed here.

16. The original poem, "The Martyr," was written by Fitz Smythe—private secretary to Emperor Norton—a character of early San Francisco. Found in San Francisco Letter, Dec. 19, 1865, collection of Willard S. Morse, Santa Monica, Calif.

THE MARTYR

Gone! Gone! Gone!
Forever and Forever!
Gone! Gone! Gone!
The tidings ne'er shall sever!
Gone! Gone! Gone!
Wherever! Oh, Wherever!
Gone! Gone! Gone!
Gone to his endeavor!

Recapitulation

Gone forever!
To Wherever!
Ne'er shall sever!
His endeavor!
From our soul's high recompense!

"I consider," wrote Mark Twain in his San Francisco Letter, "that the chief fault in this poem is that it is ill-balanced—lopsided, so to speak. There is too much 'gone' in it and not enough 'forever.' "

CHAPTER LXIII

PRESIDENT LINCOLN'S LAST MESSAGE TO THE BOYS, JUNE 24, 1865

1. Martin, Edward Winslow (pseud.) James Dabney McCabe—*Life and Public Services of Schuyler Colfax*, 1868, pp. 202–203.

2. *Virginia Daily Union*, 6-27-'65, p. co, col. 2; 6-28-'65, p. 3, cols. 2–7.

3. Colfax, Schuyler, *Life and Public Services of*, p. 202–203.

4. Abraham Lincoln to Schuyler Colfax. McCabe's *Life and Public Services of Colfax*, pp. 202–203. *Virginia Daily Union*, 6-28-'65, p. 3, cols. 2–7. Speech of Honorable Schuyler Colfax, delivered at Virginia City, Monday evening, June 26, 1865. Reported by Sumner and Cutter; see also Chapter VIII, *Life and Public Services of Schuyler Colfax*, p. 178.

5. McCabe, James Dabney, *Life and Public Services of Schuyler Colfax*, p. 179.

6. *Ibid.*

7. Laughlin, Clara E., *The Death of Lincoln*, p. 55.

8. *Virginia Daily Union*, 6-28-'65.

9. "I am engaged to go to the theatre with Mrs. Lincoln. It is the kind of an engagement I never break. Come with your friend tomorrow at ten and I shall be glad to see you.   A. LINCOLN."

Brown, G. R., *Reminiscenes of Senator William M. Stewart*, Neale Publishing Co., 1908, p. 190; see Laughlin, Clara E., *Death of Lincoln*, pp. 75-76. Perhaps the Ashmun note was the last.

10. Laughlin. Clara E., *ibid.*, p. 76.
11. Brown, G. R., *Reminiscences of Senator William M. Stewart*, Neale Publishing Co., p. 190.
12. *Virginia Daily Union*, 6–28–'65.

CHAPTER LXIV

AMENDS, JUNE 27, 1865

1. *Virginia Daily Union*, 6–28–'65, p. 3, cols. 2–7.
2. *Virginia Daily Union*, 6–28–'65, "In Memoriam."
3. "In Memoriam," *Gold Hill News*, 6–28–'65.
4. *Virginia Daily Union*, 6–28–'65, p. 3, cols. 2–7.
5. *Gold Hill Daily News*, 6–28–'65, p. 2, col. 1.
6. *Lyon County Sentinel*, 7–1–'65, p. 2, col. 1, says that Alpheus Bull supplied the marker. In spite of this reference the slabs were provided by the father of Hosea. See A. B. Grosch's letter—Angel's *Nevada*, p. 52. There is a further tradition that the Speaker brought them west with him.

CHAPTER LXV

IRONICAL WASHOE, 1865

1. Bancroft, *Chronicles*, IV, p. 51.
2. Bancroft, *Chronicles*, IV, p. 52.
3. De Quille, Dan, *Big Bonanza*, pp. 369–370.
4. Lewis, W. S., *Washington Historical Quarterly*, Vol. XIX, Oct., 1928.
5. *Gazley's Pacific Monthly*, Vol. I, No. 1, Jan., 1865, pp. 34–40. Paxson, Frederic L., *History of the American Frontier*, Houghton Mifflin Co., p. 459.
6. Angel's *Nevada*, p. 468.
7. Lord's *Comstock Lode*, p. 301.
8. Davis' *Nevada*, p. 249. For a description of Tom Peasley's funeral, see that of Buck Fanshaw in Twain's *Roughing It*, Harper & Brothers. Tom Peasley and Buck Fanshaw are one and the same. See N. P. Langford, *Vigilante Days and Ways*, McClurg.
9. Goodwin, C. C., *As I Remember Them*, p. 42.

VIRGINIA CITY,

In the centre is a view of the famous Comstock mining town. Prominent buildings in the border, r
ing right from upper left corner, are: the Wells Fargo bank and express office; the assay office of F
ing and Company; Beck's hardware store; Ford's Exchange; Bricket's recorder's office; Taylor's
vision and liquor store; Drake's carpenter shop; office of *The Territorial Enterprise;* residence of M
Bryan, Bloomfield, tobacconist; Feusier's grocery; Gardiner's livery; tunnel of the Mt. Davidson Mi
Company; blacksmith shop of Willard and Eells; Moore's pavilion; John A. Collins' residence; Sm